Autobiographical Writings

ARTHUR MACHEN

Autobiographical Writings

Edited by S. T. Joshi

Hippocampus Press
New York

Copyright © 2020 by Hippocampus Press.
Selection and editorial matter copyright © 2020 by S. T. Joshi.

Published by Hippocampus Press
P.O. Box 641, New York, NY 10156.
www.hippocampuspress.com

All rights reserved.
No part of this work may be reproduced in any form or by any means without the written permission of the publisher.

Hippocampus Press logo designed by Anastasia Damianakos.
Cover design, incorporating a photo of Arthur Machen, by Daniel V. Sauer, dansauerdesign.com

1 3 5 7 9 8 6 4 2

ISBN 978-1-61498-310-1 (paperback)
ISBN 978-1-61498-318-7 (e-book)

Contents

Introduction	7
Far Off Things	17
Things Near and Far	127
The London Adventure; or, The Art of Wandering	239
Supplementary Essays	311
Strange Roads	313
With the Gods in Spring	318
Sixty Years Since	322
A Lament for London's Lost Inns	326
One Night When I Was Frightened	330
The Ready Reporter	333
The Treasure of the Humble	341
My Murderer	346
Precious Balms	349
[Preface]	353
The Great God Pan and *The Three Impostors*	359
Hieroglyphics	378
The House of Souls	388
The Hill of Dreams	405
The Secret Glory	415
Far Off Things and *Things Near and Far*	422
Dog and Duck	431
The Other Side	438

Appendix **455**
   Eleusinia 455
   Beneath the Barley: A Note on the Origins of *Eleusinia* 466
   Introductory Letter to "Confessions of a Literary Man" 468

Bibliography **471**

Introduction

Arthur Machen's crafting of his own life—as recorded in his three autobiographies, *Far Off Things* (1922), *Things Near and Far* (1923), and *The London Adventure* (1924)—can take its place beside any of his works of fiction for its artistry and selectiveness. This is not in any sense to suggest that Machen tells deliberate falsehoods in these charming volumes; but it becomes clear that he is carefully shaping the actual events of his life—or, at least, some of them—to exhibit to the world the portrait of the happily impoverished writer, lost in nostalgia for the past (not only his own past but the far more remote past of his civilization); a man full of curious and useless learning, but one who clings to that learning in defiance of the disapproval of his forward-looking contemporaries; a man who derives Falstaffian pleasure from meat, drink, tobacco, and other tangible objects but is also a reverent, and at times aggressive, defender of the Old Faith. In the end, the image of Machen that we find in his autobiographical writings is fundamentally true, even if there are curious omissions that only an actual investigation of his life and work reveal.

Arthur Llewelyn Jones Machen[1] was born on 3 March 1863, at Caerleon-on-Usk, in southeastern Wales, near Cardiff— the former site, as Machen never ceases to remind us, of Isca Silurum, the ancient Roman town that was the home of the Second Augustan Legion. This constant reminder of a pre-Christian past colored Machen's temperament and work for the remainder of his life. As the son of a clergyman, Machen was raised in modest surroundings. He attended Hereford Cathedral School from 1874 to 1880; but, while he did well academically, he failed an examination for the Royal College of Surgeons in London, with the result that the course of his future employment was thrown into doubt. He whiled away the time writing the long poem *Eleusinia*, a vivid evocation of the Eleusinian Mysteries of ancient Greece.[2] In

---

1. He was born Arthur Llewelyn Jones. In 1874 his father adopted the name Jones-Machen, the latter derived from his wife's maiden name. Machen later dropped the hyphen and, in his published writings, almost always signed himself "Arthur Machen."
2. The poem is printed here in the Appendix, along with an essay on it written by Machen in 1931.

1881 he paid for the publication of 100 copies of the poem, but was later so embarrassed over its perceived inadequacies that he sought to destroy as many copies as he could, so that today only a few copies remain extant.

The taste for London that Machen had gained during his failed examination whetted his appetite for a new start in England's greatest metropolis, even though neither he nor his family had any idea what kind of work he could secure. He recounts in his autobiographies how he attempted (and failed) to learn shorthand, briefly worked as a tutor for small children, and then, living on nothing but green tea and tobacco, found a job with the bookseller George Redway, working as a cataloguer, translator, and so on. It was Redway who published Machen's first book, an imitation of Robert Burton entitled *The Anatomy of Tobacco* (1884)—which, inexplicably, he refers to in *Far Off Things* as *The Anatomy of Tankards*. It was Redway who commissioned him to translate the *Heptameron* of Marguerite de Navarre, which appeared in 1886.

Meanwhile, significant developments—and traumas—in Machen's personal life were occurring, very few of which are discussed in any detail in his autobiographies. His mother died on November 10, 1885, and his father on September 29, 1887; meanwhile, he had married Amelia Hogg on August 31, 1887. Amelia was thirteen years older than Machen, and it is remarkable that he refers to her—highly obliquely—in only a single line of his autobiographies, when taking note of her death on July 31, 1899: "Then a great sorrow which had long been threatened fell upon me: I was once more alone."

The death of Machen's father, and the subsequent inheritance he received, allowed Machen to become a writer of independent means for the next decade and a half; and it is no accident that it was during this time that he produced some of his most memorable work. He continued his devotion to the past in *The Chronicle of Clemendy* (1888), a strikingly faithful echo of medieval storytelling. It was also at this time that he undertook the first complete translation of Giacomo Casanova's enormously long *Memoirs;* they were published in a sumptuous twelve-volume edition in 1894. He also translated Béroalde de Verville's *Fantastic Tales* (1890).

But Machen, for all his nostalgia for the medieval and Renaissance eras (inspired in part by his fervent Anglo-Catholicism), inadvertently found himself in tune with the temper of his times—the Yellow Nineties—when he published *The Great God Pan and The Inmost Light* in 1894. "The Great God Pan," composed in 1890–91, was particularly reviled in a number of reviews as reflecting the decadence and salaciousness of the period that saw the ascendance of Oscar Wilde (with whom Machen had become acquainted as early as 1890) and Algernon Charles Swinburne; what these reviewers could not have known is that Machen himself shared their own horror at aberrant sex and sought to portray it as loathsomely as the conventions of the period allowed. In this sense it could be said that Machen became a supernatural writer largely by accident—anticipating in many ways the work of William Peter Blatty, whose *The Exorcist* (1971) similarly sought to convey a religious message (the triumph of the pious soul over satanic forces) but was read by millions as merely an entertaining and over-the-top horror novel.

Machen followed up *The Great God Pan* with *The Three Impostors* (1895), an episodic novel that reviewers rightly criticized as being too close a pastiche of Robert Louis Stevenson. Machen took that criticism to heart and, over the next two years, worked in anguish to produce a work that, both in prose style and in content, could be unequivocally deemed his own. The result was *The Hill of Dreams;* but this work was not published until 1907. Machen dryly recounts how the publisher Grant Richards, reading the book when it was completed in 1897, urged Machen never to publish it. Ten years later, Richards himself published it. It received mixed reviews, as all Machen's books did, but at least a few critics recognized that the work embodied the sincere strivings of a man whose depth of feeling incited him to write a book whose core message was the impossibility of communicating certain profound sentiments to an uncaring public. In 1899 he wrote "The White People," one of the greatest weird tales ever written; it was not published until 1904. At this time he also wrote his eccentric treatise on literature, *Hieroglyphics,* published in 1902.

With his inheritance exhausted in 1901, Machen was forced to return to the work force; but he did so in a curious manner. He joined Frank Benson's Shakespeare Repertory Company, remaining with it for the next eight years. Some of the most engaging parts of Machen's autobiographies tell of the intense camaraderie he established as a bit player with this talented group. Somehow, in between tours with Benson's company, he managed to become acquainted with Dorothie Purefoy Hudleston, whom he married on June 25, 1903. She merits not a single line in Machen's autobiographies—not because he thought little of her (by all accounts, their marriage was a happy and rewarding one, lasting until her death on March 30, 1947), but probably because Machen wished to keep this aspect of his life strictly private.

But as his stint with Benson was coming to an end, Machen once again had to think of how he could support himself. He turned—not entirely wisely—to journalism. As early as 1887 he had written a number of pieces on bibliography and rare books for *Walford's Antiquarian,* and he had also written a great many reviews, articles, and unsigned notes for *Literature,* a magazine founded in 1898 by *The Times* of London. But in 1907 Machen began writing for a leading literary paper, the *Academy,* and more popular pieces for *Vanity Fair, T.P.'s Weekly,* and some other venues. Then, in 1910, he made the fateful decision to work as a reporter for the London *Evening News.* Over the next eleven years he wrote hundreds of articles for the paper—articles that today would be considered "human interest" pieces, where Machen once again expressed his nostalgia for the Wales and London of his childhood and early maturity. Indeed, *Far Off Things* appeared in the *Evening News* from March to July 1915 in more than thirty sections as "Confessions of a Literary Man." Machen was only in his early fifties, but he had gained an experience of life and literature that allowed him to wax eloquent about an era—the 1890s—that already seemed to many as remote as the Elizabethan age.

The outbreak of World War I in August 1914 was traumatic for Machen, as it was for his entire generation. Very soon after the war began, he wrote a story, "The Bowmen" (published in the *Evening News* for 29 September 1914), that created a sensation—one that Machen did not expect and perhaps did not welcome. This account of the ghosts of the valiant English soldiers who had won the great victory over France in the battle of Agincourt (1415) coming to the aid of a beleaguered English force and overcoming its German attackers was taken as a true account, and Machen became notorious as the recounter of this story of the "angels of Mons." He spent years, even decades, averring that he had made the whole thing up; but the narrative was so uplifting to British morale that his words went for naught.

And yet, Machen should perhaps have anticipated the furor he created, precisely because he published his account in a newspaper that was chronicling the actual course of the conflict in minute detail. About a year later, he repeated the trick by serializing the novella *The Great Return* in the *Evening News* (published in book form in late 1915), and still later serializing *The Terror* in the same paper in October 1916. Machen also attempted a feeble defense of his religion amidst the horrific course of the war by writing a series of papers gathered as *War and the Christian Faith* (1918).

Machen's episodic novel *The Secret Glory* first appeared in part as a series of articles or sketches in the *Academy* in 1907–08, but did not appear in book form until 1922. It too received mixed reviews, and understandably so; the novel cannot seem to decide whether it is a satire on the English school system or a mystical account of a man's rediscovery of his spiritual roots in Wales. (Machen had earlier written a much more successful story on this same theme, in the novella *A Fragment of Life*, collected—along with several of his best horror tales—in *The House of Souls* [1906].) And the final two chapters of the novel, which tell of Ambrose Meyrick's actual return to Wales and therefore bring the work full circle, were not published at the time because the book had already become quite lengthy.[3]

But by this time Machen had become a genuine celebrity on both sides of the Atlantic, thanks in part to the decision by the American publisher Alfred A. Knopf to reprint many of Machen's books in a uniform edition. Although some critics, such as H. L. Mencken, scorned Machen as overrated, many others found merit in this belated acknowledgment of his literary eminence. An impressive limited edition of his *Works* (the Caerleon Edition) appeared from Martin Secker in nine volumes in 1923.

Machen took to writing essays on all manner of subjects in such papers as the *London Graphic*, the *Lyons Mail, John o'London's Weekly*, and others; a small number of these were gathered in such volumes as *Dog and Duck* (1924), *Dreads and Drolls* (1926), and other volumes. Knopf issued an exquisite edition of Machen's prose poems (written in 1897),

---

3. The full text of *The Secret Glory* can now be found in my edition of Machen's *Collected Fiction* (New York: Hippocampus Press, 2019).

Ornaments in Jade (1924). His American admirer Vincent Starrett issued two volumes of miscellany in 1923 and 1924. And, of course, Machen published his three autobiographies. Inexplicably, *The London Adventure* is frequently overlooked as an autobiography;[4] and while it may be the slightest and least revelatory of the three books, it does contain some engaging features.

Later events in Machen's life and work are of course not covered by his autobiographies. His transatlantic celebrity did little for his own pocketbook, and by the later 1920s he and his wife were living in dire poverty. The poet Robert Hillyer provided financial assistance to Machen for several years during this time; but a more permanent solution was attained in 1932 when Machen received a Civil List pension that paid him £100 a year, enough for him to live comfortably if frugally for the remainder of his life. Numerous literary figures, including T. S. Eliot, lobbied the English government on Machen's behalf.

In 1929 Machen and Purefoy moved to a cottage in Old Amersham, in Buckinghamshire, ending his half-century-long fascination with the metropolis of London. His later publications—the short novel *The Green Round* (1933) and the two collections *The Cosy Room* and *The Children of the Pool* (both 1936)—do not amount to much. Machen, grieved at the passing of his wife of more than four decades, himself died on 15 December 1947.

It is no accident that there has been no comprehensive biography of Arthur Machen; for his autobiographies are so vital, piquant, and compelling that they would intimidate even the bravest chronicler of Machen's life and work. His affecting account of his early days in poverty in London, where he had to use the rungs of a ladder as a bookshelf; his recollections of wandering about the London of the 1880s onward—a city that came to seem like the embodiment of a new *Arabian Nights;* his inveterate modesty, humility, and self-deprecation in speaking of his writings, his stint as an actor, and his work as a journalist: all these things warm the reader's heart, rendering Machen an affectionate and sympathetic character.

Other sides of Machen's personality as revealed in his autobiog-

---

4. An often reprinted volume, *The Autobiography of Arthur Machen,* first published in 1951, includes only *Far Off Things* and *Things Near and Far.*

raphies are perhaps less appealing. His mortifyingly silly attacks on science and philosophy become wearisome after a time, although they are sadly representative of his other nonfictional work and even enter into his fiction. Machen, so devoted to the "truth" of his religion, reacts with fury and loathing at any social, political, or intellectual tendency that might cast doubt on that "truth." He is particularly exercised by the work of the anthropologists of his day—as represented by such a work as Sir James George Frazer's *The Golden Bough* (1890–1915)—which was largely successful in accounting naturalistically for the origin of religious belief. Like so many other dogmatists, Machen uses his own ignorance of science as a gauge of the validity of science. And those who dispute the misogyny that Machen clearly reveals in such a work as "The Great God Pan" will be disconcerted by the sustained passage in *Things Near and Far* in which Machen attributes the decline of journalism in his day to the predominance of female readers.

These texts are, however, full of significant notes on the writing of Machen's most significant works, from "The Great God Pan" to *The Secret Glory*. *The London Adventure,* for all its discursiveness, provides fascinating extracts from a commonplace book in which he recorded never-written plot germs. And Machen wittily recounts the hostile reviews that nearly all his books received over the years—with the unspoken conclusion that these reviews did little to prevent him from establishing at least a foothold in the English literature of his day.

Machen, indeed, prepared a kind of loose appendix to his autobiographies in the peculiar volume *Precious Balms* (1924), one of the rarest of his publications. Here he does little except reprint those negative reviews of book after book, with no commentary whatever except a somewhat smug introduction and a concluding section of favorable reviews and articles (two of them in French). It is not entirely clear that Machen is reproducing these reviews merely to make fun of the reviewers; in some passages in his autobiographies he appears to acknowledge the validity of some reviewers' judgments. But I have chosen to reprint this book here chiefly because the reviews provide clear insights into the general attitude toward weird fiction in Machen's day, especially at the turn of the twentieth century. The later decades of the nineteenth century had seen the outpouring of an enormous quantity of "ghost stories"; but Machen's very different work—the product of a sincere philosophical stance and one that embodies a powerfully original imagination that resulted in gripping and at times unbearably grisly horrific scenarios—proved to be strong meat for reviewers, and they seemed to take their revenge by seeking to discount his work as ineffective or clumsy. Those who thought Machen was indulging merely in obscenity betray a different type of prejudice; but the cumulative effect of the reviews in *Precious Balms* is to display in vivid fashion how mightily weird fiction has had to struggle against the attacks of the timid and conventional in gaining recognition as a valid form of literary expression.

Machen did not confine his autobiographical reflections to his three formal autobiographies. Many of his essays and journalistic writings are at least implicitly or partly autobiographical; and in this volume I have reprinted only a selection of those pieces that most concentratedly embody facets of his personality. Whether it be his accounts of walks through the English countryside ("Strange Roads," "With the Gods in Spring"), his nostalgia for the tokens of the past ("Sixty Years Since," "A Lament for London's Lost Inns"), his work as a newspaperman ("The Ready Reporter"), or some peculiar incidents he witnessed or took part in ("My Murderer"), these vignettes fill in gaps in the autobiographies or add small touches that round out the picture of himself that Machen has so artfully fashioned.

By a curious coincidence, these autobiographies can take their place next to Algernon Blackwood's *Episodes Before Thirty* (1923) and Lord Dunsany's *Patches of Sunlight* (1938) as among the most poignant self-portrayals by a weird writer—or, indeed, by any writer. They permanently affect our view of Machen the man and writer, and they will serve as fodder for the scholar and critic engaged in the assessment of his literary output. But beyond all their value in those regards, they are eminently readable—and they vivify Machen as few documents could. Whatever one's opinion of his philosophy or his fiction, these autobiographies reveal Arthur Machen as one of the most appealing figures of his time.

—S. T. Joshi

A Note on This Edition

I have used the first English editions of Machen's three autobiographies—*Far Off Things* (London: Martin Secker, 1922), *Things Near and Far* (Martin Secker, 1923), and *The London Adventure* (Martin Secker, 1924)—as the basis of my text. I have slightly modified some points of style and punctuation to bring them in line with what I believe to be Machen's preferences, as discussed in my introduction to Machen's *Collected Fiction* (see note 2 above). I have also examined the serialization of *Far Off Things* ("Confessions of a Literary Man," London *Evening News*, March–July 1915) and supplied interesting variants or omitted passages in footnotes (the serialization is abbreviated as CLM). My footnotes are enclosed in brackets; Machen's few footnotes are presented without brackets. An introductory letter prefacing the first installment of the "Confessions" is presented as an appendix. The texts of the supplementary essays are derived from their original appearances, as listed in the bibliography at the rear of the volume.

The text of *Precious Balms* is somewhat eclectic. The original text (London: Spurr & Swift, 1924) printed book titles in Roman type with quotation marks. I have printed such titles in italics without quotation marks. I have attempted to distinguish references to the story "The Great God Pan" and the book *The Great God Pan* (1894). I have also added a period to such abbreviations as "Mr.," "Dr.," and so forth, in accordance with Machen's preferences. A consultation of the original texts of these reviews indicates that such periods were added more often than not. In the original publication, the names of the periodicals appeared as marginal notations; this has proven to be inconvenient, and so they appear here at the head of each review, followed by a colon.

I extend special thanks to Martin Andersson and Clark Tucker for their scrupulous proofreading.

—S. T. J.

Far Off Things

DEDICATION

To ALFRED TURNER

This is a book, my dear Turner, which I had in my heart to write for many years. The thought of it came to me with that other thought that I was growing—rather, grown—old; that the curtain had definitely been rung down on all the days of my youth. And so I got into the way of looking back, of recalling the far gone times and suns of the 'seventies and early 'eighties when the scene of my life was being set. I made up my mind that I would write about it all—some day.

Some day would undoubtedly have been Never; if it had not been for you. I had not spoken of the projected book to you or anyone else; but one fine morning in 1915 you ordered me to write it! You were then, you will remember, editing the London Evening News, *and as a reporter on your staff I had nothing to do but to obey. The book was written, appeared in the paper as "The Confessions of a Literary Man", and now reappears as* Far Off Things.

So far, good. I enjoyed writing the book enormously; and, I frankly confess, I enjoy reading it. In a word, I am not grumbling. But there is one little point that I do not mean to neglect. My complacent views as to "Far Off Things" may not be shared by other and, possibly, more competent judges. And what I want to impress on you is this: that if there is to be trouble, "you are going to have your share of it". You ordered the book to be written, you printed it in your paper, you have urged me to reprint it, not once or twice, but again and again.

Now, you remember Johnson on advising an author to print his book. "This author," said the Doctor, "when mankind are hunting him with a canister at his tail can say, 'I would not have published, had not Johnson, or Reynolds, or Musgrave, or some other good judge commended the work!'"

Now you see the purpose of this Epistle Dedicatory. It is to make it quite clear that, if there is to be any talk of canisters and tails, the order will run:

"Canisters for two!"

ARTHUR MACHEN

I

One night a year or so ago I was the guest of a famous literary society. This society, or club, it is well known, believes in celebrating literature—and all sorts of other things—in a thoroughly agreeable and human fashion. It meets not in any gloomy hall or lecture room, it has no gritty apparatus of blackboard, chalk, and bleared water-bottle. It summons its members and its guests to a well-known restaurant of the West End, it gives them red and white roses for their button-holes, and sets them down to an excellent dinner and good red wine at a gaily decked table, flower garlanded, luminous with many starry lamps.

Well, as I say, I found myself on a certain night a partaker of all this cheerfulness. I was one guest among many; there were explorers and ambassadors and great scientific personages and judges, and the author who has given the world the best laughter that it has enjoyed since Dickens died: in a word, I was in much more distinguished company than that to which I am accustomed. And after dinner the Persians (as I will call them) have a kindly and courteous custom of praising their guests; and to my astonishment and delight the speaker brought me into his oration and said the kindest and most glowing things imaginable about a translation I once made of the *Heptameron* of Margaret of Navarre. I was heartily pleased; I hold with Foker in *Pendennis* that every fellow likes a hand. Praise is grateful, especially when there has not been too much of it; but it is not to record my self-complacence that I have told this incident of the Persian banquet. As I sat at the board and heard the speaker's kindly compliments, I was visited for a twinkling part of a moment by a vision; by such a vision as they say comes to the spiritual eyes of drowning men as they sink through the green water. The scene about me was such as one will find nowhere else but in London. The multitude of lights, the decoration of the great room and the tables, above all the nature of the company and something in the very air of the place; all these were metropolitan in the sense in which the word is opposed to provincial. This is a subtlety which the provinces cannot understand, and it is natural enough that they are unable to do so. The big town in the Midlands or the North will tell you of its picture galleries, of its classical concerts, and of the serious books taken out in great numbers from its flourishing free libraries. It does not see, and, probably, will never see, that none of these things is to the point.

Well, from the heart of this London atmosphere I was suddenly transported in my vision to a darkling, solitary country lane as the dusk of a November evening closed upon it thirty long years before. And, as I think that the pure provincial can never understand the quiddity or essence of London, so I believe that for the born Londoner the country ever remains an incredible mystery. He knows that it is there—somewhere—but he has no true vision of it. In spite of himself he Londonises it, suburbanises it; he sticks a gas lamp or two in the lanes, dots some largish villas of red brick beside them, and extends the District or the Metropolitan to within easy distance of the dark wood. But here was I carried from luminous Oxford Street to the old deep lane in Gwent, which is on the borders of Wales. Nothing that a Londoner would call a town within eight miles, deep silence, deep stillness everywhere; hills and dark wintry woods growing dim in the twilight, the mountain to the west a vague, huge mass against a faint afterlight of the dead day, grey and heavy clouds massed over all the sky. I saw myself, a lad of twenty-one or thereabouts, strolling along this solitary lane on a daily errand, bound for a point about a mile from the rectory. Here a footpath over the fields crossed the road, and by the stile I would wait for the postman. I would hear him coming from far away, for he blew a horn as he walked, so that people in the scattered farms might come out with their letters if they had any. I lounged on the stile and waited, and when the postman came I would give him my packet—the day's portion of "copy" of that Heptameron translation that I was then making and sending to the publisher in York Street, Covent Garden. The postman would put the parcel in his bag, cross the road, and go striding off into the dim country beyond, finding his way on a track that no townsman could see, by field and wood and marshy places, crossing the Canthwr brook by a narrow plank, coming out somewhere on the Llanfrechfa road, and so entering at last Caerleon-on-Usk, the little silent, deserted village that was once the golden Isca of the Roman legions, that is golden for ever and immortal in the romances of King Arthur and the Graal and the Round Table.

So, in an instant's time, I journeyed from the lighted room in the big Oxford Street restaurant to the darkening lane in far-away Gwent, in far-away years. I gathered anew for that little while the savour of the autumnal wood beside which the boy of thirty years before was walking, and also the savour of his long-forgotten labours, of his old dreams of life and of letters. The speech and the dream came to an end: and the man on the other side of the table, who is probably the most skilful and witty writer of musical comedy "lyrics" in England, was saying that once on a time he had tried to write real poetry.

I shall always esteem it as the greatest piece of fortune that has fallen to me, that I was born in that noble, fallen Caerleon-on-Usk, in the heart of Gwent. My greatest fortune, I mean, from that point of view which I now more especially have in mind, the career of letters. For the older I grow the more firmly am I convinced that anything which I may have accomplished in literature is due to the fact that when my eyes were first opened in earliest childhood they had before them the vision of an enchanted land. As soon as I saw anything I saw Twyn Barlwm, that mystic tumulus, the memorial of peoples that dwelt in that region before the Celts left the Land of Summer. This guarded the southern limit of the great mountain wall in the west; a little northward was Mynydd Maen—the Mountain of the Stone—a giant, rounded billow; and still to the north mountains, and on fair, clear days one could see the pointed summit of the Holy Mountain by Abergavenny. It would shine, I remember, a pure blue in the far sunshine; it was a mountain peak in a fairy tale.[5] And then to eastward the bedroom window of Llanddewi Rectory looked over hill and valley, over high woods, quivering with leafage like the beloved Zacynthus of Ulysses, away to the forest of Wentwood, to the church tower on the hill above Caerleon. Through a cleft one might see now and again a

---

5. [In CLM the text adds here: "The Welsh name for it signifies 'the Great Rending,' for the legend was that its peak was rent asunder at the Crucifixion."]

bright yellow glint of the Severn Sea, and the cliffs of Somerset beyond. And hardly a house in sight in all the landscape, look where you would. Here the gable of a barn, here a glint of a whitewashed farmhouse, here blue wood smoke rising from an orchard grove, where an old cottage was snugly hidden; but only so much if you knew where to look. And of nights, when the dusk fell and the farmer went his rounds, you might chance to see his lantern glimmering a very spark on the hillside. This was all that shewed in a vague, dark world; and the only sounds were the faint distant barking of the sheepdog and the melancholy cry of the owls from the border of the brake.

I believe that I have seen at all events the main streets of London at every hour of the day and night. I have viewed, for example, Leicester Square between four and five of a summer morning, and have marvelled at its dismal disarray and quite miserable shabbiness of aspect. With the pure morning sun shining upon its gay places in clear splendour they are infinitely more "shocking" than they can appear at night-time to the narrowest of provincials. The Strand is a solemn street at two in the morning, Holborn has a certain vastness and windiness about it as the sky grows from black to grey, and at six the residential quarters seem full of houses of mourning, their white blinds most strictly drawn.

And at one time I had almost as full a knowledge of my native country, though not so much with respect to the category of time as to that of place. I have, it is true, seen the sky above the dark stretch of Wentwood Forest redden to the dawn, and I have lost my way and strayed in a very maze of unknown brooks and hills and woods and wild lands in the blackest hours after midnight. But the habits of the country, unlike those of London, generally fail to give reason or excuse for night wanderings. If you stayed in friendly and hospitable company much after ten of the night, it was usually a case of the spare room, newly aired sheets, one pipe more, and so to bed. This at all events on nights that were very black or tempestuous with wind and rain; for on such nights it is difficult to make out the faint footpath from stile to stile, and only the surest sense of locality will enable one to strike the felled tree or the narrow plank that, hidden by a dense growth of alders, crosses the winding of the brook. But from very early years indeed I became an enchanted student of the daylight country, which, I think, for me never was illuminated by common daylight, but rather by suns that rose from the holy seas of faery and sank down behind magic hills. I was an only child, and as soon as I could walk beyond the limits of the fields and orchards about the rectory, my father would take me with him on such parish visitations as were fairly within the stretch and strength of short legs. Indeed, I began my peregrinations at a still earlier period, for I can remember a visit to the mill, that was paid when I was a passenger in a perambulator, and aged, I suppose, about three.

Later these travels became more frequent, and I have recollections, still fresh and pleasant, of sitting still in old farmhouse kitchens while my father was about his ghostly business. Always, even in the full blaze of summer, there would be a glint of fire on the cavernous hearth and a faint blue spire of wood smoke mounting the huge hollow of the chimney. The smell of this wood smoke scented and sweetened the air, in which there was usually a hint of apples stored away in loft or cellar, somewhere behind one or other of the black tarred doors that opened from every wall in the long, low room, and here and there bevelled what should have been an angle. By the hearth stood a big curving settle on one side, on the other there was usually an arm-chair for the farmer's wife. One small window, with square leaded panes, with solid oaken mullions, looked out on the garden, and so thick were the walls—they were always heavily "battered", or sloped outward towards the ground—that there was a depth of at least three feet between the window panes and the inner wall of the room. There was whitewash within and without, renewed every spring, and it is one of the most beautiful circumstances in Gwent that this custom of whitewash prevails. To look up to a mountain side and to see the pure white of the walls of the farms and cottages established there, fronting great winds, but nestling too in a shelter of tossing trees, gives me even now the keenest pleasure. And if on a summer day one climbs up amidst those brave winds and looks down on all the rolling land of Gwent, it is dotted with these white farms, that shine radiant in the sunlight.

And these farmhouse kitchens were floored with stone, which was so purely and exquisitely kept that people said "one could eat bread and butter off Mrs. Morgan's kitchen floor". Such a place was, and still is, my notion of comfort, of the material surroundings which are fit to house a man. Now and then, in these later days, my business—never my pleasure—calls me to our Hôtel Glorieux or our Hôtel Splendide; to the places where the rooms are fifty feet high, where the walls are marble, and mirrors and gilding, where there are flowery carpets and Louis Quinze chairs and the true American heat. I think then of the kitchens of Pantyreos and Penyrhaul, as Israel in exile remembered Syon.

But it is not in summer-time that it is best to remember these places, excellent though the thought of their coolness and refreshment may be. I like to think of them as set in a framework of late autumn or deep mid-winter. I will be more curious than De Quincey: no mere bitter wind or frost, not even snow will serve my turn, though each of these has its admirable uses.

But let me have a night late in November, let us say. Every leaf has long been down, save that the beech hedgerow in the sheltered forest road will keep its tawny copper all through the winter. Rain has been sweeping along the valleys for days past in giant misty pillars, the brooks are bank high with red, foaming water; down every steep field little hedgerow streams come pouring. In the farmyards the men go about their work clad in sacks, and if they may will shelter under penthouses and find work to do in the barns.

Give me a night in the midst of such weather, and then think of the farm atop the hill, to which two good miles of deep, wandering lane go climbing, and mix the rain with a great wind from the mountain: and then think of entering the place which I have described, set now for the old act of winter. The green shutters are close fastened without the window, the settle is curved about the hearth, and that great cavern is ablaze and glorious with heaped wood and coals, and the white walls golden with the light of the leaping flames. And those within can hear the rain dashing upon shutter and upon closed door, and the fire hisses now and again as stray drops fall down the chimney; and the great wind shakes the trees and goes roaring down the hillside to the valley and moans and mutters about the housetop.

A man will leave his place, snug in shelter, in the deepest glow of the fire, and go out for a moment and open but a little of the door in the porch and see all the world black and wild and wet, and then come back to the light and heat and thank God for his home, wondering whether any are still abroad on such a night of tempest.⁶

Looking back on my native country as I first remember it, I have often regretted that I was not born say twenty or thirty years earlier. I should then have seen more of a singular social process, which I can only call the Passing of the Gentry. In my father's parish this had taken place very long before my day, or his either. Indeed, I am not quite sure that any armigerous families had ever inhabited Llanddewi; though I have a dim notion that certain old farmhouses were pointed out to me as having been "gentlemen's houses". But an adjoining parish had once held three very ancient families of small gentry. One was still in existence well within my recollection, another became extinct in the legitimate line soon after I was born, and the third had been merged in other and larger inheritances.

There were no Perrotts left, and their house had been "restored", and was occupied as a farm. I often sat under their memorials in the little church, and admired their arms, three golden pears, and their crest, a parrot; altogether a pretty example of *heraldia cantans,* or punning heraldry. Of the other two houses one was a pleasant, rambling, mouldering place, yellow-washed, verandahed, and on the whole more like a *petit manoir* in Touraine than a country house in England. The third mansion was a sixteenth-century house built in the L shape, and here dwelt in my childhood the last of the ancient gentry of the place.

Even he was descended from the old family in the female line. The old race had been named Meyrick, and they had given land in the thirteenth century that a light might burn before the altar of a neighbour-

---

6. [In CLM a paragraph is added here: "It is such a scene as always comes to my mind now on those rare nights—at the best, but two or three of them throughout all the length of winter—in which we Londoners are made aware of the presence of the wind. Now and then, even in the heart of London, with eight miles of houses on every side of me, the wind does descend and sweep down with might, howling in the chimneys quite after the country fashion. And then, as the gust shakes the houses and the rain rattles on the windows, I get forty years younger, and find myself back again in Gwent. I am struggling through the wild night, across the wild wet fields, under wild black heavens. And at last the open door and genial warmth and the kindly fire, and voices of welcome that now, alas! are silent for evermore."]

ing church for ever. The family affirmed that at one time they had owned all the land that could be seen from a certain high place near their house, and very possibly the tradition was a true one. They had remained faithful to the Latin Church through all the troubles—up to the year of Napoleon Buonaparte's sacring as Emperor by the Pope in Notre-Dame. And when the reigning squire of Lansoar heard the news he raged with fury, and saying, as the story goes, "Damn such a Pope as that!" left the Roman Church for ever. His grandson, whom I knew, always read the Bible in the Douay version and praised the Papists. Indeed, he used often to end up, addressing my father, "In fact they tell me that you're more than half a Roman Catholic yourself, and I like you none the worse for it!"

He was an extraordinary old man. In his youth he had been busy one morning packing up his portmanteau to go to Oxford. News came that his father was ruined; it was probably in the wild smash of speculation that brought down Sir Walter Scott. The young man quietly unpacked his portmanteau and took possession of the mill, not many yards from his own door. He ground corn for the farmers; he did well; he moved into Newport, and became, I think, an importer of Irish butter. Probably, also, he had his share in the industrial developments of Glamorganshire and Monmouthshire, then at the height of their prosperity. At any rate in twenty years or so the fortunes of the old house were redeemed. The drawing-room of Lansoar had been used as a barn for storing corn; in my day it was the most gracious and grave room that I have ever seen. The old family portraits were back on the walls, the old tapestried chairs were in their places, there was not a thing in the room less than a hundred years old, and the squire sat beside his hearth, looking—as I have found out since those days—exactly like Henry IV of France.

He had travelled a good deal in his time, and was supposed to have had his fancy taken by the clothes he had seen worn by the Heidelberg students. So he wore an odd sort of vestment striped with black and dull red, and gathered in with a belt of the same stuff. We called it a blouse, but it must have been something of the shape of a Norfolk jacket. In the evening he would put on a black velvet coat which, as he told me, he got from Poole's at the price of five guineas. Smoking he abominated, and it was never allowed at Lansoar, save when Mr. Williams of Llangibby was a guest.[7]

The owner of Lansoar was in many ways a kindly and benevolent old gentleman, but I think we in the country were chiefly proud of his temper. It was said to be terrific, even in a land of furious, quickly-raised rages. People told how they had seen the old man's white moustache bristling up to his eyes; this was a sign that the fire was kindled. And, as I once heard him say, "the Meyricks always get white with love and hate". It was said that his sister was the only person who met him on something like equal terms. She was an ancient gentlewoman with a tremendous aquiline nose and was more like a marquise of 1793 going proudly to instant execution than can possibly be imagined. She and her brother differed—it is much too mild a word, I am sure—so fiercely as to what were the true armorial bearings of the family that when these were to be emblazoned above the dining-room hearth a compromise had to be arranged, and two shields were painted, one on each side.

I am sorry that I was too young to observe Lansoar and its ways with intelligent interest. The people that lived there were of a race and sort that have now perished utterly out of the land; there never will be such people again. But I was banished from Lansoar for the last year or two of the old squire's life. I had left school and was at a loose end at home, and I heard I had fallen under heavy displeasure. It seemed that the descendant of the Meyricks had known a doctor who had lived in Paris on five shillings a week at the beginning of the nineteenth century; he wished to know why I was not living in London on five shillings a week in 1880. The answer would have been that I had neither five shillings nor five pence a week; but one did not answer Mr. James of Lansoar.

I am heartily sorry that the class which he represented has perished. I am sorry to think of all their houses scattered over Gwent; now mere memorials of something that is done for ever and ended. One came upon these houses in every other valley, on every other

---

7. [In CLM this passage reads: "Smoking he abominated, and it was never allowed at Lansoar, save when Mr. Iltyd Nicholl of the Ham was a visitor. But Mr. Iltyd Nicholl, of the Ham, Llantwit, in the country of Glamorgan, was no doubt 'of the tribe of the saint'—that is, the tribe of Iltyd Sant, founder of the great Cetic monastery of Llantwit in the sixth century."]

hillside, looking pleasantly towards the setting sun. They are noble old places, even though they are noble in a humble way; there are no Haddon Halls in Gwent. But these old homes of the small gentry of the borderland—now for the most part used as farmhouses—shew their lineage in the dignity of their proportions, in the carved armorial bearings of their porches. The pride of race that belonged to the Morgans, Herberts, Meyricks that once lived in them has passed into their stones, and still shines there.

There is a great book that I am hoping to write one of these fine days. I have been hoping to write it, I may say, since 1898, or '99, and somewhere about the latter year I did write as many as a dozen pages. The *magnum opus* so far conducted did not wholly displease me, and yet it was not good enough to urge me forward in the task. And so it has languished ever since then, and I am afraid I have lost the MSS. that contained all that there was of it long ago. Seriously, of course, it would not have been a great book if it had been ever so prosperously continued and ended; but it would have been at least a curious book, and even now I feel conscious of warm desire at the thought of writing it—some day. For the idea of it came to me as follows:

I had been thinking at the old century end of the work that I had done in the fifteen years or so before, and it suddenly dawned upon me that this work, pretty good or pretty bad, or as it may be, had all been the expression of one formula, one endeavour. What I had been doing was this: I had been inventing tales in which and by which I had tried to realise my boyish impressions of that wonderful magic Gwent. Say that I had walked and wandered by unknown roads, and suddenly, after climbing a gentle hill, had seen before me for the first time the valley of the Usk, just above Newbridge. I think it was on one of those strange days of summer when the sky is at once grey and luminous that I achieved this adventure. There are no clouds in the upper air, the sky is simply covered with a veil which is, as I say, both grey and luminous, and there is no breath of wind, and every leaf is still.

But now and again as the day goes on the veil will brighten, and the sun almost appear; and then here and there in the woods it is as if white moons were descending. On such a day, then, I saw that wonderful and most lovely valley; the Usk, here purged of its muddy tidal waters, now like the sky, grey and silvery and luminous, winding in mystic esses, and the dense forest bending down to it, and the grey stone bridge crossing it. Down the valley in the distance was Caerleon-on-Usk; over the hill, somewhere in the lower slopes of the forest, Caerwent, also a Roman city, was buried in the earth, and gave up now and again strange relics—fragments of the temple of "Nodens, god of the depths". I saw the lonely house between the dark forest and the silver river, and years after I wrote "The Great God Pan",[8] an endeavour to pass on the vague, indefinable sense of awe and mystery and terror that I had received.

This, then, was my process: to invent a story which would recreate those vague impressions of wonder and awe and mystery that I myself had received from the form and shape of the land of my boyhood and youth; and as I thought over this and meditated on the futility—or comparative futility—of the plot, however ingenious, which did not exist to express emotions of one kind or another, it struck me that it might be possible to reverse the process. Could one describe hills and valleys, woods and rivers, sunrise and sunset, buried temples and mouldering Roman walls so that a story should be suggested to the reader? Not, of course, a story of material incidents, not a story with a plot in the ordinary sense of the term, but an interior tale of the soul and its emotions; could such a tale be suggested in the way I have indicated? Such is to be the plan of the "great" book which is not yet written. I mention it here chiefly because I would lay stress on my doctrine that in the world of imagination the child is indeed father of the man, that the man is nothing more than the child with an improved understanding certainly, with all sorts of technical advantages in the way of information and in the arts of expression, but, on the other hand, with the disadvantages of a dimmed imaginative eye and a weakened vision. There have been a few men who have kept the awe and the surmise of earlier years and have added to those miraculous gifts the acquired accomplishments of age and instruction; and these are the only men who are entitled to the name of genius. I have said already that in my boyhood and youth I was a deep and learned student of the country about my home, and that I always saw it as a kind of fairyland. And, cross-

---

8. [In CLM this title is rendered as "The Nympholept."]

examining my memory, I find that I have in no way exaggerated or overcoloured these early and earliest impressions. Fairyland is too precise a word; I would rather say that I saw everything in something of the spirit in which the first explorers gazed on the tropical luxuriance and strangeness of the South American forests, on the rock cities of Peru, on the unconjectured seas that burst upon them from that peak in Darien, on the wholly unimagined splendours of the Mexican monarchy. So it was with me as a child. I came into a strange country, and strange it ever remained to me, so that when I left it for ever there were still hills within sight and yet untrodden, lanes and paths of which I knew the beginning but not the end. For it is to be understood that country folk are in this respect like Londoners: that they have their customary tracks and ways which lead more or less to some end or other; it is only occasionally that either goes out determined not to find his way but to lose it, to stray for the very sake of straying. Thus I walked many times in Wentwood and became familiar with the Roman road that passes for some distance along the summit of that ancient forest, but only once, I think, did I set out from the yellow verge of the Severn and cross the level Moors—a belt of fen country that might well lie between Ely and Brandon; really, no doubt "y môr", the sea—and wonder for a while at the bastioned and battlemented ruins of Caldicot Castle, and so mount up by the outer hills and woods of the forest, through Caerwent, past the Foresters' Oaks, a grove of trees that were almost awful in the magnificence of their age and their decay, and so climb to the ridge and look down on the Usk and the more familiar regions to the west.

And, as you may judge, it was only the knowledge that one must not frighten one's family out of its wits and that camping out in forests without food or drink is highly inconvenient that kept me on this comparatively straight path. So all the while, as I paced an unknown way, yet more unknowns were beckoning to me on right and left. Paths full of promise allured me into green depths, the wildest heights urged me to attempt them, cottages in orchard dells seemed so isolated from all the world that they and theirs must be a part of enchantment. And so I crossed Wentwood, and felt not that I knew it, but that it was hardly to be known.

* * *

I have already mentioned, I think, that I was an only child. Add to this statement that I had no little cousins available as play-fellows, some of these being domiciled in Anglesea, others in London; that it was only by the merest chance and on the rarest occasions that I ever saw any children at all, and I have given some notion of the extreme solitude of my upbringing. I grew up, therefore, all alone so far as other children were concerned, and though I went to school, school did not seem to make much difference to my habit of mind. I was eleven years old at the time, and I suppose I was "set" to loneliness. I passed the term as a sort of interlude amongst strangers, and came home to my friendly lanes, to my deep and shadowy and secret valleys, as a man returns to his dear ones and his dear native fields after exile amongst aliens and outlanders.

I came back, then, again and again to solitude. There were no children's parties for me, no cricket, no football, and I was heartily glad of it, for I should have abhorred all these diversions with shudderings of body and spirit. My father and mother apart, I loved to be by myself, with unlimited leisure for mooning and loafing and roaming and wandering from lane to lane, from wood to wood. Constantly I seemed to be finding new, hitherto unsuspected tracks, to be emerging from deep lanes and climbing hills so far but seen from the distance, matters of surmise, and now trodden and found to be Darien peaks giving an outlook upon strange worlds of river and forest and bracken-covered slope. Wondering at these things, I never ceased to wonder; and even when I knew a certain path and became familiar with it I never lost my sense of its marvels, as they appeared to me.

I have read curious and perplexed commentaries on that place in Sir Thomas Browne in which he declares his life up to the period of the *Religio Medici* to have been "a miracle of thirty years, which to relate were not a history, but a piece of poetry". Dr. Johnson, summing up the known events of Browne's early life, finds therein nothing in the least miraculous; Southey says the miracle was the great writer's preservation from atheism; Leslie Stephen considers that the strangeness "consists rather in Browne's view of his own history than in any unusual phenomena". "View of his own history" seems a little vague; but however critical sagacity may determine the sense of the passage, I would very willingly adopt it to describe these early years of mine, spent in that rectory amongst the wild hills of Gwent. Of my private opinion, I think there can be little doubt that when Sir Thomas Browne used the word "miraculous" he was thinking not of miracles in the accepted sense as things done contrary to the generally observed laws of nature, but rather of his vision of the world, of his sense of a constant wonder latent in all things. Stevenson, I believe, had some sense of this doctrine as applied to landscape, at least, when he said that there were certain scenes—I forget how he particularised them—which demanded their stories, which cried out, as it were, to have tales indited to fit their singular aspects. This, I think I have shewn, is a crude analysis. I should put it thus: this group of pines, this lonely shore, or whatever the scene may be, has made the soul thrill with an emotion intense but vague in the sense in which music is vague; and the man of letters does his best to realise—rather, perhaps, to actualise—this emotion by inventing a tale about the pines or the sands. Such at all events was my state through all the years of boyhood and of youth: everything to me was wonderful, everything visible was the veil of an invisible secret. Before an oddly shaped stone I was ready to fall into a sort of reverie or meditation, as if it had been a fragment of paradise or fairyland. There was a certain herb of the fields that grew plentifully in Gwent, that even now I cannot regard without a kind of reverence; it bears a spire of small yellow blossoms, and its leaves when crushed give out a very pungent, aromatic odour. This odour was to me a separate revelation or mystery, as if no one in the world had smelt it but myself, and I ceased not to admire even when a countryman told me that it was good for stone, if you gathered it "under the planet Juniper".

And here, may I say in passing, that in my opinion the country parson, with all the black-coated class, knows next to nothing of the true minds of the country folk. I feel certain that my father, if asked by a Royal Commission or some such valuable body, "What influence has astrology on your parishioners?" would have answered: "They have never heard of such a thing." In later years I have wondered as to the possible fields which extended beyond the bounds of our ignorance. I have wondered, for example, whether, by any possibility, there were waxen men, with pins in them, hidden in very secret nooks in any of the Llanddewi cottages.

But this is a mere side-issue. To return to my topic, to that attitude of the child-mind which almost says in its heart, "things are because they are wonderful", I am reminded of one of the secret societies with which I have had the pleasure of being connected. This particular society issued a little MS. volume of instructions to those who were to be initiated, and amongst these instructions was the note: "remember that nothing exists which is not God." "How can I possibly realise that?" I said to one of the members of the society. "When I read it I was looking at the tiles on each side of my fireplace in Gray's Inn, and they are of the beastliest design it is possible to imagine. I really cannot see anything of Divinity in those tiles." I do not remember how my objection was met; I don't think it was met. But, looking back, I believe that, as a child, I realised something of the spirit of the mystic injunction. Everywhere, through the darkness and the mists of the childish understanding, and yet by the light of the child's illumination, I saw *latens deitas;* the whole earth, down to the very pebbles, was but the veil of a quickening and adorable mystery. Hazlitt said that the man of genius spent his whole life in telling the world what he had known himself when he was eighteen. Waiving utterly—I am sorry to say—the title of man of genius, I would reaffirm Hazlitt's proposition on lower grounds. I would say that he who has any traffic with the affairs of the imagination has found out all the wisdom that he will ever know, in this life at all events, by the age of eighteen or thereabouts. And it is probable that Hazlitt, though he never dreamed of it, was but re-expressing those sentences in the Holy Gospels which deal with the intimate relationship between children and "the Kingdom of Heaven". In the popular conception, of course, both amongst priests and people, these texts are understood to refer to the innocence of childhood. But a little reflection will satisfy anyone that in the true sense of the word children are only innocent as a stone is innocent, as a stick is innocent; that is, they are incapable of committing the special offences which to our modern and utterly degraded system of popular ethics constitute the whole matter of morality and immorality. I remember a few years ago reading how an illustrious Primitive Methodist testified on the sacred mount of Primitive Methodism at some anniversary of the society. He said that his old grandmother had implored him when he was a boy never to drink, never to gamble, never to break the Sabbath, and, he concluded triumphantly, "I have never done any of these things."

"Therefore I am a good Christian" is the conclusion evidently suggested. This poor man, it may be said, knew no better, but I am much mistaken if the majority of our Anglican clergy would not accept his statement as a good confession of the faith. The New Testament for all these people has been written in vain; they will still believe that a good Christian is one who drinks a cup of cocoa at 9.30 and is in bed by ten sharp. And to such persons, of course, the texts which assert the necessity of becoming like little children if we would enter the Kingdom of Heaven are clear enough; it is a mere matter of early hours and plenty of cocoa—or, perhaps, of warm bread and milk. But, personally, I cannot at all symbolise with them. I look back to the time when the mountain and the tiny shining stone, the flower, and the brook were all alike signs and evidences of an ineffable mystery and beauty. I see myself all alone in the valley, under hanging woods, of a still summer evening, entranced, wondering what the secret was that was here almost told, and then, I am persuaded, I came near to the spirit of St. Thomas Aquinas: *Adoro te devote latens Deitas.*

There comes to me from very long ago the memory of a burning afternoon in the hot heart of July. I am not sure whether it was in the dry summer. This was in '68 or '69—I am not certain which—and it was notable for many things in my recollection. Firstly, the mountain caught fire. This sounds a terrific and unlikely statement, considered with relation to the temperate and reasonable geology of this land, which has known nothing for many æons of volcanoes or burning mountains. What had happened, of course, was that the heather and wild growth on the mountain had somehow been fired, and so all through that hot August I remember looking westward to the great mountain wall, and watching the dun fume that drifted along its highest places; looking with a certain dread, for there was something apocalyptic in the sight.

Another notable event was the failure of the water supply. The rectory stood almost on top of a long hill that mounted up from the valley of the Soar, there were no ponds or tanks in its curtilage and the drought of this year exhausted the water in the great butt that stood in the yard and received the streams from the roof in rainy weather. This, of course, was not drinking water; that we obtained always from a well deep in the brake, about a quarter of a mile from the house; and without contempt for other and more elaborate beverages, I may say that there are few draughts more delicious than cold well-water, dripping from the rock, and shaded in its hollow basin by the overhanging trees. Our London water is, I believe, perfectly wholesome, but it is absolutely tasteless, no doubt through the manifold purifications and purgations which it has undergone. But well-water has a savour and a character of its own, and the product of one well will often differ in a very marked degree from that of another. Before my day, oddly enough, we had in the county a connoisseur or gourmet of wells. He was a clergyman, and he had been heard to boast that he had tasted the water of every well in the forest of Wentwood. Our own well in the rectory brake was thought excellently of by good judges of clear cold water.

I think it was in this year of the burning mountain that the rectory paid a call on Mr. and Mrs. Roger Gibbon, of the Wern, on a blazing afternoon. They were very old people, and the stock of the Gibbons—I am not using their real name—was one of the most ancient and honoured in the land of Gwent. I suppose, indeed, that they would look on many dukes as parvenus of yesterday. Furthermore, this branch of the race was quite comfortable and well-to-do in money matters.

They received my father and my mother and myself with the heartiest kindness—they had known my father from his boyhood—and insisted on the necessity of some refreshment. So presently the maid came in with a tray and old Roger solemnly mixed for my father and mother, for his wife and himself, four reeking glasses of hot gin. I think that, all things considered, this was the very strangest refreshment ever offered. The old people swallowed their boiling spirit with relish, my parents took their dose with shuddering politeness, and the thermometer rose steadily. Roger and Caroline had been quarrelling about a carpet before we came, and after a decent interval the quarrel was resumed. Roger addressed himself to my mother.

"She would buy it too small. I told her it would be too small, and there it is, with three or four feet of the floor shewing. And what do you think she says, Mrs. Machen? She says she will have the bare boards painted green to match the carpet. I say that's ridiculous, don't you think so? [Without waiting for an answer, and bellowing to deaf old Caroline.] There, Caroline, I told you what everyone would say. Mrs. Machen says it's ridiculous. The idea of painting the boards green!"

And the old man, turning to my father, told him in a lower voice and with considerable enjoyment of some home-made wine that his wife had concocted. She had stored it in a cupboard in their bedroom, and Roger told how he used to lie awake at night laughing as he listened to the bottles bursting, the old lady being much too deaf to hear the reports.

Old Gibbon was an expert shot, but he could never be persuaded to use the new-fangled percussion caps. He brought down his birds to the last by means of flint and steel. He was an enthusiastic fox hunter also, but he never hunted on horseback. Up to something past the middle of his life the Llangibby Hounds had been hunted afoot, the Rector of Llangibby being the master, and afoot Roger Gibbon followed them up to his old age. And so cunning had he become in matter of wind and scent and lie of the country that he rarely failed to be in at the death. I doubt whether he knew much of the world outside of a twenty-mile radius, Caerleon being taken as the centre of the circle. But when Roger Gibbon was quite an old man people told him that he ought to see London. So he went to London. He walked out of Paddington Station and saw London, as he thought; and, filled with a great horror and disgust and terror at what he had seen, he trotted back into the station, and paced the platform till the next train for the west started. He got into that train, and returned to the Wern and to the shelter and companionship of his hills and woods, and there abode till the ending of his long days.

It was strange how in those times people were fixed in the soil, so that for many miles round everybody knew everybody, or at least knew of everybody. It is all over, I suppose, and again I think it is a pity that it is over. It was a part of the old life of the friendly fires, and the friendly faces, and when, rarely enough, in this great desert of London, I meet a friend of those old days, I think we both feel as if we were surviving tribesmen of some sept that has been "literally annihilated" or "almost decimated"—to use our modern English.

One says: "Do you remember that walk over Mynydd Fawr to the

Holy Well?" The other replies: "How good the beer at the Three Salmons tasted that day we walked all the way from Caerleon on the Old Usk Road." "Let me see; when was that?" "April, '83." And we look on one another and, lo, our heads have whitened and our eyes are beginning to grow dim.

But, as an instance of the fellowship and brotherhood that there was in the land of Gwent in the old days, here is a true story. I have told of fierce old Mr. James, of Lansoar, the ancient squire. Well, there had been a raging and tremendous quarrel between Mr. James and a neighbouring farmer called Williams, and as Williams was an honest and excellent and placable old man, there was not much doubt as to who was the aggressor. After years of hate, on one side at all events, a false rumour went about the county that Mr. James had lost all his money, in "Turkish Bonds", I think. Then did old Mr. Williams, the farmer, go up one night secretly to old Mr. James, the squire, and altogether heedless of the white face and the furious glance and the bristling moustache that greeted him, he offered all he had to his enemy.

May he remember me from his happy place.

II

By this time I hope that I have made a sort of picture of my conditions as they were up to the time that I left school at the age of seventeen. Solitude and woods and deep lanes and wonder; these were the chief elements of my life. One thing, however, I have so far omitted, that is the matter of books, which I will now consider.

And, firstly, I must record with deep thankfulness the circumstance that as soon as I could read I had the run of a thoroughly ill-selected library; or, rather, of a library that had not been selected at all. My father's collection, if that serious word may be applied to a hugger-mugger of books, had grown up anyhow and nohow, and in it the most revered stocks had mingled with the most frivolous. There were the Fathers, in the English version made by the Tractarians, and there was also no end of "yellowbacks" bought at Smith's bookstalls on railway journeys. There was a row of little Elzevir classics, "with the Sphere", bound in parchment that had grown golden with its two hundred and odd years; there was also Mr. Verdant Green in his tattered paper wrapper as my father had bought him at Oxford. Next to Verdant Green you might very likely find the Dialogues of Erasmus in seventeenth-century leather, and Borrow in his original boards—we read Borrow at Llanddewi long before there were any Borrovians—might hide an odd volume of *Martin Chuzzlewit* (in a "Railway Edition") which had tumbled to the back of the shelf. Hard by stood Copleston's *Prælectiones Academicæ,* and close to it a complete set of Brontë books, including Mrs. Gaskell's *Life,* all these in yellowish linen covers, being, I imagine, the first one-volume edition issued by the publishers. And here again Llanddewi in the woods may claim to have been in advance of its age, for we were devoted to the name of Brontë.[9]

---

9. [In CLM appear the following paragraphs: "But suppose me on a wet af-

Suppose the weather did not beckon me, I would begin to go about the house on the search of books. I might have *Wuthering Heights* in my mind and be chasing that amazing volume very closely, and be, in fact, hot on the scent, when I would be brought up sharply by my grandfather's Hebrew grammar. I always loved the shape and show of the Hebrew character, and have meant to learn the language from 1877 onwards, but have not yet thoroughly mastered the alphabet. I once, indeed, got so advanced as to be able to spell out the Yiddish posters which cover the walls in the East End of London, and I remember being much amused when I had deciphered a most mystic, reverend-looking word and found that it read "Bishopsgyte". But I believe that in Yiddish the two "yods" represent the "a" sound.[10]

Well, this Hebrew grammar would distract me from the hunt of Emily Brontë's masterpiece, and by the time I had decided that Monday would be soon enough for a serious beginning in Hebrew, while I

---

ternoon many years ago, weighing the account of things profitable and pleasant to be done for the passage of the time and my good entertainment. On the one hand, odd as it may seem, the weather, if outrageously foul, would beckon to me with a strong allurement. Odd as it may seem, I say, and yet I do not know that it is odder to put on one's clumping boots and stout leather leggings and go out and face the storm and wet, than to put on one's flannels in weather that is outrageously hot and so to play lawn tennis. ¶ I have followed each of these courses, and have found each enjoyable. So if the rain came from Caerleon in the south, or over Twyn Barlwm in the south-west, if it had fallen all through the night and all the morning, if, when dinner was done and my father had said grace after his last bit of Caerphilly cheese, I saw the storm marching in giant misty columns over the valley; then it was odds that I would put on the boots with inch-thick soles, and strap on the leather gaiters, and sally forth in a frieze great-coat. ¶ In my earlier boyhood it would be a case of three or four miles out and four or five miles back—coming back by the same way was always repugnant to me. I would seek out some abandoned lane—abandoned in favour of a new-made track, as uninteresting to me then as a motor-track is now—and presently I would be in one of the true lanes of old Gwent, with banks of red and green marl twenty feet high, hedges atop grown so wild that they were well-nigh woods, and a roadway here of the solid limestone rock, there of rich red mud, there again of mere rushing water. ¶ But, on the other hand, suppose the weather . . ."]
10. [In CLM this sentence is rendered as: "The scribe had faithfully rendered into Hebrew letters what he knew as the correct pronunciation of the word."]

meditated in the meanwhile on the beauty of the names of the four classes of accents—Emperors, Kings, Princes, and Dukes, I think—it was likely enough that I had got hold of Alison's *History of Europe,* or *The Bible in Spain,* or a book on Brasses. And by the time I had gloated over the horrors of the French Revolution as described in Alison, or had marvelled at Borrow in the character of a Protestant colporteur, or had admired the pictured brasses of Sir Robert de Septvans, Sir Roger de Trumpington—winnowing fans on the coat-armour of the one, trumpets on the shield of the other—and Abbot Delamere of St. Albans it was tea-time, and I probably spent the rest of the evening with a bound volume of *Chambers's Journal, All the Year Round, Cornhill,* or *The Welcome Guest.* These were always a great resource; and I particularly wish that I still possessed *The Welcome Guest,* a popular weekly dating from the late 'fifties of last century. It was full of work by people who afterwards became famous, and now, again, are fading into forgetfulness. John Hollingshead we still remember, though it is only the elderly who can tell much now of "the sacred lamp of burlesque", which was kept burning at the Gaiety. Hollingshead was a contributor to *The Welcome Guest,* so also were the Brothers Mayhew and the Brothers Brough, so on a great scale was George Augustus Sala, who wrote in it *Twice Round the Clock* and something that was called, I fancy, "Make Your Game or, the Adventures of the Stout Gentleman, the Thin Gentleman, and the Man with the Iron Chest". This was a "lively" account of a visit to the gaming tables then existing in Germany. The Stout Gentleman was one of the Mayhews, the Man with the Iron Chest was Sala himself; and I met the Thin Gentleman many years afterwards in a cock-loft in Catherine Street, where I was cataloguing books on magic and alchemy and the secret arts in general. The cock-loft was over the Vizetellys' publishing office, and the Thin Gentleman was old Mr. Vizetelly. We "larned" him to publish a translation of *La Terre* by sending him, an old man past seventy, to gaol for three months. He died soon afterwards; I forget whether his death took place before or after the very handsome and official and "respectable" reception and entertainment that were given to Zola on his visiting England.

I must say that I should like to see the old *Welcome Guest* volume again. I am afraid I should not admire its literature very much, for Sala, the chief contributor, had already acquired those vicious mannerisms which pleased the injudicious. He would speak of Billingsgate as a "piscatorial bourse", for instance. I am afraid I should find it all terribly old-fashioned. But I should like to hold the fat volume again and glance through its pages, for they would bring back to me the long winter evenings, and the rectory fire burning cheerfully, and the heavy red curtains drawn close over the windows, shutting out the night.

I must say that I found a great joy and resource in these old magazines. If one were in a mood averse from reading in the solid block, if the hour did not seem propitious for beginning once more *Pickwick* from the beginning, it was a delight to think of those bound volumes all in a row, and of the inexhaustible supply of mixed literature which they contained. For just as there was always the chance, and indeed the likelihood, of making new discoveries in the happy confusion of the Llanddewi library, so it was with these rows of *Household Words, Chambers's, All the Year Round, Welcome Guest,* and *Cornhill;* there was always the possibility of a find; some tale or essay hitherto overlooked or neglected might turn out to be full of matter and entertainment. And so the most unlikely events happened. You would expect to find good things of all sorts in a magazine edited by Charles Dickens, but you would hardly expect to find there the curious thing or the out-of-the-way thing. Still, it was in a volume of *Household Words* that I first read about alchemy in a short series of papers which (I have since recognised) were singularly well-informed and enlightened. I do not wish it to be understood that I myself have any strong convictions on the matter of turning inferior metals into superior, though I believe the later trend of science is certainly in favour of the theoretical possibility of such a process. Nor do I hold any distinct brief for the very fascinating doctrine which maintains, or would like to maintain, that the great alchemical books are really symbolical books; that while seeming to relate to lead and gold, to mercury and silver, they hide under these figures intimations as to a profound and ineffable transmutation of the spirit; that the experiment to which they relate is the Great Experiment of the mystics, which is the experiment of God. This, I say, is a fascinating theory; whether it have any truth in it I know not, and perhaps it is one of those questions of which Sir Thomas Browne speaks; questions difficult, indeed, and perplexed, but not beyond all conjecture. But, however this may be, I recollect that those articles in that old, half-calf bound volume of *Household Words,* while not affirming this, that, or the other doctrine as to alchemy in so many distinct words, did suggest that a few of the old alchemists, at all events, were something more than blundering simpletons engaged on a quest which was a patent absurdity, which could only have been entertained by the besotted superstition of "the dark ages", which had this one claim to our attention inasmuch as the modern science of chemistry rose from the ashes of its foolish fires.

This is not the place for a discussion of the art of Thrice Great Hermes; the matter is cited here as an example of the odd and unexpected way in which my attention, I being some eight or nine years old, was directed to a singular and perplexing subject which has engaged my curiosity at intervals ever since. I see myself sitting on a stool by the rectory hearth, propping up *Household Words* against the fender, quite ravished by the story of Nicholas Flamel, who found by chance *The Book of Abraham the Jew,* who journeyed all over Europe in search of one who would interpret its figures to him, who succeeded at last in the Operation of the Great Work, and was discovered by the King's Chamberlain living in great simplicity, eating cabbage soup with Pernelle, his wife. These fireside studies of mine must have been made forty-three or forty-four years ago, but I still think the story of Nicholas Flamel and Pernelle, his wife, an enchanting one. But then I re-read the tale of Aladdin and the Wonderful Lamp only the other day, and I am still thrilled and perplexed by that most singular and important fact; that the genie declared himself to be the servant of the Roc's Egg.

I am sorry to have to confess that the rectory shelves held no copy of *The Arabian Nights.* I made up this deficiency soon after I went to school by buying an excellent edition, issued, I think, by Routledge for a shilling. This edition is now, the booksellers tell me, out of print, and it is a pity, for now if you want the book there is nothing between an edition obviously meant for the nursery, with gaudy plates, and Lane's version for thirty shillings. I speak not of Burton, for I found myself unable to read a couple of pages of his detestable English, made more terrible by the imitations of the rhymed prose of the original. I came upon something which went very much as follows:—

Then followed the dawn of day, and the Princess finished her allotted say,

> Praise be to the Lord of Light alway, who faileth not to send the appointed ray——

and so on, at much greater length; highly ingenious, no doubt, and also infinitely foolish.

I remember once wasting hours—nay, days—in the effort to render Rabelais' "Verses written over the Great Gate of the Abbey of Thelème" into English, following as far as I could the rhyme system. Now, according to the French notion, "don" is a perfect rhyme to "pardon", and so Rabelais wrote:—

> Or donné par don,
> Ordonne pardon
> A cil qui le donne;
> Et bien guerdonne
> Tout mortel preudhom
> Or donné par don.

That is, the final sound of each line is almost identical with the final sound of every other line; and of this I made:—

> For given relief,
> Forgiven and lief
> The giver believe;
> And all men that live
> May gain the palm leaf
> For given relief.

Soon afterwards, while I was resting from this mighty effort, I read in Disraeli's *Curiosities of Literature* a quotation from Martial: Turpe est difficiles habere nugas—'Tis folly to sweat o'er a difficult trifle. I was convinced of my sin. I suppose that the real translator when confronted by such puzzles contrives to think of an indirect rather than a direct solution. For example, the right way of getting the effect of the Arabic jingle into English might be sought by the path of alliteration; or possibly blank verse might give to the English reader something of the same kind of pleasure as that enjoyed by the Oriental in reading a prose which infringes on the region of poetry. And it may be that the queer music of Rabelais could be echoed, at least, in English by the use of assonance.

Here is, indeed, a diversion, but it has arisen, legitimately enough, from that shilling, paper wrapper volume of *The Arabian Nights* bought in 1875 or '76 or thereabouts. And another event of like importance was my seeing De Quincey's *Confessions of an English Opium Eater* at Pontypool Road Station. This also I instantly bought and as instantly loved, and still love very heartily. It always vexes me to detect, as I constantly do detect in modern critics, the subtle desire to run down De Quincey. The critic is afraid to make a frontal attack—the stress of these times will win pardon for the phrase—since he knows that he will be opposed by such splendours and such terrors—"an army with banners"—as the English language can scarce shew elsewhere. He is quite aware, since he is, ex hypothesi, an able critic, that De Quincey deliberately used our tongue as if it had been a mighty organ in mightier cathedral, so that the very stones and the far-lifted vault and the hollow spaces of the towers re-echo and reverberate and thrill with tremendous fugal harmonies. And our critics are advised also that De Quincey was no mere player of clever tricks with the language; his was not the amusing Stevensonian method of counting the "l's" and estimating the value of medial "s's" and the terrifying effect of the final reiterated "r". There was none of this; he wrote in the great manner because he thought in the great manner. The critic cannot deny this; he must admit the beauty and pathos of the Ann episode and of the vision of Jerusalem; but still he will hint a fault and hesitate his dislike of this greater master. The reason is not far to seek. All realism is unpopular, and De Quincey was eminently a realist.

Now I know that I am touching here on a great question. I hope to debate it at length later on; for the moment I would merely say that I define realism as the depicting of eternal, inner realities—the "things that really are" of Plato—as opposed to the description of transitory, external surfaces; the delusory masks and dominoes with which the human heart drapes and hides itself. But, all this apart, I cannot help dwelling on the manner in which I associate these early literary discoveries of mine with the places where they were made.

You may hear friends and lovers discussing after many years the manner of their first meeting; Daphnis as Darby will remind Chloe—now Joan—how they saw one another for the first time at the Smiths' garden-party, and one plate of their bread and butter tasted slightly of onions, and the curate achieved six faults running at lawn-tennis, and it came on to rain. So I can never take up De Quincey without thinking of the dismal platform at Pontypool Road, and the joy of coming home for the holidays, and the mountains all about me as I stood and waited for my father and the trap and read the first pages of the magic book. Those great mountains, and the drive home by the green arched lanes, abounding in flowers, and the very dear look of home amidst its orchards; all these are part and parcel of my joy in the *Confessions* for ever. And so again with another noble book; with one of the noblest of all books, as I have ever esteemed it. I am a very small boy; about seven or eight years old, I conceive, and my mother takes me with her to pay a call on Mrs. Gwyn, of Llanfrechfa Rectory. The ladies talk, and I, seeking quietly for something to entertain me, light in a low bookcase on a fat, dumpy little book. I suspect it was the oddity of the shape, the extreme squabness of the volume, that first took my fancy, and then I open the pages—and I have never really closed them. For the dumpy book was a translation of *The Ingenious Gentleman, Don Quixote de la Mancha;* and those are words that will thrill a lettered man as the opening notes of certain fugues of Bach will thrill a musician. I heard nothing of the amiable talk of the ladies. I was deep in the small print—alas! it would now blind my tired eyes—and when my mother rose to go I clung so desperately and piteously to the fat little book that the kind Mrs. Gwyn said she would lend it to me, and I might take it home. For which benevolence I am ever bound to pray for her good estate, or for her soul; as it may chance to be.

So, as Hereford Station spells for me, principally, *The Arabian Nights,* as De Quincey is linked with domed mountains and green lanes and the return home: the Ingenious Gentleman advanced to greet me, mysteriously enough, in the drawing-room of the rectory of Llanfrechfa, and I shall always reckon Frechfa—the "freckled"—as among the most venerated of the Celtic saints.

For a long time, as it seems to me, I have been talking of discoveries of books; discoveries in our own Llanddewi shelves, in the shelves of neighbours, on railway bookstalls. We shall hear more of books by and by, of books found in very different places—Clare Market and the Strand of 1880 and back streets by Notting Hill Gate are even now looming before us—so for the present we may hear more of the conditions of that Gwent where I was a boy and a young man.

I have said that I was born just a little too late to witness the Passing of the Gentry. Few of them survived into my day, and I was too young to see with intelligence that which still remained to be seen of the old order. But one thing I do remember, that the gentry of those times, even when they were wealthy, lived with a simplicity that would astonish the people of to-day. Those who know *Martin Chuzzlewit* will remember how Tigg Montague, who was Montague Tigg, lunched luxuriously in the board room of his city office. The meal was brought in on a tray and consisted of "a pair of cold roast fowls, flanked by some potted meats and a cool salad". There was a bottle of champagne and a bottle of Madeira. This was the luncheon of vulgar and ostentatious luxury in the 'forties; compare it with the kind of midday meal that the modern Montague would eat at the Hôtel Splendide or the Hôtel Glorieux; the meal of the man who eats and drinks as much to impress others with his wealth as to gratify his own appetite.

Well, I have often seen "the old Lord Tredegar" eating his luncheon. My father and I would be in the coffee-room of the King's Head, Newport, waiting for the ostler to put in the pony. And there in one of the boxes sat the old lord—a very wealthy man—eating his luncheon; which was bread and cheese and a tankard of ale. And, oddly enough, on the one occasion on which I visited the Ham, the magnate thereof, Mr. Iltyd Nicholl, was enjoying a meal similar in every respect to that of Lord Tredegar—though I believe he had a little cold apple tart after his cheese. We, of the middle people, always dined at one on meat, pudding, and cheese; tea followed at five, an affair of bread and butter and jam, with, possibly, a caraway loaf. Hot buttered toast was distinctly festal. The day closed so far as meals were concerned with bread and cheese and beer at nine o'clock. On rare occasions, once in three years or so, a number of clergy who called themselves collectively the Ruridecanal Chapter came to hear a paper read and also to a dinner. This would probably consist of a salmon of Severn or Usk—which muddy waters breed incomparably the finest salmon in the world—of a saddle of Welsh mutton from the mountains, and of a rich sweet called, very lightly and unworthily, a trifle. There would be a dessert of almonds and raisins and, according to the season, home-grown apples and pears or greengages. These delicates would be displayed on a service which shewed green vine-leaves in relief against a buff ground, bordered with deep purple and gold. It was hideous, and, I should think, Spode.

In the autumn my mother used to concoct a singular dish which she called fermety. It is more generally known as frumenty; you will find it mentioned in Washington Irving's "Christmas", where the squire makes his supper off it on Christmas Eve—no doubt because it was the traditional fasting dish for the Vigil of the Nativity. It was made, so far as I can remember, of the new wheat of the year, of milk, of eggs, of currants, of raisins, of sugar, and of spices, "all working up together in one delicious gravy". No doubt a very honourable dish and a most ancient and Christian pottage; but I am not quite sure that I should like it, if it were proffered to me now. Among the farmers a few of the elder people still breakfasted on *cawl*, a broth made of fat bacon and vegetables, and decorated, oddly enough, with marigold blossoms. And a fine old man whom I once met in a lane spoke violently against tea, as a corrupting thing and a very vain novelty. For women, he said, it might serve, but the breakfast for a man was a quart of cider with a toast. But most of the farming people breakfasted on rashers of bacon, cooked by being hung on hooks before the fire in a Dutch oven. With the bacon they ate potatoes, which were done in a very savoury manner. Take cold boiled potatoes, break into small pieces, fry (or rather, *faites sauter*) in bacon fat, then press into a shallow dish, pat to a smooth surface, and brown before the fire. This is a breakfast that goes very well with a keen mountain breath of a morning.

And I believe that cheese always formed part of the farmers' breakfast, as a kind of second or cold course. This was of their own making, and was of the kind called after Caerphilly, a little town with a huge ruinous castle in a hollow of giant hills. It is a white cheese of a creamy consistency and delicate flavour, and is to be commended for the making of Welsh rarebit. The farmers, as I say, ate it at breakfast, again at twelve o'clock dinner, after hot boiled fat bacon and beans or cabbage, and again at tea, where, to their tastes, it seemed to go very well with bread and butter—I find it hard to realise in London that bread and butter can be a choice delicacy—and a sweet, such as an open-work raspberry tart. And, of course, the Caerphilly cheese appeared again at supper, and with bread and onions it was always the hedgerow snack of the man in the fields.

And the cider of that land was good. It was a greenish yellow in colour, with a glint of gold in it if held up to the light, as it were a remembrance of the August and September suns that had shone mellow on the deep orchards of Gwent. It was of full body and flavour and strength, smooth on the palate, neither sweet nor sharp; and I do not think there was anyone in Llanddewi parish so poor as not to have a barrel or two in his cellar against Christmastide and snowy nights, though to be sure in years wherein apples were a scanty crop some of the smaller folk increased the bulk of their cider by strange expedients. Pears went to the mill always, and as a matter of course. In most of the orchards there were one or two big pear trees, and possibly the wisdom of the Gwentian ancients had concluded that a slight admixture of pears with the apples improved and mellowed the cider. But in scanty years, when the man with but a few trees saw bare boughs in autumn, he went to his garden, dug up a barrow load or two of parsnips and added them to his apples. I cannot say anything as to the resultant juice, since I never tasted it.

There was no wretched poverty in Llanddewi, because almost everybody had a little land of his own. Tenant farmers there were, of course, who held of Mr. John Hanbury, of Pontypool Park, lord of the manor of Edlogan; a manor named after a certain Edlogion who was a prince of the sixth century and the protector of Cybi Sant. But besides his tenants and those of other landlords there was a numerous race of small freeholders, who owned eighty, fifty, ten acres of land, and so down till you came to a holding of a house and a garden and a mere patch by the roadside. But with a garden and a patch of land a clever cottager of the old school could do a great deal. I remember an old man named Timothy who lived in a house very small and very ancient in the midst of the fields, far, even, from a by-road; and he thought in greengages as a Stock Exchange man thinks in shares. For about his old cottage there were three or four, or maybe half a dozen, greengage trees that had been planted so long ago that they had grown almost to the dignity of timber, and spread wild branches high and low and far and wide, so that one might say that old Timothy lived in a grove or wood of greengage trees. So you may conceive how deeply the poor old man thought of these gages, beside which his little orchard of damsons and bullaces was of small account. A really plentiful crop, when the big boughs were heavy and drooping with rich green, sun-speckled fruit, meant to him abundance and luxury; and bare trees spelt on the other hand a bare winter and some pinching of poverty, though nothing beyond endurance. Timothy was a smallholder on the smallest scale, but there were many people of two, six, or twelve acres who did very well in their humble way—which I have always thought is the happy way, if one can attain to it. The man would work for a farmer in the day-time, and often be sturdy enough to do many things on his own estate on summer evenings; and all the day long his wife was busy with her pigs and bees and fowls, and perhaps with two or three cows. There was a good market for their produce at Pontypool, a town on the verge of the industrial district, for the colliers and the tinplate workers love to feed richly. I once saw a woman putting the last touches to a flat apple tart in a little tavern called Castell-y-bwch (Bucks' Castle) on the mountain side. She drew out the tart from the oven, prised open the lid of pastry, and inserted some half-pound of butter and half-pound of moist Demerara sugar, and then put back the lid and replaced the pastry in the oven; so that apple juice, sugar, butter should fuse all together. That is a fair sample of hill cookery; other people of the hills would buy fresh butter at a high price, and give what they were asked for "green" Caerphilly cheese, still melting from the press; and they loved to plaster butter heavily on hot new bread and then crown all with an equal depth of golden honey. And they had a goodly appetite also for great fat salmon, caught in the yellow Usk water; and so the fishermen of Caerleon and the little farmers of such parishes as Llanddewi profited hugely by these mountain tastes.

Many years afterwards I lived for a short while on the Chiltern Hills. Here was a different tale. In a whole parish there was, I think, barely a single small holder; the little properties had all been bought up by the great landlords. There was no comfort about the tumbledown, leaky cottages which, in many cases, depended for their drinking water supply on dirty water-butts. None of the farm labourers had fowls or pigs or bees; the farmers, their employers, did not allow the men to keep pigs or fowls lest they should be tempted to steal corn and meal.

So the poorer folk were divided into two classes—the good-humoured wastrels, who "went on the parish" at the slightest provocation and without the slightest shame, and a few more prosperous, sour, ill-mannered boors, who were consumed with an acrid "Liberalism" and with a rancorous envy of anyone better off than themselves.

But at Llanddewi the small holder of land, so far from envying or hating the great landlord, took, as it were, a pride in him. I remember Mrs. Owen Tudor, owner of nine or ten rough acres of wild land in Llanddewi, being both grieved and angry when she heard that a great and ancient Gwentian house might be forced to sell a certain portion of their estates through the pressure of bad times in the early 'eighties. She, too, was a landowner—of rushes chiefly and alder copses and bracken—and of ancient, though unblazoned, family, and if the great Morgans suffered, so also did she suffer.

It comes to my mind that I must by no means forget Sir Walter Scott and all that he did for me. And to get at him it is necessary that we enter the drawing-room at Llanddewi. I was amused the other day to see in an old curiosity shop near Lincoln's Inn Fields amongst the rarities displayed small china jars or pots with a picture of two salmon against a background of leafage on the lid. I remember eating potted salmon out of just such jars as these, and now even in my lifetime they appear to have become curious. So, perhaps, if I describe a room which was furnished in 1864 that also may be found to be curious. I may note, by the way, that we always applied the word "parlour"—which properly means drawing-room, and is still, I think, used in that sense in the United States of America—to the dining-room, which was also our living-room for general, everyday use. So Sir Walter Scott speaks of a "dining-parlour", and Mr. Pecksniff, entering Todgers's, of the "eating-parlour". And now the word only occurs in public-houses, in the phrase "parlour prices", and even that use is becoming obsolete.

But as for the Llanddewi drawing-room: the walls were covered with a white paper, on which was repeated at regular intervals a diamond-shaped design in pale, yellowish buff. The carpet was also white; on it, also at regular intervals, were bunches of very red roses and very green leaves. In the exact centre of the room was a round rosewood table standing on one leg, and consequently shaky. This was covered with a vivid green cloth, trimmed with a bright yellow border. In the centre of the cloth was a round mat, apparently made of scarlet and white tags or lengths of wool; this supported the lamp of state. It was of white china and of alabastrous appearance, and it burned colza oil. One had to wind it up at intervals as if it had been a clock. In the sitting-room, before the coming of paraffin, we usually burned "composite" candles; two when we were by ourselves, four when there was company.

Over the drawing-room mantelpiece stood a large, high mirror in a florid gilt frame. Before it were two vases of cut-glass, with alternate facets of dull white and opaque green, of a green so evil and so bilious and so hideous that I marvel how the human mind can have conceived it. And yet my heart aches, too, when, as rarely happens, I see in rubbish shops in London back streets vases of like design and colour. Somewhere in the room was a smaller vase of Bohemian glass; its designs in "ground" glass against translucent ruby. This vase, I think, must have stood on the whatnot, a triangular pyramidal piece of furniture that occupied one corner and consisted of shelves getting smaller and smaller as they got higher.

Against one wall stood a cabinet, of inlaid wood, velvet lined, with glass doors. On the shelves were kept certain pieces of Nantgarw china, some old wine-glasses with high stems, and a collection of silver shoe-buckles and knee-buckles, and two stoneware jugs. The pictures—white mounts and gilt frames—were water-colours and chromo-lithographs. Against one of the window-panes hung a painting on glass, depicting a bouquet of flowers in an alabaster jar. There was a plaster cast in a round black frame, which I connect in my mind with the Crystal Palace and the Prince Consort, and an "Art Union", whatever that may be: it displayed a very fat little girl curled up apparently amidst wheat sheaves. A long stool in bead-work stood on the hearthrug before the fire; and a fire-screen, also in bead-work, shaped like a banner, was suspended on a brass stand. On a bracket in one corner was the marble bust of Lesbia and her Sparrow; beneath it in a hanging bookcase the Waverley Novels, a brown row of golden books.

I can see myself now curled up in all odd corners of the rectory reading *Waverley, Ivanhoe, Rob Roy, Guy Mannering, Old Mortality,* and the rest of them, curled up and entranced so that I was deaf and gave no answer when they called to me, and had to be roused to life—which meant tea—with a loud and repeated summons. But what can they say who have been in fairyland? Notoriously, it is impossible to give any true report of its ineffable marvels and delights. Happiness, said De

Quincey, on his discovery of the paradise that he thought he had found in opium, could be sent down by the mail-coach; more truly I could announce my discovery that delight could be contained in small octavos and small type, in a bookshelf three feet long. I took Sir Walter to my heart with great joy, and roamed, enraptured, through his library of adventures and marvels as I roamed through the lanes and hollows, continually confronted by new enchantments and fresh pleasures. Perhaps I remember most acutely my first reading of *The Heart of Midlothian,* and this for a good but external reason. I was suffering from the toothache of my life while I was reading it; from a toothache that lasted for a week and left me in a sort of low fever—as we called it then. And I remember very well as I sat, wretched and yet rapturous, by the fire, with a warm shawl about my face, my father saying with a grim chuckle that I would never forget my first reading of *The Heart of Midlothian.* I never have forgotten it, and I have never forgotten that Sir Walter Scott's tales, with every deduction for their numerous and sometimes glaring faults, have the root of the matter in them. They are vital literature, they are of the heart of true romance. What is vital literature, what is true romance? Those are difficult questions which I once tried to answer, according to my lights, in a book called *Hieroglyphics;* here I will merely say that vital literature is something as remote as you can possibly imagine from the short stories of the late Guy de Maupassant.

The hanging bookcase in the drawing-room under the marble bust of Lesbia and her Sparrow is not only rich and golden in my memory from its being the habitation of the Waverley Novels. This had been treasure enough, indeed, to make the shelves for ever dear; but there was more than this. The bookcase held, besides Sir Walter's romances, my father's school and college prizes, dignified books in whole calf and in pigskin, adorned with the arms of Cowbridge School and Jesus College, Oxford, in rich gold. Here was the Judicious Hooker, whose judiciousness, I regret to say, I could never abide nor stomach; here that noble book, Parker's *Glossary of Gothic Architecture,* in three volumes, one of text and two of beautifully executed plates; and here was an early volume of Tennyson.

Of these two last-named books I can scarcely say which is the more precious and eminent in my recollection. The one stands for my initiation into the spirit of Gothic, and I think that is one of the most magical of all initiations. More furious and frantic nonsense has been talked about "paganism" than about almost any other subject; it will only be necessary to think of Swinburne with his "world has grown grey" phrase to indicate what manner of nonsense I have in mind. But the fact is that the heart of paganism was not exactly contrite or broken, but certainly resigned, with an austere and stoical acceptance of fate, which is not without its beauty and its majesty. The nearest modern equivalent to the classic or pagan spirit is Calvinism—the Œdipus Tyrannus is nothing but the doctrine of predestination set to solemn music—and this austere spirit stamped itself on all the finest Greek art. It is somewhat softened in Plato, for Plato drew from the East by way of Pythagoras, but the beauty of Greek tragedy, architecture, sculpture, is essentially austere and severe. It is Calvinism in marble; and judgment and inexorable vengeance on guilty sinners are sung in choral odes.

Now winter has its splendours; but with what joy do we welcome the yearly miracle of spring. We and the whole earth exult together as though we had been delivered from prison, the hedgerows and the fields are glad, and the woods are filled with singing; and men's hearts are filled with an ineffable rapture. Israel once more has come out of Egypt, from the house of bondage. And all this is expressed in the Gothic, and much more than this. It is the art of the supreme exaltation, of the inebriation of the body and soul and spirit of man. It is not resigned to dwell calmly, stoically, austerely on the level plains of this earthly life, since its joy is in this, that it has stormed the battlements of heaven. And so its far-lifted vaults and its spires rush upward, and its pinnacles are like a wood of springing trees. And its hard stones, its strong-based pillars break out as it were into song, they blossom as the rose; all the secrets of the garden and the field and the wood have been delivered unto them. And not only is all this true of building. Take a common iron nail that is to be driven into a door. The Gothic smith would so deal with that nail that its head should become a little piece of joy and fantasy, a little portion of paradise. Nay, take the letter A, as the Romans gave it to us; a plain, well-built, business-like letter, admirably fulfilling its purpose, with no nonsense about it. Now look at a thirteenth-century illuminated manuscript and seek out this A. It has every kind of "nonsense" about it; of that nonsense that makes earth into heaven. It is not only that it glows with rich raised gold, that it is most imperially vested in blue and in scarlet, but its frigid form has relaxed into beauty; it is no longer a mere letter, it is as a wild rose-tree in a hedge. From it spring curves of infinite grace, which enclose the page of text, and hair-line branches break from the main stem and blossom out into flowers of paradise: so the wild roses, delicate, enchanting, sway and quiver over the green field in the month of June.

So much for the *Glossary;* now for the other volume, the little early Tennyson. My attention was directed to this in an odd manner. One of the masters at school had called me a "lotus-eater", and I was much pleased with the sound of the phrase, though the master did not mean to be complimentary, and I had no notion as to what a lotus-eater really was. But in the course of the next holidays, rummaging at random among the books at the rectory, as my custom was, I opened the Tennyson and found the poem of "The Lotos-Eaters" with the "Choric Song" annexed. I began to read that I might be instructed as to the exact nature of my crime. I read on, enchanted, and it was then, in my twelfth or thirteenth year, that I first delighted in poetry as poetry, for its own sake, apart from any story it might tell.

And here I find an extraordinary difficulty in "making a distinction", as the casuists say, between two very different kinds of literary pleasure. For some time I had enjoyed great literature in such books as *Don Quixote* and Sir Walter Scott's romances; but "The Lotos-Eaters"—which is also, I think, great literature—gave me a quite new and peculiar delight. Hitherto it had been the story which had charmed me; but now I found myself delighting in the music and melody of verse, in the "atmosphere" of the poem, in the "colour" of the words—to use terms of which I disapprove, but for which I can find no efficient substitutes. I suspect, indeed, that I found in Tennyson's poem the transmuted and golden image of my own solitary and meditative habit of mind; and this may have counted for something in the sum of my delight. The master, a cheery, excellent young man as I remember him, may have made a correct diagnosis; I had been a lotus-eater for years without knowing it, and so recognised Ulysses' entranced companions as my true comrades in dreams. It may have been so; but in any case I have always dated my inoculation with the specific virus of literature from my reading of those verses in the little calf-bound volume.

III

Some years ago I was asked by the editor of a well-known paper to write a short series of articles about London. The subject seems ambitious enough, and indeed London considered either physically or intellectually is so vast and mighty a world, that the study of any one—of even the smallest and least considerable—of its aspects may well be the task of a lifetime. But, so far as I can remember, my instructions were of the liberal and catholic kind. I mean, I was not required to write of the great city as the goal of the timber merchant or of the dealer in precious stones, or of the makers of chasubles, or of the fashioner of wigs, but rather to depict it as the end sought by all these, and by myriads more. And so I set about the task in my usual spirit, firmly convinced, that is, that better men had said all that there was to say on the matter brought before me, and yet resolved to do my best and to try to make something of the job in one way or another. So I set to work, and found, strangely enough, that though I was writing about London, I was also writing a mystical treatise, on a text which I will not divulge in this place. But for the beginning of my series I remember that I went back a good many years to the time when London began to call to me. I often speculate now in these later days as to how it would have been with me if this call had never come. For I have certain friends—very few of them—still living in Gwent and on its borders who have not heard the summons. The special family that I have in mind has lived in those regions for more centuries than I can tell. It would be a bold and learned Welsh herald who would trace them to their beginnings on the Celtic side, but on the Norman they go back to Sir Payne Turberville, the companion of Fitzhamon, and even in Wales a story of nine hundred years is a long story.

Well, coming down a little through the ages, the Rowlands that I knew—of course, their grandfather knew my grandfather—are still on the soil. Certainly a younger son has crossed the Severn, but the two others have not moved their habitations more than ten or twelve miles in the last fifty years. From half-way between Newport and Cardiff to Newport, from Newport to a mile east of Newport, then to four miles east of Newport, at last to three miles west of Cardiff: they will surely be laid in the land of their fathers at the end. So it might have been with me, perhaps, if it had not been for the blood of certain Scottish sailors intermingled with the stay-at-home stock of Gwent. But I often wonder, as I say, how it would have happened to me if I had found a home under the shadow of Twyn Barlwm instead of becoming a dweller in the tents of London. Tents, I say advisedly, for, with the rarest exceptions, Londoners have no homes. This was true in a great measure nearly two hundred years ago, when Dr. Johnson first came to London from Lichfield; it is now all but universally true.

But, anyhow, the call of London, partly external and partly internal, came to me, and for some months before I left the old land for the first time I was imagining London and making a picture of it in my mind, and longing for it. I turned up the old magazines and re-read Sala's *Twice Round the Clock*. I came upon the strange phrase, "the City", in stories, and wondered what the City signified. And I began to have an appetite for London papers. For it should be understood that at Llanddewi Rectory a London paper was a thing of the rarest appearance. I think I can remember that when the Prince of Wales—afterwards King Edward VII, of happy memory—was dangerously ill, my father made some kind of arrangement—I cannot think what it could have been—by which he got the *Echo* of those days, not only on week days, but on Sunday afternoons. And in ordinary times, when we went into Newport on market days, we might possibly bring back a *Standard* or a *Telegraph*, but likely enough not. We saw the *Western Mail* occasionally, the *Hereford Times* once a week; weekly also came the *Guardian*, an excellent paper, but with more of Oxford, Pater, and Freeman, and Deans, and Dignitaries in it than of London or Londoners. Indeed, I remember how the news of the fall of Khartoum came to the rectory. I had been spending the evening with some friends across a few miles of midnight and black copse, and ragged field and wild, broken, and wandering brook land, and I remember that not a star was to be seen as I came home, wondering all the while if I ever should find my way. One of my friends had been in Newport that day, and had seen a paper, and so when I got back at last and found my father smoking his pipe by the fire, I announced the news in a tag of Apocalyptic Greek: Khartoum he polis he megale peptoke, peptoke; Khartoum the mighty city, has fallen, has fallen. And sometimes I wonder now in these days, when I am nearer to the heart of newspapers, whether our work in Fleet Street, with its anxious, flurried yell over the telephone, its tic-tac of tapes, its slither and rattle and clatter of linotypes, its frantic haste of men, its final roar and thunder of machinery ever gets itself delivered at last on a midnight hillside so queerly as the tragic news of Khartoum was delivered in the "parlour" of Llanddewi Rectory.

But the days came when above the clear voice of the brook in the hidden valley, above the murmur of the trees in the heart of the greenwood there sounded from beyond the hills to my heart a clearer voice, a mightier murmur. London called me, and all documents relating to this new unknown world became matters of the highest consequence and significance, and so London papers must by all means be obtained.

Far and long ago that spring and summer of 1880 now seem to me. It was then that London began to summon, and I was filled with an eager curiosity to know all about the new world which I was to visit.

As I have explained, the London paper made a very rare and occasional appearance at Llanddewi-among-the-Hills, and I don't think that any of us felt any aching need of it. But now for me *Standard* and *Telegraph* became mystic documents of the highest interest and most vital consequence; these were the charts to the Nova Terra Incognita; every line in them came from the heart of the mystery and was written by men who were learned in all the wisdom of London. London papers I must have; that was certain; so I set out to get them.

The nearest point at which these precious rarities were obtainable was Pontypool Road Station, about four miles distant from Llanddewi Rectory. It was the place where I had bought my copy of "De Quincey" some years earlier, and is now sacred to me on that account. But in this month of April thirty-five years ago I thought little of De Quincey or of his visions. Columbus, I suspect, while he watched the fitting of his caravel forgot any mere literary enthusiasms that he might have once possessed; for him there was but one object and that was the tremendous, marvellous, terrible venture into the unknown that he was soon to make. So it was with me; London loomed up before me, wonderful, mystical as Assyrian Babylon, as full of unheard-of things and great unveilings as any magic city in an Eastern tale. It loomed up with incredible pinnacles—to quote Tennyson on another city—and in its mighty shadow all lesser objects disappeared. De Quincey? After all he was not without value, since he spoke of Oxford Street; still, I wanted later news of the City of the Enchanters. So three or four times a week I walked the four miles to Pontypool Road, taking the short cut across the fields which leaves the by-way at Croeswen and brings one out on the high road from Newport to Abergavenny, somewhere about a mile from the station, near the lane which wanders through a very solitary country into Usk.

Pontypool Road Station lies, as I have said, under mountains, or rather under the huge domed hills which we in Gwent call mountains. It is one of the many meeting-points between the fields and the "works", and is always associated in my mind with a noise of clanking machinery and a reek of black oily smoke of rich flavour, which this generation would not recognise, since it is only to be imitated by blowing out a tallow candle that has long wanted snuffing; and now there are neither tallow candles nor snuffers. Here, then, of a "celestial" agent of W. H. Smith I bought my papers; usually the *Standard* and the *Daily Telegraph*. The *Morning Post* was, I think, twopence in those days, and twopence was too much to give for a daily paper, and, moreover, we had a vague belief that the *Morning Post* was almost exclusively concerned with the social doings of the aristocracy, splendid matters, doubtless, but no affairs of mine. With these two papers, then, and once a week with a copy of *Truth*, I would make my way out of the station and along the high road till I came to the stile and the lonely path across the fields, and alone under a tree or in the shelter of a friendly hedge I would open my papers, cut their pages, and plunge into their garden of delights. One of my chief interests in these journals—perhaps my chiefest interest—was the theatre; and I am sure I cannot say why this was so. As far as I can remember I had up to this time witnessed three performances of stage plays, and of these three one was certainly not "legitimate", being a drama of the circus called *Dick Turpin's Ride to York*. Its chief incidents were firing pistols and leaping over five-barred gates, and I must have been about seven when I saw it at Cardiff. Then in '76 I was at Dublin, and saw *Our Boys,* and was very heartily bored, and finally in '78 or '79 I went with a school-fellow to the skating-rink at Hereford—I remember the former as well as the latter rinking mania—and enjoyed a touring company's rendering of *Pinafore.* And, looking back, I believe that it was then that the delightful poison began to work; then when in that ramshackle barn of a place in the Hereford backstreet the curtain went up on the Saturday afternoon, and eight men dressed as sailors began to sing:—

> We sail the ocean blue,
>   And our saucy ship's a beauty;
> We're gallant men and true,
>   And attentive to our duty.

I remember that, young as I was, I could not help feeling that eight was a very small number for the male chorus. This circumstance confirms me in a belief which I have long entertained that Heaven meant me to be a stage-manager. True, I could never master simple addition, and a stage-manager has to keep accounts. Still, I should not have been the first stage-manager whose ledgers were filled with "comptes fantastiques".

But here I am under my tree or my hedge on a sunny morning of that Gwentian spring of so many years ago, eagerly opening the paper and turning to the theatrical advertisements in that part of the journal which I have in later years learned to call the "leader page". I read about Mr. Henry Irving at the Lyceum and Mr. Toole at the Folly—I do not think the vanished theatre was known as Toole's in those days. Mme. Modjeska and Mr. Forbes-Robertson were, I believe, at the Court, Dion Boucicault's play, *The Shaughraun,* was running at the Adelphi—or, stay, was this old house of melodrama then the home of *The Danites?* In Wych Street, at the Opera Comique, was *The Pirates of Penzance; Madame Favart* enchanted at the Strand; *Les Cloches de Corneville* was at the Globe or the Olympic, I forget which. And, said each advertisement, "for cast see under the clock".

I was vividly interested in that phrase, "For cast see under the clock", which I read in the sibylline leaves of my London papers. The real meaning of the words never occurred to me; I conceived that somewhere, in some dimly-imagined central place of London, there was a great clock on a high square tower, and that this tower was so prominent an architectural feature as to be known all over London as "the clock". And at the base of this tower, so I proceeded in my fancy, there were displayed bills or posters, containing the casts of all the plays of all the theatres. I never found that mighty tower in London, but it was many years before it dawned on me that "the clock" was merely the pictured clock-face in the newspaper itself, under which the full casts were then printed.

As I have said, I cannot quite make out the sources of this intense interest of mine in the theatre. But I suspect that for the time I had got into that strange frame of mind to which Thackeray alluded when he asked a man if he were "fond of the play". Thackeray's friend replied, I think, to the effect that it depended on the play, whereupon Thackeray told him that he didn't understand in the least what the phrase "fond of the play" implied. Thackeray was right; for this attitude of mind is universal, not particular; and oddly enough, I believe it is very little related to any serious interest in the drama as a form of art. There is so vast a gulf between the theatre of to-day and that of thirty-five years ago that I do not know whether it is now possible for anybody to be "fond of the play" in the old sense; but if there be such people left, I am sure that they have not the faintest interest in the proposals to build and endow a national theatre. For to those in the happy state to which Thackeray alluded, the theatre was loved not for itself, but as a symbol of gaiety; I would almost say of metropolitanism as opposed to provincialism. I have known countrymen relating their adventures in London almost to wink as they included a visit to the Globe or the Strand in the list of their pleasures; the theatre represented to them the "chimes at midnight" mood.

Thackeray meant—do you like the mingled gas and orange odours of the theatre, do you like the sound of the orchestra tuning, the sight of the footlights suddenly lightening, can you project your self readily into the fantastic world disclosed by the rising curtain, and afterwards, do you like a midnight chop at Evans's, with Welsh rarebit to follow, and foaming tankards of brown stout, and then "something hot"; in fine, do you like to be out and about and in the midst of gaiety at hours of the night when your uncles and aunts and all quiet country people are abed and fast asleep? That is what Thackeray meant by his question, and I suppose that our modern, serious lovers of the drama would regard the man who was fond of the play in this sense as an utter reprobate, a stumbling-block and a stone of offence. But it was in that sense that I pored devoutly over everything relating to the theatre that I found in my newspapers, as I delayed in my walks home from Pontypool Road, not being able to refrain any longer.

Well, the day dawned at last for dreams to come true—or as true as they ever come. My father and I set out one fine Monday morning for Paddington, starting, I think, at about eleven o'clock from Newport, and getting to London by five in the afternoon. This was then the best train in the day; for the Severn Tunnel was not yet made, and we went all the way round by Gloucester. It was a six hours' journey, and now one can get from London to Newport in two hours and a half. At Westbourne Park we changed and got into the Underground system, and so came to the Temple Station on the Embankment. Thence it was a short walk to the private hotel in Surrey Street where my father had always stayed on his infrequent visits to town. I have forgotten the name of the hotel;—Bradshaw's office is built on the site of it—it was Williams's, or Smith's, or Evans's, or some such title, and as I believe was then the way, it was understood to be more or less the preserve of people from the west. I suppose there were other little hotels for parsons and small squires of the east and north and south; for all the streets that go down from the Strand to the river were then occupied by these private hotels and by lodging-houses. Craven Street, by Charing Cross, is the only one of these streets that has at all preserved the old manner, which, let me say, was a dingy and dim but on the whole a comfortable manner. Our hotel was just opposite the pit door of the old Strand Theatre, and in a former visit my father and mother, sitting at their window, had had the gratification of seeing Mrs. Swanborough sitting at her window over the way knitting busily. Now all our ladies, however smart, have become knitters, but if I had been writing these reminiscences a few years ago I should have asked: "Can you imagine a London manageress of these days sitting and knitting in her room at the theatre?"

We went out for a short stroll before eating, and for the first time I saw the Strand, and it instantly went to my head and to my heart, and

I have never loved another street in quite the same way. My Strand is gone for ever; some of it is a wild rock-garden of purple flowers, some of it is imposing new buildings; but one way or another, the spirit is wholly departed. But on that June night in 1880 I walked up Surrey Street and stood on the Strand pavement and looked before me and to right and to left and gasped. No man has ever seen London; but at that moment I was very near to the vision—the *theoria*—of London.

After the astounding glimpse at the Strand we went back to the private hotel in Surrey Street and had something to eat. I am not sure, but I think the meal consisted of tea and ham and eggs, the latter beautifully poached. I know that my mind holds a recollection of this simple dish very admirably done in connection with Smith's, or whatever the place was called; and I believe it was eaten in the evening of our arrival. And I may say in passing that the hotel had a pleasant, well-worn, homely look about it; very plain, but extremely comfortable. I think that my bedroom carpet was threadbare and that the bed was a feather bed; at all events one slept sublimely there under the roof, under the London stars.

Then for the Strand again, now sunset flushed, beginning to twinkle with multitudinous lamps—I had hardly seen a lamp-lit street before—and so to the Opera Comique, where they were playing *The Pirates of Penzance*. The Opera Comique was somewhere in Wych Street, which has gone the way of the streets of Babylon and Troy; purple blossoms and big hotels and other theatres that I know not grow now in the place where it once stood. We went to the upper boxes of the Opera Comique and enjoyed ourselves very well. I remember my father being especially pleased with the Pirate King's defence of his profession: "Compared with respectability it's almost honest," or words to that effect. But, oddly enough, I was a little disappointed. There was not the sense of gaiety that I had expected. For one thing the music reminded me of the classic glees and madrigals which I had heard discoursed by the Philharmonic Society at Hereford, where I was at school, and I did not want to be reminded of Hereford. And the female chorus hardly looked as thoughtless as I could have wished; it seemed to me that they might very well have come fresh from the rectory like myself. Of course, it was all very well to be ladylike, and so forth; but what I asked of the stage was careless devilry, the suggestion, at all events, of naughtiness. In fact, my attitude was perilously near to that of the Arkansas audiences as analysed by the Duke in *Huckleberry Finn:* "What they wanted was low comedy—and maybe something ruther worse than low comedy." But I was not really quite so bad as the "Arkansaw lunkheads". We went on another night to *Les Cloches de Corneville,* a most harmless production, I am sure; and *that* was what I wanted. I was enchanted from the rising of the curtain; there was the sunlit scene in Normandy, charming, smiling, and a whole row of pretty girls, evidently as thoughtless as the lightest heart could wish, dancing down to the footlights and singing:—

> Just look at that,
> Just look at this,
> Don't you think we're not amiss?
> A glance give here,
> A glance give there,
> Tell us if you think we're dear.

And—not one of these girls looked as if she could have come from any conceivable rectory. Decidedly, *Les Cloches de Corneville* was the comic opera for my money. What a pleasing thrill the scene afforded when the entire village, for some reason that I cannot well remember, dressed up as Crusaders and Crusaderesses, and came suddenly into the room of Gaspard, the miser, and the big bell began to toll and the gold was poured out in a torrent on the ground. "When the heir returneth, then shall ring the bell, so the legend runneth, so the old men tell"; in some such words was this grand peripeteia announced in the text. So the heir no doubt returned and married the extra pretty girl whose name I have forgotten—she was not Serpolette, I know, for Serpolette was comic, delightfully, impudently comic, but still comic, and so no mate for the hero. Serpolette, I think, having regard to the Unities, ought to have married the thin but amusing assistant of the Bailie; but I do not know whether this were so. But I am sure everybody was happy ever after, and of *Les Cloches* and other comic operas like it I say, in the words of Coleridge's friend: "Them's the jockeys for me!"

I have never been able to make up my mind as to the respective merits of *Les Cloches de Corneville* and *Madame Favart,* which was running at the Strand. *Les Cloches* had the more coherent plot of the two, and the great scene of the miser and the crusaders was more effective in its stagey way than anything in *Madame Favart,* but, then, Florence St. John was Madame Favart, and to old playgoers I need say no more. And Marius, a delightful French comedian, was in the cast; and there were those songs dear to memory: "Ave, my mother", "The Artless Thing," "To Age's Dull December," and

> Pair of lovers meet,
> Stolen vows are sweet,
> Sighs, etcetera.
> Love is all in all,
> On a garden wall,
> Never heed papa.

This was sung by Marius, who had no voice in particular, but an infinite Gallic relish and unction and finish in everything that he did. The fourth piece that we went to in this wonderful week was *The Daughter of the Drum Major,* at the Alhambra, then a theatre, with an extremely roomy, comfortable pit. This last piece made but little impression on me. From my recollection, it seems to have been more in the modern mode, that is, a mere excuse for shewing off a "beauty chorus" without the little touch of thin, theatrical but pleasant romance that delighted me in the two other plays. But the poverty of the play was atoned for by the happy circumstance that before going to it we dined at the Cavour. And the Cavour in 1880 was exactly like the Cavour in 1915, save in this one matter, that on the earlier date there was included in the price of the dinner a bottle of violet wine.

Looking back through the years and comparing the London of the early 'eighties with the London of to-day, one circumstance emerges very clearly in my mind: that is, that the early London had an infinitely "smarter", wealthier air than the later. I say "air" advisedly, to make it clear that I knew nothing of the real interior life of the place, or of the resources of its rich inhabitants. I judged of London purely by its exterior aspects, as one may judge of a passing stranger in the street, and decide that he goes to an expensive tailor, without knowing anything of the condition of his banking account. So, I say that the outward show and lineaments of the London of 1880 were much more refulgent and splendid than those of the last few years. I was a good deal surprised when the truth of this first dawned on me some three or four years ago. For I believe that as a matter of fact the new London is a much wealthier, more luxurious, more extravagant place than the old. The rich people of to-day spend hundreds instead of tens, thousands for the hundreds of their fathers; the "pace" of the splendid has increased enormously in the last thirty-five years; and all the facilities for expending very large sums of money have also increased to a huge extent. So well was I convinced of all this when I fell to comparing the London of my boyhood with the London of my middle age that at first I thought that there must be a fallacy somewhere, and I was very willing to believe that those early impressions of mine were illusions, natural enough in a lad who had never seen any more splendid streets than those which the Newport and Cardiff of those days had to shew, than the venerable, peaceful, ancient ways of Hereford, whose stillness was only broken by the deep, sweet chiming of the cathedral bells. But when, interested, I went into the facts of the question, I found that I had not been mistaken in my first view—i.e., that London was a smarter-looking place thirty years ago than at the present day, and this for several reasons.

To begin with, there is the trifling matter of men's dress. I do not know whether we have yet realised the fact that the frock coat is rapidly becoming "costume", verging, that is, towards the status of levee dress. Already, I believe, it is only worn on occasions of semi-state, at functions where the King is expected, at smart weddings, and so forth. Before long it will probably attain the singular twofold state of "evening dress", which is worn all day long by waiters and by what are conveniently called gentlemen after seven o'clock in the evening. So very likely the frock coat will soon be seen on the backs of the maître d'hôtel, the hotel manager, the shopwalker, the major-domo—if there be any majores-domo left—as a kind of uniform or livery, while it will also be the afternoon wear of dukes at great social functions. And so with the silk hat; it has not gone so far on the road of obsolescence as the frock coat, but, unless I mistake, it has entered on that sad way.

Here, then, is the point of contrast. Between 'eighty and 'ninety—and later still—practically every man in London went about his business and his pleasure with a high hat on his head. Every man, I say, above the rank of the mechanic; certainly all the clerkly class; Mr.

Guppy and his friends were still faithful to this headdress; which, be it remembered, was once universal all over England, so that even smock-frocked farm labourers wore it. As for the London of pleasure, the West End, it would have been quite impossible to conceive a man of the faintest social pretensions being seen abroad in anything else. And now, I go up and down Piccadilly, Bond Street, the Row at the height of the London season, and see—a few silk hats and morning coats, it is true—but the majority of well-dressed men in "lounge" suits and grey soft hats and black and grey bowlers.

Now let it be clearly understood that I have no passion for black coats and shiny hats myself, nor for the dazzling white linen which has largely given way to soft, unstarched stuffs. But it is not to be denied that all those habits had a "smart" appearance, and that a pavement crowded with shiny black hats, shiny white cuffs and collars, and long black frock coats made a much more imposing show than the pavement of to-day, on which the men's dress is very much as they please. The modern men look extremely comfortable and well at their ease; but they do not scintillate in the old style. A soft grey hat does not flash back the rays of the sun.

Then, another point and a most important one: the coming of the motor. I suppose the kind of motor-impelled vehicle which one is likely to see in Hyde Park may very well have cost seven or eight or nine or ten times as much as the horse-drawn carriages which I remember going round and round so gay and so glorious. Well, I have watched the modern procession of motor-cars, and they are about as impressive as a career of light locomotive engines. It may indeed in course of time become fashionable to go up and down the Row in express locomotives capable of drawing their hundred coaches at a hundred miles an hour, but the effect would not be smart. Now, the old equipages were undeniably the last word of smartness; in themselves they were enough to tell the stranger that he had come to the very centre of the earth, of its riches and its splendours. There were the high-bred, high-spirited, high-stepping horses, in the first place, groomed to the last extreme of shiny, satiny perfection, tossing their heads proudly and champing their bits and doing the most wonderful things with their legs. The bright sunlight of those past London summers shone on their glossy coats, shone in the patent leather of the harness, shone and glittered on the plated bolts and buckles and ornaments. And the carriages were of graceful form, and the servants of those days sometimes wore gorgeous liveries; and scores of those brilliant equipages followed on one another in an unending dazzling procession. That was the old way; now there are some "Snorting Billies" that choke and snarl and splutter as they dodge furtively and meanly in and out of the Park, like mechanical rabbits bolting for their burrows.

While I contrast the London of my young days and the London of my old—or present—days, I would like it to be remembered that I am, so far, only contrasting the two cities from one point of view, the point of view of smartness. I have not been saying that 1880 London was more sensible than 1915 London; but merely that the former struck an outsider as a more brilliant place than the modern city. The fact is that I have the most cordial approval for all social pomps and splendours, so long as I am not required to take part therein. I hate wearing frock coats and silk hats and shiny shirts; but I am very well pleased to sit in the pit, as it were, and watch those exalted persons who are cast for the decorative parts going through their brilliant performances. And, after all, if a man finds that plate armour is uncomfortable, that is no reason why he should not delight in seeing other people wearing it, and wearing it with dignity. And in speaking of the Hyde Park and Rotten Row of the old days I mentioned that there were some gorgeous servants' liveries still left in 1880. And while we are on that matter, I may say that I have never sympathised at all with those persons who have found something mean and ridiculous in a manservant in purple and gold or in blue and crimson, unless, that is, the point be taken that only a splendid duty should be dignified with a splendid vestment, and in that objection I admit there is some force. Not that I agree for one moment that there is anything contemptible in "menial" service; but I am willing to allow that it may not be altogether seemly for a faithful fellow, whose business is to hold on behind a carriage and wait at dinner, to outshine a bishop in pontificals. But I suspect that the people who sneered at poor Jeames and his plush were not actuated by this reasonable motive, but rather by that vile "Liberal" objection to splendour as splendour. The man who found "Blazes" ridiculous would probably find the King in his Coronation robes equally ridiculous. And so you may go on, up the scale and down the scale; but the only logical alternative to splendour is Dr. Johnson's proposed suit of bull's hide—all beyond that is superfluity and vain show, according to the doctrine of the wretches who in times not long past sold antique civic ornaments, such as chains and maces, on the ground that the Mayor of Little Pedlington did not need such gauds to help him in his customary task of sentencing "drunks".

There is one more point in connection with the Row. Twenty-five years ago the appointed hour was five o'clock in the afternoon. Then people sat in the chairs and walked up and down and looked at the carriages, and I remember a friend observing to me this singularity, that though the place was public and open to anybody, still only those persons who were dressed in the regulation costume—frock coat and silk hat for men—ever came near the sacred ground. The people in lounge suits and bowler hats stood apart, and watched the show from some distance. Well, the hour of the Row is now in the morning; but there is a greater change. There are still "smart" people there; but there are also people who cannot by any possibility be described as smart, not even if they be judged by the very lax standards of these days.

In another matter the London of to-day is much less impressive in its outward show than the London of 1880; that is in the aspect of its principal streets. There are still excellent shops in Bond Street, Regent Street, and Piccadilly; but there is no longer in any of them that air of exclusiveness and expensiveness that I can remember, and this is particularly true of Regent Street. In 1880 you felt as soon as you turned up the Quadrant that anything you might buy therein would certainly be dear; the very stones and stucco exuded costliness and the essential attars of luxury. I feel convinced that the cigars of Regent Street were of a more curious aroma than cigars bought in any other street, that it was the very place wherein to purchase a great green flagon of rare scent as a present for a lady, that if you happened to want a Monte Cristo emerald this was the quarter wherein to search for it. That was my impression, but lest it should be mere fancy, a year or so ago I asked one of the older shopkeepers whether the street was quite what he and I remembered it. He said very emphatically it was not at all what it had been; and I feel sure that he was right, and that in a less degree the other principal shopping centres have declined from their former splendour.

And this for two reasons; first, the curious modern tendency of the best and most luxurious shops to scatter and disperse themselves abroad about the side streets of the West End, leaving gaps which are filled in most cases by dealers in cheaper wares. And secondly, the coming of the popular tea-shop has, in my opinion, done a very great deal to "unsmarten" the streets of which I am speaking. Let it not be understood for one moment that I would speak despitefully of cheap tea-shops; that would indeed be vilely thankless in one who has often made the principal meal of the day at an A.B.C.—large coffee, threepence; milk cake, twopence; butter, a penny—and has been grateful that for once in a way he has dined. But, it cannot be pretended that a milk cake is a costly or a curious dish, or that a plate of cold meat for sixpence or eightpence is an opimian banquet; and so, when I pass a popular tea-shop or eating-house, I feel that my dream of luxury and expense is broken; and that something of glitter and splendour has passed away from the West End of London.

I spent the years from the summer of 1880 to the winter of 1886 in a singular sort of apprenticeship to life and London and letters and to most other things. Sometimes I was in London; then for months at a time I was out of it, back again in my old haunts of Gwent. I had hot fits of desire for the town when I was forced to stay in the country; and then, settled, or apparently settled, in the heart of London, its immensities and its solitudes overwhelmed me, the faint, hot breath of its streets sickened me, so that my heart ached for the thought of the green wood by the valley of the Soar, and for the thought of friendly faces.

They say that in old Japan they had a wonderful and secret art of tempering their sword blades. Now the steel was placed in the white heat of the fire, now it was withdrawn and plunged into the water of an icy torrent; and then again the trial of the furnace. So heat and cold were alternated, according to an ancient and hidden tradition, till at last the craftsman obtained an exquisite and true and perfect blade, fit for the adorned scabbard of a great lord of Japan. When I think of those early years of mine I should be reminded of the process of the Japanese sword-craftsman—if only the heart were as tractable as steel. The Kabbalists, I believe, take the view—a gloomy one—that the innermost essence of man's spirit goes out from the world in much the same state as that in which it came into the world; and it is certainly true that some men seem incorrigible; neither fire nor ice will temper them aright.

During these early years of my London experience I lived under very varying conditions. I lived with families, and I lived alone; I lived in the suburbs and in the centre; I had enough to eat, and then narrowly escaped starvation. My first habitat was in the High Street of a southern suburb. My memory holds a picture of an ancient street of dignified red-brick houses, a Georgian church, and a stream of quite inky blackness. The old houses had old gardens behind them, green enough, but with a certain grime upon them that made them strange to eyes unused to this combination of soot and leafage. But it was quite easy in those days to get from the suburb to the open country.

Not that I desired any such excursions, for my notion of an ideal residence was then a lodging in one of the streets or courts or passages going down from the Strand to the Thames. This was a dream that I realised years afterwards, when many waters (not of the Thames) had passed over my head. It was well enough, and I used to go out and get my breakfast at the "chocolate as in Spain" shop at the west end of the Strand, on the north side. It was well enough, I say, but it was not absolute paradise. And, furthermore, and in an interior parenthesis, let me say that the chocolate at the old Strand shop was not as in Spain, though very decent chocolate. The Spanish service of chocolate—I encountered it when I was in Gascony—consists in this, first that the chocolate is made extremely strong and thick, and secondly that with it comes a goblet of ice-cold well-water, to be drunk after the chocolate, on the principle, I suppose, of the Scots who drink water, not with whisky, but after it.

Well, to return to the more or less—chiefly less—direct current of my tale, after my sojourn in the southern suburb came a return to the country, where I remained eight or nine months. It was during this exodus or hegira, I think, that I was excommunicated by old Mr. James, of Lansoar, because I was loafing at home instead of living on five shillings a week in London. But my long sojourn in Gwent was in fact due to a very dismal discovery having been made of me by certain persons called examiners. They found me utterly incapable of the simple rules of arithmetic; and hence I was debarred from the career which I had been contemplating. And here I would say that I am almost proud of myself for my quite extraordinary arithmetical incapacity. I am not merely dull and slow, but desperate. I am so wanting in the mere faculty of counting as to be curious, like those tribes of savages that can say "One, two, three, four, five . . . many." There are people who make a living by exhibiting their arithmetical skill in the music-halls; someone writes on the blackboard a multiplication sum of fifteen figures multiplied by fifteen figures, and a second or two after the last figure is drawn the arithmetical artist utters the result. Well, I am at the opposite end of the scale, and I have sometimes wondered whether "Incompetent Machen" would not be quite a good turn. It would make anybody laugh to hear me doing a sum in simple addition. It is like "Forty-seven and nine, forty-seven and nine, forty-seven and nine." I ponder. Then a brilliant idea strikes me. I pretend the problem is "forty-seven and ten". I get the result, fifty-seven, deduct one and proceed.

Well, I came to London again in the summer of '81, thinking of another and quite a different career, which did not involve, on the face of it, that little difficulty of arithmetic. Again I was in a suburb, and again in an old one, but this time the quarter was in the far west. I stayed in Turnham Green, then a place of many amenities standing amongst fields and gardens and riparian lawns, which, long ago, have been buried beneath piles of cheap bricks and mortar, for a year and a half, and then again I altered my plans, or fate rather altered them for me. I started on a new tack and kept it for a month, and then somehow slid into a backwater, in which I was afloat and nothing more than afloat. Summoning this period into recollection, I find my position very much like to that of certain ancient and outworn barges, grass-grown, flower-grown, that I have come upon suddenly in improbable back alleys of water, in the midst of a maze of by-streets at Brentford; but, locally and literally, I was then living in a small room, a very small room, in Clarendon Road, Notting Hill Gate.[11]

I have already stated that when I first came up to London I had no

---

11. [In CLM the following paragraph appears here: "Looking over the preceding article in this series of confessions, I perceive a certain danger of which I must beware. In that article, as I see, I give dates with some precision, I mention divers suburbs and quarters of London by name, I have even furnished the title of a street in which I once lived. Now all this is much too scientific—by science comes death—and here is the very place for a digression."]

thought of literature as a career. Indeed, I never have thought of it as a career, but only as a destiny. Still, my meaning is that it in no wise dawned upon me as I travelled up from Newport to London in the early summer of 1880 that writing of any kind or sort was to be a great part of my life's business. And yet, before I had lived a month in the old red house by the inky stream, I was trying to write, in the intervals of a very different task, in an atmosphere which was utterly remote from literature of any kind. How was this? Partly, I suppose, because of the very large proportion of Celtic blood in my veins. It is quite true that the Celt—the Welsh Celt, at all events—has directly contributed very little to great literature. This I have always maintained, and always shall maintain; and I think all impartial judges will allow that if Welsh literature were annihilated at this moment the loss to the world's grand roll of masterpieces would be insignificant. I, speaking from the point of view of my own peculiar interests, I should be very sorry to miss my copy of the *Mabinogion,* and there are certain stanzas of the poem called *Y Beddau*—"Vain is it to seek for the grave of Arthur"—which have a singular and enchanting and wizard music; but in neither case is there any question of a literary masterpiece.

Yet there is in Celtdom a certain literary feeling which does not exist in Anglo-Saxondom. It is diffused, no doubt, and appreciative rather than creative, and lacking in the sterner, critical spirit which is so necessary to all creative work; still it is there, and it is delighted with the rolling sound of the noble phrase. It perceives the music of words and the relation of that music to the world. I was taking a lesson in Welsh pronunciation some time ago, and uttered the phrase "yn oes oesodd"—from ages to ages. "That is right," said my Welsh friend, "speak it so that it makes a sound like the wind about the mountains." And, with or without the leave of the literary rationalists, I would say that the spirit of that sentence is very near to the heart of true literature.

So far then, as a man three-parts Celt, I was by nature inclined to the work of words, and there was, moreover, a feeble literary strain in my own family. There was a second cousin, or Welsh uncle, I am not certain which, who had composed a five-act heroic blank verse drama, called *Inez de Castro,* which was almost, but not quite, represented by the famous Mrs. Somebody at the Lane in the early 'fifties. And then, more potent still, was the heredity of bookishness, the growing up among books that had accrued from grandfathers and uncles and cousins, all men who had lived all their days amongst books, and had sat over country hearths on mountain sides, reading this leathern Colloquies of Erasmus, this little Horace in mellow parchment, with the Sphere of Elzevir.

And then there was the old-fashioned grammar school education, of which it must be said, by friends and foes, that it is an education in words. One spent one's time, unconsciously, in weighing the values of words in English and Greek and Latin, in rendering one tongue into another, in estimating the exact sense of an English sentence before translating it into one or another of the old tongues. So that a boy who could do decent Latin prose must first have mastered the exact sense and significance of his English original, and then he must also have made himself understand to a certain extent, not only the logic but the polite habit of each language. I remember when I was a very small boy rendering "Put to the sword" literally into "Gladio positi". "Well," said my master, "there is no reason on earth why the Romans shouldn't have said 'gladio positi', but as a matter of fact they *did* say 'ferro occisi'—killed with iron." And if one thinks of it, he who has mastered that little lesson has also mastered the larger lesson that literature is above logic, that there are matters in it which transcend plain common sense. And so, the long and the short of it was, that in 1880 I began to try to write.

Now I believe that one of the most tortuous and difficult questions that engages philosophy is the theory of cause and effect. I think, though I am not quite sure, that in one of Mr. Balfour's philosophical books this matter is treated, and the familiar case of a sportsman's pulling a trigger, firing a gun, and thereby bringing down a bird, is made an instance. What is the "cause" of the bird's death? Roughly speaking, of course, the pulling of the trigger; but roughly speaking is not the same thing as philosophically speaking; and if anyone be so simple as to conclude that roughly speaking means truly speaking and that philosophy is all nonsense, let me remind him that when he enjoys his after-dinner cigar in his arm-chair he is not conscious of the fact that he is being whirled through space, like a top, at the most terrific speed.

So, if I remember rightly, Mr. Balfour left the philosophical "cause" of the bird's death an open question, if not a question altogether beyond determination of human wit; and thus it is with the impulse that sends off a harmless young fellow on the career of letters. One can talk of the causes that impel a grain of corn to grow from the ground; sound seed, good soil, good farming; dry weather, wet weather, each in its season; but at the last the engendering of the green shoot remains a mystery. And so it is a mystery that near midsummer in 1880 I suddenly began to write horrible rubbish in a little manuscript book with a scarlet cover; rubbish that had rhymes to it.

But if ultimate causes lie beyond those flaming walls of the world that put bounds to all our inquisition, it is not so hard to trace those causes which are proximate. The bird dies because the shot hit it in a vital part, the corn sprouts because it is put into the ground—and I began to write because I bought a copy of Swinburne's *Songs Before Sunrise*.

I forget how I heard of this name, which once loomed so fiery and strange a portent, which still, in the estimation of many excellent judges, stands for a great literary achievement. I know it was while I was down in the country, because I can remember one of our clergy, an Eton and Christchurch man, telling me gossip about the poet, who had in those early days retired from the world to Putney. It is to be supposed that I had read something concerning Swinburne in one of those wonderful London papers that came over our hills from another world, that might almost have fallen from the stars they were so wholly marvellous. But, somehow or other, I was possessed by an eager curiosity concerning this Swinburne, convinced in advance—I cannot remember how—that here I should surely find an unexpected, unsurmised treasure. And so, one hot, shiny afternoon, I came up from the old Georgian suburb by the black stream, crossed Hungerford Bridge, and made my way into the Strand; into that Strand which is as lost as Atlantis. And going eastward past many vanished things, past the rich odours of Messrs. Rimell's soap-boiling, I came to St. Mary-le-Strand, and the entrance of Holywell Street. At the southern corner of this street, facing the east end of the church, there stood Denny's bookshop, and, gold in my pocket, I went in with a bold appearance, and said, "Have you got Swinburne's *Songs Before Sunrise?*" The shopman did not seem in the least astonished at my question. He said he had got the book, and produced it, and shewed it me, and the very cover was such as I had never seen before, provocative, therefore, in a high degree. And so I bought the book and carried it out of Denny's into the sunlight in a great amazement.

For, be it remembered, one did not go into a provincial bookshop in that easy way and say, "Have you got this or that?" For the chances were about a thousand to one that they hadn't got it, and never would have it. It is odd, but I cannot remember exactly the nature of the stock of the average country bookseller; my impression is of Bibles, Prayer Books, Church Services, and Pitman's Shorthand Manuals. So, if you wanted a book in the county town, you did not say, "Have you got so-and-so?" but "Will you get me so-and-so?" and in four or five days you called and the book was ready. But I had a notion that in this wonderful London the bookshop would actually have the book that you wanted, there actually in presence, and waiting for you on its shelves. I had a notion, I say, but again, it seemed almost incredible that there should be such shops in the world, and so when the bookseller under St. Mary-le-Strand said "Yes," quite simply, and handed me the *Songs Before Sunrise* in two or three seconds, I was amazed and exultant too; the legend of London, though marvellous, was evidently a true one.

Now I have a friend who is very fond of preaching the doctrine of what he calls the cataclysm. He holds that we are all much bettered by an occasional earthquake, moral, mental, or spiritual. He says that volcanoes which suddenly burst out from under our feet are the finest tonics in the world, that violent thunderstorms, cloud-bursts, and tornadoes clear our mental skies. The treatment is heroic, but my friend may be right; certainly that volume of *Songs Before Sunrise* was to me quite cataclysmic. First there was the literary manner of the book, which to me was wholly strange and new and wonderful, and then there was the tremendous boldness of it all, the denial of everything that I had been brought up to believe most sure and sacred; the book was positively strewn with the fragments of shattered altars and the torn limbs of kings and priests.

How do the lines go? I quote from memory, but they run something like this:—

> Thou hast taken all, Galilæan, but these thou shalt not take;
> The laurel, the doves and the pæan, the breasts of the nymph in the brake.

Clearly this was a terrible, a tremendous fellow, an earth-shaking, heaven-storming poet. And so between my endeavours to qualify for passing the preliminary examination of the Royal College of Surgeons, I began to write; I should think the most horrible drivel that ever has been written since rhymes first jingled. I can't remember, oddly enough, whether I tried to imitate Swinburne; I know one copy of verses was "inspired" by a picture called "Harmony", which I think was hung in the Academy of 1880. It depicted a mediæval maiden playing the organ, while a mediæval youth watched her in a dazed and love-stricken condition. This is positively the only one of these early horrors of mine, of which I have any recollection; my memory is purged of the rest of them, I am glad to say. I merely mention these things because they illustrate a very singular point in literary psychology; in universal psychology, for the matter of that. For I believe it is a rule that almost every literary career, certainly every literary career which is to be concerned with the imaginative side of literature, begins with the writing of verses. Nay, people who are to live lives quite remote from literature will often try to write poetry in their youth; and on the face of it, this is a great puzzle. For poetry, be it remembered, is the most "artificial" kind of literary composition, it is immeasurably the most difficult, it is by far the most remote from that which is commonly called life. Why, then, does the inexperienced beginner, devoid of all technical ability, invariably essay this most difficult technical task on his entry into the literary career?

The problem of the boy in the back room, not far from the dark stream of the Wandle, writing verses in the red notebook, is really one of the enigmas of the universe; it is rather a Chinese-box puzzle; riddle is within riddle.

For if we start at the beginning of things, or at what seems to us to be the beginning of things, we are met by the question as to why there should be any such thing as poetry in the universe. I need not say how much wider this question is than it seems; how it must be asked about all the arts, about fugues and cathedrals and romances and dances. It is an immense question; immense when one considers that with nine people out of ten the great criterion is, "Does it pay?" That is, will it result in a larger supply of fine champagne, four ale, roast legs of pork, and mousses royales to the population? Will this scheme of things enable Sir John to keep a fifth motor-car, or will it get Bill meat three times a day? That is, at last, the test by which we judge all things. It is an old and approved British test; by it Macaulay condemned the whole of Greek philosophy, because that philosophy did not lead up to the invention of the steam engine. Now, it is quite clear that poetry, speaking generally, pays neither the producer nor the consumer of it; it does not lead to motor-cars, beefsteaks, vintage clarets, or four ale. It is not even moral; not a single man has ever been induced to drink ginger-beer instead of beer by reading Keats.

I must pause for a moment; I fear that it may be thought that I am trying to be funny or—more injurious accusation!—trying to be clever. I am not trying to be either; I am stating the simple facts of the case. Hardly a month passes by without some indignant person pointing out in the Press that Engineering and Commercial Chemistry are infinitely more useful—i.e., lead to more beefsteaks—than Latin and Greek; and that when Oxford and Cambridge find out that obvious truth they may become of some service to the State. Indeed, it is only a few weeks ago since a gentleman wrote to a paper shewing that military training was better for a boy—i.e., would make him the better soldier—than "silly old" Greek plays. And let me acknowledge that these contentions are perfectly true; just as it is perfectly true that fur coats are much warmer than Alcaics. So, I say, here is the problem: the common, widely accepted test of the right to existence of everything: does it pay, does it add to the physical comforts of life, is quite clearly opposed to the existence of poetry, and yet poetry exists. Therefore, either the poets and the lovers of poetry are mad, or else the common judgment is . . . let us say, mistaken. I need scarcely say that I incline to the latter solution of the problem, and so qua human being, I am not ashamed of trying to write poetry by the Wandle, though I recognise, qua Arthur Machen, that I was, very decidedly, not born a poet.

For I firmly hold the doctrine that the natural, the arch-natural expression of man, so far as he is to be distinguished from pigs and dogs and goats, is in the arts, and through the arts and by the arts. It is not by reason, as reason is commonly understood, that man is distinguished from the other animals; but by art. I can quite well conceive the Black Ants sending the message "Hill 27 fell before the Red Ant attack early this afternoon," but I cannot conceive either Red or Black Ants writing odes or building miniature cathedrals. The arts, then, are man's difference, that which makes him to be what he is; and when he speaks through them he is using the utterance which is proper to him, as man. For, if we once set aside the "does it pay" nonsense, which is evidently nonsense and pestilent nonsense at that, we come clearly and freely to the truth that man is concerned with beauty, and with the ecstasy or rapture that proceeds from the creation of beauty and from the contemplation of it. And youth, as I think I have pointed out before, is the time of revelation. It is children who possess the "kingdom of heaven", to them are vouchsafed glimpses of that paradise which is the true home of man, and so it is that the boy with literature in his blood naturally makes his first efforts in the region of poetry, which is the heart and core of all literature.

The heart and core; for, as in the individual man, so in the whole history of men literature begins always with poetry, just as speech began with song. First, the magic incantation, sung about strange secret fires in hidden places by wild men, then the ballad or lyric, then Homer, then Herodotus, with the odours of the sanctuary of poetry still about him, though he has come down into the market-place of prose. And it is not necessary to go farther in time or space than the Northumberland of a few years ago to hear phrases common enough, things of everyday, set to enchanting melodies. I shall never forget how once in the years of my wandering I came one wet autumn afternoon to a little town called Morpeth. It struck me as a dingy place enough, "un petit trou de province, sale, noir, boueux", and my lodging was dingy, and musty too, in a house kept by an old invalid woman who moved about in a wheel chair and grumbled if a window were opened. But when it came to the question of the stroller's tea, the servant-maid, who came, I think, from the wild places of that land, said consolingly: "You need not trouble yourselves; you shall have your tea in half an hour." No doubt the girl was mortal, but she spoke the tongue of the immortals; her phrase about our tea was chanted to an exquisite melody that might have come from the Gradual—or from fairyland.

The natural man, then, is a singer and a poet, and so we may say that all artists are in reality survivals from an earlier time, and so it is that even in these later days the lad, with something of the youth and true nature of his race restored to him for a brief hour, sits in solitary places and endeavours to exercise his birthright. Alas! he stutters deplorably in his speech as he delays by the Wandle, inditing verses; but it is thus that he would declare that he is a citizen of no mean city; he would fain say through those sorry rhymes, *Civis cœlestis sum.*

IV

Well, I saw the first of Augustus Harris's autumn dramas at Drury Lane, heard the newsboys calling out the death of Miss Neilson one misty evening up and down the Strand, and went back to Gwent in the character of a bad penny; and so fell to writing of those autumn and winter nights, when all the house was still.

Poor wretch! For this is the misery of literature, that it has no technique in the sense that music and painting have each its own technique. The young painter and the young composer, having acquired a certain mechanical skill in the elements of their arts, have studios and schools which they can attend. They have masters who lead them in their several ways, or who tell them, if necessary, to abandon those ways with all convenient speed. But for the lad with letters on the brain there is no help, no guidance; nor is there the possibility of any direction in the literary path. Now and then people send me manuscripts, and ask for my opinion; I give it because I am weak, but I always tell them that in literature the other man's opinion is not worth twopence.

No; the only course is to go on stumbling and struggling and blundering like a man lost in a dense thicket on a dark night; a thicket, I say, of rebounding boughs that punish with the sting of a whip-lash, of thorns that most savagely lacerate the flesh—it is the flesh of the heart, alas! that they tear—of sharp rocks of agony and black pools of despair. Such is the obscure wood of the literary life; such, at least, it was to me. You struggle to find your way; but again and again you ask yourself whether, for you, there is any way. You think you have hit upon the lucky track at last. And lo! before your feet is the black pit. And such is not alone the adventure of little, ineffectual, struggling men. How old was glorious Cervantes, now serene for ever amongst the immortals, when he found his way to that village of La Mancha?

Fifty, I think, or almost fifty. And he had been striving for years to write plays, and poetry, and short stories of passion and sentiment; and it was only the roar of applause that thundered up from the world when the Knight and the Squire were seen riding over the hill that convinced Cervantes that at last he had discovered his true path; if indeed he ever were convinced in his heart of the magnitude and majesty of the achievement of *Don Quixote.*

And if these things are done with the great, what will be done with the little? If the clear-voiced rulers of the everlasting choir are to suffer so and agonise, what of miserable little Welshmen stammering and stuttering by the Wandle, in the obscure rectory amongst the hills, in waste places by Shepherd's Bush, in gloomy Great Russell Street, where the ghosts of dead, disappointed authors go sighing to and fro? For the fate of the little literary man there is no articulate speech that is sufficient; one must fall back on aoi or oimoi, or alas, or some such vague lament of unutterable woe.

Now one of the first agonies of the learner in letters is the discovery of the horrid gulf that yawns between the conception and the execution. Some years before this winter of 1880, when I was at school, I had read the tale of Owain in the Mabinogion, of the magic sudden storm, and of the singing of the birds after it. And going out for a walk one half-holiday with a school-fellow, just such a sudden storm, as it seemed to me, overtook us as we went down into a beautiful valley not far from Hereford; and after it there was a like joyful singing of birds in the trees. And somehow the magic atmosphere of the old tale, mingled with the enacting, as it were, of one of its chief circumstances, left on my mind a very strong and singular impression which, when the desire of literature came upon me, I yearned to put into words. I did so, in the blank verse form, and sent the "poem" to the *Gentleman's Magazine,* and this I think was my first attempt to get into print. I need not say that my nonsense was returned to me, with thanks; but I wish I knew why I chose that particular magazine. It must have had some especial attraction for me, since ten years later I sent Sylvanus Urban a prose article, which he accepted and paid for at the appropriate eighteenth-century rate of a guinea a sheet; that is sixteen pages. But I must say in all fairness that Sylvanus warned me in advance of his rate of payment.

But that gulf between the idea as it glows warm and radiant in the author's heart, and its cold and faulty realisation in words is an early nightmare, and a late one, too. For the beginner, if he suffer from many terrible disappointments, has also the consolations of hope, fallacious though these may prove to be. This scheme that looked so well has certainly come to the saddest grief, but there may be better luck next time; if this road have led to nothing but a blank wall of failure, that way may rise from the valley and climb the hill and lead into a fair land. It is later in the life of the literary man, when he has tried all roads and made all the experiments, that his final sorrow comes upon him. He may not be forced to say, perhaps, that he has been a total failure; he may, indeed, be able to chronicle achievements of a minor kind, successes in the estimation of others. But now, with riper understanding, he perceives, as he did not perceive in the days of his youth, the depth of the gulf between the idea and the word, between the emotion that thrilled him to his very heart and soul, and the sorry page of print into which that emotion stands translated. He dreamed in fire; he has worked in clay.

I did not know (happily for myself) of these things in the ending of the year 1880; and so, when all the rectory was abed and asleep, I sat up by a dying fire writing a "poem" on a classic subject.

The classic "poem" was finished some time in the winter of 1880–81, and then I performed a bold action. I sent the manuscript—I can see it now, written in a sprawly hand on both sides of ordinary letter paper—to a Hereford stationer, and bade him print me one hundred copies thereof. He, strangely enough, did so, and I saw myself in print for the first time. I have been looking at my copy of this work, I should think the only copy in existence, and wondering whether I would quote a few lines from it. I have decided against this course. But, after all, I was only seventeen when I wrote *Eleusinia*.[12]

But the little pamphlet had its influence on my life. My relations decided, after reading it, that journalism was the career for me; a decision that then seemed to me both reasonable and pleasant, which now strikes me with amazement, nay with stupefaction. Since those days I have found out a good many things concerning both poetry and journalism; and looking over that old copy of *Eleusinia,* I have meditated on

---

12. [In CLM Machen refers to the poem under the title "Cabeiria."]

what career I should advise for the author of that work if he were now to consult me. I give it up; I abandon the problem utterly. And yet, strange as it seems, strange most of all to me, my relations were justified after all. I did become a journalist, just thirty years afterwards. But by 1910, those who had arranged this destiny for me were long dead and delivered from all their troubles. I remember my father, who knew about as much of the matter as I did, sketching out my future career. I was to go to London to learn the business first of all, shorthand, of course, and all that sort of thing. A chief portion of the task, he said, half jocularly, would be to lurk in the entrance-halls of great houses and write down the names of distinguished guests on the nights of grand receptions. And then, eventually, some few hundreds would come to me, and with this I was to buy an interest in a small local paper, and so, I suppose, write leaders and live happily ever after. The programme has not been carried out literally. The few hundreds have been more agreeably spent long years ago, and my editor never sent me to get the names of distinguished guests at great houses—knowing, wise man, that I should make a sad mess of such a business. But one of my first "assignments" in journalism was to describe a Giant Apple. I chased after that apple from Bond Street to Covent Garden, from Covent Garden back to Bond Street, and wrote in my paper about its smiling face, wishing my poor father were alive to hear the story of my long-deferred entrance into the art and mystery of the journalist. He would have laughed consumedly; and from my dear remembrance of him, I think he would have found a quotation from Horace to meet the case. Once, I recollect, it turned out that the odd man at the rectory, supposed to be a bachelor, had abandoned a wife and twelve children—all of them small ones, for aught I know—somewhere in Gloucestershire. A policeman came for poor Robert, and my father was very sorry for the man, even though he were a sad dog, and a notorious toper of ale. But the rector thought of the phrase: "Raro antecedentem scelestum deseruit pœna," and cheered up amazingly.

Well, on the strength of the verses about the Eleusinian mysteries, I am to be a journalist, and consequently, as it was thought in those days, I must learn shorthand, so that I may be able to write a hundred and fifty words in a minute. And here again comes a chapter as sad as that which I have written on my arithmetic. I never learnt shorthand effectively, because I was too stupid to learn it. The queer thing is that when I was quite a little boy at school this art of shorthand had a strange and mysterious attraction for me. Why? I am sure I don't know; why did the small boys of my generation love dark lanterns? Robert Louis Stevenson has written an enchanting essay on the fascination of this instrument of the mysteries; but I am not quite sure that even he has penetrated to the heart of the enigma. For I, though a lonely child, knew the joy of the dark lantern, and it was a great and exceeding joy. The glowing of heat that rose from its roof—corrugated, I think?—the rank smell of its oils were charms that somehow carried me over the borders of this common world into an exquisite region of wonder and surmise. And now I come to look back into days horribly distant—the shorthand question must wait for a while—I perceive that there was a perfect ritual, or ceremonial rather, of the Dark Lantern, the origins of which are as obscure to me as are the origins of other primitive mysteries. Of one thing only I am certain, and I speak with all due deference to the author of *The Golden Bough*, not forgetting Miss Jane Harrison; the lantern service of my early boyhood had no reference whatever to the young crops or to the sprouting of the corn. As I lit the wick I did not say, "O Sun! shine thou also on the land and make it warm so that there may be many cabbages, so that green peas may not be lacking to the lamb which is equally nurtured by thy beams." Of course, I am quite willing to allow that, as a general rule, an anxiety about the spring crops fully explains the origin of all painting, all sculpture, all architecture, all poetry, all drama, all music, all religion, all romance: I admit that the Holy Gospels are really all about spring cabbage, that martyrdom and mass are spring cabbage, that Arthur is really arator, the ploughman; that Galahad, denoting the achievement and end of the great quest, is Caulahad, the cabbage god. I admit all this because it is so entirely reasonable and satisfactory, and, indeed, self-evident; but though all Frazerdom should rise up against me, I cannot allow that when I lit my dark lantern I was inviting the sun to help the crops.

There was some sort of obscure connection—I seem to remember—between Dark Lanterns and Masks. They were both properties in singular mysteries of a formless character which were enacted in dark shrubberies on dark nights, just before bed-time. It was well understood, I know, that these objects must be kept in secret places, and must not by any means be seen by the uninitiated; and the uninitiated were everybody besides myself. And here, I believe, I was following unconsciously, but most strictly, the rules of all primitive mysteries throughout the world. The Greeks of the historical period had become lax; they carried about the mystic fan of Iacchus in public procession. But amongst the Blackfellows of Australia, where the rites are much nearer to the original purity of their institution, the mystic fan is not seen, only heard. Therefore the Dark Lantern and the Mask were kept hidden in an obscure cranny of the coach-house, which was at the end of an overshadowed drive at some distance from the rectory. They were produced under the cover of the darkness, these sacramental instruments, clouds and stars and the dim boughs of trees and tangled undergrowth alone saw them. There were certain solemn words which accompanied the ostension of the objects, but they were in a language which I have long forgotten. But some day, when the turmoil has died down, when the clouds have cleared for the sunset and the apparition of the evening star, as I sit by a western shore awaiting the boat of Avalon, I shall write my last treatise, under the title of *The Dark Lantern and the Mask, libellus vere mysticus.* And here I give notice to all good and lawful men that I am duly seized of the above title, so that they may abstain from intromitting with the same.

This digression of the dark lantern proceeded, naturally enough, from my speaking of shorthand. This art, I said, appealed to me when I was a boy, and its appeal was that of a kind of mystery writing, of a script not in common use. For my acquaintance did not lie in journalistic circles. I knew nobody who could write shorthand or understood anything about it, and so the three books of Pitman—*Teacher, Manual,* and *Reporter*—were three mystery books, so far as my small world was concerned. But now, in later years, having written that famous poem on the initiation of Eleusis, I was to be a journalist, and to be a journalist I must learn shorthand. And then I found Phonography a mystery indeed, and too great a mystery for me, since I could not attain to it. I muddled about with it for three or four years; I actually made some use of it in one of my queer employments, but I never wrote it decently. I was too fumble-fisted; try as I would, I could not form the characters with elegance or accuracy. My p's and b's would wobble and bend till they looked like f's and v's, if I tried to halve a letter I quartered it. A kindly reporter gave me a hint: "Don't bother about the thick and thin lines," he said, "I never do." And no doubt the skilled shorthand writer can play all manner of tricks with the system, but I was not a skilled writer, and I took the reporter's advice and made bad worse. My last shorthand lesson was taken in 1885, long after I had ceased to think of journalism as a profession. Indeed, I cannot now remember why I continued to waste my time over a craft that I could not master; but I suppose I thought the endeavour gave an air of respectability and solidity to my proceedings that they would have lacked without it. From June 1881 to December 1882 I was more or less vaguely bent on the journalist's career. I remember feeling somewhat discouraged during this period by reading an advertisement for a journalistic position in a London paper. The applicant could write shorthand at the rate of one hundred and fifty words a minute, he understood all about reporting, he was an expert at "leaderettes", and quite willing to take a turn at the case—all for thirty shillings a week. This did not seem promising, but I need not have disturbed myself; my journalistic days were not yet, nor for many years to come. In the meanwhile I read variously and became thoroughly familiar with Boswell's Johnson (in Mr. Percy Fitzgerald's edition). And one windy, gusty night, when the costers' flares in the back streets were burning with a rushing sound, I came upon a secondhand bookshop on the main road between Hammersmith and Turnham Green, and went in and found an odd volume of William Morris's *Earthly Paradise*. Now followed the old trouble, and in a worse form. As Swinburne's *Songs Before Sunrise* had first set me versifying, so the *Earthly Paradise* reinforced the original virus. And now I had acquired some slight facility of a worthless sort, and so I began to imitate William Morris, and spent the odd hours of six good months in writing a sham-Greek tale in rhymed couplets; which I tore up thirty years ago. And then I discovered Herrick, and tried to imitate that inimitable writer; but this effort, though vain in itself, was not so wholly vain. For it brought me, as it were, into the seventeenth century, into an age which I have loved ever since with a peculiar devotion. Ten years later I went on pilgrimage to Dean Prior and Dean Churchtown, and in spite of the restored church, trod the lanes under the moor with reverence, since Herrick's feet had passed by those ways.

But now towards the end of the year 1882, after I had known London, on and off, for nearly two and a half years, all that feeling of its immense gaiety with which I had approached it in the first place was dropping from me. I began to realise, very gradually and by dismal degrees, that the gaieties of London were commodities that had to be bought with money, and that I had none. The theatre had ceased to charm me, and I am very sorry to say that it has never charmed me since; that is from the point of view of the man sitting in the pit. By the end of '82 I had quite definitely ceased to be "fond of the play".

For now London began to assume for me its terrible aspect. It was rather a goblin's castle than a city of delights; if indeed it had not become a place of punishment wherein I was condemned to hard labour through many dreary and hopeless years.

V

In that wonderful volume which is called the Grand Saint Graal we are told how the hermit Nasciens received a magic book from paradise. It was divided into portions, and one of these portions was intituled "Here Begin Terrors." I can find no words that might more fitly introduce the tale of my solitary life in London. I was only twenty; I was poor; I was desolate. And I frizzled all the time (or most of it) on the fire of my own futility; I longed to make literature, and I could only write nonsense.

I was employed for a time in a house of business in a street north of the Strand and parallel to it, which, I suppose, must have been Chandos Street. I know that it was still paved with cobble-stones. My employers were publishers—the firm has for many years ceased to exist—and I was something or other in what is called the "editorial" department. But to the best of my belief publishing books was but a minor part of the energies of the house, and I should think a later growth. The real staple was wholesale stationery; there was an important "line" of copy-books, there was a great deal done with ornamental and decorated albums, and also with pictorial calendars. The Shakespeare calendar of the House is still in existence, or was in existence a year or two ago, and it bears the name of the vanished firm. Mr. (afterwards Sir) Walter Besant had been the "editor" of Messrs. Chandos and Co., but just before I made my first trial of business life he had resigned, and his place was taken by a very kindly literary gentleman, whose name I have forgotten. Afterwards he edited a series, if not several series, of anthologies, and was, I believe, appointed Professor of English Literature at some Indian seminary of learning. I do not know whether he is still alive. Well, it was my business to assist this gentleman. I think I was engaged as his "secretary", but I was known in the House as his "clurk". I am trying to recollect what I actually did to assist him.

My first job on the morning of my arrival I can remember. I made a copy of Mr. Gladstone's Latin version of the well-known hymn, "Rock of Ages": "Jesu, pro me perforatus," it began. And then I had to take down in shorthand and afterwards write in longhand a stern letter to somebody who had made a mistake in the name of King Alfred's grandmother. This error had occurred in one of a series of Board School history books that the firm was publishing; and this circumstance alone gave me a loathing and hatred for the whole business, since I thought then, and think still, that the name of King Alfred's grandmother is not of the faintest consequence to any reasonable being. It is the kind of fact which would interest a German deeply; he would spend years of his life to find out all about it; but such is not the occupation of a gentleman.

In the afternoon of that day we became a little livelier. My chief contributed a London letter to some Scottish paper—he came from the northern part of this island—and again my shorthand was required. The London letter was distinctly gay in its tone, it dealt in a cheerful spirit with some early incidents in the career of a certain admirable actress whose talents then engaged and delighted us. As I took it down it struck me as over worldly for the readers of the *Haddaneuk Herald,* and sure enough my man reconsidered the matter and struck out the gaieties from the copy. And how did that famous shorthand of mine serve me? Not so vilely, considering all things. I had a quick memory then, and remembered many of the phrases that had been dictated, and I could read quite a lot of the characters that I had formed, and others gave me a vague sort of intimation of the sense; just as the neumes helped the church-singers of the earlier ages; they were quite useful if you knew the tune.

I search my memory for further details of my occupation with Chandos and Co. I think that the Shakespeare Calendar occupied me during odd hours for a week or more. This was January, and I was set to the preparation of the calendar for the next year. It was not a difficult task, and I was furnished with a sort of album, containing the Shakespeare calendars for the past six or seven years, and my only business was to make a new almanack out of these old elements. Thus January 1, 1884, gave the Shakespearean quotation that had been assigned to December 27, 1877; for January 2 I chose a motto that had pertained to February 6, 1882, and so forth. It was easy, but dull. And

I was dull, too, or I would have invented Shakespearean lines that Shakespeare never wrote, and trusted to the all but universal ignorance of Shakespeare. I did something like that when I was an older and a merrier man. I persuaded a friend of mine, a young fellow of literary tastes, that one of the most famous phrases ascribed to Shakespeare was in reality a gag, invented by Mr. F. R. Benson's stage manager. "Do you mean to say," said my friend, "that this Mr. Randle Ayrton invented 'a poor thing, but mine own'?" "Certainly," I replied. "Then," said he, "Ayrton must be a most wonderful man." And I wonder how many of my readers know exactly how the matter stands—without referring to the play?

And then what else did I do for my pound a week in Chandos Street? Chiefly, I think I took down and transcribed a daily report to the head office of the firm, which was in Belfast or Dundee or some such town. I don't remember in the least what it was about, whether it dealt with King Alfred's grandmother's name or with other matters. But I had to write about two quarto pages daily of this report, and put D 1 in the margin. I think D 1 meant Literary Department; but the whole thing was the terror of my life. For it had to be neatly written, with a fair and level margin on each side; and this I could by no means achieve. Again and again my D 1 was condemned as a ragged and untidy performance, and I had to copy it out all over again, as if I had been a careless schoolboy—as, indeed, I was from the firm's point of view.

And I sit in my corner, trying to write a round, clear, clerkly hand, trying to remember that of the two forms of the small "t" one was much to be preferred, trying to observe the rule that "today" must be written as one word, not two, and that for commercial purposes "draft" must be spelt with "f", not with "ugh"; and thinking of the nightingale in the thorn bush by the Soar, in the still valley.

Here I was, then, in Chandos Street, a peg of no particular shape at all in a perfectly round hole, feeling very miserable indeed. We were, I believe, somewhat cramped for room, and I had a desk in the album department. Here three very cheerful and kindly young fellows of about my own age did something with handsome albums. I don't know in the least what they did; so far as I could see they took albums out of tissue paper and put them back into tissue paper all day long. One of them, the senior of the room—he must have been three or four years older than any of us—was just about to make a real start in life. He used to tell me all about it when we were alone together for a minute or two, as sometimes happened. There was a young lady whom he was to marry in a few months' time, and he had made arrangements for setting up as a stationer in Harlesden, and he meant to push Chandos's stuff—albums and everything—and to do well and be happy. "Poor man, and then he died," to quote one of Dr. Johnson's muttered undertones. I do not know how far his short life at Harlesden was successful or felicitous. But as for me, I hated it all. It was not that the work was hard, but that I took no interest in it, and saw no reason why it should be done at all, or why anybody alive should do it. So I looked about me, and through the favour of a friend I got a little teaching of small children at twenty-five shillings a week. Then I gave notice to Messrs. Chandos. They were very kind; they offered me twenty-five shillings a week to stay, but I thanked them and said no. It was the business atmosphere of the place that I detested; I have always agreed with the small boy in *Nicholas Nickleby* who uttered the great maxim, "Never Perform Business." The teaching which followed was certainly not exciting, but I did not mind it. Indeed, having to teach Euclid, I found to my amazement that it was about something, and actually was a coherent and reasoned scheme of things, not a mere madhouse puzzle, as I had always imagined. But then my own geometrical instruction had been limited. It consisted simply in this: Fourteen Euclids were served out to fourteen small boys. The mathematical master then said: "Learn the Definitions, Axioms, and Postulates." That was my first and my last lesson in geometry; though I duly went through the accustomed books of Euclid, trying to learn by heart what was to me mere unmeaning gibberish.

At this time and for the next year and a half I was living in Clarendon Road, Notting Hill Gate—or Holland Park, to give the politer subdirection. I am sorry to say that I had not a garret, since the houses of that quarter, being comparatively modern, do not possess the sloping roofs which have seen the miseries of so many lettered men. Still, my room had its merits. It was, of course, at the top of the house, and it was much smaller than any monastic "cell" that I have ever seen. From recollection I should estimate its dimensions as ten feet by five. It held a bed, a washstand, a small table, and one chair; and so it was very fortunate that I had few visitors. Outside, on the landing, I kept my big wooden box with all my possessions—and these not many—in it. And there was a very notable circumstance about this landing. On the wall was suspended, lengthwise, a step-ladder by which one could climb through a trap door to the roof in case of fire, and so between the rungs or steps of this ladder I disposed my library. For anything I know, the books tasted as well thus housed as they did at a later period when I kept them in an eighteenth-century bookcase of noble dark mahogany, behind glass doors. There was no fireplace in my room, and I was often very cold. I would sit in my shabby old great-coat, reading or writing, and if I were writing I would every now and then stand up and warm my hands over the gas-jet, to prevent my fingers getting numb. I remember envying a man very much indeed on a certain night in late winter or early spring. It was a very cold night; there was a bitter north-easter blowing, and the wind seemed to pierce right through my old coat and to set my very bones shivering and aching. I had gone abroad, because I was weary of my den, because I was sick with reading and in no humour for writing, because I felt I must have some change, however slight. But it was an evil and a bitter blast, so I turned back after a little while, coming down one of the steep streets that lead from Notting Hill Gate Station to Clarendon Road. And halfway home I came upon a man encamped on the road by the pavement. He was watching over some barrows and tools and other instruments of street repair, and he sat in a sort of canvas wigwam, well sheltered from the wind that was chilling me to the heart. His coat, too, looked thick and heavy, and he had a warm comforter round his neck, and before him was a glowing, ardent brazier of red-hot coals. He held his hands and his nose over the radiant heat, and smoked a black clay pipe; and I think he had a can of beer beside him. I envied that man with all my heart; I don't think I have ever envied any man so much.

Occasionally I had applications for the loan of a book from my step-ladder library. These came from the lodgers on the ground floor, an Armenian and his wife, who annoyed the landlady by sleeping in cushions piled about the carpet and hanging their blankets in front of the doors and windows. It was the Armenian lady who had literary tastes, and her desire was always for "a story-book". I never saw her or her husband, but I often heard him calling Mary, the servant. He would stand at the top of the kitchen stairs and shout "Marry! Marry!" and then, reflectively, and after a short interval, "Damn that girl." He gave a fine, Oriental force to the common English "damn". Other lodgers that I remember were a young Greek and a chorus girl, mates for a single summer. They occupied the first floor and were succeeded by a family from Ireland. I have a confused notion that there was something a little queer about the head of this household. He was, I think, a major, and I know he was Evangelical. As I went down the stairs I heard him more than once uttering in loud, earnest tones the words, "Let us pray." This was startling; and one of his daughters would always shut the door of their room with a bang on these occasions, and that was startling, too.

The little table in my little room turned out to be a very useful piece of furniture. I not only read at it and wrote on it, but I used it as a larder. In the corner nearest the angle of the wall by the window I kept my provisions, that is to say, a loaf of bread and a canister of green tea. Morning and evening the landlady or "Marry" would bring me up a tray on which were a plate, a knife, a teapot, a cup and saucer, and a jug of hot water. With the aid of a kettle and a spirit lamp, which came, I think, from under that serviceable table—one may fairly say from the cellar—I made the hot water to boil and brewed a great pot of strong green tea.

In the first months of this life of mine an early dinner was added to the fees of my teaching; later, my pupils changed, and the dinner disappeared. I then used to spend the hour in the middle of the day in wanderings about Turnham Green and the waste places round Gunnersbury, making my meal on a large Captain's biscuit and a glass of beer. I varied this repast by taking it in various public-houses. In those days there were still pleasing and ancient taverns scattered along those western roads. One I remember in particular, a very old, tumbledown house, set at the edge of the market gardens, which then approached almost to Turnham Green. There was not a straight line about this old, old house, its roof-tree dipped and wavered, and the roof was of mellowed tiles, and one end of the place was quite overwhelmed by a huge billow of ivy. I used to think that highwaymen must have lurked in the little room where I took my biscuit and glass of ale; and the food and drink tasted much better on that account. The old tavern, and its leaning sheds and ragged outbuildings, its red roof and its green ivy; all are gone long ago. There is a row of raw houses where it stood, and I hate them. Sometimes I did not have any beer, either because I did not want any, or because it struck me as too great a luxury. Then I would buy a small bag of currant biscuits and take them to the region of the market gardens and devour them, sitting on a gate or sheltering behind a hedge. I don't know how it is, but these feasts are always connected in my mind with a grey and gloomy sky and a very cold wind, so that I shiver when I think of flat, square biscuits in which currants are embedded. But I have a reverence for them, too. There were, I confess, days of gross debauch. Once a week, or once a fortnight at the least, I went to a goodly and spacious and ancient tavern on the high road, and had a grilled chop, potatoes, bread, and beer; which came to one and a penny or one and twopence. *Les Cotelettes de Mouton, Sauce Bénie* the dish is called by the experts of the *haute cuisine*. I can recommend it. And in the evenings I sometimes exceeded, though not so violently. I would, nine evenings out of ten, buy my provision of bread at a shop at the bottom of the long main road, opposite or nearly opposite to Uxbridge Road Station. The shop kept a very choice kind of gingerbread, and I would buy a couple of bricks of this gingerbread, and munch them with a high relish as a supplement to the common bread.

 As the spring of 1883 advanced, and the weather improved and the evenings lengthened, I began the habit of rambling abroad in the hope of finding something that could be called country. I would sometimes pursue Clarendon Road northward and get into all sorts of regions of which I never had any clear notion. They are obscure to me now, and a sort of nightmare. I see myself getting terribly entangled with a canal which seemed to cross my path in a manner contrary to the laws of reason. I turn a corner and am confronted with an awful cemetery, a terrible city of white gravestones and shattered marble pillars and granite urns, and every sort of horrid heathenry. This, I suppose, must have been Kensal Green: it added new terror to death. I think I came upon Kensal Green again and again; it was like the Malay, an enemy for months. I would break off by way of Portobello Road and entangle myself in Notting Hill, and presently I would come upon the goblin city; I might wander into the Harrow Road, but at last the ghost-stones would appal me. Maida Vale was treacherous, Paddington false—inevitably, it seemed, my path led me to the detested habitation of the dead.

Be it remembered that my horror at the sight of Kensal Green Cemetery was due to this, that, odd as it may seem to townsfolk, I had never seen a cemetery before. Well I knew the old graveyards of Gwent, solemn amongst the swelling hills, peaceful in the shadow of very ancient yews. I knew well these garths. There was Henllis, high up on the mountain side, in the place of roaring winds, under the faery dome of Twyn Barlwm. I had lingered there of autumn evenings while the sun set red over the mountains, and a drift of rain came with the gathering darkness, as the yew boughs beat upon the east window of the church. There were graves there with flourished inscriptions, deeply cut, and queer Welsh rhymes—*dyma gareg dêg:*—

> Here's a rare stone—of death.
> Beneath it lies
> A rarer dust, that shall arise
> By heavenly breath alone; and climb the skies—
> We trust.

I knew the churchyard of Llanddewi, looking down the steep hillside into the chanting valley of the Soar, and Kemeys, between the Forest and the Usk, and Partrishw, in the heart of the wild mountains beyond Abergavenny. These places of the dead were solemn with old religion, and the tones of *Dirige* and *De Profundis* and *Requiem Æternam* sang still about them on their hills; but this white ghostly city of corruption—there was nothing but horror in it! Still, I see myself on these wanderings, beating to and fro in the stony wilderness, entangled, as I say, in the endless mazes of unknown streets. Now I would succeed in breaking away. I would pass that sad zone of destruction and disgrace that always lies just beyond the furthest points of the suburb. These are the places where the hedges are half ruined, half remaining, where the little winding brook is defiled, but not yet a drain, where one tree lies felled and withered, while its fellow is still all green. Here curbstones impinge on the fields, and shew where new, rabid streets are to rush up the sweet hillside and capture it; here the well under the thorn is choked with a cartload of cheap bricks lately deposited. I would pass over these dismal regions and come, as I thought, into the fair open country, and then suddenly at the turn of the lane I would be confronted by red ranks of brand-new villas: this might be Harlesden or the outposts of Willesden.

I think that on the especial occasion that I have in mind the red row of houses must have been some portion or fragment of Harlesden. I remember that, like the cemetery, this impressed me as a wholly new and unforeseen horror, something as strange and terrible as the apparition of a rattlesnake or a boa-constrictor might be to an English child, wandering a little away into the orchard or the wood near the house. I had never lived in a world that might have prepared me for such things; in Gwent—in my day, at all events—there was no such phenomenon as this sudden and violent irruption of red brick in the midst of a green field; and thus when I came round the corner of a peaceful lane and saw in the midst of elms and meadows this staring spectacle, I was as aghast as Robinson Crusoe when he saw the track of the foot on the sand of his desert island.

. . . And here I would make a parenthesis, and say that so long as my writing habits had any concern with the imagination I never departed from the one formula. This not consciously; in fact, I have a secret doctrine to the effect that in literature no imaginative effects are achieved by logical predetermination. I have told, I think, how I was confronted suddenly and for the first time with the awe and solemnity and mystery of the valley of the Usk, and of the house called Bartholly hanging solitary between the deep forest and the winding esses of the river. This spectacle remained in my heart for years, and at last I transliterated it, clumsily enough, in the story of "The Great God Pan", which, as a friendly critic once said, "does at least make one believe in the devil, if it does nothing else". Here, of course, was my real failure; I translated awe, at worst awfulness, into evil; again, I say, one dreams in fire and works in clay. But, at all events, my method never altered. More legitimately than in the instance of "The Great God Pan" I made the horrid apparition of the crude new houses in the midst of green pastures the seed of my tale, "The Inmost Light", which was originally bound up with "The Great God Pan". And so the man in my story, resting in green fields, looked up and saw a face that chilled his blood gazing at him from the back of one of those red houses that once had frightened me, when I was a sorry lad of twenty, wandering about the verges of London. The doctor of my tale lived in Harlesden.

And if I may pursue this subject farther I would suggest that the whole matter of imaginative literature depends upon this faculty of seeing the universe, from the æonian pebble of the wayside to the raw suburban street, as something new, unheard of, marvellous, finally, miraculous. The good people—amongst whom I naturally class myself—feel that everything is miraculous; they are continually amazed at the strangeness of the proportion of all things. The bad people, or scientists as they are sometimes called, maintain that nothing is properly an object of awe or wonder since everything can be explained. They are duly punished.[13]

If we go more deeply into this text of Horror and Harlesden, it will become apparent, I think, that what is called genius is not only of many varying degrees of intensity, but also very distinctly of two parts or functions. There is the passive side of genius, that faculty which is amazed by the strange, mysterious, admirable spectacle of the world, which is enchanted and rapt out of our common airs by hints and omens of an adorable beauty everywhere latent beneath the veil of appearance. Now I think that every man or almost every man is born with the potentiality at all events of this function of genius. *Os homini sublime dedit, cœlumque tueri:* man, as distinct from the other animals, carries his head on high so that he may look upon the heavens; and I think that we may say that this sentence has an interior as well as an exterior meaning. The beasts look downward, to the earth, not only in the letter but in the spirit; they are creatures of material sensation, living by far the greatest part of their lives in a world of hot and cold, hunger and thirst and satisfaction. Man, on the other hand, is by his nature designed to look upward, to gaze into the heavens that are all about him, to discern the eternal in things temporal. Or, as the Priestess of the Holy Bottle defines and distinguishes: the beasts are made to drink water, but men to drink wine. This, the receptive or passive part

---

13. [CLM adds the following: "The Italian man of science ends by believing in the 'miracles' of Eusapia Palladino, and the French *nouvelliste* writes a crazy tale of how a man's chairs and tables charged at him as he was entering the drive of his own house, leaving the rooms all empty."]

of genius, is, I say, given to every human being, at least potentially. We receive, each one of us, the magic bean, and if we will plant it it will undoubtedly grow and become our ladder to the stars and the cloud castles. Unfortunately the modern process, so oddly named civilisation, is as killing to this kind of gardening as the canker to the rose; and thus it is that if I want a really nice chair, I must either buy a chair that is from a hundred to a hundred and fifty years old, or else a careful copy or replica of such a chair. It may appear strange to Tottenham Court Road and the modern furniture trade; but it is none the less true that you cannot design so much as a nice arm-chair unless you have gone a little way at all events up the magic beanstalk.

Still, many of us have our portion of the passive or perceptive faculty of genius; we are moved by the wonder of the world; we know ourselves as citizens of an incredible city, we catch stray glimpses of faery Atlantis, drowned beneath the ocean of sense. But it is one thing to dream dreams; and quite another to interpret them, and in this active faculty of interpretation, or translation of the heavenly tongues into earthly speech, there are infinite degrees of excellence. And the masters in this craft of interpretation are few indeed. And the final conclusion—a sad one for me—is that if I could have "translated" the Horror of Harlesden competently I should have been a man of genius.

Still, I see myself all through that year 1883 tramping, loafing, strolling along interminable streets and roads lying to the north-west and the west of London, a shabby, sorry figure; and always alone. I remember walking to Hendon and back—this must have been on a whole holiday—and to this day I can't think how I found my way there, through what clues I struck from the north parts of Clarendon Road into the Harrow Road, and how I knew when to leave the Edgware Road and bend to the right. Anyhow, I got there and back, tired enough and glad of the half-loaf of bread that awaited me.

Then I became learned in Wormwood Scrubs and its possibilities. It was and is a very barren and bleak place itself, but in those days there was an attractive corner on the Acton side of the waste, that I was fond of contemplating. This was a sort of huddle of old cottages and barns and outhouses with a fringe of elms about them. It did my eyes good then as now to look on something that was old and worn with use and mellow; my eyes that were bleared and aching with the rawness and newness of multitudinous London. To me an old cottage, with its little latticed porch and its tangled garden patch, was veritable balm; I would gaze on such a place with refreshment and delight, as desert travellers must gaze on the cold pools and green leafage of an unexpected oasis. I used to light on these little, humble, pleasant retreats in my walks—there were many more of such cottages in the outskirts of London then than now—and make impossible plans for migrating from the urbanity of Clarendon Road into one of these hidden places, where there would be a garden for me to walk in, and perhaps a summer-house overgrown with white roses, and a little low room with oldish furniture. But I found no such place, and still went prowling in a kind of torment of the spirit by the highways and byways of the west. Acton used to do me good; it was then more like a country town than a modern suburb. On the right hand, as you came up from the Uxbridge Road under the railway bridge, there were then some grave and dignified houses of the early Georgian period, with broad lawns before them and big gardens behind them. On the left was the Priory, with spacious and park-like grounds and many greeny elms. Legends about the first Lord Lytton hung about the Priory, and it was whispered that the old lady who kept the lodge-gate had in her day written daring poetry, of the erotic kind. There are laundries and rows and rows of little houses now where the Priory stood; the Georgian houses on the other side of the road have all been pulled down. But I have a notion that the last time I went that way I saw a second-hand bookshop on the London side of the railway bridge, where in '83 I bought an old, odd volume of Cowley's poems.

The second-hand bookshop, which includes the bookstall, is one of the many things that I have dabbled in; but I have never been sworn to the hunt over the old shelves as to a devouring passion. I lack the great incentive: the love of rare books on account of their rarity. I have a great respect for the collector of such things, and I often envy him his sudden joys of discovery; it must be like finding a golden treasure in a rubbish heap; but I could never follow his example. Still, I often used to amuse myself by grubbing about the dusty shelves for an odd hour or two, turning over vast masses of insignificance—of insignificance for me, at all events—conning titles, diving into prefaces, glancing doubtfully over strange pages, wondering whether this or that or the other would bring me the best entertainment for the few shillings that I had to spend. In these new days the young man with a thirst for literature has his labours simplified; the classics of the world are ready for him, nicely printed, in a handy form, and at a low price. He has simply to go into a shop, put down his shilling, and get his book, and it is all over. This would never have done for me. When I bought a book I required and obtained a long drawn-out, deliberated pleasure; I considered that the possession of three-and-sixpence or five shillings entitled me to a whole afternoon's rich enjoyment. Just as ladies of the suburbs make arrangements—as I understand—to come up to town and do a little shopping, and have a delicate cress-sandwich or two in Regent Street, and then go to a matinée at the theatre, and have creamy cakes for tea before they start back for the red villas: so did I use to travel from Notting Hill Gate to Charing Cross, and stroll up Villiers Street, and walk along the Strand, relishing its savours, which never grew stale to me. For I do believe that the old Strand, before they destroyed it with their porphyries and their marbles and Babylonian fooleries and façades of all sorts, was the very finest street in all the world. I know quite well its manifest and manifold weaknesses and faults, if it were to be regarded from the point of view of a classical town-architect. There was no plan, no design about it, no uniformity; its houses were of all shapes, sizes, periods, and heights; it had no more been designed than a wild hedgerow has been designed. And there, exactly, was its infinite and subtle and curious charm. Nothing could be more urban or urbane than the Strand; and yet it had grown, as the green brake grows, as the cathedrals and the country houses of England grew from age to age, gathering beauty as they increased. The Strand was an altogether English street, and it was the very heart of London. In it, or beside it, were the theatres and the bookshops and the cookshops; to north and south odd passages and stairs and archways admitted the curious into the oddest places and quarters. You were weary of the traffic and the pattering feet? Then you could turn into New Inn or Clement's Inn and enjoy deep silence. You wanted to see the old hugger-mugger of the London back streets, dark taverns of the eighteenth century, where men had lain hidden from the hangman? Here was Clare Market for you. You had heard that "Elzevirs" were very rare and curious books, and would like to see an Elzevir? You would lose your opinion of their rarity, for you would see as many Elzevirs as any man could desire in Holywell Street, where I believe they were to be bought by the sack, as if they had been coals. And Elzevirs apart; the naughty prints and books of Holywell Street were as good as a play. For I believe that the Row had turned naughty somewhere in the early 'fifties; it had then got in its stocks—and had kept them. Here were the works of G. M. W. Reynolds in large volumes; *Mysteries of the Court of St. James,* and such weariness. Here was the faded coloured engraving of a young female of extreme gaiety—with ringlets, and the appearance of the chambermaid in the once-famous print, "Sherry, sir". And with all the curiosity, and variety, and oddity and richness of the Strand, it had the while a manner of snug homeliness and cosiness and comfort about it which was quite inimitable. To be in the Strand was like drinking punch and reading Dickens. One felt it was such a warmhearted, hospitable street, if one only had a little money. Unfortunately, I was never on dining terms, as it were, with the Strand; but I always felt that if it only knew me it would have called me "old boy" and given me its choicest saddles of mutton and its oldest port, and I felt grateful. Somehow I always warmed my hands when I got into the Strand . . . and they were often chilly enough.

Such, then, was my preparation for a book-foray in the heart of London, this relished, leisurely, savoury walk along the Strand; and then I might dive into Clare Market by Clement's Inn and look for mystery books in a certain shop that I knew there. I bought one of the most curious—I do not say the best—books in the world, Vaughan's *Lumen de Lumine,* in a shop in Clare Market, and still I should be much obliged if someone would tell me what *Lumen de Lumine* is about. Or I might try Denny's, at the western end of Booksellers' Row, or like enough go grovelling round the shelves of Reeves and Turner, who were then in the southern bend of the Strand, opposite to St. Clement Dane's Church.

One dull afternoon, I remember, I ran to earth in this shop on a lower shelf a dim, brown elderly-looking book in cloth covers called *Ferrier's Institutes of Metaphysic.* It repaid me many times over for the couple of shillings that I gave for it. I took Ferrier home in delight to the little room in Clarendon Road, and made a great deal of green tea, and found the dry bread of quite admirable flavour, and smoked pipes and read the new book far into the night. Before I went to bed Ferrier had quite convinced me of the truth of the proposition—which looked odd at first—that we can only be ignorant of that which we can know. This means, of course, that no man can be ignorant of the existence of four-sided triangles; which is evident enough. But as I fell asleep, I felt I had had a tremendous day.

I look back upon myself in that little room in Clarendon Road with some amazement. I come in from one of my long, prowling walks—I may have been to Hounslow to look for the Heath, or I may have been to Hampton Court—and make my meal of bread and tea, and then settle down to tobacco and literature. I find that my landlady turns off the gas at the meter at midnight, so I provide myself with carriage candles, which I fix up somehow on the table. I read on night after night. It may be Homer's *Odyssey,* or it may be *Don Quixote*—to which I have been faithful ever since I found the book in the drawing-room of Llanfrechfa Rectory—it may be that singular magazine of oddities, Disraeli's *Curiosities of Literature,* it may be Burton's *Anatomy of Melancholy;* a great refuge, this last, a world of literature in itself. Or I am reading Pepys for the first time, with ravishment, or Pomponius Mela *De Situ Orbis* in a noble Stephanus quarto, or Harris's *Hermes,* or Hargrave Jennings on the Rosicrucians; this last one of the craziest and most entertaining of books, which had a little later an odd influence on my fortunes. It was a sad blow to me to find out afterwards, chiefly through the medium of A. E. Waite's *Real History of the Rosicrucians,* that, as a cold matter of fact, there were no Rosicrucians. A Lutheran pastor who had read Paracelsus, wrote, early in the seventeenth century, a pamphlet describing a secret order which had no existence outside of his brain. Naturally enough, societies arose which imitated, so far as they could, the imaginary organisation described by the fantastic Johannes Valentinus Andrea; I should not be surprised, indeed, to be told that such societies are now in being in modern London; but these orders are late "fakes"; the 'seventies and 'eighties of the last century saw their beginnings. There are no Rosicrucians—and there never were any.

Or I am reading Carlyle—*Sartor Resartus* or the Johnson and Burns and Walter Scott Essays—and I must say that I think a good many young men of this age would be all the better for a Carlyle course. For though Carlyle was not the prophet of full inspiration that the time just before my own imagined, though he exalted brute force into a place that belongs to the Divine Wisdom, though his original Calvinism hung like a dark and obscuring cloud over all his life, yet I know not any man of these days that is worthy to dust Carlyle's hat or to clean his pipe for him.

There is a passage in the Johnson essay telling how the poor, agonised, heroic doctor made for himself a boat of the transient driftwood and enduring iron, and sailed down Fleet Ditch, "the roaring mother of dead dogs", to the City that hath foundations; the phrases ring still in my heart, noble music; worthier stuff than the prophecies of to-day—or should I say of yesterday? These, so far as I can make out, bid us abstain from meat and beer and tobacco, and the State shall give us a pound a day and save our souls alive. This message does not ring in my heart a noble music; I think Carlyle would have called it "a damned potato gospel". I read Carlyle, then, in my little room, and find a strange encouragement and strength in him. His picture of life is of a bitter struggle, and so indeed I find it—at twenty. Man, in Carlyle, is a poor wretch in thin and ragged clothes, out on a blasted heath, with all the heavens and all the clouds crashing and pouring upon him; blackness over him, hailstorms and fire showers his portion in the world. Get into whatever kennel or doghole you can find, says Carlyle, and shelter yourself from the blast so long as you can keep it, and be thankful. I liked the doctrine then, and it still seems to me a very good philosophy.

So I read and meditated night after night, and I am amazed at the utter loneliness of it all, when I contrast this life of mine with the beginnings of other men of letters. These others have often gathered friends of all sorts, both useful and pleasant, at the University; they have come of well-known stocks, every step they take is eased for them, their way is pointed out, there are hands to help them over the rough and difficult places. Or, even if they have not been at Oxford or Cambridge, if they have not come of "kent folk", they know, somehow or other, young fellows of their own age, with whom they can engage in endless talk about letters over eternal pipes and ever-welling tankards. One informs another, one, consciously or unconsciously, charts the other's way for him. I am often made quite envious when I see and hear how a young man, fresh on the town, drops so easily, so pleasantly, so delightfully into a quite distinguished place in literature before he is twenty-five. He enters the world of letters as a perfectly well-bred man enters a room full of a great and distinguished company, knowing exactly what to say, and how to say it; everyone is charmed to see him; he is at home at once; and almost a classic in a year or two.

And I, all alone in my little room, friendless, desolate; conscious to my very heart of my stuttering awkwardness whenever I thought of attempting the great speech of literature; wandering, bewildered, in the world of imagination, not knowing whither I went, feeling my way like a blind man, stumbling like a blind man, like a blind man striking my head against the wall, for me no help, no friends, no counsel, no comfort.

Somehow or other, out of a welter of reading of the most miscellaneous and shapeless sort, out of long walks and long meditations, out of moonings and loafings by Brentford and the parts thereto adjacent, there rose up in the spring of 1883 the beginnings of something that had a vague resemblance to a book. I had finished that miserable "poem" which attempted the manner of William Morris, and from that time my attacks of verse-writing became brief and trifling, causing no uneasiness. And, this trouble happily over, I became immersed in the study of scholastic logic, and gave many days and nights to Whately's *Elements*. I got Thomson also, and dallied with the quantification of the predicate, but I found such devices too new-fangled; what I wanted was the logic of the mediæval schools, and in this I took a singular and intense delight.

And here is a paradox, which may be worthy the consideration of the curious: that age which was above all the age of logic, was also the age of the most luxuriant and splendid imagination. The scholars and thinkers of the Middle Ages have been reproached with idolising the logical process to a point of utter extravagance, with treating the syllogism as a sort of divining rod by which all the treasures of the spiritual, intellectual, and physical worlds could be discovered and drawn up from the dark womb and chaos of things into the light of the sun. These reproaches, I think, have chiefly proceeded from people to whom exact thinking has proved unpleasant and unprofitable; but it is certainly true that the logical art was deeply and profoundly and constantly studied in the thirteenth century—which was the age of the marvellous imagery, the great magistry of the Gothic cathedrals, of the Arthurian romances, of Dante. Nay, it is interesting to note that Coleridge and De Quincey, two main agents of the "renascence of wonder" at the beginning of the nineteenth century, were both practised logicians. It would seem, therefore, that the dream and the syllogism have between them a certain secret alliance and bond, and so, naturally enough, two of the most extravagant dreams, *Alice in Wonderland,* and *Alice Through the Looking-Glass,* were the visions of a master of logic. As for the Snark, I can inform the inquisitive as to his true abode. He dwells in the place that is called Bocardo.

And so I steeped myself in these rare and entrancing studies, for such they seemed, and still seem to me. And thus I would sit on a bench on that bald, arid, detestable Shepherd's Bush Green, and be in reality, though not in actuality—let us for the moment adapt our discourse to the matter, and make the distinction—in cool, grey cloisters of the Middle Ages, walking in the silvery light with the Master of the Sentences, with the Angelic Doctor, listening to the high, interminable argument of the Schools. High, indeed, as dealing with immortal essences, not with monkeys' guts; interminable also in the manner of the cathedral rushing upwards to the stars which it cannot attain, of the old modes in which there are no true closes, but rather hints of undying melodies far beyond their endings; interminable, according to the dictum of one of these dark-robed Masters; *omnia exeunt in mysterium.* For there is a quest to which there is no term, nor bound, nor limit: *pelagus vastissimum.* Meditating these things, the jangling of the old horse trams might disturb me, and I would carry my quiddities to green fields by Hanger Hill, or to solitary places in Osterley Park, beyond Brentford, and so muse till the shadows came and sent me homeward under the twinkling, wavering lamps of those far-off days. Then for much tobacco, the disjunctive hypothetical syllogism and the strict rigour of the game. I am afraid very little of the old science has remained with me, but now and then I come with some amusement on distinguished personages engaged in what they suppose is argument. I see no arguments; but undistributed middle terms are thick as October leaves in Wentwood.

From such a soil, then, the thing that had certain resemblances to a book rose up and gradually took shape, so far as it ever had any shape. It came up out of my logic books and out of Burton's *Anatomy of Melancholy,* and so it was called *The Anatomy of Tankards.* For, having enough sense, even though I was only twenty, to know that I could not write a serious treatise concerning the high doctrines that entranced me, I wrote a grave burlesque of what I loved. I examined into the essence of the tankard, I sought deeply into its quiddity, I divided its properties from its accidents, and distinguished again between the separable and inseparable accidents. I shewed philosophically and conclusively that if there were no tankards there would be no men, that is, no rational or civilised men. For the ancient Greeks truly taught that man was raised from the brutish to the spiritual state by Bacchus, the giver of the vine. By wine is man made divine; and a diviner, says Bacbuc: and since wine must be contained before it can be drunk, it is clear that without tankards man cannot become divine; that is, cannot be man at all, in the proper sense of the term. And so on, and so on, with an infinite deal of easy dictionary learning, with much twisting of my logic formulæ; it was all too elaborate, elephantine, prolonged; a little thing that might have been well enough in its way drawn out into a big thing, and so spoiled. Still, I was only twenty, and twenty is apt to worry its bone long after all the meat has disappeared.

But if I could only have written the real book—that is, the dreamed, intended book—and not the actual book! Then, I promise you, you should have had high fantasies; not only arguments that began with a pebble by the way and rose upward to the evening star, that deduced all the shining worlds in an ineffable sorites from one mere letter of the alphabet. You should not only have been in at the death when Achilles caught at last the tortoise and passed him by, spurning his body into that utter void where parallel straight lines meet; you should have had an English Rabelais.

I remember taking my thoughts of the book up to Ealing Common one autumn evening. The work was drawing to a close, and I stood meditating the matter, looking from the height down towards Brentford. There was a wild sunset, scarlet and green and gold, and as it were, gardens of Persian roses, far in the evening sky. I stood by an old twisted oak, and thought of my book as I would have made it, and sighed, and so went home and made it as I could.

VI

The kind of life that I have been trying to indicate lasted for about eighteen months, and then my pupils mysteriously disappeared. Mysteriously, I say, for I have completely forgotten what became of them, and by what ways they left me. At all events, they vanished, and I, being destitute, returned to Gwent and my old home. There they were almost as poor as poverty, but they were glad to see me. And I, waking in the morning to the brave breath from the mountain, wandering in the sunshine—it was summer-time—about the gardens and the orchards, revisiting the green, delicious heart of the twisted brake, listening once more to the water bubbling from the rock; I thought I had been translated from hell to paradise.

For, be it remembered, I have dealt gently with the days of Clarendon Road. I have spoken for the most part of the happier hours, of eager reading, of finding an enchanting book on dusty shelves, on the delights of the mind, on the capacity of changing dreary, common Shepherd's Bush into the cloistered walks of the Schools, on the joy of obtaining some kind of literary utterance. I have said little of the black days and the waste nights, of the desolation that would sometimes engulf me as it were with a deep flood. For many weeks at a time I never spoke to any human being; save to my pupils on Euclid and Cæsar, and this was a speech that was no speech. And being born, I believe, with at least the usual instincts of human fellowship and a great love of all genial interchanges of thought and opinion, this silence seared my spirit; to the interior sense I must have shewn as something burnt and blasted with ice-winds and fires. Indeed, when I was released from this life in the manner that I have described, I came out, as it were, a prisoner from the black pit of his dungeon, all confused, trembling, and afraid, scarce able to bear the light of genial affection. For a long while I spoke but little, and then with difficulty; I was fast losing the habit of speech. Indeed, the eighteen months in Clarendon Road had been a very grave experience; but I think that what affected my relations most in my demeanour was this: for a long time I would cut myself a piece of dry bread at tea, and munch it mechanically, having forgotten all about the use of butter. This struck them as dreadful; one might be poor, but to eat dry bread was more than poverty; it was beggary. When my aunt first noticed this trick of mine, she pushed the butter dish towards me, saying in a disturbed voice that there was no need for *that* any more.

And for many days I was in a sort of swoon of delight. I had no desire for activities of any kind; I had all the happy languor of the convalescent about me. It was bliss to stroll gently in that delicious air, to watch the mists vanishing from the mountain-side in the morning, to see again the old white farms beneath Twyn Barlwm and Mynydd Maen gleaming in the sunlight, to lie in deep green shade and to feel that I was at home again; that my troubles were over. I did not fret myself by enquiring as to whether they would not begin again. Indeed, in this first passion of relief, I loved to imagine myself as dwelling for the rest of my days amidst friendly faces in a friendly land, and devoting, say, fifty years to healing the wounds of eighteen months. It is a sorry thing to be but twenty-one and to feel so.

But it is thus, I suppose, that the man of the imaginative cast of mind pays, and pays heavily, for whatever qualities he may possess, and it will always be a question whether the price exacted be not too dear and beyond all proportion to the value received. But the case, I apprehend, is this: Mr. Masefield has said, very finely, that literature is the art of presenting the world as it were *in excess*. To the lovers in Mr. Stephen Phillips's drama of *Paolo and Francesca* the earth appears a greener green, the heavens a bluer blue; all beautiful things are raised to a higher power by the fire of their passion; the whole world is alchemised. And this state, which is a result of love, is the condition of imaginative work in literature, and so the man who is to make romances sees everything and feels everything acutely, or, as Mr. Masefield says, excessively. Now there would be nothing amiss in this state of things if these exalted and intensified perceptions could be utilised when there was a question of making a book and then abrogated and laid aside with pen and ink and paper. Unluckily, however, this cannot be so managed; and too often the dealer in dreams finds that his magic magnifying glass is tight fixed to his eyes and cannot be moved. And thus a mere common bore or nuisance appears to him as dreadful as Nero or Heliogabalus, the possibility of missing a train is as tragical as *Hamlet,* and the pettiest griefs swell into the hugest sorrows.

I, in truth, had suffered; I had been through a dreary and a dismal experience enough; but my pains had racked me to excess; the pinpricks, unpleasant in plain earnest, had become stabs of a poisoned dagger. And so I came back to Gwent as to Avalon; there to heal me of my grievous wounds. So, as I say, it was mercifully given to me to saunter under the apple trees in July and August weather, to watch the sun and the wind on the quivering woods, to wander alone, and yet how deeply consoled and medicined, by the winding Soar Valley. Now and again I recollected, as I hope we shall recollect earthly torments in Paradise, as things over and paid for, the interminable, cruel labyrinths of London. I saw myself again, a half-starved, unhappy, desolate wretch astray in those intolerable, friendless, stony mazes of Notting Hill and Paddington and Harrow Road; I came again by obscene, obscure paths to Kensal Green, the place of the whited sepulchres. Or the hideous raw row of suburban houses would suddenly confront me, surging up, a foul growth, from the green meadow, or the sick reek of the brickfields by Acton Vale blew in my nostrils. And the grim little room and solitude for the end of every journey!

I recollected these things, but though only days or weeks had been interposed between my happy state and my endurance of them they were as torments suffered in some remote æon. I said to myself, "I am as they that rest at last," and almost heard the words *In Convertendo:* with whatso in that psalm is after written.

Among the books that I kept in my step-ladder library in Clarendon Road I mentioned that queer piece of sham learning and entertaining extravagance *The Rosicrucians: Their Rites and Mysteries,* by Hargrave (or Hargreave?) Jennings. I said that this odd volume had eventually a curious influence on my life; and this was as follows: I was reading Herodotus and that portion of Herodotus which treats of Egypt—I have long ago forgotten the Muse which names the book—and Herodotus, it will be remembered, was very deeply interested in the Mysteries of the Egyptian religion. In treating of these occult things of Osiris the historian mentions certain singular matters which were highly pertinent to Mr. Jennings's thesis—if Mr. Jennings could be said to have had anything so definite as a thesis. But *The Rosicrucians* contained no mention of that which Herodotus had seen when night was on the Nile, so I ventured to write to the ingenious author, pointing out the particular passage which, I thought, would interest him. Mr. Jennings did not answer my letter; he was odd to extremity in most things, but in this particular he conformed perfectly to all the literary men whom I encountered in my early days. I came into contact with four or five men of a certain reputation; or perhaps I should say I came within sight of them; and they could very easily have flung me a word or two of encouragement, which would have been very precious to me then. But I never had that word, and so was forced to go on and do my best without it; the better way, no doubt, but a hard way. But though the author of *The Rosicrucians* did not reply to my letter, he passed my name and address to another man, a young fellow who had just set up as a publisher, and was going to issue one of the astounding Jennings books. So Davenport, the publisher, sent me his catalogue of new and second-hand books, and I, on reading it, sent him the manuscript of my *Anatomy of Tankards*.

Here a parenthesis, if not several parentheses. We are now in 1884, and I had finished the *Anatomy* in the autumn of 1883. Soon after it was ended I sent the MS. to a gentleman who was then but in a small way. He is now a very eminent publisher indeed, and loved so much by his authors—by some of them at all events—as to be known as "Uncle". Well, "Uncle" (though, alas! it was not fated that he should ever be uncle-in-letters of mine) sent back the MS. in due season with a letter that almost made up for any disappointment my first "boomerang" may have occasioned.

His letter delighted me, not because it was specially complimentary, nor because it gave evidence of a careful and critical reading of the rejected manuscript, but because it was almost a replica of the publisher's letter which introduces Mr. Tobias Smollett's admirable epistolary romance, *Humphry Clinker*. My actual publisher so resembled Smollett's feigned bookseller in the manner of his letter that I should suppose the one had deliberately made the other his model, did I not know "Uncle" to be far too good a man to read such a book as

Humphry Clinker. I have not got my Smollett by me, I am sorry to say, so I cannot quote, but I may mention that both publishers made a very liberal use of the dash, or mark of parenthesis, and were curious in avoiding the word "I".

My letter ran somewhat as follows:—

"Dear Sir,

"Referring to your favour of the 17th ult., enclosing MS. of work, 'Anatomy of Tankards'—have read MS. with interest—fear it would hardly command large sale—have had little encouragement to speculate lately—would recommend topic of more general public interest—hoping to have pleasure of hearing from you on some future occasion.

"Etc. etc."

I was delighted, only a few years ago, to find that "Uncle's" hand has not lost its epistolary cunning. A distinguished friend of mine had been good enough of his own motion—not with my knowledge—to write to this publisher suggesting that a book by me would ornament his catalogue. The publisher approached me by letter. I wrote to him briefly, saying that I was just finishing a romance. He wrote back: "Sorry you speak of a romance—fear there is very little sale for those old things—however", etc. etc.

I did not trouble to go into whatever might lie beyond the portals of "however". But note the phrase, "those old things". It seems to me more precious than gold that has passed the furnace.

But to return from this backwater of narrative; I found Mr. Davenport established in an old street in the quarter of Covent Garden. I got to know this street well afterwards, and to like it, too, for all its associations and circumstances. Over the way, opposite to Davenport's offices, was the house where they said De Quincey had written his great book; there were theatrical shops all tinsel and wigs and grease paints close at hand, and on market days the street was all apack with carts and waggons and clamorous with marketmen who are still a rough and primitive and jovial race. Indeed, the market overflowed into York Street and submerged it, and I have had to leap over an undergrowth of green, springing ferns established on the office steps. Mr. Davenport had written me a very agreeable letter, and we had a very agreeable interview. The book on his publication-list which had attracted my attention was called *Tavern Talk and Maltworms' Gossip*, and an admirable little anthology it was, compiled (as I found out afterwards) by Davenport himself. I thought there was a certain congruity between this book and my *Anatomy of Tankards,* hence the despatch of the manuscript to York Street. The publisher liked my book very much. He wanted to publish it badly; but there were certain preliminaries to be adjusted before this could be done, and I did not see how the obstacle could be surmounted. This conference took place at that singular hour of my career when my pupils seemed to melt away from me, as though they had been morning dew. I was just bound for the country, and the publisher agreed to hold the little matter of which I have spoken in suspense.

So I went westward, and there in Gwent there were kind people who had known my father all his days, and my grandfather before him, and so, for the sake of "the family", they helped me to arrange those "preliminaries". And, after all, perhaps it is fair enough that a man should pay his footing when he enters the craft.[1]

So here was another element or elixir in the potion of my bliss, that I was drinking among those dearly-beloved hills and woods of Gwent. The bad old days were all over, and my torments were past; Clarendon Road and all its sad concatenations were like a black wrack of cloud seen far down on the horizon, as the sun rises splendid on a bright and happy day. I was come to the territory of Caerleon-on-Usk which was Avalon; and every herb of the fields and all the leaves of the wood, and the waters of all wells and streams were appointed for my healing. And my book was going to be published; I was to see myself in print, between covers—vegetable vellum they turned out to be—and I should be reviewed in London newspapers; and, not a doubt of it, be

---

1. [In CLM there is an additional paragraph after a section break: "I am reminded, oddly enough, of an initiation ceremony described in a queer French book of the seventeenth century, called 'Le Moyen de Parfenir.' The craft was that of the Butchers, and the Apprentice was stripped naked. Then he was ordered to put his clothes on again, and this done, the Warden uttered the sentence: 'Now you are a Master Butcher; you have dressed a calf.' I would not say that when seventeenth-century France called a man a calf it intended any very high compliment to his wisdom."]

happy ever after.

Mr. Pecksniff, it will be remembered, spoke of the melancholy sweetness of youthful hopes. "I remember thinking once myself, in the days of my childhood, that pickled onions grew on trees, and that every elephant was born with an impregnable castle on his back. I have not found the fact to be so; far from it." Nor have I found "the fact" to be so. Still, these visions of fair print and title-pages and reviews are very pleasant in the green of youth, and they helped to make that summer of 1884 delightful for me. I "worked in" the thought of the coming proof-sheets—even the anticipation of a proof-sheet is almost too much joy at twenty-one—into my escape from hard bondage, into the summer sunlight, into the odours of the solemn woods at night, into the cool breath of the brook, into the twilight fires of the sky above Twyn Barlwm. They were brave days while they lasted.

And now and again I had gallant tramps over the country with my old friend Bill Rowlands. I saw Bill a couple of years ago, after an interval of a quarter of a century, and Bill wore a long black coat and a solemn collar, having been a clerk in holy orders for many years. But when I began to speak of the little tavern at Castell-y-Bwch there was a twinkle in Bill's eye, and at the mention of the chimes of Usk, we both laughed till we cried—and perhaps we did cry internally. But I said to Bill, "Now I am going to take you to the Café Royal; it's the best I can do for you. But I wish it were the Three Salmons at Usk!"—where, if I remember rightly, we had bread and cheese and a great deal of beer and hot brandy and water to follow.

But that was a great day. We had gone over hill and dale, through the depths of woods and over waste lands, finding footpaths in the most unsuspected places that we had never dreamed of. And I remember that these footpaths gave me a singular impression of travelling in time—backwards, not forwards, as in Mr. Wells's enchantment. For the track of feet was but barely marked, and seemed on the point to fade away altogether, and the stiles that we climbed were of old, old oak, whitened and riven with age, and the outlets of these paths were into deep, forgotten lanes where no one came. And if one passed a house, it was roofless and ruinous; its gable-wall standing grey, with fifteenth-century corbel stones. The garden wall was fallen into a heap of stones, and the fruit trees were dead or straggled into wildness. So it seemed to me that we had fallen on old ways that were not of our day at all, and no one, perhaps, had been there for fifty or a hundred years, and if we saw anyone it would not be a man of our time. Bill, I am convinced, thought nothing of all this; his talk was of B.N.C. and mad tricks and all the mirth in the world, and I warmed the chilled hands of my spirit at his gaiety, as I had longed to warm my bodily hands at the watchman's brazier, glowing red in the cold London street. So Bill and I came at last into Caerleon, having succeeded by much extraordinary wandering in making five miles into ten, and at Caerleon we drank old ale at the Hanbury Arms, which is a mediæval hostelry, close to the Roman tower by the river. And then nothing would satisfy us but to go to Usk by the old road; again, ten miles instead of five, but with our "short cut" imposed upon it, a good fifteen miles.

The way goes over the river; on the right are King Arthur's Round Table and the relics of the Roman city wall of Isca Silurum, as the Second Augustan Legion, garrisoned at Caerleon, called the place. Then through the village, still known in my days as Caerleon-ultra-pontem, and so into that most wonderful, enchanted, delicious road that winds under the hillside, under deep Wentwood, above the solemn curves and esses of the river. We passed Bulmore, which does not mean a moor of bulls, but pwll mawr, the great pool, of the Usk river. It is a farmhouse now, but once a retired officer of the 2nd Augustan had his villa here, and his graveyard also: and here, I think, in the orchard, as they were planting some young trees, they found the stone inscribed: *Ave, Julia, carissima conjux; in æternum vale.* Hail, Julia, dearest wife; farewell for ever.

And here, to the best of my belief, Bill was telling me how an undergraduate friend of his at B.N.C., a schoolfellow of mine, found himself under the painful necessity of screwing up the Dean in his rooms; the screws employed being coffin-screws, headless, that is, and not to be extracted without enormous pains.

We went on our way by the river, and passed under Kemeys, a noble grey old house, with mullioned windows and Elizabethan chimneys. There is such a peace about this place, such a sweetness from the wood, such a refreshment from the water, so grave a repose upon it, that I translated to Kemeys one of my heroes, a clerk in Shepherd's Bush. This clerk had found out that all the bustle and activity of modern life are delusions and wild errors, and his reward was to be that he should end his days at Kemeys, sheltered from all turmoil and vanity, garnered from the evil world.

The peace of Kemeys was the peace of all the valley of the Usk, and what balms it exhibited to my spirit only those can know who have been bred in such places, and have experienced the jar and dust and racket of some great town, and then have returned to the old groves.

My friend Bill and I went swinging along the winding lane beside the winding river, and as we went the sound of pouring waters sang to us. For now the over-runnings of the wells of Wentwood came from the hill as rivulets, and about each stream its twisted thicket grew, accompanying it all down the steep, to the river below. We passed little Kemeys church, watching above the pools of the Usk, and then on the hillside, almost in the shadow of the forest, was Bartholly, that solitary house which awed me for years, so that I made my awe into a tale. And here was Newbridge, crossing a river that had now ceased to be tidal and yellow, and had become glassy clear, and so on northward, and it seemed into silences and solitudes that grew ever deeper and more solemn, more evidently declaring the great art-magic of God that has made all the world. The day drew on, the sun sank below wild unknown hills—neither of us had ever been this way before—and the green world was dim for a while, and then was lighted up with the red flames of the afterglow. The evening redness appeared, and in those fires the ash tree became of immortal growth, the round hills rose above no earthly land, the winding river was a faery stream. Then, veil upon veil rising from the level, rising from the fountains in the wood, mists closing in upon us.

My friend Bill said we should never get to Usk at this rate; he felt sure that there must be a short cut across the fields. So we took the first stile that appeared and set out over country that was utterly unknown to us; and the marvel was that we ever got to Usk at all—or to anywhere for the matter of that. I have a confused recollection of walking for hours in a gathering darkness, through jungles and brakes of dark wood, climbing hills that rose fantastic as out of dreamland, going down into dusky valleys where white mist rose icy from the courses of the brooks, threading an uncertain way through quaking marshland, and the regions of the distance as vague as shapes of smoke.

The bells were ringing nine when we came out of this dim world into Usk, and to the lights and cheerfulness of the Three Salmons, to ale and to laughter. There was a wonderful old fellow, a Water Bailiff, making the mirth of that cheerful, ancient parlour; and he told us of the tricks he had played on poachers and fishermen till we roared again. He was a fellow of strange disguises; if one of his stories were to be believed he had caught the most famous salmon poacher of the Usk by assuming the gait and utterance of a calf seeking for its mother at midnight. The tale may have been true; it was certainly an excellent entertainment.

Such was one of our days; and again we would go wandering over the mountains to west and to northward; climbing up into great high wild places of yellow gorse and grey limestone rocks, stretching and mounting onward and still beyond, so that one said in one's heart "for ever and ever. Amen". High up there; the sunlight on that golden gorse, on the yellow lichens that encrusted the rocks ringed in old Druid circles, the great sweet wind that blew there, the heart of youth that rejoiced there, all the dear shining land of Gwent far below us, glorious; it is all an old song.

And there was a day on which we mounted over Mynydd Maen and came down into a valley in the very heart of the mountains, and walked there all the day, and in the evening returned again over the mountain at the southern end, winding under Twyn Barlwm as the twilight fell. It is only music, I think, that could image the wonder of the red sky over the faery dome, and the gathering dusk of the night as it fell on the rocks of that high land, on the streams rushing vehemently down into the darkness of the valley, on the lower woods, on the white farms, gleaming and then vanishing away. Only by music, if at all, can such things be expressed, since they are ineffable; not to be uttered in any literal or logical speech of men. And if one looks a little more closely into the nature of things it will become pretty plain, I think, that all that really matters and really exists is ineffable; that both the world without us—the tree and the brook and the hill—and the world within us do perpetually and necessarily transcend all our powers of utterance, whether to ourselves or to others. Night and day, sunrise and moonrise, and the noble assemblage of the stars, are continually exhibited to us, and we are forced to confess that not for one moment can we proclaim these appearances adequately. We stammer confusedly about them, much as a savage who had been taken through the National Gallery might stammer a few broken sentences, the applicability of which would be more or less dubious. "Woman—very bright round head," might be the Blackfellow's "description" of a famous Madonna; and a Turner would be summed up as "plenty clouds—one big tree". And in like manner we, confronted, not only with things remote and majestic, but with things familiar and near at hand, stutter a few lame sentences, endeavouring to describe what we have seen. And thus all literature can be but an approximation to the truth; not the "truth" of science, for that is a figment of the brain, a non-existent monster, like dragons, griffins, and basilisks; but to that truth which Keats perceived to be identical with beauty. And it is further evident that even this approximation to the truth of things is a matter of the utmost difficulty and not very far from a miracle, inasmuch as in a generation of men there are only two or three who achieve it, who in consequence are hailed as men of the highest genius.

Of course, there are persons for whom "truth" implies "even gilt-edged securities slumped heavily", or some such statement. To them, I tender my sincere apologies.

The proof-sheets of my book began to appear early in that autumn of '84; they made me rapturous reading. And while I was correcting them, with a vast sense of the importance and dignity of the task, Davenport, the publisher, was writing to me, asking if I had any ideas for new books, and throwing out suggestions of his own.

Now this was very pleasant, for it all tended to persuade me, in spite of any doubts and fears of mine, that I was really a literary man. I would read Davenport's letters again and again, and deliberate gravely with myself over the answering of them; I enjoyed this very much indeed. But the correspondence led to no practical result; because I could not then—or ever—perform the Indian mango trick. The expert conjurers of the East, as is well known—in magazine fiction—will put a seed into a flower pot, cover up for a second or two, and lo! there is a little plant. Again the concealment; the plant has grown, and so forth, till within the space of five minutes you can gather ripe mangoes from the tree that you saw sown. This is the mango trick of fiction; that of fact, as I have seen it, is about the dreariest and most ineffective piece of conjuring imaginable. But, as I say, I could never imitate those fabled Orientals. If Mr. Murray and Mr. Longman were to jostle one another on my doorstep, clamouring for a masterpiece, and offering Arabian terms, it would make no difference; if I had no book within me, I should not be able to produce one on demand. In practice, I have found that I take about ten years to grow these things; though I have one in my mind now that was first thought of in 1898–99 and is not yet begun.

So Mr. Davenport's letters produced no literature, interesting though they were; and I must say that a less sluggish mind would have found them stimulating in a high degree. But the literary publisher struck on cold iron; he suggested, I remember, a volume of scathing criticism—"like Mozley's Essays"—as likely to receive his most favourable attention. But, really, I could not think of anybody that I particularly wanted to scathe—now, perhaps, I could oblige a publisher in search of anathemas and Ernulphus curses—and I had not read Mozley, nor have I read him to this day. Then I, on my side, suggested a book to be called *A Quiet Life,* this being, in fact, a description of the life that I was then gratefully and gladly leading. I sent a specimen chapter, and so far as I remember Davenport counselled me to defer the writing of *that* sort of book till I was eighty or thereabouts. I daresay he was right. Then my half-dozen copies of *The Anatomy of Tankards* reached me; and I believe that as soon as I saw the book printed and complete in its (vegetable) vellum boards I began to be ashamed of it. I think that this was hard lines, but the trick has been played on me again and again; and I do believe that a moderate, not excessive, dose of the good conceit of oneself is one of the chiefest boons that parents should beg from fairy godmothers for their offspring. For life is necessarily full of such buffetings and duckings, such kicks and blows and pummellings, that balms and elixirs and medicaments of healing are most urgently indicated, and there is nothing equal to this same rectified spirit of conceit. It may tend to make a man an ass, but it is better—or more agreeable, anyhow—to be an ass than to be miserable.

Then came the reviews, and they did me some good, for, as far as I remember them, they were kindly and indulgent. I think the critic of the *St. James's Gazette,* then in its glory under the editorship of Greenwood, spoke of "this witty and humorous book", while he said, with absolute justice, that I had ruined the popularity of my parodies by their prolixity. Then the publisher, despairing, I suppose, of getting any ideas out of me, produced a notion of his own. He sent me three or four French texts of the *Heptameron,* and bade me render it into the best English that I had within me; and so I did forthwith, for the sum of twenty pounds sterling. I wrote every night when the house was still, and every day I carried the roll of copy down the lane to meet the postman on his way to Caerleon-on-Usk.

And so my story has come round full circle. In the first of these chapters I told how the kindly speaker at the Persian Club, praising my version of the French classic, transported me in an instant from that shining banqueting hall in the heart of London, over the bridge of thirty years, into the shadows of the deep lane. Again it was the autumn evening, and the November twilight was passing into the gloom of night. There was a white ghost of the day in the sky far down in the west; but the bare woods were darkening under the leaden clouds; the familiar country grew into a wild land.

And I, with time to spare, walk slowly, meditatively down the hill, holding my manuscript, hoping that the day's portion has been well done. As I come to the stile there sounds faint through the rising of the melancholy night wind the note of the postman's horn. He has climbed the steep road that leads from Llandegveth village and is now two or three fields away.

It grows very dark; the waiting figure by the stile vanishes into the gloom. I can see it no more.

THE END

NOTE

Far Off Things was written in 1915, and, the work not being of an encyclopædic nature, no effort has been made to bring it up to date.

The book called *The Anatomy of Tankards* in the text was called in fact *The Anatomy of Tobacco.* Simple-hearted American collectors are now willing to give four pounds for a copy of it.

Things Near and Far

I

The road from Newport to Caerleon-on-Usk winds, as it comes near to the old Roman, fabulous city, with the winding of the tawny river which I have always supposed must be somewhat of the colour of the Tiber. This road was made early in the nineteenth century when stage-coaching came to perfection, for the old road between the two towns passed over the Roman bridge—blown down the river by a great storm in the seventeen-nineties—and climbed the break-neck hill to Christchurch. Well, this new road as I remember it was terraced, as it were, high above the Usk to the west, and above it to the east rose a vast wood, or what seemed a vast wood in 1870, called St. Julian's Wood, of some fame as a ghostly place. It was cut down long ago by an owner who thought timber of high growth better than ghosts.

On the one side, then, the steep dark ascent of St. Julian's Wood; on the other, the swift fall of the bank to the yellow river, where, likely enough, there would be a man in a coracle fishing for salmon. And then there came a certain turn, where suddenly one saw the long, great wall of the mountain in the west, and the high dome of Twyn Barlwm, a prehistoric tumulus; and down below, an island in the green meadows by the river, the little white Caerleon, shining in the sun. There is a grey wall on one side of it, a very old and mouldering wall to look at, and indeed it is old enough, for it is all that remains of the Roman wall of Isca Silurum, headquarters of the Second Augustan Legion.

But there, white in the sun of some summer afternoon of fifty years ago or so, Caerleon still stands for me shining, beautiful, a little white city in a dream, with the white road coming down the hill from Newport, down out of St. Julian's Wood, and so to the level river meadows, and so winding in a curve and coming to the town over the bridge.

That is my vision of the place where I was born; no doubt the recollection of driving home beside my father on some shining summer afternoon of long ago; but of later years another vision of the same white town and white road has come to me. I have "made this up", as the children say, though, no doubt, it is all true. The time now goes back from the early 'seventies to the early 'fifties, and two young ladies are setting out from the Vicarage—it stood practically in the churchyard, pretty well in the position of that other, that illustrious Vicarage at Haworth, and my Aunt Maria could never see any reason why a vicarage should not be in a churchyard—the two young ladies closed the Vicarage door, and made their way down the deserted street, where the grass was green between the cobble-stones, and so passed over the bridge and into the Newport road. They were going to meet John, home from Jesus College, Oxford; and no doubt they talked eagerly of how well John was doing at Oxford, and wondered when he would be ordained, and where his first curacy would be, and what a good clergyman he would make, and how they hoped he would marry somebody nice, and what a pity it was that John was not at home when Mr. Tennyson came to Caerleon and stayed at the Hanbury Arms, and smoked a black clay tobacco pipe with his feet on the mantelpiece; very odd, but poets always were odd people and "Airy Fairy Lilian" was very pretty. The Vicar had called of course, and had been a little shocked at the pipe; still, Papa was always so amiable and ready to make allowances.

"Your grandfather," Aunt Maria said to me years afterwards, "was a most amiable man, but he could not bear radishes or the *Adeste fideles.*"

Well, the two young ladies, Anne and Maria, shading themselves from the heat of the sun with their fringed parasols, pace decorously along the Newport road discussing these and many other matters; parish matters, of helping poor people and old people and sick people; county matters, the great doings that there would be at the Park when Sir (?) Hanbury Leigh was to have a great party from London on August 12th to shoot grouse on the mountain; Church matters; how a Mr. Leonard had just been given the living of Kemeys Commander and had actually been heard to say, "I call myself a Catholic priest", and, in spite of the Creeds, wasn't that going rather far? And what would John say to that? And, somehow, I fancy the talk came circling again and again back to John, and how glad he would be to be at home again, and how lucky it was that Mrs. Williams Pantyreos had come in that very morning because John always said that he never got butter like the Pantyreos butter anywhere, and how it was to be hoped that the weather would keep up till Wednesday when they were all going to drive to Aunt Mary's at Abergavenny—except Mamma, who said, "Young gadabout ne'er won a clout"—and how this beautiful sunshine must be doing Cousin Blanche's cough a great deal of good: John would like to see Cousin Blanche again.

And so on, and so on, and the two sisters walk along the white limestone road, picking a flower now and again, for Anne paints flowers and Maria is much interested in Botany—I am not sure whether she had acquired Miss Pratt's three-volume work on the subject at that date. And the evening draws along, and the sun hangs over the huge round of Mynydd Maen in the west, and the scents of St. Julian's dark, deep wood fill the stilled air; till Maria says suddenly: "Anne! here is the omnibus at last, and, there! I believe I can see John's face."

The old dim yellow and faded chocolate omnibus from the Bull—I remember it in its last days just before they made the line, and never will I speak of *this* omnibus as a 'bus—comes lumbering on its way, and the old driver, recognising the "two Miss Joneses the Vicarage" and knowing that Master John is inside, causes it to stop. John, a mild-looking young man with little side whiskers, gets out and kisses his sisters; and the three then get in, and the omnibus lumbers down the hill towards Caerleon, the three chattering of Oxford, of plans and prospects, of Caerleon news and how happy Papa looked at breakfast. And so the evening draws on and the shadows deepen and the walls of white Caerleon glimmer and grow phantasmal like the old grey Roman wall as they cross the bridge and the Usk swims to high tide, the tawny yellow tinged with something of the sunset redness that glows over the mountain. The three are talking and chattering all the while, making plans for holidays and happiness and long bright years and the joy of life—a correct joy, but still joy—before them, and John is enquiring eagerly after Cousin Blanche and nodding and smiling to the Bluecoat boys and girls and saying: "I'll unpack my box to-night and shew you my prizes—Parker's *Gothic Architecture,* in three volumes, and Hooker and a lot more," and they are hoping again and again that Wednesday will be fine, and Blanche is sure to be quite well by this, and John is feeling his young cheeks grow a little red when—it is night.

Alas! They are all dead, years and years ago. The kind Vicar and his grim, good wife are dead. Poor Cousin Blanche perished of consumption in her fresh youth; no summer sun could allay the racking of that cough of hers. Anne followed her, by the same way to the same end: I have the *Holy Dying* that John, my father, gave her. There are two inscriptions in it; one facing the rubricated title-page, now "foxed" with time. This runs:

> To Anne E. Jones
> from her affectionate
> Brother John Edward
> On her Birthday, and in
> remembrance of the 29th
> September, 1857*
> April 16th, 1858.

The other, on the recto of the leaf, is as follows:

> Johannes Edvardus Jones,
> In memoriam A.E.J.J.
> Quæ obdormvit in Jesu
> 29 mo Martii MDCCCLIX

And those of the party that lived longer knew more of sorrow, and more of broken hopes and of dreams that never came true. And thus, advisedly, I begin this second chapter in the story of a young man's dreams and hopes and adventures. *Ego quoque*—I am forgetting my Latin tags—I, too, have walked on the white road to Caerleon.

To walk a little faster, to comply, in fact, with the request of the whiting in Lewis Carrol's beautiful Idyll, the end of 1884 and the beginning of 1885 found me in something of a backwater. *The Anatomy of Tobacco*, the book I had written in the 10 by 6 cell in Clarendon Road, Notting Hill Gate, had been published in the autumn of 1884, and soon after I had set about the translating of the *Heptameron*. Every evening I

---

*The date, I think, of their father's death.

worked at this task till it was ended; and now it was done, and there seemed nothing to do next. I wandered up and down the country about Llanddewi Rectory in my old way, lost myself in networks of deep lanes, coming out of them to view woods that were strange and the prospect of hills that guarded undiscovered lands. Thus on my wider and more prolonged travels, but I had haunts near home, nooks and retreats where nobody ever came. There was an unfrequented lane, very dark, very deep, that led from a hamlet called Common Cefn Llwyn—the Ridge of the Grove—to Llanfrechfa, used scarcely at all save by labouring men going to their work in the early morning and returning in the evening. All the length of this lane there was only one house in sight—the farms in Gwent are mostly in the heart of the fields, remote even from the byways—and this one house must have fallen into ruin eighty or a hundred years ago. From what remained one judged that it had been the *petit manoir* of some dead and forgotten race of little squires; it was of grey stone, of fifteenth-century workmanship, and the corbels supporting the chimney were still sound and clean cut. All about the old broken house were the ruins of the garden, apple trees and plum trees run wild, hedges that had become brakes, a confusion of degenerate flowers; and by the tumbledown stile that led to this deserted place I would linger for an hour or more, wondering and dreaming and setting my heart on the hopeless endeavour of letters. Weather made no difference to my goings; a heavy greatcoat, boots with soles an inch thick, and leather gaiters up to the knee, made a wild wet winter's day a thing to be defied and enjoyed; and indeed I loved to get abroad on such days and see all the wells of the hills overflowing and rushing down to swell the Soar or the Canthwr, red and foaming, and making whirlpools of barmy froth as they fell into the brooks. And then, when the rain changed to snow, what a delight to stand on some high, lonely place and look out on the wide, white land, and on the hills where the dark pines stood in a ring about some ancient farm: to see the wonder of the icy sunlight, of the violet winter sky. These were my great adventures, and I know not whether in reality there are any greater, since it is a great thing to stand on the very verges of an unknown world.

So the winter of '84–85 went on and I dreamed and wondered and did nothing, though I was nearing the age at which many a young man has produced his first novel with success and acclaim. I never could do these things, and still I cannot do them. I knew that I had no business to be loafing and mooning about the rectory, a burden on my poor father—the "John" of that happy return of the 'fifties had by this time experienced sorrows and pains and miseries of all sorts. My mother had been a hopeless invalid for fifteen years, my father's health had failed and he had become very deaf, the poor "living" of Llanddewi Fach had grown poorer still through the agricultural smash of 1880, he was in dire and perpetual straits for money, he underwent most of the mortifications which are allotted to the poor. It makes me grieve to this day to remember with what piteous sadness he would lean his head on his hand; he had lost hope; nothing had any savour for him any more. And seeing this, I was distressed to be an additional weight in the heavy pack of sorrows and trials that he bore daily, and I tried to get all sorts of employments for which I was utterly unfit, which would not have harboured me for twenty-four hours. Nothing came of these attempts, and so the time went on till we were in June, 1885. Then there was a letter from the publisher of *The Anatomy of Tobacco* to the effect that he thought he could find me some odd jobs of work if I would come up to London; and so I returned again to the well-remembered cell in Clarendon Road.

With mixed feelings. I was glad indeed at the prospect of doing something for myself and so removing a little from the weary burden at the rectory: but, I had not forgotten the *peine forte et dure;* the dry bread, enough and no more than enough, the water from a bitter runnel of a sorrowful street, the heavy weight of perpetual loneliness. "Alone in London" has become a phrase, it is a title associated, I think, with some flaring melodrama; but the reality is a deadly thing. I was only twenty-two; and I shuddered a little one June night when I went out and bade farewell to the brooks and the woods and the flowers; to the scent of the evening air.

All sorts of odd jobs and queer jobs awaited me. I was given a big folio book full of cuttings on a particular subject, and the publisher asked me to make a selection from these and so compile a book of oddments. Then, there were novels submitted to him that I was to read and advise upon: a weary business when the said novels were as a rule foolish things written in varieties of straggly and scraggy scripts.

But the principal business was the making of the Catalogue. For the publisher of York Street was also a second-hand bookseller. He had a mass of odd literature stored in a garret in Catherine Street, and on these volumes I was let loose; my main business being to write notes under the titles, notes describing the content of the books and setting that content in an alluring manner before the collector.

It was as odd a library as any man could desire to see. Occultism in one sense or another was the subject of most of the books. There were the principal and the more obscure treatises on Alchemy, on Astrology, on Magic; old Latin volumes most of them. Here were books about Witchcraft, Diabolical Possession, "Fascination", or the Evil Eye; here comments on the Kabbala. Ghosts and Apparitions were a large family, Secret Societies of all sorts hung on the skirts of the Rosicrucians and Freemasons, and so found a place in the collection. Then the semi-religious, semi-occult, semi-philosophical sects and schools were represented: we dealt in Gnostics and Mithraists, we harboured the Neoplatonists, we conversed with the Quietists and the Swedenborgians. These were the ancients; and beside them were the modern throng of Diviners and Stargazers and Psychometrists and Animal Magnetists and Mesmerists and Spiritualists and Psychic Researchers. In a word, the collection in the Catherine Street garret represented thoroughly enough that inclination of the human mind which may be a survival from the rites of the black swamp and the cave or—an anticipation of a wisdom and knowledge that are to come, transcending all the science of our day.

Which? It seems to me a vast question, and I am sure it is utterly insoluble. Of course, an enormous mass of occultism, ancient and modern, may be brushed aside at once without the labour of any curious investigation. Madame Blavatsky, for example, her coadjutors and assessors and successors need not detain us. I do not mean that every pronouncement of Theosophy is false or fraudulent. A liar is not to be defined as a man who never by any chance speaks the truth. A thief occasionally comes honestly by what he has. I mean that the specific doctrines and circumstances of Theosophy: the Mahatma stories, the saucers that fell from the ceiling, the vases that were found mysteriously reposing in empty cupboards, the Messiahship of a gentleman whose name I choose to forget: all this is rubbish, not worth a moment's consideration. And so with Spiritualism; though in a less degree. For I am strongly inclined to believe that very odd things do sometimes happen amongst those who "sit", that some queer—and probably undesirable—psychic region is entered; and all this quite beyond and beside the intention or understanding of those present at the séance. You never know what may happen when a small boy pokes his fingers carelessly among the wheels and works of a clock. But as to the profession of the Spiritualists; that they are able to communicate with ghosts, *that* need not trouble us. Their photographs of fairies need not trouble us. Their revelations as to the life of the world to come as given through the Rev. Vale Owen need not trouble us. Though here is a "phenomenon" which seems to me of no little interest. How can a man who is confessedly perfectly honest and straightforward conjure himself into the belief that when he takes up a pencil an intelligence apart from himself guides his hand as he writes? I suppose the answer involves the doctrine of dual or multiple personality; and *that* is mysterious enough in all conscience. Yet, apart from all the nonsense, apart from the state of mind of the average Spiritualist—one of them, a very eminent one in his day, said that the clause of the Creed: "I look for the Resurrection of the Dead" meant "I expect to see some physical manifestations of the departed"—apart from all this I still think as I have said that very strange and inexplicable things do sometimes happen. Here is nothing to do with ghosts: but the evidence that the famous medium Home rose into the air, floated out of an open window high on a Scottish castle tower, and floated in again at another open window: the evidence here is good; that is, if levitation, as they call it, were a criminal offence and Home had been put on his trial he would have been convicted. It will be seen that I am not exactly a fanatical Spiritualist: but I had rather be of the straightest sect of Rappers and Banjo Wielders than of that company which understands all the whole frame and scheme of the universe so thoroughly and completely that it is absolutely certain that levitation is impossible, that a man cannot rise into the air unless he is mechanically and materially impelled and supported, that no evidence, however direct and unimpeachable, can establish this for a fact. I do not understand the universe; consequently I do not dare to advance any such proposition. And further; let me diminish a little a proposition that I have only just dared to make. I have said that all the ghost business, all the Vale Owen sort of business, is rubbish and foolery. Well, I believe most heartily and profoundly that it *is* rubbish, nonsense, unveridical to the last degree; in fact, and in the proper sense of the word, a lie. Yet; let us beware. Not one of us understands the universe. Even in the Higher Mathematics, the Queen of profane sciences, very odd things are reported to happen. So, possibly, the following account may really correspond with the truth of things.

The room is in total darkness. One of the sitters proclaims with exultation that his nose has been tweaked by *Joey,* who, on this side, was a clown. *John King,* understood to have been a master-mariner, sings "Tom Bowling" in a falsetto voice through a speaking trumpet. On this, *Cardinal Newman,* known to be a lover of music, is gratified and utters the word "Benedictine". There is a sudden scream of joy in a female voice: "Oh! darling Katy, thank you, thank you, *thank you!* Oh, *please,* may we have the lights turned up for a moment? Katy promised me a lock of her beautiful golden hair, and I am *sure* I felt it float down on my hand." The lights are turned up. A strand of yellow hair is, sure enough, reposing on the lady's hand. It had evidently been treated with spiritual peroxide, made, no doubt, of Ethers, like the ghostly whiskey and sodas in *Raymond.* Then the room is darkened and the Medium takes up the tale.

"This spirit's name is Milton. Henry—no, John Milton, the author of the *Faery Queen.* He says that he is very happy. He spends most of his time with Shakespeare and Ben Jonson. Shakespeare has confessed to him that all his plays were written by Bacon. The evidence will be found in a brass box under the Tube station at Liverpool Street. Pope often has tea with him. He says they don't use alcohol there."

There is a sudden crash. "Avast!" comes with a roar through the trumpet. *John King* has returned, bringing with him an *American Indian* who speaks in the idiom of a Nigger Minstrel practising in the East End of London and will call the Medium his "Midi". Whereupon *Katy* puts a beautiful warm arm round the neck of a gentleman sitter and the gramophone plays "Abide with me". All repeat the Lord's Prayer, and Sir Arthur Conan Doyle expresses his intense gratification.

Well; it may be so. But I hope it isn't, and I shall never believe that it is so.

Well; there I laboured in the Catherine Street garret amidst all this, and much more than this. Down below were the publishing offices of old Mr. Vizetelly, who was issuing English translations of Zola at the time, and was at last sent to gaol for publishing an English version of *La Terre,* an obscene book that every judicious Bishop of Central France should put in the hands of newly ordained priests—if it is to be accepted that the physician ought to have some knowledge of the constitutions of his patients and of the diseases from which they are suffering. It was a sumptuous and rich garret—a street now passes over the site of the house—filled with that mysterious odour that used to prevail in oldish London houses that were not too carefully swept and washed and polished, and there day after day I worked, reading and annotating, and all alone. Now and then in the older books I came across striking sentences. There was Oswaldus Crollius, for example— I suppose his real name was Osvald Kroll—who is quoted by one of the characters in "The Great God Pan". "In every grain of wheat," says Oswaldus, "there lies hidden the soul of a Star." A wonderful saying; a declaration, I suppose, that all matter is one, manifested under many forms; and, so far as I can gather, modern science is rapidly coming round to the view of this obscure speculator of the seventeenth century; and, in fact, to the doctrine of the alchemists. But I would advise any curious person who desires to investigate this singular chamber of the human mind to beware of over-thoroughness. Let him dip lightly from the vellum quarto into the leather duodecimo, glancing at a chapter here, a sentence there; but let him avoid all deep and systematic study of Crollius and of Vaughan, the brother of the Silurist, and of all their tribe. For if you go too far you will be disenchanted. Open Robert Fludd, otherwise Robertus de Fluctibus, and find the sentence: *Transmutemini, transmutemini de lapidibus mortuis in lapides philosophicos vivos*—Be ye changed, be ye changed from dead stones into living and life-giving stones. This is a great word indeed, exalted and exultant; but beware of mastering Fludd's system—if confusion can be called a system—of muddled alchemy, physical science, metaphysics, and mysticism. Get Knorr von Rosenroth's *Kabbala Denudata,* vellum, in quarto, and find out a little about the Sephiroth: about Kether, the Crown; Tiphereth, Beauty; Gedulah, Mercy; Geburah, Justice or Severity. Really, you will discover very curious things, and the more easily, if instead of Knorr von Rosenroth, you choose A. E. Waite's *Doctrine and Literature of the Kabalah.* It is odd, for example, to discover that the side of Mercy is the masculine side, that Justice or Severity is feminine; and that all will go amiss till these two are united in Benignity. Again, it is interesting from another point of view to discover that three of the Sephiroth are called the Kingdom, the Victory, and the Glory. Is there any connection between these and the ancient liturgical response to the Pater Noster: "For Thine is the Kingdom, the Power, and the Glory"? And then that matter of Lilith and Samael and the Shells or Cortices, the husks of spirits from a ruined world that brought about the Fall of Man; the strange mystery of that place "which is called Zion and Jerusalem"—duly here comparing Böhme on the Recovery of Paradise when innocent man and maid are joined in love—all this is a wonderful and fascinating region of thought. And beautiful indeed is the saying of one of the Fathers of Kabbalism: that when the lost Letters of Tetragrammaton, the Divine Name, are found there shall be mercy on every side. And here, perhaps, but not certainly, light may be thrown on certain obscure matters of Freemasonry. Dip then, and read and wander in the Kabbala; but do not become a Kabbalist. For if you do, you will end by transliterating your name and the names of your friends into Hebrew letters and finding out all sorts of marvellous things, till at last you back Winners—which turn out to be Losers—on purely Kabbalistic principles.

And here, by the way, I may remark that I have long meditated writing an article called "The Aryan Kabbala", keeping the requirements of occult magazines strictly in view. It would make a pretty article. I should begin by a brief note on the Hebrew Kabbala, explaining how the Sephiroth tell in a kind of magic shorthand the whole history and mystery of man and all the worlds from their source to their end. The Tree of Life—as the Sephiroth arranged in a certain scheme are called—is, in fact, I would point out, at once an account of how all things came into being and a map and an analysis of all things as they now are. As an occult friend once said to me by my hearth in Gray's Inn: "The Tree of Life can be applied to that poker." The Tree of Life, then, is a key to the secret generation and being of all souls and all heavens; it will also analyse for you the little flower growing in a cranny of the wall.

Well; this made clear, I would go on to say: "But what if there be a Kabbala and a Tree of Life of the Aryans as well as of the Semites?

What if it tells all the hidden secrets of our beginning and our journey and our ending? What if its august symbols are known to all of us, in everyday and common use amongst us, remaining all the while as undiscerned as the most sacred and mystic hieroglyphics? What if the office boy and the grocer handle every day the signs which tell The Secret of Secrets?"

And then, after all due amplifications and ponderous circumnavigations it would all come out. The Aryan Kabbala is, in fact, the Decad; the ten first numbers. They embody an age-old tradition dating from the time when the ancestors of the Greek and the Welshman, the Persian and the Teuton were all one people. They contained the secret mystery religion of this primitive race, they sank by degrees from their first august significance to become instruments of common use and commercial convenience, just as vestments became clothes. The proof is easy enough. Take the first number of the Decade: one in English, ἕν (in the neuter) in Greek, unus in Latin, Un (pronounced "een") in Welsh, ein in German. And then compare another series of words in these languages: wine, οἶνος, vinum, gwin, wein. Then: two, δύο, duo, dau, zwei; and compare with: water, ὕδωρ, udus, wy (and dwr), wasser. I drop the other terms, or Sephiroth, of the Decad—in Mrs. Boffin's presence—and come to the last two numerals: nine, ἐννέα, novem, naw, neun, compared with: new, νέος, novus, newydd, neu. Then finally ten, δέκα, decem, deg, zehn: compare with deck (bedeck), δόξα, decor, teg, schön.

The conclusion, I hope, is evident: we (and all things) proceed from Unity, which is wine, decline to Duality (or a weakened, fallen nature), which is water. Then, after passing through many changes, adventures, transformations, transmutations—undescribed for the reason given—we are renovated, made New—"I will make all things new"—in the last number but one of the Decad, and, in the final term, which is Ten, are reunified in Beauty and Glory.

There! It seems to me wonderfully plausible, and I really think I should have written the article and sent it to some suitable quarter. It is all nonsense, of course, but . . . does that matter?

Well, all that business of the Aryan Kabbala is an absurd digression, but it illustrates well enough the frame of mind likely to be induced by the study of a good many of the books in the Catherine Street garret.

Take the interlude and add to it the rich odours of the frowsy, neglected room stuffed with confusions of old books and pamphlets, add to it the old, delightful, picturesque London that was undisturbed in those days. Holywell Street and Wych Street were all in their glory in 1885, a glory compounded of sixteenth-century gables, bawdy books and matters congruous therewith, parchment Elzevirs, dark courts and archways, hidden taverns, and ancient slumminess. There were no great, blatant Australia Houses or Colonial Edifices of any kind about the Strand in those times: instead, we had the beauty and the green lawns of Clement's Inn and the solemn square of New Inn, and Clare Market communicating tortuously with Great Queen Street by the most evil-smelling byways that I have ever experienced—and something of jollity in the air that seems to me to have vanished utterly. Take all these elements and things; and you have me as I worked high up in the vanished house in Catherine Street, preparing the Catalogue that was to be called: *The Literature of Occultism and Archæology*—when the gas lamps in the Strand shone with a brighter light than the arc lamps of to-day.

II

Such was the scene of my life in the summer of the year 1885. By my odd jobs; a little "reading", a little compiling, and a good deal of catalogue making, I just managed to live, earning perhaps as much as a pound a week, one week with another. I do not remember exactly the precise terms on which I worked, but I know that I had a good deal of time on my hands. Part of this time I spent in trying to learn shorthand. I can't think why, for at this period of my life I had no newspaper or secretarial employment in view. I am inclined to think that trying to learn shorthand had become a mechanical habit with me. Then, I resumed my old mooning walks out of London, going westward usually or always, sometimes Acton way and sometimes through Brentford—that curious, dirty, and most fascinating place—to Osterley Park, where in those days you could walk and wander anywhere you pleased, so long, I suppose, as you did not glue your nose to the windows of that mansion. And then I fell to writing again.

Now here is a mystery. It is held, and very properly, that people should keep their mouths shut unless they have something to say; similarly that a man has no business to write unless he has something in his heart which, he feels, cries out to be expressed. But here was I not knowing in the least what I wanted to say, but resolved, even at the cost of much pain and misery, to say it; that is, to write it. There are, of course, people who are said to talk for talking's sake; and so, I suppose, I was suffering from the analogous vice of writing for writing's sake, otherwise known as the *cacoethes scribendi*. I fancy a volume of Hazlitt had fallen into my hands; it had strayed, very likely, into the Catherine Street library, and at first I began to try to write essays, more or less in imitation of this inimitable author. I need scarcely say that I made sad work of it; and happily, no scrap of manuscript survives. And then I fell on Rabelais and on Balzac's *Contes Drolatiques,* and wondered and admired hugely and studied both deeply in my long night watches under the gas-jet in the little room in Clarendon Road. I would dine sumptuously on half a loaf of dry bread, green tea made as I liked it, without milk or sugar, with plenty of tobacco by way of dessert; and then to my books and to my wonder. It was not a bad life on the whole, sweetened as it was by the enthusiasm for letters; but the loneliness was an oppression and sometimes a horror. Weeks passed without any human converse beyond brief business dialogue; still, since then I have known far worse days. Poverty and loneliness; these are doubtless evils hard to bear; but they are light indeed; nay, they have their dignity, and the gas-jet of Clarendon Road is not altogether without a halo—when I weigh all this and set it in the balances beside the intolerable degradation of the service of Carmelite House. I often thought in those latter and most hideous days that my case was somewhat that of a man who had been captured by a malignant tribe of anthropoid apes or Yahoos and was by them tormented and unspeakably degraded; and there was this additional shame and horror: that my degradation and misery were witnessed by rational creatures like myself. I remember how in my last year in the employment of *The Evening News,* I was out on some idiotic errand which led me up Wellington Street, past York Street, where George Redway, the publisher of *The Anatomy of Tobacco* and of *The Literature of Occultism and Archæology,* had his place of business. In a line, pretty well, with York Street I could see that new street which runs over the site of Old Vizetelly's office where the famous fusty garret was. The streets—Wellington Street, Bow Street, York Street—are not much changed in the last forty years, and the gap formed by the new street made me see myself a cloudy young man of twenty-two up in the air labouring amongst the dusty ancient books; all this and all the recollections of the days of dry bread, tea, tobacco, and the hopeless but not dishonourable endeavour of literature; all this contrasted with the shameful circumstances of my life as a weary old man of fifty-eight, a man who had known struggles and sorrows and losses; all this, I say, overwhelmed me suddenly. It was almost more than I could endure.

But we go too fast. We are still in the days of the cloudy young man, who is clear that fine literature is an infinitely noble thing, but is not clear upon any other subject whatever. I had my queer books in the mornings and my long lonely walks in the afternoons, and my great books in the evening and far into the night. I remember reading Dante in Longfellow's translation, from beginning to end, and though I could not by any manner of means lift up my heart and mind to the mountain-peak of the Paradise, I divined the majesty I could not comprehend. Don Quixote was always with me, and good company and meat and drink and lights and fire always to me; and so I pass along the dim London streets revolving all these mighty works, a ghostly man amidst the hurrying multitude of the living, and go far afield under dim trees in the West, or sit solitary on a bench near the river in Kew Gardens, looking towards Syon; all the while in a lonely but not an unhappy dream.

It came suddenly to me one night. I was lying awake in my bed; and then it came to me that I would write a Great Romance. A Great Romance! I know it is funny; but it is sorry too. I didn't in the least know what the said Great Romance was to be about; save this, that Rabelais was to have something to do with it, and that my own county, beloved Gwent, was to have much more to do with it. That does not sound very definite; but I believe it is more definite than the actual vision which appeared to me, for this was rather a warm and golden and wonderful glow and radiance than any scheme for a book. I know I lay happy and trembling for a long time and fell asleep happy and awoke happy in the morning, and went out forthwith to buy pens and paper. I had both already, but I felt that the occasion was more than a special one and called for very special purchases. So, at the stationer's shop, near the Holland Park end of Clarendon Road, I got ruled quarto paper, and "Viaduct" pens, and two penholders, and I am pleased that I am writing all this with a surviving penholder of those two; a poor old thing chewed to a stump and battered grievously in its metallic parts. So here was paper, here were pens and penholders; and of course the rest was easy.

There was only this little difficulty. The golden and glowing vision of the night, the announcing of the Great Romance, declined to be more specific. It had no hints to give, it seemed, as to plot; it still veiled the subject of this wonderful book in the dimmest, most religious obscurity. The paper and the pens were ready; but how to begin writing the first line? I had not the faintest notion, so I proceeded to write Prologues and Epilogues, with commentaries on the *magnum opus* which was not even begun. Two of these oddities survive, the Dedication to Humphrey, Duke of Gloucester, as the Patron of men of letters; a dreadful quip founded on the old saying about "dining with Duke Humphrey", which meant that you had not had any dinner. This was worked out with all elaboration and with an attempt at the great manner of Bacon in his most magistral mood. It ran in this vein:

> Truly, then, do we poor folk (men of letters) owe what service we are able to pay Your Grace, who in spite of mean dress and poverty (justly accounted by Mr. Hobbes for shame and dishonour) is pleased to entertain us at that board, where so great a multitude of our brotherhood has feasted before. For your illustrious line hath now for many generations made it a peculiar glory to supply the needs of lettered men; and as we sit at meat it seems (methinks) as if these mighty men of old did sit beside us and taste with us once more the mingled cup we drink. The ingenious author of Don Quixote de la Mancha must, I suppose, have often dined with the Duke of his age, Mr. Peter Corneille and Mr. Otway, Senhor Camoens, Rare Old Ben, Signori Tasso and Ariosto not seldom: while young Mr. Chatterton the poet did not only dine, but break his fast, take his morning draught, and sup with your Grace's great-grandfather, till at last he died of a mere repletion.

There! Very solemn and portentous fun, indeed; but what is so solemn as a youngster of twenty-two? Canterbury Cathedral and Westminster Abbey seem gay and light and airy by comparison. *I* like it still, to be sure; but then I am prejudiced, and indeed, there is one sentence that still affects me; that phrase about "the mighty men of old" who seem "to sit beside us and taste with us once more the mingled cup we drink". For in that sentence I see something of the spirit which sustained me, the cloudy young man, the dreamy and obscure and inarticulate young man, of those long-ago days, all through the fire and the darkness of poverty and loneliness and weariness and disillusion. Let us still, if you please, ride the high horse and be as magnificent as we can: I saw myself and, to be frank, I still see myself, as the youngest novice in a great and noble monastic house. The novice is by no means a promising member of the congregation, the Abbot and the Prior and the Master of the Novices have the gravest doubts as to his vocation: the other novices are inclined to indulge in remarks of a jocular and contemptuous kind. But the little, obscure, and despised candidate for the triple cord sits in his low place at the board and looks at the pictures on the walls: on the faces where torment and exultation shine with twin fires: on Blessed Bernardus a Baculo, who was beaten to death by the Danes in the ninth century, on the Venerable Servant of God, Marcellinus, who was impaled by the Turk, on St. Eugenius de Compostella, who was shut by the Moors in a horrible dungeon of filth for forty years and at last his visage shone and gave light to the tormentors when they came to end him, on Venerable Raymondus Anglus, who was slowly sliced into little pieces in Cathay, on Blessed Gregory Perrot, whom the ministers of the Virgin Queen attended to at Tyburn in 1590: on all these brilliant successes of the convent does the little novice gaze with admiring wonder. Well he knows that his picture will never hang on the wall; still, and after all, he is a member of the congregation to which these, the lucky and happy, belonged; in a faint sort they are his brothers; they are *commensales, cohæredes, et sodales.*

Very fine, indeed; but in the meantime I am scratching with a somewhat hopeless pen under Clarendon Road gaslight, taking difficulties for solution to lonely places such as Perivale, to the unfrequented parts of Hampton Court; or else, by contrast, to the long black High Street of Brentford, with its creeks and backwaters of the river, where grass and flowers grow on the decks of derelict barges. I find no oracles to help me in any of these promising quarters; there are some very sad nights in the little room over the dry bread, tea and tobacco, and the helpless pen. Finally, in a kind of despair, I begin something of which the first scene is to be laid in Gwent, which, later, is to have a voyage in it—there is a great voyage in Rabelais to the Oracle of the Holy Bottle. I read the first chapter. It is quite hopeless; and yet I do not give up hope; I resolve to try again.

But all this time, while the Great Romance refused to move, my worldly affairs were moving fast, and decidedly in the way of destruction. I suppose, having finished the Catalogue, I had done all that the publisher wanted of me. At all events, the stream of employment, never auriferous to any great extent, dwindled and dried up. I had a little, a very little money in hand, I could not possibly call on those poor people at home for help; my landlady in Clarendon Road had a hard struggle of it, I fancy, and I would not cadge on her kindness, even though my board and lodging were far from being luxurious. It seemed to me that at the end of the week I must just walk out of 23 Clarendon Road and go on walking towards the West till I couldn't walk any longer. I admit that the plan was vague, as vague as the plot of the Great Romance, but I could think of no other. And in the meantime—I had three or four days before me—I would write the Epilogue for my book: which was not yet begun.

I set about this task with the utmost relish and enjoyment. For once, I knew what to write about; that was my own position; not in a plain and literal manner, but after the fashion of a decorated fantasy. It would never do to say: "Here am I, a stupid lad who is not worth twopence to anybody, who thinks he can write and can hardly get half a dozen words to stagger on the paper; here am I going out to die in a ditch or to live in a ward of the workhouse": that would never have served. I agree with Mr. Sampson Brass in holding that the truth is often highly unpleasant and inconvenient. Hence the Epilogue to the unwritten book, which survives in the written book, *The Chronicle of Clemendy*, a work which is neither great nor a romance, but which answers the description admirably in all other respects. And as the Dedication was made to Humphrey Duke of Gloucester, so the Epilogue is concerned with the same nobleman. So here we are:

> A few days ago His Grace did take me aside into his cabinet, and looking kindly upon me (though some call him a stern and awful noble) said: "Why, Master Leolinus, you look but sickly, poor gentleman, poor gentleman, I protest you're but a shadow, do not your Abbreviatures bring you in a goodly revenue?" (Note the elegant reference to my mysterious shorthand.) "Not so, Your Grace," answered I, "to the present time I have abbreviated all in vain, and were it not for the hospitality of your table, I know not how I should win through." "How goes it then with your Silurian Histories?" (The Great Romance.) . . . "With them, may it please Your Grace, it fares excellently well, and this morning I have made an end of writing the First Journey, containing many agreeable histories and choice discourses." "I believe indeed it will be a rare book, fit to read to the monks of Tintern while they dine. But yet I will have you lay it aside a little, since I have a good piece of preferment for you, an office (or I mistake you) altogether to your taste. What say you, Master Scholar, to the Lordship of an Island and no less an Island than Farre Joyaunce in the Western Seas? How stand you thitherwards? Will you take ship present-

ly?" At hearing this, I was, as you may guess, half bewildered with sudden joy, that is apt to bring tears into the eyes of them that have toiled in many a weary struggle with adversity: I could but kneel and kiss His Grace's hand, and say "My Lord."

Of course, the allusions to "First Journeys" and "Silurian Histories" were put in months later, when I had at length found out what my book was about; at the time, October, 1885, I had not written one word of it. So the Epilogue went on its mellifluous way, and thus ended:

> But here is my Paumier, with his parchments, to advise with me concerning a grant of Water Baylage to the Abbey of St. Michael, and also concerning the ceremonies observed in the island at Christmastide. He tells me that the voyage will surely be a rough and tempestuous one, but with the captain of the *Salutation* there need be no fear. And so farewell, till the anchor be dropped in the Sure Haven of Farre Joyaunce.

And indeed, as I was writing the last page of the Epilogue, a letter came for me. I had written to Mr. Quaritch, stating my experience in cataloguing, and asking for employment. Mr. Quaritch wrote very civilly stating that he did not want any cataloguers, but people who knew how to sell books. And I wrote on to my final flourish, with all the more relish. "Ceremonies observed in the island at Christmastide", indeed! Ceremonies observed at Reading Workhouse, more likely!

But the next morning came a letter from Aunt Maria, that Maria who had walked with Anne to meet John on the white Caerleon road. My mother was dying; and they sent me the money for the fare, that I might come home.

III

It is a debatable point, I suppose, whether life, taking it all round, by and large, as Mr. Bixby said, is a horrible business. On the one hand, most of us are excessively sorry to quit this world, so, clearly, there must be something to be said for it. But, on the other hand, how endless are the devices which we find to give a seasoning to a dish which is, perhaps, rather insipid than nauseous. I have eaten cold mutton with relish—after smothering it in about half a dozen different condiments, sauces, relishes, and salads. So look at all the games we play with desperate earnestness, with a vigour and delight and, sometimes, an asceticism which we give to no office routine or serious employment of our lives. Perhaps we may try and define what "life" means a little later; but, under all ordinary and respectable conventions, I presume that the business of which I have been dimly aware on this day of writing can in no wise be classed as one of the serious employments of life; as, in any sense, a vital part of life according to accepted doctrine, religious, scientific, or philosophical. The business of which, I say, I have been dimly aware; for all I have seen of it has been Grove Road, Grove End Road, and Circus Road and all the roads adjacent lined on both sides with motor cars of all sizes, splendours and miseries; the affair being the last day of the Oxford and Cambridge Cricket Match. And, looking at all this fairly, it comes to this: here are two wickets placed at a certain specified distance from one another on a stretch of turf, and here are men with bats and here are men with balls. Will the men with balls succeed in hitting the wickets, or will the men with bats succeed in hitting those balls away to remote parts of the turf? And on the whole: are the eleven young men of Oxford or the eleven young men of Cambridge the smarter and more skilled at these pursuits and in the subsidiary pursuit called "fielding", or the art of stopping the ball which the man has hit with the bat from going to a remote part of the stretch of turf? That, in the very rough, is cricket;

and I want to ask the clergy (if they have any time to spare from their self-appointed tasks of meddling in politics, "disapproving" of bookstall novels, and serving tables) what they honestly think Saint Paul would have said, if he had seen twenty-two of his most promising young converts engaged in this cricket business, applauded by a vast multitude of the saints? I desire to put this question not with a wish to "score"—to use an idiom of the game which we are discussing—but with an honest longing for information. That is: will theologians maintain that the 'Varsity Match and First Class County Cricket generally is a part of serious life, or a serious part of life? Or, will the scientific people or the philosophical people declare that this game, played as it is played at Lord's with desperate earnestness, is a necessary part of the bodily and mental well-being of the human race? I say the game as played at Lord's, that is the great game; for the case of the old-fashioned, village cricket on the green was somewhat different. Then you had a number of people with two or three hours of leisure before them who found a good deal of fun and relaxation and amusement in bowling balls and hitting balls and running after balls, with intervals of supping of ale, sitting on the bench under the shady tree in front of the village inn; this is a very different matter from the high cricket of our times, just as diverting yourself with a ball, a racket, and a net is remote from Mlle. Lenglen's game at lawn tennis.

And these are the comparatively mild forms of sport. What of rowing till you are blue in the face, what of climbing frightful mountain-peaks, with half an inch of rock between you and a fall of a thousand feet? Why do people do all these things voluntarily, gladly, enthusiastically? I can only suppose that they do these things to make life tolerable, even entertaining, just as I add tomato sauce, Worcester sauce, pickles, beetroot, cucumber, and salad to the cold mutton, to make *that* tolerable and even appetising. It would seem indeed that life must be an awful business, if you have to plaster yourself on the walls of a sheer Alp before you can endure it. This is "drowning" your cold mutton in strong sauce with a vengeance.

And all this by way of a tentative explanation of why I ever wrote anything at all, and still more why I have gone on writing, with brief remissions, ever since the autumn of 1880. This problem, as I have hinted already, is a profound mystery. For, taking first the plain view of the man in the street, and applying his plain and simple test, I have just been running through a list of my books from 1881 to 1922, and reckoning—it was an easy task—how much money I have made by them. The list contains eighteen titles. Of these, the *Heptameron, Fantastic Tales, Casanova* represent more or less laborious translations—*Casanova* runs to twelve sizeable volumes. And my total receipts for these eighteen volumes, for these forty-two years of toil, amount to the sum of six hundred and thirty-five pounds. That is, I have been paid at the rate of fifteen pounds and a few shillings per annum. It seems clear, then, that my literary activities cannot be adequately accounted for on the hypothesis of mere greed and money-grubbing.

And, then, taking another side of the question: consider the debit of toil and endeavour and mortification and disappointment that these forty-two years of book-writing have cost me. I believe that business men, engaged in manufacture, always "write off" a considerable sum for legitimate wear and tear and depreciation of plant. What about the wear and tear of mind and heart and that T,e,a,r, which is pronounced in another manner; what about the depreciation of the plant—a highly important one—of self-confidence that my writing has inflicted on me? I have described some of the pains I endured when I set out to write the thing which afterwards became the *Chronicle of Clemendy*, and that was only the beginning of months of hard and agonising labour. And then I remember another occasion. The "idea" which turned into "The Great God Pan" came to me; again that delicious glow of delight. Now at last I had got hold of a real notion; I had a curious tale, a rare fantasy set in a rarer atmosphere to work upon: I thrilled at my heart as the explorer must thrill as he comes suddenly to the verge of the dark forest, or to the summit of the high mountain and sees before him a new and wonderful and undiscovered land. Well I remember how all this exquisite bliss was bestowed on me, one dark and foggy afternoon of 1890–91, in rooms in Guilford Street, not far from "The Foundling". The foul air shone bright, the dingy street, the dingy room were irradiated: here was happiness almost too keen to be endured. With no delay I got notebook and pencil and proceeded to "lay out" the story; that is, to set down the various scenes and incidents by which the plot was to be developed. Afterwards; the writing, and on the whole I was not altogether so ill-contented—though I daresay that I ought to have been disgusted—till it came to the last chapter. And that simply would not be written. I tried again and again; it was impossible. I could hit on no incident that would convey the required emotion; and at last I put away the uncompleted MS. in despair; I was within an ace of tearing it to bits. But think of the suffering, the misery, the bitter disappointment of those evenings. True it was all a silly thing, a toy; but an authority quoted in *The Water Babies* says that one of the saddest sights in the world is a child crying over a broken toy. My scheme was all silly, I allow; but I had set my heart on it, I had glowed with pride over it: and here it was all broken to pieces in my hands, a sorry, spoilt, piteous thing. True, I found some sort of an ending six months later; but that was not the same. There was no fun in that. You remember the party in the cabrioily that called on Mrs. Bardell? There was a dispute about the precise situation of Mrs. Bardell's house, and finally the driver, who had dismounted, led the horse by the bridle to the house with the red door.

> Here was a mean and low way of arriving at a friend's house! No dashing up with all the fire and fury of the animal; no jumping down of the driver; no loud knocking at the door; no opening of the apron with a crash at the very last moment. . . . The whole edge of the thing had been taken off; it was flatter than walking.

So with me and my story: I got to the house with the red door eventually; but the whole edge of the thing had been taken off. And so it has been with most of my books; I get, somehow or other, to the house with the red door, or to a house which I try to persuade myself is just as good; but on the way in the cabrioily I have suffered so many disappointments that I am in no condition to enjoy the pleasure of Mrs. Bardell's society. I remember that, in writing *The Hill of Dreams*, I sat down every night for three weeks with blank paper before me, trying to get the second chapter. On some nights I wrote half a dozen lines, on other nights a couple of pages—before the evening's work went, hopeless, into the drawer. A few months later, having fallen on the wrong path, I had the pleasure of casting aside about 30,000 words that I had written; and by the time the book was at last ended there were two neat piles of MS. in my drawer; the one a little higher than the other. The bigger pile consisted of the folios that I had written and had been forced to reject. And think of what that means: a heartbreak to every other page and the comment of the author on himself and to himself: "You fool! Why do you pass your life in rending your heart, in trying to do the thing that you can't do? Why weren't you brought up to sit by a brazier in the streets, to see that nobody steals the planks and railings and the wood pavement: to do something that with an effort you might be able to do?" Or, to return to our former metaphor: "Don't you see that you haven't the knack of the toy maker? Then why will you persist in trying to make toys which always break in your hands, while you fill the air with lamentable boohoos?"

And yet, as I have said, such has been my employment, with intermissions, from 1880 to 1922. It was like that in 1885–86. Night after night, when my father had knocked out his last pipe at eleven o'clock, did I draw out my papers from the table-drawer and set them under the lamp. Winds came from the mountain of the west and shook the trees about the house and sighed and wailed; snows came from the mountains of the north and whitened the terraced lawn, black clouds drifted over Wentwood, the winter rains scourged the land; and still I wrote on in the silent house; struggling against the bitter conviction of my incapacity, as a man struggles and claws at the crumbling earth when his foot has slipped and he is over the edge of the cliff. Yet, stubborn, I wrote on late into the night, far into the morning, and as the year advanced I often drew the heavy crimson curtain and looked out after I had put away my papers in the drawer, and saw a red or golden dawn streaming above the forest in the east. And as to the work itself? Let us not enquire too curiously; though I have always been proud of my parody of the terms of an ancient writ. *Diem clausit extremum,* he has ended his last day, was the title of the writ, which is moved now and then even in these days: my writ was called *Cyathum hausit extremum:* he has drained his last cup. And then there is the *merum et mixtum cervisium,* and the Charter of *Terra Sabulosa* or Sandy Soil, and the offices of Tankard Marshal and *Clericus Spigotti,* or Clerk of the Spigot; all choice jests—to adopt the manner of the work in question. But, as I say, let us not enquire too curiously into the merits of *The Chronicle of Clemendy.* I am content to abide by the verdict of M. Octave Uzanne, who is held, I believe, to be a good judge of letters. He said that it was "le renouveau de la Renaissance", and that I was sure of my place beside Rabelais and Boccaccio, on the serene, immortal seats. I am surrendering my judgment wholly to that of M. Octave Uzanne.

By the way; I do not know how it was, but the only copy sent out for review was addressed to *Le Livre,* which was then edited by M. Uzanne. Somehow, no review copies found their way to the English papers. But the MS. had been shewn to a pushing young literary gentleman, and he said that if it were properly "cut" it might make a good Christmas book for boys.

And then, again, the question returns: why did I compel myself to undergo all the toil and misery and disappointment that the writing of this *Chronicle of Clemendy* involved? It was my own choice, nobody stood over me with a stick to force me to do it. Why? Why do men row themselves into blueness and incipient heart disease at Henley and Putney? Why do men expose themselves to horrors, miseries, and the instant risk of death on all the most desperate mountains of the world? The answer is the same in all these cases: that cold mutton (or life) is in itself intolerable; that *Le Gigot de Mouton froid, Sauce Cyanide de Potasse* is better than the same dish *nature.*

And, going further, the reason of this odd state of things is plain enough. The fact is, that what we commonly call life is not life at all. All the things that are considered serious, important, and vital: the faithful earning of a living, the going to the City every morning to copy letters, keep accounts or float companies; the toils of the Chancery barrister, of the factory hand, of the doctor, of the shop-keeper, of the mining engineer, the affairs of all the serious and necessary employments of life; these things are not life at all. They are the curse of life, or, as it is sometimes called, the curse of Adam; as the theologians might have told us if they had not been too busy over the "curse of alcohol", over the dubious moral influence of "the pictures", over the decidedly frivolous character of the lighter fiction of the day, and the demoralising effects of putting a bob on the winner—this dreadful offence, I believe, is held to "harden the heart" more quickly and thoroughly than any other method. But this curse of getting a livelihood remains profoundly unnatural to man, in spite of his long experience of it: hence his frantic efforts to escape from what he erroneously calls life by running himself red in the face at Lord's, by rowing himself blue in the face at Henley, by drinking methylated spirit, by "putting on" those criminal bobs, by playing mind-torturing games like chess, by knocking small balls into small holes, by climbing Alps—and even by writing books. He will do anything to get away from what are called the serious facts of life and follow any track however desperate, trivial, perilous, or painful, if only those serious facts can be evaded and forgotten, though it be but for a few hours. And so I wrote on, night after night, till the August of 1886 saw my task ended; and I immediately began to think of what I could write next.

IV

I have just been trying to reckon up the various quarters which I have occupied in my forty-two years on-and-off life in London. When I first came up to town in 1880—the year when the play was the thing—I stayed at Wandsworth in an old Georgian house near the ugly Georgian church. I looked for it a few years ago, but I could not find it; I suspect that shops now flourish on its site and on the site of its grave old garden. Then, in 1881–2 I was domiciled in a house fronting Turnham Green; here, too, were ample lawns and gardens which, for all I know, may remain still. Clarendon Road, as I have mentioned once or twice, entertained me in '83, '84, and again in '85, and when I returned to London at the beginning of '87 I lodged for a time in Upper Bedford Place, Russell Square. This place I left for an amusing reason. I had been out rather late. The festivity was not furious; simply a little and most informal dance given by Mrs. Augusta Webster, in those days an admired poetess; and I suppose that it was half-past one when I got home from Hammersmith. I was moving softly up the stairs, and was a good deal puzzled to hear the clanking noise of metal on metal, as I passed the door of the first-floor bedroom. However, I supposed that somebody was ill and that the fire was being kept up. But the next morning, the landlady addressed me gravely. She said that Mr. and Mrs. Sogden had been very much alarmed by hearing footsteps in the middle of the night, and had made preparations for receiving burglars; and on the whole the landlady thought that I should be much more comfortable at her sister's in Great Russell Street, where no ladies were taken and things "were more Bohemian". And, indeed, she was quite right. The garret—a real garret, with a sloping roof and a dormer window—looked out on Dyott Street, the last remnant of the old rookery of St. Giles; the house was late seventeenth century or quite early eighteenth, and the room, with tea and bread and butter breakfast included, only cost ten-

and-six a week. Later in the year, I moved across the street and lived for a while over a stained-glass business; then I crossed again and lived over a tailor's shop. January, 1890, found me in two rooms in Soho Street—undoubted seventeenth century, panelled, with beautifully deep wooden cornices. And here took place the battle of the fleas.

I had moved in, as I say, early in the year, in cold weather. The rooms seemed quite all right, and the black tom cat of the premises was a remarkable and consistent character whom it was a privilege to know. His daily plan of dining with every one in the house, from his own family in the basement to the people in the attics, finally welcoming the cat's-meat man with loud shrieks, shewed, I thought, Mind. And, as I say, the cornice; well, I wish that I had been draughtsman enough to draw a section of it. Well, everything was as pleasant as it could be; and there, at the door, was all Soho to explore and investigate, and I suppose I need not say that Soho offered then, and still offers, I am glad to note, a large and curious field wherein the contemplative mind loves to expatiate.

Very well; but the weather got warmer: and the fleas appeared. At first as single spies; and then in battalions. They swarmed everywhere. They made life hideous and intolerable. I did not see what was to be done. My furniture, such as it was, occupied the rooms; it would be highly inconvenient for me to move. The advertised specifics were useless. I isolated a flea—they were fair, large fleas—with a little of the powder, under a wine glass and watched his behaviour. He seemed happy, though perhaps a little torpid; he reminded me of a stout, red-faced old gentleman who has had two or three glasses of "hot Scotch", and is inclined to fall asleep by the tavern fire. Clearly, such mild measures were useless against the busy multitudes which swarmed all over my rooms. Then, I had a notion, a much more brilliant notion than anything that I have known in the region of literature. I have an odd and random vein of practicality within me, and it came out in the Soho Street emergency. I took a large sheet of newspaper and brushed it over with treacle and laid it on the bedroom floor and waited for an hour or two. At the end of that time, a dozen or so of fleas were sticking fast to the treacle. I experienced the happy glow of the inventor; and now there was no dismal reaction. By the evening there were at least six dozen fleas captured and out of action. I thought I might say, Eureka.

But then there came a difficulty. I discovered a certain property in treacle, which, so far as I know, is not recorded in scientific textbooks. The matter of the work—to use the term of alchemy—was, I found, susceptible to weather. In certain states of the atmosphere, in place of being sticky, it became crystalline and as hard as glass. I do not know whether this interesting property of treacle can be utilised for forecasting purposes. But this hardness rendered it useless for my immediate end. The large, fair fleas hopped on to the trap and hopped away. I surveyed the problem anew. Again the flash akin to genius. I thought of fly-papers and bought half a dozen. The battle was over in a few weeks. I kept a careful daily account, and in a month, or perhaps five weeks, I had captured over three thousand fleas. And I had purged the first floor of 12 Soho Street utterly of all the race. I recollect well one night's bag. I had been to see *A Pair of Spectacles* at the Garrick, and when I came home I found I had got 120 fine fleas.

And then, having won this notable victory, a very odd distaste for London came upon me. I am not joking; the sentiment had nothing to do with the insects whom I had defeated; but, somehow, London sickened me. Its faint, hot summer airs were an oppression, its swarming streets a tribulation; I thought of cold wells in the hills and running brooks and the breath of the wood and the mountain in the early morning—and I resolved to be a countryman again. So I took a cottage high up on the Chiltern Hills, and while certain alterations were being made, I left for Tours, Touraine, France.

The Rabelaisian enthusiasm was still upon me. I had just issued a translation (called *Fantastic Tales*) of that extraordinary and enigmatic book, *Le Moyen de Parvenir*, by Béroalde de Verville, who was a canon of Tours Cathedral. So to Touraine I went; to see the land of Rabelais, of Béroalde, of Balzac. And the odd thing is, that my first Sunday afternoon in Tours—I got there on a Saturday—was a severe disappointment. The fact was that I had taken Doré's wonderful illustrations to the *Contes Drolatiques* for granted. I supposed that the enchanted heights, the profound and sombre valleys, the airy abysses of these amazing plates represented, with a little exaggeration, perhaps, the veritable scenery of Touraine. You remember the picture shewing how that sinful little page climbed the heights of Marmoutiers to confess his sin to the Abbot? Well, that Sunday afternoon, early in September, 1890, I set out from the Faisan, in the Rue Royale, to see the tremendous ascent of Marmoutiers. I crossed the bridge over the Loire, most of it sand with a swift stream here and there, and arrived at Portillon, where the conductor of the steam tram was calling out "Marmoutiers, Rochecorbon, Vouvray" in a melodious chant. But I walked along the road to Marmoutiers. Alas! there were no terrific heights, as in the picture. Imagine something like the high ground near the river at Henley; nothing higher, nothing as high. Instead of the dark green woods of Henley, golden rocks and golden earth shining in a very happy sun; little villas, larger villas, everywhere with gardens that were gardens indeed. Green walled closes, with rich green lawns; fountains in the midst of them, flowering shrubs and flowery creepers blossoming and trailing everywhere; kitchen gardens where the peaches glowed and burned dark against the hot white walls, where the pears on the dwarf trees were as shapes of golden honey: at last the old *clôture* of the Abbey of Marmoutiers with pepper-pot turrets at intervals, close to the road, and inside the enclosure, the modern buildings of a convent school: and the mellow river cliff behind all. It was delightful; but it was not a bit like Doré. I confess, my heart sank. And then going on by the river road, I got to Rochecorbon. Still the warm cliff overhung the road, underneath it a small hamlet with a tavern, "A la Lanterne de Rochecorbon", and perched on the edge of the cliff the Lantern, an odd structure which looked something like an ancient factory chimney, and was, I suppose, the sole relic of the ancient castle celebrated by Balzac. It took me some time before I could get Doré's Touraine out of my mind and enjoy the Touraine of actuality on its own merits. And these are many. There were great moments on this first visit to the garden of France.

I was staying at the Faisan in the Rue Royale—that street which Balzac, who was born in it, praises as being "always royal, always imperial", which in these later days has taken to calling itself the Rue Nationale—a delicious inn indeed. I got the recommendation from Thackeray. Philip stayed there once. He calls it the "Faisan d'Or". It had three courtyards, or rather a courtyard and two gardens, both closed in by the hotel walls. You entered the courtyard under the archway in the Rue Royale; to the left was the dining-room hung with tapestries depicting in an ancient mode the famous castles of Touraine;

on the right was the kitchen, all bright with glowing copper pots, and the big round cook standing at the open door or bending over his furnace, occasionally shaking one of his pots knowingly and beaming on you as you sat at your little table in the courtyard as much as to say: "You will find it good." Around this great man were four or five boys, all in white like their chief, who seemed to be busy all day long in washing vegetables, in chopping meat and herbs fine for *farses,* in manifold culinary employments, running out now and again and shaking showers from bags full of wet lettuce or endive leaves. At the back were the stables, and on market days the yard of the Faisan was full, like an English inn yard, of all manner of queer traps and shandridans from the country. And beyond this courtyard, at the back of the house, were the two gardens, secret, retired, and delicious. Such green turf was there in these chosen places, so pleasant a music in one of them of a singing fountain, so glowing the flowers about it with the water drops glittering on them, so sweet the shade of overhanging boughs—there are here and there gardens that address the heart and spirit and not the florist, as Poe knew well.

And thinking of the Faisan at Tours and of its curious delights, how is it that much money—one may say the wealth of the whole world—cannot buy anything like this in London? Money will get you a set of rooms thirty feet or so in height from floor to ceiling, it will buy you the use of suites of furniture that make you wonder when you wake up in the morning whether by any chance you can have turned into Louis XV in your sleep; it will buy you bathrooms all marble and tessellated pavement, dining-rooms as marblous and Louisquinzious as your private suites; but delights such as are afforded by the Faisan at Tours it will by no means buy. It is a pity; at least I think so. But then I can never fancy that I am Louis XV even for a moment, and that, I suppose, is the reason why I don't like living in the style of that monarch, why I don't even like lunching or dining in palatial halls built and furnished in his favourite manner. And I doubt whether the grandest of all grand hotels in our London could furnish you with a bottle of Vouvray Nature of a named *clos,* for any money that your millionaire's purse could proffer.

And the mention of that admirable amber wine of Vouvray, the wine wherein an argent bead rises at intervals through the mellow gold, reminds me of my first night at the Faisan. All down the tables were portly decanters of wine, red and white. I chose red, and found it a new sensation in wine vastly to my taste. It was, of course, an ordinary wine, and a little wine, I think of the kind called Joué Noble, from the place of its growth, a parish by the Cher river. It was scented like flowers in June; it was in its entirely unpretending way quite exquisite. I drank it with relish, and towards the end of dinner I had accounted for about three-parts of the decanter. Swiftly came the head waiter and bore it away and as swiftly put another and a full decanter in its place. It was almost too much; "temperance" enthusiasts would say a great deal too much. I thought solemnly to myself as I smoked a grateful pipe after dinner in the courtyard: "This night I have had as much good red wine as ever I could drink." And this was one of the great moments of my visit to Touraine.

And then there was Chinon. The train passes through the deep darkness of Chinon Forest, and you leave the station and come out into the sunlight. Here is a narrow river valley: the clear Vienne in the middle of it; to the left a gently rising land, rich with vines; to the right a long, golden, precipitous cliff, golden in such a sunlight as we never see in England. As in the backgrounds of the old Italian masters, the trees stand out clearly, vividly, distinctly against the sky; so was it at Chinon. That long, mouldering, and golden cliff was surmounted by the walls of the old castle, golden and mouldering also, irradiated; and from the river to the cliff the town climbed up; narrow ways, winding ways, steep ways, and every here and there the grey-blue *tourelles* of the fifteenth-century houses piercing upwards; and the dark mass of the forest stretching far and far away beyond. And then the thought that the man who had received one of the great visions of reality once walked these ways, and looked on a scene that had not much changed since his time; that the golden and rich sunlight had shone on him also, in the hour when the amazing, terrible, tremendous figures and symbols of the vision of Pantagruel, Panurge, Friar John, the three who are yet one came to him, we must conjecture, in clouds and darkness and uncertainties, as he listened to the new song of the vineyards, and the vine and the outpoured wine: all this was made a great moment also. I sat on a sort of bridge—if I remember—joining the two parts of the ruined castle, sat on golden stones, and looked down on the Chinon of the grey-blue *tourelles,* on the shining Vienne, and the gentle vine-covered slope, and I thought of the cloudy young man stumbling over that hard French of Rabelais far into the night, in obscure Clarendon Road, long ago. It was not long ago; this was of '90 and that was of '85, but hard pains make long years. I went down the hill again, past the fountain, and drank the red wine of Chinon solemnly, reverently in a dark tavern in one of the dark, narrow streets. It was called "Le Caveau de Rabelais".

I came back to London in the autumn and took rooms in Guilford Street till that cottage on the Chilterns should be ready for occupation. Then from 1891 I lived in the country, and found it nothing, and came back to London in the autumn of 1893, to an "upper part" in Great Russell Street, a little westward of the British Museum. It was then that I began to explore London, and to realise its vastness, its immensities. Things are relative; I began now to appreciate the fact that if you set out, without a map, from your house at 36 Great Russell Street and walk for an hour eastward or northward you are in fact in an unknown region, a new world. Continually you stand on a peak in Darien, and look out on undiscovered territories, inhabited by peoples of whom you know nothing. I would go along Great Russell Street, and turn up into Russell Square, and then go by Guilford Street, crossing Gray's Inn Road, and so find myself, like the knight in the song, "ten leagues beyond the wide world's end". I would go northward, up the Gray's Inn Road, and then turn to the right, descend into a valley and climb a height and so come to a region which was to me as the ultimate parts of Libya, and the lands of the Mountains of the Moon. I shall never forget the awe with which I first came upon the other Baker Street, the Baker Street which would enter no taxi-driver's mind; those houses climbing up the hill into Lloyd Square, stucco houses with classic pediments, but all tottering, askew, and falling into decay; the jerry building of 1820–30. And, I remember, seeing on one of the leaning and doubtful doors here the brass plate of someone who said that he was a "Buhl Maker". I wonder. Did someone really labour in this forsaken, climbing street in that rich eighteenth-century art of brass and tortoise-shell, fashioning curious cabinets and escritoires! How unlikely it seemed; more unlikely than another announcement on a modest door in the recesses of Camden Town, to the effect that here were made Shell Boxes.

Often I went up Baker Street and stood in Lloyd's Square and looked down on London, on Gilbert Scott's horrible, villainous sham-Gothic St. Pancras Station and on all the vague, smoky, weary streets about it. Here, one evening, the sun flamed suddenly and struck the windows of a school below and lit fires in them: hence the lines—in "A Fragment of Life"—entitled: "Lines written on looking down from a Height in London on a Board School suddenly lit up by the sun."

And here I would say that the matter of Wonder—that is the matter of the arts—is everywhere offered to us. It is, I am sure, true, as the feeble though pious Keble wrote, that:

> The daily round, the common task
> Will furnish all we need to ask.

And it is utterly true that he who cannot find wonder, mystery, awe, the sense of a new world and an undiscovered realm in the places by the Gray's Inn Road will never find those secrets elsewhere, not in the heart of Africa, not in the fabled hidden cities of Tibet. "The matter of our work is everywhere present," wrote the old alchemists, and that is the truth. All the wonders lie within a stone's-throw of King's Cross Station.

I remember that when, later on, I wrote a book on the principles of literary criticism called *Hieroglyphics,* a good many of the reviewers found grave fault with my dictum that all fine literature is the work of ecstasy and the inspirer of ecstasy. "In other words," said these clever fellows, "a good book is a book that you happen to like. But other people may have very different tastes and likings; no doubt many people experience ecstasy in reading a newspaper feuilleton. Is the feuilleton therefore fine literature?" The objection, I hasten to say, is perfectly legitimate. Tens of thousands, or hundreds of thousands of people, I have no doubt, read the newspaper feuilleton in an ecstasy of delight. I once found myself, to my dumb, almost awestruck horror, in a drawing-room where a number of tolerably well-educated people were engaged in taking the works of . . . well, Miss Thingumbob, seriously. Doubtless, then, there are many people who find rarities and wonders in matter that you and I pronounce to be contemptible or detestable or just nothing at all: my reviewers were perfectly right. But if you accept their ruling you put an end to criticism of all sorts. I could form a large company of coalheavers, financiers, sporting noblemen, gardeners, journalists, ladies of quality, actors, scavengers—I was going to add bishops, but they rarely speak the honest truth—and myself who had very much rather not see the famous Primavera and the famous Monna Lisa Gioconda than see them, who had rather—again I include myself—listen to George Robey's songs and gags and wheezes than to *Hamlet*. But what does that prove? Simply, I suppose, that so far as the pictures and the play are concerned my friends and myself cannot rise to these particular heights. As an old friend of mine once observed very well, "We all of us have some windows that are darkened." My friend is a musician, and remembering his maxim, I was much diverted one day by hearing him speak with easy contempt of the composer of *Acis and Galatea*. But it is true that each one of us has some darkened windows: Oscar Wilde confessed to me once, with shame be it said, that he thought absinthe a detestable drink. But no inference can be drawn from this undoubted fact. It always stirs in me a certain feeling of impatience when I see the solemn correspondence, the more solemn leading articles under the dread heading, "What is Wrong with the Church?" It is alleged, I am sure with complete truth, that a great many people do not go to church; and the conclusion is drawn that the Church must be very gravely at fault. Now this may be true also—I think it is—but it is a conclusion not to be deduced from the minor premiss, the sole premiss stated. Scholastic logic, the only logic that is worth twopence, the "new logic" being, as an Oxford graduate once very sensibly observed to me, merely "nonsense about things", is now unfashionable, so, I suppose I shall be thought somewhat boorish for exhibiting the newspaper syllogism at full length, supplying the suppressed major. But here it is:

That which is unpopular is worthless.

The Church is unpopular.

Therefore, the Church is worthless.

In other words, as one of the ladies in the cabrioily—to which I have already alluded—observed: "Most Votes carries the day." Very well; but how does the attendance on the pictures in the National Gallery compare with the attendance at "the pictures"? And shall we try the experiment of "knocking" the music-halls, the revue houses, and the musical comedy houses by running Bach's Organ and Clavier Fugues at popular prices? Perhaps the purse of Rockefeller might survive the experiment; certainly no other purse would hold anything after a year of it. Mr. Walkley of *The Times* proposes to solve the difficulty of criticism by making the critic address himself to ὅ χαριείς, the well-graced and accomplished man. But who is he? Each one of us is a good judge—in his own judgment. And technical instruction is nothing. No one in his senses would seek anything vital as to Greek or Latin poetry from a classical don at Oxford or Cambridge. Keats, poor, shabby John, who had only been to a commercial academy, knew more about Greek poetry than a wilderness of classical tutors.

But, I was going to say, all these considerations apply to the known and recognised arts, to literature, music, painting, architecture. In all these I am willing to admit I may be hopelessly wrong—I have said that I had much rather hear Robey than *Hamlet*—but I will listen to no objections or criticisms as to the Ars Magna of London, of which I claim to be the inventor, the professor, and the whole school. Here I am artist and judge at once, and possess the whole matter of the art within myself. For, let it be quite clearly understood, the Great Art of London has nothing to do with any map or guide-book or antiquarian knowledge, admirable as these are; and indeed Peter Cunningham's *London* is to me one of the choicest of books. But the Great Art is a matter of quite another sphere; and as to maps, for example, if known they must be forgotten. How would the Odyssey have read, do you imagine, if Ulysses had been furnished with Admiralty Charts, giving the soundings in fathoms, even to the exact depth of water in the harbourage of Calypso's isle? And all historical associations; they too must be laid aside. Mr. Pickwick at Bury St. Edmunds has nothing to do with the history of the famous abbey. Of all this the follower of the London Art must purge himself when he sets out on his adventures. For the essence of this art is that it must be an adventure into the unknown, and perhaps it may be found that this, at last, is the matter of all the arts.

And it was this art of London that I followed, while I lived in Great Russell Street between '93 and '95, and still more earnestly afterwards when I was living at Verulam Buildings, Gray's Inn. Sometimes I took a friend with me on my journeys, but not often. The secret of it all was hidden from them, and they were apt to become violent. On one grey day that I remember I had personally conducted a man on a most interesting exploration of the obscurer byways of Islington. He grew silent as the streets grew greyer and the squares dimmer and the remoteness of the whole region from any conceivable London that he knew filtered through his soul. His London was Piccadilly, the Haymarket, St. James's, and the many polite neighbourhoods where there are flats and calls are paid and tea is taken and literary and theatrical and artistic circles meet and gather. But this London that was a grey wilderness, these streets that went to the beyond and beyond, these squares which nobody that my friend could ever have known could ever inhabit: it was all too much for him. His face darkened with terror and hate, and with a poisonous glance at me he struck his golden-headed cane violently on the pavement, and stopping dead, exclaimed: "I wish to God I could see a hansom!"

So, of course, I never took him to Barnsbury. As for Brentford, that is the Great Magisterium, the Hidden Secret. There is a Secret Society of those initiated in Brentford, and so darkly is the mystery kept that there have been cases in which members have known each other intimately for twenty years before the passwords have been exchanged.

V

I have been talking of rooms in Gray's Inn, of trips to Touraine; and I suppose it will have become evident that the days of the Clarendon Road cell, of dry bread and green tea meals were over. This was, in fact, the case. Between '87 and '92 I "came into money", that is, into what I called money. My mother died in 1885, my father in 1887; distant and ancient relatives in Scotland who had lived to fabulous ages died at last, and thus moneys that should have come to my mother came to me. And I was no longer the lonely man of the earlier chapters.

Reckoning up the various sums which I inherited, I calculate that if they had been invested I should have had enough whereon to live narrowly and meanly for the next thirty years. Somewhere about 1921 a long lease would have fallen in, and two-thirds of my income would have disappeared. I should then have been left with sixty pounds a year at the outside, and even with the "aconomy" recommended by Captain Costigan, there is very little to be done in these days with £60 per annum. But I did not invest my fortune in sound securities. Perhaps I might have done so if it had fallen in a lump on my lap; but this was not the way of it. It came in bits and parcels: £700 one year, £500 eighteen months afterwards. So I adopted the simple, manly course of putting my money as I got it into a box, as it were, and dipping my hand into the box when I needed a few gold pieces. I wish it were possible to do this literally: it must be magnificent to live on a chestful of gold; but I compromised by getting a cheque-book.

And I have always been glad that I made this business-like arrangement. By it I was enabled to live for eleven or twelve years under pleasant and humane conditions. Not in luxury, be it understood, for luxury has always been utterly detestable to me. Detestable to me, I say with emphasis; I do not say that luxury is detestable in itself. If men like to have it so, by all means let them dwell in marble halls, with vassals and serfs and wine-stewards at their side. Let them be as Louisquinzious as ever they please in their homes and at their hotels; for all I care, they may take their ease in snuggeries, all gold and mirrors and marbles, fifty feet high, a hundred feet high, if they like it so. But to me, a poor clerk, all this has ever been nauseous. When I plied my sorry trade of journalist, I disliked most things involved in that vile business, but I hated my occasional missions to the Hôtel Splendide and the Hôtel Glorieux. I would be sent to these places to find out, say, the exact method employed by the new chef, M. Mirobolant, in cooking red herrings for the famous Joy Teas in the Venetian Hall—everybody has heard of the Joy Teas at the Splendide, and of the Joy Band of twenty kettle-drums, fifty tea-trays, ten trombones, and thirty bassoons. Well, I would be sent to the Splendide on this errand; or, perhaps, to the Glorieux to find out whether it were true that the principals of the Russian Ballet sucked their morning tea through raspberry jam and declared that this was necessary to their art. I would visit one or other of these establishments and sit down on Louis Quinze or Louis Seize chairs and wait there in my dingy old cloak, while "Reception" and "Enquiries" smiled to see such an incongruous figure before them, while the guests of the hotel smiled also as they went in and out, till at last the manager arrived, fretful enough, usually, at being dragged from his business or his leisure to answer idiotic questions. I used to wonder on these Splendide or Glorieux days what I had done to deserve such humiliations. The only thing that somewhat consoled me was the thought that, whatever pains the Doctor may have suffered, while he waited in Lord Chesterfield's outward rooms or was repulsed from that nobleman's door, my case was more humiliating still, since an English nobleman of race is a much greater personage than the shiniest of hotel managers. And perhaps, also, I fancied that I was beginning to follow a little in the faithful steps of Venerable Raymondus Anglus, who was slowly sliced into little pieces in Cathay.

Rather, I am afraid, in the steps of a relative of my own, some distant Cousin Machen, whom business, I suppose, took to Cathay in the 'fifties and 'sixties of the last century. It so fell out that while this gentleman was in China we declared one of our infamous Opium Wars against the Dragon Throne and the Vermilion Pencil. Promptly the local mandarin seized Cousin Machen and put him in a cage. They then travelled him round the Chinese "Smalls". When the cortège got to a village or town, my cousin's custodians touched him up smartly with their spears. Cousin Machen would then dance with anguish, and, I am sure, most ungracefully, and the happy villagers, howling with mirth, and voting Cousin Machen good goods, would pelt the poor man with undesirable matters. He got away from them, but I have heard my relations say that in extreme old age the mere word "China" was enough to bring a sweat of horror pouring down his face. And I am in a position to sympathise fully with Cousin Machen——

Well, I was saying, I think, that I never cared for luxury, and so did not waste my bit of money on it. But if luxury tempts me not at all, I care a great deal for homely comfort, and I lived in considerable comfort in the days of which I am speaking. I think that my annual budget was between four and five hundred a year, and let me tell an amazed generation that for five hundred a year or rather less two people could live very sufficiently in the 'eighties and 'nineties. Your saddle of mutton and your sirloin of beef were of the best, lamb at Easter—is there anything better than spring lamb with its skin roasted to a golden-brown?—was easily attainable; fowls and ducks, grouse and partridges and pheasants, with now and then that most delicious bird the woodcock, were no rarities. And asparagus might well appear quite early in the spring, and green peas in advance of the main crop. And sometimes one felt that it would be amusing to go out to dinner for a change: well, the bill of the Soho restaurant never gave an indigestion afterwards. Sometimes the Soho dinners were quite good, they were always amusing; and in those days there was such a thing as decent Chianti. It came to the cheerful table in flasks of very thin glass, and between the cork and the wine was a stratum of olive oil. This the waiter flicked off on to the linoleum with a swift gesture. The last Chianti of this order that I tasted was in 1902. I saw great gallon flasks of it standing in the window of a small shop opposite the stage door of the Palace, and bought one of these flasks—it cost six shillings, if I remember—and bore it tenderly to my dressing-room at the St. James's Theatre. It was the last night of *Paolo and Francesca,* and we drank the Chianti merrily in trunk hose and armour when the play was done. And Herbert Dansey, who was really a noble Florentine, "degli Tassinari", vowed you could get no better Chianti in all Tuscany.

Or again, one didn't fancy roast beef, and yet one didn't want to go out dining. There was the middle course; Salame or Mortadella, half a round of ripe Brie and a bottle of a sufficient red or white wine. And a half-bottle of Benedictine only cost four-and-six. And the whole of the small banquet ran into very little: they were cheap days, and the Income Tax was inconsiderable then. But I was forgetting. I had no income, so I saved the expense of the tax. And under these conditions, living very pleasantly, with a month in France every year, I cultivated literature between 1890–1900. I refrained, utterly, I am glad to say, from the impious folly of wondering what would happen when the money should have come to an end. When that day came, why, that day could see to it.

Living very pleasantly; that is, apart from my chosen sport of making books. I have already discussed the strange paradox of writing, of writing, that is, when it is entirely divorced from all commercial considerations. I wrote purely to please myself; and what a queer pleasure it was! To write, or to try to write, means involving oneself in endless difficulties, contrarieties, torments, despairs, and yet I wrote on, and I suppose for the reason which I have given, the necessity laid upon most of us to create another and a fantastic life in order that the life of actuality may be endurable. Look at the golfer: observe how he toils and frets in that fantastic world that he has made for himself, a world wherein he who can say, "I did the fourth hole in two" is happy; while the wretch who had to hit the little white ball six or seven times before it finally popped into that fourth hole goes out miserably into the night. It is fantastic nonsense; but for all that the golfers are in the right.

Still, there may be a little more in the sport of literature; and if the golfers feel hurt by this remark, let them remember that a man always praises his own game. We understand so little of the real scheme of things that, for all we know, golf may be the end for which man was made, as, according to Coleridge, snuff was the final term of the human nose. But waiving this possibility—I think a remote one—I would contend that literature has more in it on the whole. Being an art as well as a sport, there is a question of making something, and very occasionally of making something that will divert or enchant others, besides the maker; whereas the sport which is nothing but a sport has no such by-products as *Don Quixote* or *Pickwick*. Of course the man who plays a game, such as golf or cricket, often gives pleasure—or amusement, at all events—to many spectators; but when the match is over and the last ball bowled nothing permanent remains. So far as others are concerned the player of games is much in the position of the player of plays. The actor thrills the house or rocks it with laughter; but the curtain falls and all is over. We know that the best judges of the eighteenth century found Garrick natural, simple, affecting; but we know no more. We have pictures of Garrick in his favourite situations; but I at least have no distinct image in my mind of what it was really like to be in the front row of the pit at Drury Lane and see and hear Garrick play.

And, this apart, I cannot help thinking that the pleasures of the literary game are more intense and more exquisite than the pleasures of the other games. I know this is a very difficult question; there is no final answer to it. But I feel sure that the happiness of Charles Dickens on writing the last words of *David Copperfield* was greater than the happiness of the cricketer at Lord's who carries out his bat for a faultless innings of two hundred against the most difficult bowling and the best fielding in England. I do not know that this is so, but I conjecture that it is so, chiefly because the joys of the writer of a great romance are so varied and so complex in comparison with the joys of the man who has played a perfect innings. In a sense, perhaps, the first-rate cricketer has achieved the more perfect performance: he has met every difficulty splendidly, his judgment as to running has been impeccable, he has not given a single chance. The writer, on the other hand, is—I think we may say—never perfect: consider those last chapters of *Don Quixote;* consider Steerforth and that infernal . . . woman, Agnes; the Grandfather and Little Nell. Yet the man of the book has traversed such an infinitely wider region than the man of the bat and ball: he has perhaps rectified the work of the Creator and made himself anew and made himself much better; and so he has worked with all the world, fashioning a new life, discovering wonders where before there were no wonders, shewing secrets that had been hidden from the foundation of things, peering now and again, as Poe and Hawthorne peered, into the places of thick darkness, and, above all, voyaging into the unknown, perpetually climbing the steep white track that vanishes over the hill.

VI

We are, I think, in the period 1890–1900; or, perhaps, to be more accurate, let us say 1889–1899. Between these dates I made a translation of *Le Moyen de Parvenir*, an early seventeenth-century book by an odd follower of Rabelais. I wrote "The Great God Pan," "The Inmost Light," *The Three Impostors, The Hill of Dreams,* a short collection of experiments called *Ornaments in Jade, Hieroglyphics,* "The White People," the first part of "A Fragment of Life," and "The Red Hand." As I have said, I had inherited a little capital and spent it, and at ample leisure wrote these books and tales, instead of doing honest work. In the words of some character in *The Three Impostors,* I regarded my various legacies as an endowment of research.

Now, as to the first title on this list, I was inspired to translate *Le Moyen de Parvenir* by that earlier Rabelaisian enthusiasm, which had lasted on. I found the book (in the original edition, I think), a little dumpy volume, while I was in the employment of a firm of second-hand booksellers who lived not far from Leicester Square. I have been called a modest man in an after-dinner speech, and I hope I am one; but I am sure I was modest in 1888. For, finding that I could not get a "rise" on the £60 a year which York Street afforded me, I tried Leicester Square and asked as much as £80; thirty shillings a week. I think the firm were amused; but they gave it me, and I set about cataloguing books for them.

I did this under odd conditions. When I made my application, the Brothers—let us say—took me down to the place in the basement where my work would have to be done. Once, I suppose, it had been the underground back-kitchen of the house. The kitchen was occupied by two other employees of the firm. One of them kept the accounts; the other treated "foxed" plates and pages in baths and made them fresh again, and "grangerised" and packed up books that had been bought. And the kitchen had the illumination from the solid glass over which people walked as they passed the shop, and some sort of air from the outer world. But my workshop had neither one nor the other. Save for gas, it was in total darkness. Its air was dead. And the House asked me very fairly whether I thought I could stand it. I said I could, and so I went to work.

I was never any good at cataloguing, real, technical cataloguing. I was explaining the other day to a friend of mine, a most accomplished and learned cataloguer, how I despised his work. "This business," I said, "of putting little slanty lines between the words of a title-page. A pitiable job," I proceeded, "it must be so since I could never make anything of it." But, the truth is, I never had any heart for the work. I don't care twopence whether a book is in the first edition or in the tenth; nay, if the tenth is the best edition, I would rather have it. To me it appears mere childishness to consider whether Lowndes—I think that is one of the authorities—has seen three copies of some particular book or three hundred; the only question being: is the book worth reading or not? Then, when it comes to measuring an Elzevir, say, with a graduated rule, and pronouncing a little book three inches and a half high to be a "tall copy", my common sense revolts. In other words, I am sure that Bibliography is a capital game, but it is not my game. I disliked my work of cataloguing; but I loathed another branch of my work, that was indexing. Everybody knows about "grangerising". You take a book, say, Smith's *Life of Nollekens*. In it many eighteenth-century personages are mentioned, and many London streets and public places. The indexer has to read through the book, noting every person, every place, and compile an index. And on this index the grangeriser, the bookseller, goes to work hunting his stock of plates, hunting certain well-known sources for pictures with which he can stuff the original work. He will destroy a dozen or a hundred or a thousand other books of less value to produce a kind of monster: "*The Life of Nollekens,* by Joseph Smith, 1 vol., 8vo., 17—. Enlarged to 3 vols. quarto, and furnished with 250 extra illustrations, comprising portraits, views, plans, maps, and original and facsimile letters from Blank, Dash, Chose, and other famous persons of the period. Purple Levant Morocco Jansenist; in watered purple silk case, gilt. Price: A great deal."

There. I am afraid I have forgotten the trick of the business, and my friend the expert cataloguer will say that it is a good thing indeed that I have changed my trade; but it is something like that. Well, indexing is a horrible job; a weariness, a nuisance; a matter of covering the table with innumerable little slips of paper that flow over on to the floor; and one must be careful and accurate, and I have always hated being careful and accurate—unless I happen to be interested in what I am doing. Besides, I hold that "grangerising" is both barbarous and silly. So I didn't like my work, but I liked the Brothers. They were always most courteous. Near our establishment was a shop where a very old gentleman sold precious things. His shop windows were made of small squares of glass. Above them was an inscription to the effect that the firm were "Goldsmiths and Silversmiths to Their Majesties the King and Queen and to Her Royal Highness the Duchess of Kent". And the old gentleman who kept this shop wore what we call evening-dress all day long, and advanced to meet his customers with an inclined head, his hands clasped together. The Brothers were a good deal younger, but they were of the same school. They had a way of putting things. For example, Brother Charles was trying to teach me how to catalogue their very beautiful collection of French eighteenth-century illustrated books, the sort of books that have illustrations by Fragonard.

"And if, Mr. Machen," said Brother Charles, "if it strikes you that any of these plates are brilliant impressions—well, we have no objection to your saying so."

It may be mentioned that the firm dealt occasionally in works which would not be suitable for the "center table" of a New England parlour. For themselves, for their own private taste, they read George Eliot and thought her by far the greatest novelist that the English Nation had ever produced. I am sure that they would have held *Peregrine Pickle*—save in the rare first impression—to be a low book, and Dickens, I conjecture, would have struck them as funny and vulgar. But, still, selling books was their business, and it was not their affair as booksellers to censor the morals of the works they sold. They dealt in rare books.

Well, one morning as I walked down from Great Russell Street to the shop, I was reading of the trial and conviction of a minor bookseller of Charing Cross Road. This Mr. Jackson, or whatever his name was, had been found guilty of selling obscene books, and had been sent to gaol, for nine months, if I remember. I mentioned the matter to Brother Ned as I entered.

"You've seen about Jackson?" I said.

"Yes, Mr. Machen," said Brother Ned, with a certain moral austerity of demeanour that was new to me. "We *have* seen about Mr. Jackson, and we wish to state at once that we have no sympathy with Mr. Jackson; none whatever. There is a *right* way, Mr. Machen, of doing these things and a *wrong* way."

Mr. Jackson, I may say, did not deal in rare books. His prices were low, he appealed to the general public. I hasten to add that on the whole I sympathise with the Brothers on this matter. And I add also: that after more recent experiences of mine I am very loath to find fault with any persons who treat those in their employment as human beings, with the decent civilities, courtesies, and considerations that are befitting between man and man. In those days I had no knowledge of the anthropoids; still, I appreciated the pleasant treatment I received.

Yet, with all their pleasant manners, I am afraid that the Brothers did not find in me the ideal cataloguer. Anyhow, one day Brother Ned came down to my darksome place with a queer little quarto in his hand, a quarto in a dull paper wrapper. He had it open, marked with a slip of paper, at a certain page, and so far as I remember, without any particular preface or explanation, he asked me to begin making a translation of the work from that point. I said: "Certainly, Mr. Edward," and began to translate without more ado.

And here I may say that my career as a French translator has always struck me as highly humorous. At the good old grammar school where I was educated and educated very well, I think that the headmaster thoroughly agreed with the boys that Foreign Languages were a silly game that, for various reasons, one had to play. Education was Latin and Greek, but a notion had arisen in these late days that one ought to learn French, and so there was a French master. But he wore neither cap nor gown, and so he was not a real master, and so, again, his language was not a real language. Therefore: poor M. Ménard! And I am afraid that he was a very bad master. If his authority had been supported, and if we had tried our best, I do not think we should have learned much; as it was, the French lessons, three times a week, were a farce. I knew no French when I left Hereford Cathedral School in 1880, that is, I could not have conjugated the verb *Aimer* to save my life. I had read no French to speak of. Then, in my desolation in Clarendon Road, I had somehow come across *Gil Blas* and had managed, being interested, to get through it. Then, the York Street publisher had sent me down the sixteenth-century *Heptameron* and had ordered me to translate it, and I did so, somehow. And now, Brother Ned ordered me to translate from the dumpy quarto which he handed me; and forthwith I set about translating, not troubling what it was, what it was about, not caring two straws that I had not the thread of the narrative, nor worrying over the fact that I knew nothing whatever about the enigmatic "M.M." or the mysterious "C.C." into whose singular adventures I now plunged gaily. Thus I began the translation of the famous *Memoirs of Casanova,* and I think the money balance between the Brothers and myself was readjusted. For if I had been dear as a cataloguer, at thirty shillings a week, I was decidedly cheap as a translator. Casanova is a work that runs into twelve sizeable volumes, and the task of turning it into English took me a year, and I think the cost to the firm will be held to have been strictly moderate.

And what about these strange Memoirs of the charlatan adventurer? Well, not long ago I was called upon to write an introduction to a reissue of the version I had made in the 'eighties. I found this an extremely difficult task. The obvious solution of the difficulty, the writing a sort of *précis* of the book and calling it an Introduction, did not appeal to me. It was some time before the "moral" of the Memoirs disengaged itself. The Introduction when written proved to be an essay on the futility of trying to tell the whole truth about the relations between men and women. This is what Casanova, who was highly qualified, in a certain sense, for the undertaking, tried to do; and the more "frank", the more "outspoken" his page the more the secret escapes from it; the more openly he reveals, the more deeply he conceals the mysteries. For the fact is that all the real secrets are ineffable; the secrets of love, and the secrets of the wood; the secrets of the flower and the secrets of the flame; and the secrets of the Faith. As I point out in my Introduction, you can enumerate the scientific facts—such of them as are known—relating to any subject. You can define a horse, for example, as Bitzer defined it in *Hard Times.*

"Quadruped. Graminivorous. Forty teeth, namely twenty-four grinders, four eye-teeth, and twelve incisive. Sheds coat in the spring; in marshy countries sheds hoofs, too. Hoofs hard, but requiring to be shod with iron. Age known by marks in mouth."

And so you may discourse of the pistils and stamens of the lilies of the field, and divide the fowls of the air into genera and species and subspecies and count the teeth of Keats: and when all is done you know—nothing. Nothing that is of the essence of your matter, nothing of its "quiddity", a word that we have ceased to use, I suppose, because we have no use for it, having forgotten that there is such a thing as that essence which is present in all things, which indeed makes them to be what they are, which is nevertheless unsearchable and ineffable. And all this is true, not only of the matters which the plain man, the man in the street, is inclined to sniff at, but of all things, of man himself and of the universe of noumena and phenomena which is presented to him. If you talk to the plain, practical man about Mystic Theology, Mystic Love, Poetry, Romance, he will, very likely, brush you aside with his "In my opinion that's all imagination"—and serve you right for talking to him on such subjects at all. The dear fellow has no notion of the fact that he has never seen a point, a line, a square, or a triangle, and that he never will see any one of these things—in this life at all events. He has seen black marks on paper which he has been told are lines and squares and triangles. Being at heart thoroughly credulous, he believes what he is told, but if he will dig up his old "Euclid" and read the definitions, he will find that no mortal eyes can ever see a square or a circle, since a line is length without breadth and a plane surface is length and breadth without thickness. There is nothing in the nature of things to prevent a man from seeing a dragon or a griffin, a gorgon or a unicorn. Nobody as a matter of fact has seen a woman whose hair consisted of snakes, nor a horse from whose forehead a horn projected; though very early man most probably did see dragons—known to science as pterodactyls—and monsters more improbable than griffins. At any rate, none of these zoological fancies violates the fundamental laws of the intellect; the monsters of heraldry and mythology do not exist, but there is no reason in the nature of things nor in the laws of the mind why they should not exist. But no man hath seen a line at any time, since the manifestation of length without breadth is a contradiction in terms. And the plain man is probably inclined to believe in the existence of vulgar fractions; he may tell you that he makes use of them daily in his calculations. But let him study the story of the race between Achilles and the Tortoise, and note to what monstrous results his belief in elementary arithmetic inevitably conducts him; results which are more intolerable than a madman's dreams.

And then, again, there are wider, more universal conceptions than anything contained in the geometry and arithmetic books. In a little book of mine with the bad title of *War and the Christian Faith*—the publisher chose the title—I speak thus of Space and Time:

> "Take two insistent and unavoidable examples (of the things which are unsearchable and indefinable), space and time. No man who strolls from his arm-chair to the mantelpiece and watches the hands of the clock move round can deny the existence of either, since he has walked from point to point in one and seen the other measured before his eyes. But as to understanding space and time, what highest philosophy can attain to such a pitch? The limitless cannot so much as be imagined in the mind, nor imagined in a nightmare: but that space which you have traversed of some eight or ten feet is limitless, and must be so.
>
> "It is a sea without a shore. And time, that which your two-guinea clock ticks off for you, as you watch the dial: it had no beginning that you can picture; it can have no end save with God. You cannot understand; you must believe; and so on your very hearth-rug the infinities and eternities are before you and confront you, as truly as the clock face confronts you."

And the conclusion of the whole matter is that we live and move in a world of profound and ineffable mystery; that all things from the most abstract to the most concrete are involved in this mystery, and, *therefore,* that Casanova as an exponent of love is a futile fellow. He was a Voltairean; he approached the question as he would say without prejudices, as the foolish among us would say, without any nonsense, or, as the still more foolish among us would say, in a scientific spirit. And the result is exactly what might be expected: nothing. Love is defined and expounded in the spirit of Bitzer defining a horse; and one perceives that science misapplied is just gibberish, nothing more or less. Otherwise, taking Casanova's Memoirs from a lower standpoint, they are in many places vastly entertaining. He knew all Europe from Petersburg and Constantinople to London and Madrid; he was familiar with the palace and the gutter; he was the friend of kings and philosophers and popes—and also of the scum of the eighteenth-century earth. One cannot understand the period as a whole without knowing Casanova.

So I translated and translated day after day; but in a few months' time the black hole in which I worked began very violently to disagree with me. I got ill, and it was clear that some change must be made. The Brothers, as always, were courteous and considerate: why not do the work at home? I assented very willingly, worked at the task for five hours every day, and every Saturday took my parcel of copy to the shop and got my thirty shillings, the week's wages.

And here I must make a boast, which is not wholly a boast: the second part of this sentence I shall explain no farther. I finished the translation of the Memoirs, but the book was not immediately issued. On the completion of my job the Brothers needed me no more. I imagine that they wanted a real, expert, technical cataloguer, not a literary man of sorts; and my having worked for them for some months at my own home and not in the shop made it easy for them to get rid of me quietly; rather, to let me fade away, without the least suspicion of firmness, much less of harshness. And they were always very glad to see me when I chose to look them up, either on business or merely as a friendly caller. I remember, for example, that when I had finished the translation of *Le Moyen de Parvenir* and was "subscribing" the book with "the trade", I called at the shop and was received with a genial and kindly courtesy that I have not forgotten, though it is a long time since 1890; but then I do not forget. And lest it should be suspected by some persons that under a veil of benignity I am "getting at" the Brothers all the time, I hasten to say that this is not so; to say this in the strongest manner possible. True, thirty shillings a week was not good pay for decent French-English translating, even in 1889; but it was the wages that I had asked myself, having been thoroughly convinced by my experiences of the six preceding years that I was such a dismal and incapable ass that if I just managed to escape the Governorship of the Island of Farre Joyaunce—otherwise the ditch or the workhouse—it was as much as I could expect. So I asked my thirty shillings a week and hoped in my heart that it was not too much; and I am not blaming the Brothers in the least because they did not press more upon me. And, however that may be, they were always courteous and kindly in all communications that passed between us; and for that they shall be in my grateful memory so long as I live. I have said already, I think, how once during the last year of my employment on the *Evening News,* finding myself in old haunts of long ago, Wellington Street, Bow Street, York Street, anguish possessed me as I remembered how I had once starved and had known something like happiness while I toiled over the ancient occult books in the Catherine Street garret; anguish possessed me as I recollected the happy time in misery. And, as I said to a friend soon afterwards: "In those days I was getting considerably less money in a whole year than I am now getting in a month; and yet . . ."

Again, I say, if our clergy would but mind their business. If instead of enquiring into the exact cut of bodices, instead of passing anxious hours as to the pernicious corruptions of the Fox-Trot and the Bunny Hug, instead of working with all their hearts and souls to make sure that no one can possibly get a glass of bitter beer after ten o'clock, instead of unmasking the inferno of the race-course, the utter levity of much of our railway literature; if, instead of all this accursed drivel, cant, and imbecility, they would but say Mass and preach the Gospel, and otherwise quite abide in peace! Let them go to the Book, and there they will find that the most horrible sin denounced in it is neither gambling, drinking, nor wantoning, but the sin of shaming a man, of bitterly insulting him, of making him mean in his own eyes, of making him despise his own self as something unutterably fouled and scorned and bewrayed. What is the text? Something like: but he that sayeth to his brother, "Thou fool," shall be in danger of hell fire.

I am drawing a contrast between 1889 and 1921, and hence I say that the Brothers always treated me with the common decency due from one human being to another, though they were rich and I was poor, though they were men of business and I an idiot in all matters of business, though they were masters and I was man.

And now as to the famous boast. As I said, I ceased to be in the employment of these good men. I went into the country, up on the Chiltern Hills. We neither saw nor heard anything of each other. But all the while those legacies of which I have spoken came dropping slow, and in 1893, when I had made up my mind to return to London, I think I must have had in bank something between three and four thousand pounds. I was assailed by an unworthy pang of prudence, by one of the foolish notions that the world's people take for wisdom. It struck me that this living on capital, taking the pieces of eight by fistfuls out of the chest, would never do; that the money ought to be invested, preferably in some business in which I could contribute work as well as money. I looked about me, I advertised, I saw some people in the City and found nothing promising from my point of view, though I found here and there such curiosities as London, I believe, only affords. For example, in a very dim sort of cock-loft in an old house in the heart of the City, I hit upon a firm of general agents who had answered my advertisement. There were two of them: one, a young, rosy, out-in-the-open sort of man, the other elderly, frock-coated, with a kind of dissenting beard on his chin. He talked of the version of Horace's odes that he was shortly bringing out at his own expense, and discussed with me the true pronunciation of the Latin language with much intelligence. The junior partner's talk was of trawling, and indeed he said that the firm was a sort of trawling concern—in City waters.

But nothing came of it, and at last I bethought me of the Brothers. Brother Charles was as genial as ever. He saw my point. He said: "We are going to issue Casanova at last; why not put a thousand pounds into that for a start?" I agreed, and the matter was settled. And then, very nervously, with a good deal of hesitation, with a certain difficulty in the choice of words, Brother Charles said:

"Of course, Mr. Machen, we quite recognise the . . . er . . . circumstances in which you made your most admirable translation of the book. It was . . . er . . . in a manner . . . er . . . task-work; yes, *task-work*. Well . . . the case is now, to certain degree . . . altered; you have an interest in the prosperity of the venture, and, in short, we rather wondered whether you would like to . . . to . . . *revise* your manuscript."

"Mr. Charles," I replied, "I did the job as well as I could; and I don't think I can make it any better."

VII

Béroalde de Verville proved to be what the elder members of the theatrical profession used to call "a pill". Only the other day I was reading a French account of this author. The critic said in the course of his remarks that many people who had gone to the *Moyen de Parvenir* in search of unpleasantness had turned back from the quest, deterred by the difficulty of the language. And I don't know that it is more difficult for a modern Frenchman than for an Englishman. It is written in a sort of Babylonish dialect which is not exactly French though it looks like it; as Meredith looks like English to the casual glance. And then, it is not only difficult, but obscure; not only are the sentences queerly constructed, but the subject-matter is of a highly dubious and cloudy character: when you have found out what Béroalde is saying, you begin to wonder what he is saying it about. And, then, there are bits of old dialect peppered about this excessively odd volume. I remember coming upon two words: "iquent hesne". I sat down in front of them, and looked at them from every angle. I don't know how I found out at last that "iquent hesne" was a sort of seventeenth-century French "Zummerzet" for "cette chêne"—"thicky oak". Again the *Moyen* is thick with puns, of the kind that used to be called in the golden days of Burlesque "outrageous": and the time I wasted in trying to turn these silly French tricks into sillier English contortions! On the whole, I would say that *Le Moyen de Parvenir* in literature is as a cathedral constructed entirely of gargoyles would be in architecture. Rabelais is full of gargoyles, "apes and owls and antics", as he calls them, on the outside of the jar. But within, as he rightly claims, there are precious medicines, aromatic balms of singular power and virtue. And so far as I can judge, Béroalde is all oddity and nothing else. He cost me a year's hard labour; the version was issued and is now valued by collectors; and that is all that need be said.

And now—in 1890—I began to try a little journalism of the more or less literary kind. I began, I think, by writing "Turnovers" for the *Globe,* and miscellaneous articles for the *St. James's Gazette,* and at length stories for the latter paper, which was then edited by Mr.—now Sir—Sydney Lowe. The *Globe* is extinct, the *St. James's Gazette* is merged and submerged in the *Evening Standard;* there are no papers of such metal now in existence. The difference between them and the evening papers of the day is a very simple one: the former were meant to please the educated, the latter are designed to entertain the uneducated, and the uneducated may be equated, very largely indeed, with women. It is an odd paradox: there is no doubt, I suppose, that the instruction—or, if you like, education—of women has made immense strides in the last thirty years; and yet it is true that when a newspaper editor says to himself: "We have an immense number of women readers and we must see that they get what they like," the result is drivel. This sort of thing:

> Madame has just discovered a new craze. Jewelled clay pipes and shag tobacco delicately sprinkled with gold-dust are now quite *démodés* when once we cross the borders of Balham; but my lady prides herself on her collection of hookahs, the water-pipes of the gorgeous East.
>
> It is quite the thing, I hear, amongst really smart women to give "Hookah Teas". Everybody wears Oriental costume, and sits on cushions piled on the floor, and delicately draws in the aroma of the rarest Turkish Tobacco, scented by its passage through rosewater or lavender-water. At Lady Clarinda Belsize's Hookah Tea last Wednesday, two native musicians played the tom-tom and the *guzla* behind a curtain, or *purdah,* as I am told it is called. Of course *yashmaks* were worn by all the guests.

There; it is not worth parodying. And there is another sort of terrible tosh which deals with the doings of "The Summer Girl" and "The Winter Girl" and "The Marathon Girl": all of it a very feeble imitation of the cheapest American journalism. In the 'nineties this kind of thing existed, but it was confined to the columns of one or two ladies' papers. In those days, I would not say that the editors of evening papers brought out their journals exclusively for the benefit of the members of the best clubs of St. James's and Pall Mall; but I certainly should say that they had the clubs in their mind's eye; that they presumed a certain standard of education and culture in their readers. All that ended when the evening *Westminster Gazette* came to an end.

But indeed there would be little harm done if a column or two columns or three columns were reserved for the "Hookah Tea" stuff and the "Caravan Girl" stuff and all similar stuff. You could skip these columns if you didn't like them, just as I skip the racing columns, in which I am not interested. But "the women" rule the whole paper. Not only must the editor put in matter which he knows they will like, he must keep out matter which he knows they won't like. And the result is . . . the result as we know it. As the "literary editor" of a big London paper acutely observed to me not long ago, the case of the newspaper article is exactly as the case of chops and steaks, beefsteak puddings and saddles of mutton that were of old. "The women" have spoilt all. What do they know or care about man's food? To them there is nothing to choose between a chop fried white and hard and greasy in the frying-pan and a chop which has been purged of all excess by the ardent heat beneath the gridiron, which beneath a coat half black, half golden-brown, preserves its delicious juices, which sizzles on the plate as William or Charles serves it, which, opened by the eager knife, shews within a hue like that of a blush-rose in June. These are not matters to enchant the wayward heart of a young girl, and when once she sets foot inside the tavern coffee-room, farewell to all such solid merits. There was once a noble tavern called Herbert's, famous for two generations. Men who had spent half a lifetime in Africa or India or in the islands of the South Seas were sustained by the thought of the beefsteak pudding at Herbert's. The times changed and the old tavern with them. Going there in these later days, I used to wonder why all the meats seemed to taste alike, why there was no distinctive and peculiar relish about any of the dishes. I found out the reason why one day. I had business, oddly enough, in Herbert's kitchen. One of the cooks shewed me the joints roasting on the jack; and I perceived that three different meats were cooking at the one fire, while beneath, in a common pan, their juices mingled, ready for the basting ladle. It is not much wonder, I think, that veal and lamb and beef taste all much alike in this unhappy place, once so high, now fallen so low. One night I was dining there, and a member of the party asked the waiter to bring him some Stilton. "I beg your pardon, sir," said the man, "we only have *English* cheeses." It sounds impossible; but I heard this with my ears. In the old days Herbert's was exclusively masculine in its custom; I do not know what would have happened to that waiter then. I hardly think that his death would have been an easy one.

But to "the women" all this is of no account. They know nothing about man's food, as I say, and they care less. I do not blame them; I do not blame myself for being ignorant of the difference between Hopsac and Gaberdine: but how would *they* like it if I poked my nose into their Oxford Street shops and insisted on these shops being carried on to suit my taste?

So through this monstrous incursion of women, with the war and the nursery hours of to-day, the old tavern life has gone; utterly and for ever, I am afraid. A good thing has gone. The old mahogany boxes with bright brass work and green curtains, the light twinkling in the dark polished surfaces that were all about the room, the flaming fire with the plates warming by it, the plain food, the best of its kind, cooked in the best possible manner, the mighty tankards of mighty ale, the port that *was* port afterwards, in itself a great gift and a curious grace, and later—say about eleven o'clock—Charles appearing with a large china bowl and a bottle under his arm, following up these things with lump sugar, lemons, and the hot water: it is all over. And it is not only the good material things that have been taken away: the good meats and the good drinks, the glowing mahogany and the cheerful blaze and crackle of the fire: with them has gone, I suspect, a certain genial habit of the mind and soul which was congruous with all the circumstances of the old-fashioned tavern, which was congruous also with good men and good books and choice poetry, with all the rich zest and relish and unction which made the Victorian age of letters a great age; and, in its measure, a worthy successor to three other illustrious tavern ages: the Shakespearian, the Caroline, and the Johnsonian. Think of Falstaff and his tavern bill and his warning against thin potations, think of Herrick and his address to Ben, his fond remembrance of the taverns "where we such clusters had as made us nobly wild not mad", think of Johnson squeezing the orange into the bowl with antick gestures, saying, "Who's for *poonsh?*" think of Tennyson and that blest pint of port at the vanished Cock Tavern, think of Dickens, that great lover of tavern feasts and immortaliser of them: think of all this, my poor young man, and beat your breast. There are no jolly taverns for you, and your favourite authors do not write like men—"my son Cartwright writes all like a man", said Ben Jonson—but like psycho-analytical chemists.

And as I was saying, as with the taverns, so with the papers. When I wrote a little for them, in 1890 or thereabouts, it was allowable to assume a certain amount of literacy, a certain knowledge in the reader. Now that is over. I know the case of a man who, I am certain, pretends ignorance that he may continue to be employed. As it happens, he is an expert in food and drink; but I have known him number Beaujolais with the wines of Bordeaux in a newspaper article, and speak of curry powder and pickles as ordinary ingredients in veal and ham pie. I believe he knows much better; but he has probably found out that a misstatement or two gives an easy careless air that is much admired. Nobody can call a writer of this kind a pedant. A highly accomplished journalist said to me a few years ago: "Always remember that we appeal, not to the cabman, but to the cabman's wife." And another instance, though I am afraid it is somewhat tinged with self-praise. I had written a brief article for the *Evening News* on a topic that had been given to me; I was to explain *why* it is that a "mean street" of to-day is, generally, hideous and appalling, while a row of sixteenth-century cottages is, generally, a delight to see. I did as I always do when I can, I took the particular instance and placed it under a general principle. I said the chief horror of the modern street was not to be sought in the poverty of the design, though that was, doubtless, bad enough, but in the fact that in the street of to-day each house is a replica of the other, so that the effect to the eye is, if the street be long enough, the prolongation of one house to infinity, in an endless series of repetitions. And I pointed out that even if you admired some particular picture or statue immensely, it would be rather awful to traverse a long gallery in which the picture or the statue were repeated again and again as far as the eye could see. And then, on the other hand, I shewed how the sixteenth-century cottages were each of them individuals, each with some slight difference from the cottage next door, each with its variety in door or window or pent-house. And hence, I urged, a continual slight surprise to the beholder, and taking the supposed row as a whole, that strangeness in the proportion which Bacon declared, most profoundly, to be necessary to the highest beauty. Well, I got this with difficulty into the prescribed 500 words—"nobody will read anything over 500 words"—and said to myself: "Now that Patmore is dead, nobody else could have written that article. But . . . there will be a row." There was. Lord Northcliffe gave the little essay the honour of a special mention in one of his famous *communiqués*—as I believe they were called. He spoke of it with venom as "a wiseacre article". I am sure he was perfectly right from his point of view. The fault was mine. "When I am in Rome, I fast on Saturdays," said one of the Fathers.

Things have changed indeed. I was mentioning Coventry Patmore. In the Introduction to the *Religio Poetæ*, a collection of short essays of the profoundest wisdom, he acknowledges his obligations to Greenwood, once editor of the *St. James's Gazette*. Some of these essays had appeared in that journal: the fact is quite stupefying considered in the light of the journalism of to-day. Education increases; ignorance grows deeper.

Let me not be understood as claiming that my newspaper work of thirty-two years ago was characterised by the profoundest wisdom. Very far from it; my articles were harmless and agreeable enough, I think, in a small way; and writing them, I first began to get a hint of my true subject; the country of my childhood and my youth. And I thus began to move away from the exotic Rabelaisian influence, both as to manner and to matter: to perceive that not the splendid Loire but the humble Soar brook, winding and shining in deep valleys and obscured by dark alder thickets, was my native stream. I began to see that I was a citizen of Caerleon-on-Usk, and not of Tours or of Chinon, and that the old grey manor-houses and the white farms of Gwent had their beauty and significance, though they were not castles in Touraine. There was something of all this, of course, in *The Chronicle of Clemendy*, the Great Romance which was neither great nor a romance; but in this everything was viewed and everything expressed in an exotic medium: now I saw that a blossoming thorn bush in the valley of the Soar and the nightingale singing in it and the river level about Caerleon and the red fires of sunset over the mountain in the west were all in themselves and by themselves fit matter for the work; that they needed not to be disguised in a French literary habit of four hundred years ago.

It was in this summer of 1890 that I wrote the first chapter of

"The Great God Pan". I have told the whole story in the Introduction to the latest edition of that fantasy, which is published by Messrs. Simpkin, Marshall, and whether I should weary my readers I know not, but I do know that I should weary myself if I told it all over again. The tale was written in bits, in the intervals between severe literary cramps, as I have mentioned in this present volume, and it was published by Mr. John Lane, of the Bodley Head, at the end of 1894, when yellow bookery was at its yellowest. And it aroused a certain amount of attention. There was a storm—in a doll's teacup.

The other day a friend of mine said genially to me:

"I have just been reading that 'Great God Pan' of yours over again, and I really don't see that there's much in it to make a sensation of."

I am sure he was quite right. But a sensation there was, of a minor kind. It had some mysterious property in it, this little book, which caused good men to froth at the mouth, greatly to my delight. I have quoted a good many of the reviews in the Introduction to the Simpkin, Marshall edition: things like this:

"We are afraid he only succeeds in being ridiculous. The book is, on the whole, the most acutely and intentionally disagreeable we have yet seen in English. We could say more, but refrain from doing so for fear of giving such a work advertisement."—*Manchester Guardian.*

"This book is gruesome, ghastly, and dull . . . the majority of readers will turn from it in utter disgust."—*Lady's Pictorial.*

"These tricks have also their ludicrous side."—*Guardian.*

And so forth. It is very well, but I cannot help saying, as an old craftsman and an old reviewer, that it might have been better. I have no fault to find with the technique of the *Guardian;* but the *Lady's Pictorial* should have left out the "gruesome" and the "ghastly" and also, I am inclined to think, the "disgust". There are readers who like the gruesome and the ghastly; there are readers whose curiosity is stimulated by the term "disgust". I am afraid, for example, that if the account of legal proceedings, civil or criminal, is headed "Disgusting Details", there are minds so prurient as to be rather attracted than repelled, and I am sure that the gentle scribe of the *Lady's Pictorial* did not wish to paint my little book in attractive colours. And so with the *Manchester*

Guardian. "Ridiculous" is admirable; but "acutely and intentionally disagreeable" is something of a signal set to attract those prurient readers whose existence I have regretted; and the last sentence says too much. Mr. Harry Quilter, something of a figure in those days, did better. He pointed out in an article in the *Contemporary Review*—also something of a figure in those days—that the only explanation he could give of such favourable notices as the book had received was that the author must have a great many friends engaged in journalism. I wrote a temperate letter to Mr. Quilter in which I said I was very sorry, but I didn't know any journalists at all—which happened to be the truth. He wrote back to remind me, as he said, that there was "an Inmost Light to which you may yet be true"—"The Inmost Light" is the title of a tale which was included in the first edition of *The Great God Pan*.

One of the saddest books in the world is Mrs. Gaskell's wonderful *Life of Charlotte Brontë*. But there is one tragi-comical touch. Poor valiant, simple, stricken Charlotte was being entertained in town by Mr. and Mrs. Smith. There was a dinner-party, given, I suppose, in her honour, and she writes to an old friend:

"There were only seven gentlemen at dinner besides Mr. Smith, but of these five were critics—men more dreaded in the world of letters than you can conceive. I did not know how much their presence and conversation had excited me till they were gone, and the reaction commenced. When I had retired for the night, I wished to sleep—the effort to do so was vain. I could not close my eyes. Night passed; morning came, and I rose without having known a moment's slumber."

Who were these terrible five? We do not know, and it is possible enough that if we heard their names we should not have heard of their names, though, likely enough, George Henry Lewes was one of them. It is odd and pathetic too to think that a great woman such as Charlotte Brontë should have allowed the brilliant repartees and tremendous reputation of George Henry Lewes to break her rest. And just before this passage there is another, as strange and as pathetic. A severe review of *Shirley* appeared in *The Times*. Mr. and Mrs. Smith kindly "mislaid" the paper. But Charlotte insisted on pressing the thorn to her bosom. She would see *The Times*.

> "Mrs. Smith took her work, and tried not to observe the countenance, which the other tried to hide between the huge sheets; but she could not help becoming aware of tears stealing down the face and dropping on the lap."

And all over a review, an unfavourable review! It is very strange, or, at least, it seems so to me, since like Jim the nigger, I don't never cry ska'sely over reviews, and I have always contrived to get my usual sleep.

But I have left out one curious specimen of the *Great God Pan* reviews, a specimen which leads up to a curious passage. The *Westminster Gazette* said:

> "It is an incoherent nightmare of sex and the supposed horrible mysteries behind it, such as might conceivably possess a man who was given to a morbid brooding over these matters, but which would soon lead to insanity if unrestrained . . . innocuous from its absurdity."

I was talking over old literary doings and the affairs of the 'nineties with a friend one day in the spring of 1921. My friend was asking me about my early books and their reception. I gave him a lurid account of the castigations which I had received on account of *The Great God Pan*.

"Why," said I, "the *Westminster* practically told me that if I didn't take care I should end up in a lunatic asylum."

"Well," replied the man, meaning to be funny, "haven't you? I understood you were at Carmelite House?"

"No," I returned, also meaning to be funny, "I haven't. All the lunatic asylums that I've heard of have been managed by a *doctor*."

During the latter part of my stay in the country (1891–93) I wrote two books. I have forgotten the names of both of them. They were very bad, and I tore them up, with the exception of one episode—to put it mildly, not a very good story—which appears in *The Three Impostors* under the title of "The Novel of the Dark Valley". And it was in the early spring of 1894 that I set about the writing of the said *Three Impostors*, a book which testifies to the vast respect I entertained for the fantastic, *New Arabian Nights* manner of R. L. Stevenson, to those curious researches in the byways of London which I have described already, and also, I hope, to a certain originality of experiment in the tale of terror, as exemplified in the stories of the Professor who was taken by the fairies, and of the young student of law who swallowed the White Powder. And when I had finished, with a sort of recognition that I had squeezed this particular orange to death, I remember saying to my old friend A. E. Waite: "I shall never give anybody a White Powder again." And then I was immediately called on to do that very thing which I had vowed I would not do. I actually got an "order", and—this shews that I was a mere intruder, not a true craftsman—I have rarely been so miserable, miserable that is, as a man of letters, in my life.

It was like this. As I have remarked, *The Great God Pan* had made a storm in a Tiny Tot's teacup. And about the same time, a young gentleman named H. G. Wells had made a very real, and a most deserved sensation with a book called *The Time Machine;* a book indeed. And a new weekly paper was projected by Mr. Raven Hill and Mr. Girdlestone, a paper that was to be called *The Unicorn.* And both Mr. Wells and myself were asked to contribute; I was to do a series of horror stories. I won't deny that I swelled a little and was cheered and elated by the fact of my being asked to write by anybody; nay, I really tried my best to feel important and puffed up. And then I set about writing that series of tales of horror. I was not puffed up for long. As I say, I had realised that for me the Stevensonian manner was ended. And now I was to begin all over again; to recook that cabbage which was already boiled to death! I wrote four stories in a kind of agony, my pen shrieking "rubbish!" at me with every stroke. I remember literally sobbing in a kind of hysteria of despair with my head on my hands; and this shews that there are some men who cannot be helped. The only thing that got me through at all was an endeavour to transplant the manner of Apuleius into English soil; but the four tales were sorry things when all was said. I was glad when *The Unicorn* ceased to exist after two or three numbers, before a single one of those tales of mine had appeared in it. Mr. Wells had one story in *The Unicorn,* "The Cone", which he reprinted in the collection called *The Country of the Blind.* Such was the affair, and I think it explains the irritation which I have always experienced when I have been asked to write a continuation of *The Three Impostors,* or something in the manner of *The Three Impostors.* I knew that all this was done and ended; that, for me, the vein was worked out and exhausted: utterly. I shall always recur to the metaphor of the white road that you see from afar climbing over the hill into unconjectured regions. For me that is literature; the journey of discovery; the finding of a new world. When once I have toiled painfully up that long road, and have stood on the other side of the dark wood, and have looked upon the land beyond; then all the joy, all the delight and thrill and wonder are over for me. Columbus could not discover America twice. I never can say to myself: "Look here! Let's pretend that we've never been this way before, that we don't know in the least what's beyond that turn of the road, that anything may happen beyond that pine tree." It won't do.

And that is one reason why I beg my bread in my sixtieth year.

For, all that I have written on this matter is, doubtless, very fine; but we must confess that when it is a case of literature being exchanged for the money of the publisher—and the public—the affair becomes a commercial one. And, in business, you buy a brand. Let me try to imagine it! I am a wealthy man, and I have found and my guests have found that last hamper of Champagne admirable. I go to my wine merchant and order another hamper of the same vintage. Nay, he has not got it; he will be happy to supply me with a wine of entirely different character; or, to press the analogy a little extravagantly, he no longer deals in Champagne at all, he doesn't think much of Champagne, it is an elegant lemonade, as one of Murger's characters expresses it, but he will be delighted to send me six dozen of a rare Château wine of Bordeaux, an infinitely finer wine, as he assures me. But I want Champagne! I am not going to stand such treatment for one moment! The man must be mad! *De me fabula narratur;* all my life I have been pressing my Bordeaux on people who had begun to think that there might be something to be said for my small Champagne.

And I quite see the point. I have never read one of the horror stories of Mr. W. W. Jacobs, though I am told that they are admirable. For me, Mr. Jacobs must speak through an everlasting Night Watchman, through an eternal countryman draining the last dregs of his beer on the settle at the *Cauliflower:* with these immortals I am happy.

The Three Impostors was published by John Lane some time in 1895. But before sending the manuscript to Mr. Lane, I had tried Mr. Heinemann. The firm wrote me a most delightful letter, full of the most charming things, which I had some difficulty in swallowing, though an author's throat is capable of astounding feats where praise is concerned. I was to go and see them, and I did so, my heart beating high. I saw a member of the firm. He was better than the letter for a swelling soul. He read extracts from the reader's report, and these were more splendid still. He outlined delightful terms; he pressed on me the necessity of my having something on account of royalties in advance: a happy possibility that had not even dawned on me in 1894–95. He hoped that the House of Heinemann might ever have the privilege of publishing my beautiful books. "Better than the best of Stevenson"; thus he read from the optimistic reader's report. Thus elated, glorious, happy indeed, went down Mr. Arthur Machen, man of letters—now there could be no doubt of it!—from the amiable office, even into Bedford Street, seen for the first time to be a shining thoroughfare, a veritable golden pathway of Paradise, leading to the golden Strand, nay, to the golden world, where all desires were accomplished, and the faithful servant is rewarded: "Enter thou into the joy of thy Publisher."

After all, I said to myself, the old toils, the old labours, those unhappy nights, those sick days of despair were not altogether wasted. Indeed, I tried to do my best; indeed, I grudged no labour; indeed, I was patient and tore up the sorry page; I knew that I must persevere and still persevere. And I knew that the other books were well meant but futile after all; that I had not really touched the mark, though I pretended that I had, and did my best to persuade myself that it was so. But now; "I have really written something that is good, that is, even, very good; that one of the best publishers in London praises and praises highly." I never thought of the money that all this must mean, that never entered a moment into my mind; my only meditation was that for fifteen years I had done all I could do, and that now I was to enter into my reward. O golden Strand, that day, golden Great Russell Street when I came home to tell my news, golden happy world which rewards at last all humble faithful endeavour: golden world inhabited by good men, by publishers of all men most good.

It was a pure matter of form; the waiting for the agreement, a matter of a week or so, as the kind gentlemen in the office informed me. And in three weeks, somewhere about the middle of January, 1895, came the MS. of *The Three Impostors* back to me, with a formal, printed slip from the House of Heinemann, regretting that it was unable to accept the enclosed manuscript. Well does A. E. Waite declare that there is an element of waggery in the constitution of the universe. Never did the proud policeman in the old pantomime, foiled by the buttered slide of the clown, come down with a thump so boisterously undignified. So, rolling in the mud, I lay sprawling, my legs in the air. I was silly enough to write a somewhat exasperated letter to my friend in the office. He answered me in a befitting manner, in a tone of grave rebuke: he said that if I had realised the cares of the publisher's life I would not have written "so caustically".

VIII

The *Three Impostors* came back then from Messrs. Heinemann, and as soon as I got over the little bump I have just mentioned, I thought that I would try to make the book a bit better. One of the "novels" or introduced tales displeased me, so I am sure it must have been very bad indeed. I am not certain, but I think it was about a benevolent City man, of considerable means, who occupied an old red brick house somewhere at the back of Acton and occasionally, I suppose at the full moon, turned into a were-wolf. I can see nothing against the plot; and I believe there is a considerable body of unimpeachable evidence in favour of the hypothesis that the human consciousness is occasionally displaced by the bestial consciousness: the Malays, for instance, are apt at times to fancy themselves wild cats and to behave accordingly. But, somehow, it wouldn't do. The transformation of the City man was highly unsatisfactory and unconvincing: so I tore up the tale, and wrote instead of it the surprising narrative of Professor Gregg and his disastrous search for the fairies among the hills of my native country. In the machinery of the story I introduced a hypothesis that was then new; I think I read of it in some paper written by Sir Oliver Lodge. The theory was, that when the lights are low, or turned out, at the spiritualist séance, and objects are found, when the lights go up, to have been brought from all quarters of the room and laid in the centre of the table; or when the people sitting in the dark round the table hear the piano near the door being played, the theory was that these marvels are not necessarily due to the presence and intervention of ghosts. I believe that it was the case of Eusapia Palladino that was engaging Sir Oliver Lodge's attention just then; and he advanced the striking hypothesis that the piano was played and the objects fetched from the sideboard by a kind of extension of the medium's body. I forget whether the distinguished Professor used the instance; but I know that the impression conveyed to my mind was that something happened similar to the protrusion and withdrawal of a snail's horns: Eusapia's arm became twice or thrice its usual length, performed the required feat whatever it was, and then shrank again to its normal size. This hypothesis was novel in those days; now it is widely known and credited amongst spiritualists. They have found a name for the mysterious substance which projects itself from the medium's body: it is called ectoplasm. In all probability the whole theory is a pack of nonsense, and the "phenomena" are the tricks of clever cheats: still, what do we know? At all events, I worked it all into my fairy tale, mixing up the old view that the fairy tales, the stories of Little People, are in fact traditions of the aborigines of these islands, small, dark men who took refuge under the hills from the invading Celt; with this view of the capacities of the human body, and my view, still newer, that the fairies may still be found under the hills, and that they are far from being pleasant little people. That was the recipe for the tale, and I give it in spite of a friendly rebuke I once received from poor H. B. Irving. He was talking to me about the Introduction I had written to *The Great God Pan*.

"You shouldn't have done it," he said. "You destroy the illusion. Never take people behind the scenes. I never do."

But it really doesn't matter. And, further, I have a suspicion that it is often much more interesting "behind" than "in front". I have seen some very fine theatrical storms in my time; they did these things very well in the days of the elder Irving at the Lyceum, but I never enjoyed any of those tempests half so much as a storm I once watched from the wings, while Sir Frank Benson was playing King Lear. Everything, of course, was pitchy dark, save where a farthing light was glimmering in some odd corner. By this light crouched a squat form, that of the assistant stage-manager. In one hand he held the Prompt Copy of the Play, with all the cues duly indicated in it. He held it up as close as he could to the miserable glimmer, and had evidently as much as he could do to see the script with its various interlineations and noughts and crosses, and all sorts of queer hieroglyphics which mean a great deal to a stage-manager's eye. But in the other hand he held a drumstick, and coming nearer I saw that the big drum was beside him on the boards, and that near at hand dim figures stood ready for some mysterious service. A voice is heard from somewhere:

> "Blow, winds, and crack your cheeks! Rage! Blow
> You cataracts and hurricanes, spout
> Till you have drench'd our steeples, drown'd the cocks,
> You sulphurous and thought-executing fires,
> Vaunt-couriers to oak-cleaving thunderbolts,
> Singe my white head; and thou, all-shaking thunder—"

And so on. And all the while the man with the big drum was commenting on the text. At certain points, bang! would come the drumstick on the drum, and that gave the cue to the man who stood by the thunder-sheet, which he caused to waggle violently, and at the same moment "Props" released his lightnings. It was far better behind than in front, to my taste, at all events. And so a man of letters of very great distinction once said to me:

"I've been reading your *Great God Pan*. I didn't make much of it. Confused, it seemed to me. But when I read the Introduction, I said to myself: 'Good heavens! Here's a man who writes as well as I do!'"

And I may say that the literary gentleman meant this as a very great compliment; indeed so it was.

Well, we have been speaking a little of the stage. And in the earlier rehearsals of a play a good deal is taken for granted, or indicated by the gentleman in charge. I am speaking of the old days, be it understood, and of the Shakespearean Touring Company in the provinces. The company is assembling in the wings in small groups, one strolling in after another, some of them with the cheerful look of those who have partaken of refreshment. On the whole the men keep together, and the women talk to each other. The curtain is down, and by it is a deal table and a couple of windsor chairs—or it may be a couple of golden thrones. At the table sit the stage-manager and his assistant, occupied with the prompt copies and various documents connected with the business of the morning. Above their heads burns the T-piece; piping in the shape of a capital T, with the top bar pierced and flaming with gas-jets. The stage-manager looks at his watch. "Five past eleven! All ready for the Procession! March off."

The stage-manager has risen from his windsor chair—or throne, as the case may be—and is looking up stage with his back to the curtain. As he says "March off," he indicates the music that isn't there:

"Too-too, too-too—too-too, tootery-too, too-too," in something like the time and tune of the music as it will be "on the night"; stamping with one foot on the stage to increase the realism of the performance. The old stage direction reads something like: "A sennet within. Culverins shot off," and accordingly the stage-manager interrupts his "too-tooing" at intervals:

"Too-too, tootery-too! Bang!" bringing his practicable foot down on the boards with a terrific crash.

"Too-too-too, too-too: Bang!"

Then: "March over. Flourish of Trumpets. Tara-tara-tara, ta-ta-ta. Curtain up! Tara-tara, ta-ta-ta-tatara. Procession on."

The Procession of Knights and Ladies which has been forming in the dusty obscurity of the wings begins to advance and cross an imaginary line which marks the place where the scenery will be on the night. They make more especially for a position up stage (L.U.E.) where there will be, at the proper time, a Gothic archway. The "taras" are still going on. They are violently interrupted.

"Where's the Rush-strewer?" howls the stage-manager. "Mr. Machen! (fff) Mr. Machen! Lobbit! (To the hovering call-boy) Call Mr. Machen! (To the Procession) Go back. I am going to have this done properly, if we have to stay all day for it."

The call-boy rushes violently into the darkness. His voice is heard vociferating "Mr. Machen!" in passages and on stairs. Finally, Mr. Machen appears, looking flurried or sulky, as the case may be. The stage-manager, who had been discussing beer with Mr. Machen a short quarter of an hour before, in a friendly and familiar manner, is now, very properly, distant and official.

"Mr. Machen, I wish you would contrive to be more punctual. Better be an hour too soon on the stage than a second too late. You can't learn to act, you know, by staying away from rehearsal!"

Mr. Machen murmurs something about "ten minutes allowed for variation of clocks". The stage-manager grunts impatiently. Mr. Machen places himself at the head of the procession with an imaginary bundle of rushes on his left arm. The too-tooing, the banging, the tara-ing are done all over again, and at last the stage-manager announces: "Flourish over"—and the play begins.

In other words, after the little difficulties and delays that I have indicated, *The Three Impostors* was published in the Keynotes Series at the

Bodley Head. It didn't do so well as *The Great God Pan.* The title was a bad one. Then, as my French colleague, the late P. J. Toulet, said to me afterwards: *"Ce livre est trop fumiste, ou pas assez fumiste";* the farce and the tragedy in it were not well mixed. And again, there had been some ugly scandals in the summer of '95, which had made people impatient with reading matter that was not obviously and obtrusively "healthy"; and so, for one reason or another, *The Three Impostors* failed to set the Fleet Ditch on fire.

Whereupon I began to think about my next book. I had done, as I have said, with Stevensonianism and White Powders; now we were to have something entirely new. "Tara, tara, tara!"—in the stage-manager's manner. This time there was to be no doubt of it. "Everybody ready for the Great Romance!"

I started fair. There was to be something different from the former books: I knew that. But I hadn't the remotest notion of what this new book was to be about. I used to go out in the morning and pace the more deserted Bloomsbury squares and wonder very much what it would be like. I got the hint I wanted at last from a most interesting essay by Mr. Charles Whibley, written by way of Introduction to *Tristram Shandy.* Mr. Whibley was discussing the picaresque in literature. He pointed out that while *Gil Blas* and its early Spanish originals represented the picaresque of the body, and *Don Quixote* was picaresque both of mind and body, *Tristram Shandy* was picaresque of the mind alone. The wandering in that extraordinary book is, in other words, noumenal, not phenomenal. I caught hold of that notion: the thought that a literary idea may be presented from the mental as well as the physical side of things, and said to myself: "I will write a 'Robinson Crusoe' of the mind." That was the beginning of *The Hill of Dreams.* It was to represent loneliness not of body on a desert island, but loneliness of soul and mind and spirit in the midst of myriads and myriads of men. I had some practical experience of this state to help me; not altogether in vain had I been constrained to dwell in Clarendon Road and to have my habitation in the tents of Notting Hill Gate. I immediately marked down all these old experiences as a valuable asset in the undertaking of my task: I knew what it was to live on a little in a little room, what it meant to wander day after day, week after week, month after month through the *inextricabilis error* of the London streets, to tread a grey labyrinth whose paths had no issue, no escape, no end. I had known as a mere lad how terrible it was on a gloomy winter's evening to go out because the little room had become intolerable, to go out walking through those multitudinous streets stretching to beyond and beyond, to see the light of kindly fires leaping on the walls, to see friendly faces welcoming father or husband or brother, to hear laughter or a song sounding from within, perhaps to catch a half glimpse of the faces of the lovers as they looked out, happy, into the dark night. All this had been my daily practice and use for a long while; I was qualified then, in a measure, to describe the fate of a Robinson Crusoe cast on the desert island of the tremendous and terrible London. Thus was accomplished what Garrick called, much to the Doctor's amusement, the "first concoction" of the book.

I am sorry that I cannot trace the further steps in its elaboration with a like minuteness. All this time I was getting my green-mounted review cuttings of *The Three Impostors*. I have kept them, I know, for I keep all my reviews, but I cannot lay my hands on them. I believe, though, that their general import was that I was something of a pretentious ass and that my horrors were all humbug; and for some obscure reason, which I cannot undertake to explain, these notices cheered me on immensely in my new work.

"I cannot undertake to explain"; that is the very truth. Why should a man whose only life consists in writing books feel highly elated at being told on good authority that he is utterly and entirely incapable of doing anything of the kind; that he is clever, perhaps, in a thin sort of way, but that his most prized effects at which he has evidently toiled—as the reviewer declares—with most laborious pains miss fire completely; that his endeavours to be this, that, and the other are really pathetic in their utter failure; that his lightnings and thunderings are effects of the property man? I do not know why this should be so, and perhaps if I knew I should not tell; but I think I know that there are deep things in psychology, in the real psychology, not in the muckheap of the psycho-analytical chemists. At all events, I know that when I read a review which ended, say, with: "We can only wish Mr. Machen better luck with his next bag of thaumaturgic tricks," I would be much uplifted, and go out and pace Mecklenburgh Square and the old graveyard by Heathcote Street in a happy mood of invention, feeling that the new book lay all simple and plain before me.

So, thus cheered and highly comforted, I went on my daily tours about the Bloomsbury squares, about waste places abutting on the King's Cross Road, about the wonderlands of Barnsbury, taking with me the problem of this great book that was to be made; this book that was to be the better part of me. Why, it was only the other day that a friend, who is curious like myself, in the remaining oddities of London, took me for a short stroll near the Gray's Inn Road.

"I think," said he, "that I can shew you something that you will like."

In his voice was the pride of the collector, who takes his keys, opens his safe, and draws out the rich case, containing *Pickwick* in the original numbers, with the cancelled plates, unopened leaves, all the advertisements preserved, perfect condition, autograph letter signed "Charles Dickens", giving the source of the character of Sam Weller in separate portfolio: all the pride of one who possesses such a treasure was in the voice of my friend.

He led me round corner after corner, by turns and ways that became more and more obscure. Then, elated, he said: "There!"

In the by-street I saw a queer house, standing in a sunken yard away from the pavement. It was painted in cream colour, and grotesque heads, intended to be mediæval, were peppered over its frontage. I knew it well.

"I never expected to see that again," I said. "I thought it would have been pulled down long ago; like the 'Rows' that once led from Great Coram Street. And, unless I am mistaken, we shall find Hebrew letters inscribed on plaster shields applied to the house front."

The Hebrew inscriptions were still there; very faint, but still there. I had last seen them in '95–'96 when I was entangled in the most intricate problems of *The Hill of Dreams*.

I have told already some of the troubles of the book: the battle of the second chapter, the notion sought in vain for three weeks: the affair of the fifth chapter when I lost my way completely and wrote many thousands of words that had to be rejected. Nearly all the journey, from the autumn of 1895 to the spring of 1897, there were doubts and trials and questionings: after all, was it not hopeless; would it not be better to tear it up and start afresh on a new book? In the summer of 1896, when

I was in the thick of these perplexities, I spent a month in Provence and Languedoc, visiting places the very names of which are incantations: Arles, Avignon, Nîmes, Montpellier, Beaucaire, famed Tarascon by Rhone; and I saw how the sun can shine on the white cliff road by Marsilho—to give the city its Provençal name, which you must pronounce, as near as may be, Mar-see-yo-ho. And the changing of the colours of the sea there, as the sun sank and brief twilight gathered and the moon rose: here were marvels and beauties that sank deeply into the heart.

A wonderful land, indeed. The olive garths, of such a silvery, dim green as our northern seas sometimes put on near the land, the scented rosemary growing as a weed by the roadside, the walls of Avignon seen by sunset light, the great Roman arenas, still in use for bull-fights, a matter not remote from their original purpose, the Temple of Diana at Nîmes, no ruin, but a perfect building into which the priest of Diana might well enter as you viewed the portal from the modern street; and above all the splendour of that southern sun shining on white rocks, on the dark cypresses, on the white arch which looked as clear and fine as if it had been built a year, which was eighteen hundred years old or more: all these are Provence; not at all forgetting the Bouillabaisse which Pascal makes in the Old Port, Pascal who roasts his incomparable partridges before a fire of vine boughs. More than once I felt that I had made a journey rather in time than space, that these black cypresses and clear white walls and green and silvery olives were present not in our day but in the old Roman world.

The last few days of my visit to Provence I spent in a little hotel at a place called Roucas Blanc, not far from Marseilles. The hotel, sheltered by the white rock and the dark green woods, had been built on the very verge of the sea, and in the morning I would open the door-window of my apartment and stand on a platform, but a few feet above the water. I would lean over the low wall, and wonder at the jewelled glory of the Mediterranean blue beneath the mounting sun—and my heart was at home, in Gray's Inn, in my old Japanese bureau, in the litter of papers that awaited me there, in the wretched book that I was struggling to make. *Aqui esta encerrado el alma del licenciado.* What have I said of the paradox of life, that its actualities are so nauseous that men will do anything to escape from them? And here was I, free to enjoy the sun on the Provençal sea and the wonder of the Roman world, hankering after the world of anguish and difficulty and disappointment that I had made for myself in grim Verulam Buildings, amidst the London fogs.

And so I got back and found that the labour of months had been wasted, and set to work to break and remake. The book was finished, somehow, in the March of 1897, and just then, as if he had come upon his cue, a new publisher, Mr. Grant Richards, wrote to me asking if I had any manuscripts that I should like to have published. I saw him and left *The Hill of Dreams* with him. He did not take long to make up his mind about it. He would have none of it, and he wrote advising me by no means to publish the book; for, he said, it would do me no credit. What he meant was that it was not in the least like *The Three Impostors,* and it took him ten years before he saw light on the subject, for it was the firm of Grant Richards that published *The Hill of Dreams* in 1907.

Some amusing reviews appeared. The *Daily Graphic* said, very truly, that the book was not of much practical interest, and the *Outlook* confirmed this dictum by stating that there was "scarcely a place for it in the widest utilitarian view". "Will readily impress a reader of quiet tastes," declared the gentler *Scotsman.* "Nothing that more quickly tends to tedium," corrected the *Manchester Guardian:* naturally enough, if the *Athenæum* was right in saying that "the main matter of regret is the utter formlessness and the arid inhumanity of his work". "Well written, but written not quite well enough," was the fatal sentence of the *Chronicle.* And so on, and so on. I will not disguise the fact that some of the notices were very good indeed; but it has always been the other sort of review that has heartened me, and so forthwith I set about writing a book in high spirits. This turned out to be *The Secret Glory,* which was published in the spring of 1922. This book also was on the whole very well reviewed, though it is as queer as queer can be—I am afraid I must say that the bridge is not nearly so well kept now as in the brave days of old. But one reviewer stood out boldly, and him I will quote in full, and so make an end of talking about reviews, which some authors jeer at, which I treasure with reverent care.

"Even if we wished, we could not tell the story of *The Secret Glory.* Mr. Machen manages to combine an onslaught on the public-school system with some watery Paterian mysticism. Personally, we have an equal dislike of those who belaud and those who denigrate the public-school system. Besides, 'there ain't no sich person'; there are as many systems as there are public schools. But Ambrose Meyrick, if he could have been jerked for a moment by his creator into a semblance of real existence, would justify the worst outrages wrought upon him by his equally incredible *alma mater*. He is a sentimental philanderer with æsthetic Catholicism, a mystical Celtic dreamer, a Soho Bohemian (before Soho was ruined, of course); but these crimes are as nothing compared to his incorrigible penchant for 'poetic prose.' Mr. Machen has encouraged him in it. He will have a great deal more to answer for in the day of judgment than the schoolmaster who tried to beat him out of it."

There! That notice, which appeared in *The Nation and the Athenæum*, was signed by Mr. J. Middleton Murry, generally recognised as being one of the most eminent literary critics of the day, if he is not rather to be accounted as the most eminent literary critic of the day. He is also, as a fellow-writer assured me, regarded as "the leader of the younger intelligentsia". Anyhow, I like a man who speaks his mind. I try to do so myself, sometimes.

And "there!" again. I think I have written enough about the manner in which I thought of my books, the manner in which I wrote my books, the manner in which I broke down more or less lamentably in the beginning, the middle, and the end of my books, the manner in which they were welcomed by eager publishers, and the manner in which they finally tottered into print and were acclaimed by the Press. Enough has been said on all these topics, and perhaps a good deal too much for the patience of a weary world.

Let us now be brief on this matter. The year 1898 I spent in the service of *Literature,* a weekly journal that had just been started by *The Times.* In 1899 I wrote *Hieroglyphics* and "The White People", and the first chapter of "A Fragment of Life". Then a great sorrow which had long been threatened fell upon me: I was once more alone.

IX

It was somewhere about the autumn of 1899 that I began to be conscious that the world was being presented to me at a new angle. I find now an extreme difficulty in the choice of words to convey my meaning; "a new angle" is clumsy enough, "here in this world he changed his life" is far too high in its associations; but there certainly came to be a strangeness in the proportion of things, both in things exterior and interior. And it is in these latter that I held and still hold that the true wonder, the true mystery, the true miracle reside. There is the old proverb, of course: "Seeing is believing" and, for once, the old proverb is widely astray. All phenomenal perception is apt to be deceitful, and very often is deceitful. This is in the nature of things, as Berkeley pointed out a very long time ago. That castle tower that looks round in the distance is found to be square when you get a little nearer to it; the red and golden glory and the magic architecture of the sunset cloud would change, if you were in it, into something like a London fog. And if it be objected: "Yes, exactly; when you are far away from an object you see it incorrectly, but when you come near it you see it correctly"—that is not so. If you were near enough to the tower, with your nose within six inches of it, you only see a certain limited extent of stone surface; the tower, *qua* tower, has entirely disappeared. But you see the stone surface accurately? No, you don't. The ant crawling up it has a widely different vision and perception of that stone surface from your vision and perception; and a microscope gives yet another vision, different from either; and as magnification must be infinite in potentiality, though not *in actu*, it is quite clear that no one can ever see the truth of any external object presented to the eyes: there must always be, in theory and perhaps, eventually, in fact, another microscope of still higher magnifying power, which will entirely change the aspect of the thing seen. And thus, without tedious specification and example of all the other senses, I mustn't even call the poker stiff, lest the man in the chair on the other side of the fire take it up and tie it into a knot before my eyes, proving that I have been talking foolishly. And get the rarest Bordeaux that money can buy, and offer Bill the navvy a glass; and watch his face as he calls for ale to wash that muck, that . . . something muck, out of his mouth.

All this, of course, is mere philosophic A.B.C., and if I thought this book likely to penetrate into philosophic circles I should apologise for a clumsy rehash of Berkeley's irresistible conclusions; but I do not think that the readers of *Mind* will trouble themselves about me; and I am afraid that those of us who have not been rectified by the study of philosophy are still inclined to think that seeing is believing and that some things are hard and others soft, and so on. And, no doubt, there is a kind of relative and highly inferior sort of truth in these propositions: don't knock your head against a stone wall, for instance, is a perfectly sound bit of practical advice, since, considered in relation to your skull, the stone wall *is* hard and will hurt. And so with "seeing is believing": in nine hundred and ninety-nine cases out of a thousand you will be absolutely correct in saying: "Hullo! There's old Secretan walking up the garden path." But there is that thousandth—or millionth—case in which it turns out that old Secretan was busy in Tibet or busy dying at the moment you were quite certain that you saw him approaching the hall-door of The Cedars: and then where is your "seeing is believing" maxim? I had a curious instance of this in the midst of the famous "Angels of Mons" controversy. An officer of very high distinction wrote to me from the front, and described a most remarkable experience which had been vouchsafed to him and to others during the retreat of August, 1914. The battle of Le Cateau was fought on August 26th. My correspondent's division, as he writes—his letter is quoted at length in the Introduction to the second edition of *The Bowmen*—was heavily shelled, "had a bad time of it", but retired in good order. It was on the march all the night of the 26th, and throughout August 27th, with only about two hours' rest.

"By the night of the 27th we were all absolutely worn out with fatigue—both bodily and mental fatigue. No doubt we also suffered to a certain extent from shock; but the retirement still continued in excellent order, and I feel sure that our mental faculties were still quite sound and in good working condition. On the night of the 27th I was riding along in the column with two other officers. We had been talking and doing our best to keep from falling asleep on our horses. As we rode along I became conscious of the fact that, in the fields on both sides of the road along which we were marching, I could see a very large body of horsemen. These horsemen had the appearance of squadrons of cavalry, and they seemed to be riding across the fields and going in the same direction as we were going, and keeping level with us. The night was not very dark, and I fancied that I could see squadron upon squadron of these cavalrymen quite distinctly. I did not say a word about it at first, but I watched them for about twenty minutes. The other two officers had stopped talking. At last one of them asked me if I saw anything in the fields. I then told him what I had seen. The third officer then confessed that he too had been watching these horsemen for the past twenty minutes. So convinced were we that they were really cavalry that, at the next halt, one of the officers took a party of men out to reconnoitre, and found no one there. . . . The same phenomenon was seen by many men in our column. . . . I myself am absolutely convinced that I saw these horsemen; and I feel sure that they did not exist only in my imagination."

Now I have not the faintest notion what really happened to the Colonel, to the two officers, and to many of the men in the column. What concerns us for the moment is that these people were at first perfectly certain that they saw sensible objects, that is, cavalrymen, and then were perfectly certain that there were no sensible objects to see; and therefore it may be concluded from this instance and from many instances, of like sort, that the senses are deceptive; that the world of the senses is very largely a world of illusion and delusion. To give a sharp example of what I mean: I would say that the old story of the oak and the dryad is much nearer to the real and final truth about the oak than the scientific classification and description of the tree in a manual of Dendrology. Not that I believe that a spirit in the shape of a beautiful woman of another order of being to our own is somehow bound up with the life of the oak tree; but I do believe that the truth about the oak tree—as about all else—is a great mystery, which is quite beyond the purview of all sensible—that is scientific—perception and enquiry.

And so, when I speak of that singular rearrangement of the world into which I entered in the late summer of 1899, I do not desire to lay much stress on the sensible, or material, phenomena which were presented to me. I marvel, but I marvel with caution, remembering the manifold deceits of the senses, the phantasmagoria or shadow shew that they are always displaying before us; remembering also that when the super-normal is manifested it is usually, in nine cases out of ten, irrelevant and insignificant. For example, in the case of old Secretan, seen walking up the path to the hall-door of The Cedars, but discovered afterwards to have an undoubted *alibi*, either on his dying bed or in Tibet. Suppose the latter case, suppose that Secretan returns and that you collar him and ask him if he remembers what he was doing about five o'clock of the afternoon of June 28th.

"What makes you ask that?" he may reply, likely enough. "I thought it rum at the time. Here's the entry in my diary. 'June 28th. Had rank goat and tea with rancid butter in it in the afternoon. Thought of the jolly tea and tennis parties at The Cedars and wondered how old Jones was getting on in the City.'"

And, it seems shocking, but it is probably the truth, that if Secretan had been really engaged, not in Tibet but in dying, his thought, the force which projected his shadow on that gravel path of The Cedars, Thames Ditton, was: "Beastly taste in my mouth! Wish I could get round to old Jones's and wash it out with a glass of his pre-war whiskey. Eh?" . . . and the silence.

And all this, as I say, is irrelevant and insignificant; and then again the rats and snakes and other objects seen by the delirium tremens patient; they really don't matter—save to the patient aforesaid, who, of course, is quite sure that they are there. So, again, I distrust the senses, and though I wondered and still wonder, I make nothing much of the great gusts of incense that were blown in those days into my nostrils, of the odours of rare gums that seemed to fume before invisible altars in Holborn, in Claremont Square, in grey streets of Clerkenwell, of the savours of the sanctuary that were perceived by me in all manner of grim London wastes and wanderings. One would like to think of the Knights of the Grail who were ware of the "odour of all the rarest spiceries in the world" before the Vision was given to them: but . . . if one is not a Knight of the Grail, but far otherwise?

Then, again, there was that morning, a bright, keen morning of November it seems in my recollection, when I was walking up Rosebery Avenue with a friend, and suddenly became aware of a strange sensation, and as suddenly recollected the old proverb: "walking on air". I remember thinking at the time: "this is incredible"; and yet it was a fact. The pavement of that horrible street had suddenly become, not air, certainly, but resilient; the impact of my feet upon it was buoyant; the sensation was delicious. I may mention that that very morning I had made a certain interior resolution; but I do not venture for one moment to connect this with that; I only tell what happened to me. I make no deductions, nor do I venture to conclude anything: remembering always that neither seeing nor smelling nor feeling is necessarily believing. But so it was, exactly as I have told it.

And then there was one afternoon in my sitting-room at 4 Verulam Buildings, Gray's Inn. I was sitting in my chair, and the wall trembled and the pictures on the wall shook and shivered before my eyes, as if a sudden wind had blown into the room. Let me hasten to say that there was no wind, no actual wind, that is; and that I knew at the time that there was no wind, and was, in consequence, not a little alarmed, not knowing what would happen next. And I must already correct my phrase: I have said that the pictures on the wall opposite to the window that looked on the garden of the Inn "shook and shivered". It is not quite just: trembled, dilated, became misty in their outlines; seemed on the point of disappearing altogether, and then shuddered and contracted back again into their proper form and solidity: that is the closest description of what I witnessed: with a shaking heart, and with a sense that something, I knew not what, was also being shaken to its foundations. This is all wonderful? I suppose that it is; but let me here say firmly that I consider an act of kindness to a wretched mangy kitten to be much more important.

But now comes a puzzle. We are highly composite beings. We all know that a stomach-ache may make a man very miserable, and I believe that science is beginning to admit that misery may give a man a very bad stomach-ache. There are old phrases about a "sinking heart", and a man's heart being "in his boots". Well, it seems that the heart does not sink, but that the stomach does, when subjected to certain emotional perturbations. Only this morning I was reading in the paper of new radiographic experiments which shewed that under certain stimulations of horror or fear or grief the stomach sometimes falls from one to three inches, and the doctor who was conducting the experiments declared that there was the brighter side; that he had mentioned possible "pints of bitter" to some of his subjects, with the result that there was a perceptible and upward movement of the organ in question. And so the play goes round in a ring, with a constant action and reaction of the physical and mental—or psychical, or spiritual—and it will often be difficult to say where the prime cause resides: in the stomach, in the brain, or in the immortal spirit. I have already professed my belief that the true wonder, the true miracle are of the spirit, not of the body; I here confess that in certain cases I find it difficult to disentangle the two worlds of our apprehension, that is to say definitely that the sensible thing, the phenomenal thing, is always and invariably without any true significance.

And so with that afternoon's work in Gray's Inn. The shivering pictures that seemed on the point to dissolve and return into chaos, the sensible thrill of delight that accompanied this strange manifestation—I had forgotten that part of the experience—such phenomena as these may be producible, for all I know, by drugs. You can, at all events, see far more wonderful things than anything that I saw by taking a sufficient dose of Anhelonium Lewinii and then shutting your eyes. But . . .

I had better begin at the beginning. That afternoon I was in a state of very dreadful misery and desolation and dereliction of soul. It is strange, but the most dreadful pangs of grief are generally, I think, bearable in the moment of their impact. With the wounds of the spirit, it is as with the wounds of the body; a certain anæsthesia accompanies the actual fall of the blow. I once fell backwards from some little height, and my skull lighting on the edge of a brick, I remained unconscious for more than half an hour. And I remember distinctly that the sensation at the very moment of the crash was that of being lifted and gently laid on the softest of all downy pillows; it was only when I raised myself slowly, not in the least aware that I had been unconscious, that I felt the pain of the great bleeding wound at the back of my head, and a dismal, heavy throbbing of the brow. So with the wounds of the soul; I had borne what had to be borne with some measure of solidity and stolidity; the torture of six years of lamentable expectation had, as I supposed, seared and burned my spirit into dull, insensitive acquiescence: but I was mistaken. A horror of soul that cannot be uttered descended upon me, on that dim, far-off afternoon in Gray's Inn; I was beside myself with dismay and torment; I could not endure my own being. And then a process suggested itself to me, as having the possibility of relief, and without crediting what I had heard of this process or indeed having any precise knowledge of it or of its results, I did what had to be done—I hasten to add without any more exalted motives than those which urge a man with a raging toothache to get laudanum and take it with all convenient speed. I suffered from a more raging pain than that of any toothache, and I wanted that pain to be dulled; that was all.

Well, I made my experiment, expecting, very doubtfully, almost incredulously, certain results. The results that I obtained were totally different from my expectations. I couldn't have hypnotised, or "magnetised", or mesmerised, or suggested, or Couéd, or in any way bedevilled myself into the obtained condition for the good reason that I had never heard of it, had no faintest notion of it, and was, in fact, as I have stated, not a little alarmed by it, half-thinking, if the truth be told, that I was very near to death. I may state, by the way, that in the course of a pretty extensive acquaintance with "occult" company, I only once heard of anything at all comparable with this strange adventure of mine. A man was running on, foolishly and uncritically enough, about his various occult experiences—they were of little interest as a whole—and talked at last of some sojourn that he had made amongst the Moors of Northern Africa. Here, he said, he had met a man who had known wonders, and he proceeded to tell them. There was nothing very wonderful, so far as I can remember; but the Moor or Arab of the story had an experience like enough to mine—I need not say that I had not mentioned it nor so much as hinted it to my occult acquaintance. The African also had seen the walls shiver and prepare for dissolution, had felt that the world was shaken, and that his heart was shaken within him. Mr. Jones-Robinson told the tale without any sense, apparently, that it had any special significance; it was part of his occult pack, that was all; and he went on to some sick rubbish about the "correspondence" of the Tarot Trumps with the letters of the Hebrew Alphabet; and this nonsense he discussed with real relish and a high sense of its infinite importance. I think that he alone knew the real "attribution" of the aforesaid Tarot Trumps, but he "had received it under pledge and was not at liberty to speak"—for which inhibition I was deeply thankful, having little patience for solemn hanky-panky or Abracadabras of any sort. But in ending his story of the Enchanted Moor, he said that this man, who had seen the material world quivering and fading before his eyes, had received, in some manner not indicated, a command or an intimation that he must "leave everything"; and this he could not do, having a wife and children. And I must say at once that being pretty well acquainted with Jones-Robinson and all his type, I should have paid no more attention to his story of the Moor than I paid to his story of the Tarot Trumps—if it had not been for something which I knew and kept to myself. As it was, I heard the tale and the injunction, and wondered deeply, and still wonder.

But now to our point: the connection between material or sensible things and spiritual things, the question whether the former are ever of any real consequence or significance. As I have said before, the evidence that Home the medium rose "miraculously"—to adopt a convenient shorthand—into the air seems to me good; but is such a phenomenon of any more true consequence than the phenomenon of Hydrogen gas rising into the air from the admixture of water, zinc, and sulphuric acid? And so, were the incense clouds that came to my nostrils in places where, assuredly, no material incense smoked, of consequence? Was the billowy and resilient pavement of detestable Rosebery Avenue of consequence? Were the pictures that shivered and wavered on the unstable wall of consequence? I do not know; but I am sure that the state which followed this last experience was of high consequence. For when I rose, afraid, and broke off the process in which I had been engaged, I found to my utter amazement that everything within had been changed. Amazement; for the utmost that I had hoped from my experiment was a temporary dulling of the consciousness, a brief opium oblivion of my troubles. And what I received was not mere dull lack of painful sensation, but a peace of the spirit that was quite ineffable, a knowledge that all hurts and doles and wounds were healed, that that which was broken was reunited. Everything, of body and of mind, was resolved into an infinite and an exquisite delight; into a joy so great that—let this be duly noted—it became almost intolerable in its ecstasy. I remember thinking at the time: "There is wine so strong that no earthly vessels can hold it": joy threatened to become an agony, that must shatter all. Emily Brontë, describing the state of Heathcliff soon before his death, has described just such a condition; I have often wondered how she knew of it.

But this was later. For that day and for many days afterwards I was dissolved in bliss, into a sort of rapture of life which has no parallel that I can think of, which has, therefore, no analogies by which it may be made more plain. The vine and the exultation of the vine are solemn and ancient and approved figures of the joys of the interior life, but these are not quite to my purpose. I can only fall back on little things, and quite material things. My chambers in Verulam Buildings were towards the northern portion of the Inn, and the traffic of Theobald's Road was distinct enough, distinct enough, often, to be an annoyance. But this night, the "ping, ping!" of the omnibus bell, the grind of the many wheels upon the cobble-stones sounded to me as marvellous and tremendous chords reverberating from some mighty organ; filling the air, filling the soul and the whole being with rapture immeasurable. And another trifle, as insignificant, ever more insignificant, perhaps. In the ordinary state of existence the sense of touch is exercised constantly, but almost unconsciously. Now and again it is used with intent; the buyer of old furniture acquires a sort of thumb-and-finger craft; he passes the tips of his fingers over the edges of the bureau or cabinet, and they help him to decide whether the object is an antique or a novelty. And so, I suppose, a woman choosing stuffs uses her fingers in much the same manner, learning something about the silk or velvet by the process. But in general, and very conveniently, you take up pen or pencil, or place your hand on the back of the chair without any distinct consciousness of the impact of your flesh on these exterior objects: unless, that is, your hand encounter some unexpected object which insists on notice, such as a pin point or a rusty nail. But in these strange days of which I am speaking touch became an exquisite and conscious pleasure; I could not so much as place my hand on the table before me without experiencing a thrill of delight which was not merely sensuous, but carried with it, mysteriously and wonderfully, the message of a secret and interior joy.

And one more instance. I had always been subject to headaches which visited me at intervals of five, six, or seven weeks, and invariably lasted for twenty-four hours. The pain was distressing, and any movement of the head raised it into a racking, throbbing agony; I should imagine that I suffered from a kind of migraine or megrims. Late one night during the time of which I am speaking I felt the first approaches of one of these tiresome attacks. I said to myself: "I wonder whether I can stop it," and I placed the tip of the forefinger of the left hand upon my forehead. I felt the sense as of a dull shock: and the pain was gone. And though I have had my share of pains and aches since then, I have never been revisited by that particular kind of headache from that day to this.

And there was yet another matter. In a little book of mine called *The Great Return,* which nobody has heard of, I have told how the Holy Grail came back for a brief while to Britain after long years. And describing some of the things that were seen and known during that happy visitation, I have written:

"The 'glow' as they call it seems more difficult to explain (than certain other matters duly related). For they say that all through the nine days, and indeed after the time had ended, there never was a man weary or sick at heart in Llantrisant, or in the country round it. For if a man felt that his work of the body or the mind was going to be too much for his strength, then there would come to him of a sudden a warm glow and a thrilling all over him and he felt as strong as a giant, and happier than he had ever been in his life before, so that lawyer and hedger each rejoiced in the task that was before him, as if it were sport and play."

Thus in the story, and thus it was with me in fact, in that autumn and winter of 1899–1900. It was with a singular surprise that I read, in St. Adamnan, many years afterwards, how St. Columba's monks, toiling in the fields, experienced now and again the very sensation—if it be just to speak of it as a sensation—that I have described. They, too, weary with their work of reclaiming the barren land of their isle, would know that sudden glow of joy and strength and courage; and they believed that it was the prayer of their Father in God, Columba, strengthening them and inspiring them, as he knelt before the altar of the Perpetual Choir. And lest it be said that I had read Adamnan when I was a boy and had forgotten all about it consciously though I had retained it subconsciously, I must solemnly declare that this was not the case; and that when this strange experience first befell me, I was overwhelmed with astonishment, and could scarcely credit that which was actually happening. I have hesitated as to whether it should be, in strictness, called a sensation, and I still hesitate. It seems to me, and I think that I can trust my recollection, that the two worlds of sense and spirit were admirably and wonderfully mingled, so that it was difficult, or rather impossible, to distinguish the outward and sensible glow from the inward and spiritual grace. *Magnum vere sacramentum.* And all this, be it remembered, would fall out in dim Bloomsbury squares, in noisy, clattering Gray's Inn Road, in a train on the Underground, amongst hustling crowds in common streets. I mention this, not forgetful of a pretty severe rebuke which I received from a very high literary quarter on account of that little book, *The Great Return,* which I have just cited. The critic noted the fact that in my book the Holy Grail was manifested to the common people, to common modern people, to Welsh tradesmen and farmers. He seemed to think this very low. It may be low, but perhaps things happen in this way sometimes; and so with me: I, by no manner of means a knight, received joys and knew wonders while the trams clanged along the Clerkenwell Road in the grey winter afternoon. So it was, and it appears to me necessary to tell the truth. As Coventry Patmore says, quoting from an earlier writer: "Let us not deny in the darkness that which we have known in the light."

And beyond all this, beyond these experiences in which things of the body and things of the spirit were mingled, there was a better world of which I saw the verges. There was no more grief; there was no more resentment, there was no more anger. I began to know a little of *Caritas.* The griefs that flood the heart with agony, the great sorrows of life, these were seen to be but passing trifles of no moment, like the sorrow of a little child which is past and forgotten before its tears are dry. I remember tearing up an old diary which I had kept in the bitter days of Clarendon Road, a record of struggles and starvings and desolations; I tore it up because it no longer signified anything to me. The words, I daresay, were strong enough, but the tale had become of no meaning at all. I glanced at one page and another of the tattered old notebook before I rent it, with a kind of mild curiosity as to the state of mind of the silly stranger who had written all this, and had whined so dismally. At all events, it had nothing to do with me, and so it went into fragments and into the fire. If it could be restored to me now, I should read it all with interest and whine again and foam again *sæva indignatione;* but then I have long returned into that darkness in which, I suppose, most of our lives are spent.

There is one thing that I hope I may be spared, that is the comment of the Oriental Occult Ass. I confess that I have written all this with difficulty, and with doubt as to the decency of writing it at all, especially when the tale, if it is to be a true tale, makes it necessary for me to seem to compare, for one little moment, the saints of the company and following of St. Columba with myself. But I do hope that nobody will say: "Why, this is only Ruja-Puja! You get it all in the first chapter of the Anangasataga Raja! It's all perfectly elementary. Little Hindu children learn their A B C out of it in the Svanka Visatvara. Why, when the Swami Vishnakanandaram Jam Ghosh was over here last summer he mentioned all these phenomena as things you have to forget before you set out on the Way. As he put it so beautifully: 'The sun arises. It gleams on the Lotus. The petals of the *bhulji* flower expand. The stars are no longer seen.' Yes, isn't he wonderful? Fancy anybody still bothering about Keats and those silly people!"

I hope, I say, that I shall be spared that. I can bear better I think the (more or less) Occidental Idiot, who will speak of Shin—the letter of the Hebrew Alphabet, not the delicate portion of our anatomy—attribute it to the Tarot Trump called the Fool, and just throw in a reference to Salt, Sulphur, and Mercury.

As for me, I make no deductions, I infer nothing, I refrain from saying "therefore". Like Sancho Panza: "I come from my own vineyard; I know nothing." Perhaps I may venture to say that I have seen a lousy, lazy tramp drinking from a roadside stream that drips cold and pure from the rock in burning weather. Then the wastrel passes on his ill way, refreshed indeed, but as lousy and lazy as ever.

De torrente in via bibet: propterea exaltabit caput.

X

Mr. Charles O'Malley,
    Castle O'Malley, Co. Galway.

That was the inscription of a card which had just been placed in my hand, as I walked along Southampton Row—on which I found myself stupidly gazing in real old Southampton Row, not the staring, blatant street that bears the name now—one fine day in the summer of 1900.

Ten minutes or so before I had been taking my morning stroll in the company of my bulldog, Juggernaut. I was accosted very politely by a stoutish, youngish, clean-shaven gentleman, well dressed, with the mere suspicion of an Irish accent.

He had said without preface of any kind:

"A fine dog you've got, sir. I should be very glad if you'd come up with me and shew it to a lady I know who lives in the flats opposite."

I assented at once, feeling thoroughly in the scene, as they say on the stage. I followed him and we displayed the dog Juggernaut, certainly a noble specimen of his noble race, to the lady who, I may say at once, was a lady, and appeared to be on terms of polite acquaintance with the gentleman. Jug was admired, and the gentleman and I went down into the street again. The lady had not evinced the faintest astonishment at the introduction of a total stranger with a bulldog into her flat. When we were both down on the pavement of Southampton Row, the amateur of bulldogs gave me his card, and told me that I should be welcome and more than welcome if ever I found myself near Castle O'Malley, in County Galway. And so he vanished—if he ever were there, as to which I held and still hold, in a fantastic sort of way, vague doubts.

No, the flat was a perfectly quiet and unostentatious one. Nothing to drink was produced; there were no K.O. drops. The lady did not ask me to look in again some evening for a quiet game of cards with a few congenial friends. Mr. O'Malley did not say that he had salvaged a Spanish galleon wrecked beneath the rocks on which Castle O'Malley was built, and that in consequence he had more money than he knew what to do with. And I missed nothing from my pocket. That is one of the reasons why I hate rationalism, since, when it is called in, in a little difficulty or perplexity, its advices and explanations are always so stupid, so wide of the mark, so absolutely futile. Finally, from that day to this, I have never seen Mr. Charles O'Malley, of Castle O'Malley, Co. Galway, nor have I heard of him. I have forgotten to say that he did not so much as ask me my name.

I only wish that I had kept some kind of note of the very strange period which I had entered. It came about gradually, the merging of Syon into Bagdad; and I have a much dimmer recollection of the latter city. For its essence, as will be seen in the anecdote of the O'Malley, was lack of purpose, a certain fantastic confusion, a sense that something without any ratio might happen at any moment. Nothing began, nothing ended: strange people were apt to separate themselves from the crowd, to engage in queer discourse without intelligible motive or meaning, and then to sink back again, leaving no trace behind. And when events lack logical sequence or connection, it is difficult to retain them in the memory. But I believe that I do remember that on this very day of the O'Malley incident ten total strangers addressed me, without any very manifest reason and to no discernible end. We encountered in all sorts of places, in the street, in the restaurant, in the vanished Café de l'Europe in Leicester Square; the strangers uttered their mysterious messages, which to me were as incomprehensible as if they had been in cipher, and so vanished away. Indeed, looking back, I begin to wonder whether I were constantly being mistaken for someone else, who must have been exactly like me; this Someone Else being evidently a prominent member of a secret society, who would be aware of the signs and passwords of the order. For all I know, when Mr. O'Malley praised poor old Jug—he has long years ago gone to be a gargoyle on the parapet of some great Gothic church of the skies—I should have answered: "Yes, he is a fine dog, but green bulldogs with blue spots are finer." Then, it may be, the interview would have become coherent, and tending to some end, and the lady in the flat would have pressed the secret panel and have disclosed . . . I really don't know what.

That very day, I mean the day of the incident of the Bulldog, Mr. O'Malley and the Lady in the Flat, I was sitting in the Café de l'Europe with a friend, discussing various matters, when, as we rose to go, a young man of a somewhat colourless and unpretending appearance, who had been sitting at the other side of the table, suddenly observed:

"I have been very much interested, sir, in your conversation, and I should very much like to hear more of it."

Again, I was in the scene. I gave him my address in Gray's Inn, and he called to see me several times, always coming at night and staying pretty late, asking me many questions about interior things. I think it was only on his last visit that I found out his odd manner of leaving the Inn, when he went away at one or half-past one in the morning. He was ignorant of the fact that the Raymond Buildings Gate and the Holborn Gate have watchers by them who will open the portals all the long night; and so when he left me he would climb the spiked wall which separates Verulam Buildings from Gray's Inn Road and make off into the gaslight. He, too, vanished, and I saw him no more.

It was some time earlier in this year that I became conscious of a very odd circumstance. It will perhaps have been noticed that I have become insensibly Stevensonian in my diction, as I have spoken of the Incident of the Bulldog, or of this or of that. That is so because the atmosphere in which I lived was becoming remarkably like the atmosphere of *The Three Impostors,* which, as I have remarked, is derived from the "New Arabian" manner of R. L. Stevenson. Not only did strange and unknown and unexplained people start up from every corner, from every café table, and engage me in obscure mazes of talk, quite in the Arabian manner, but I presently became aware that something very odd indeed was happening: certain characters in *The Three Impostors* shewed signs of coming to life, a feat which, perhaps, they had failed to perform before. I was once talking to a dark young man, of quiet and retiring aspect, who wore glasses—he and I had met at a place where we had to be blindfolded before we could see the light—and he told me a queer tale of the manner in which his life was in daily jeopardy. He described the doings of a fiend in human form, a man who was well known to be an expert in Black Magic, a man who hung up naked women in cupboards by hooks which pierced the flesh of their arms. This monster—I may say that there is such a person, though I can by no means go bail for the actuality of any of the misdeeds charged against him—had, for some reason which I do not recollect, taken a dislike to my dark young friend. In consequence, so I was assured, he had hired a gang in Lambeth, who were grievously to maim or preferably to slaughter the dark young man; each member of the gang receiving a retaining fee of eight shillings and sixpence a day—a sum, by the way, that sounds as if it were the face value of some mediæval coin long obsolete. I listened in wonder, for there are some absurdities so enormous that they seem to have a stunning effect on the common sense, paralysing it for the moment and inhibiting its action. It was only when I got home that it dawned upon me that I had been listening to the Young Man in Spectacles, and that he came out of *The Three Impostors.* And soon Miss Lally, another character from the book, appeared, and like her prototype discoursed most amazing tales, was the heroine of incredible adventures, would appear and disappear in a quite inexplicable manner, relating always histories before unheard of, a personage wholly diverting, enigmatic, and enchanting.

And the odd thing is that it was as if these two had parts to play for a season, and played them—till the prompter's bell sounded, and the curtain fell and the lights went out. Both Miss Lally and the Young Man in Spectacles still live; but they have become useful members of society and eminently successful, as I believe, in their several employments. Thus do the King and Queen in the play go home to their flats or their lodgings after the show and enjoy cold beef, pickles, and a comfortable bottle of beer.

And now I am going at last to say a good word for literature. I have said, again and again, even to tedium, that the only good that I can see in it is that it is one of the many ways of escaping from life, to be classified with Alpine Climbing, Chess, Methylated Spirit, and Prussic Acid. The way I have always seen it is like this: I go out on a Sunday afternoon in March with the black north-easter blowing to take a walk up Gower Street. I say to myself: "O come! I can't stand this," and go home and write—or try to write—a chapter in *The Hill of Dreams.* Many people will say that the chapter is much worse than the street, and I daresay that they are right; but, anyhow, it was different: it was, for me, the nearest way out of Gower Street and the black north-easter. But I believe that there may be a little more in literature than this. It is certainly the escape from life; but perhaps it is also the only means of realising and shewing life, or, at least, certain aspects of life. Here is an example to my hand. Here am I, not trying to write literature, but doing my best to tell a true tale, and I find that I can make nothing of it. I can set down the facts, or rather such of them as I remember, but I am quite conscious that I am not, in the real sense of the word, telling the truth; that is, I am not giving any sense of the very extraordinary atmosphere in which I lived in the year 1900, of the curious and indescribable impression which the events of those days made upon me; the sense that everything had altered, that everything was very strange, that I lived in daily intercourse with people who would have been impossible, unimaginable, a year before; that the figure of the world was changed utterly for me—of all this I can give no true picture, dealing as I am with what are called facts. I maintained long ago in *Hieroglyphics* that facts as facts do not signify anything or communicate anything; and I am sure that I was right, when I confess that, as a purveyor of exact information, I can make nothing of the year 1900. But, avoiding the facts, I have got a good deal nearer to the truth in the last chapter of *The Secret Glory,* which describes the doings and feelings of two young people who are paying their first visit to London. *I* never bolted up to town with the house-master's parlourmaid; but truth must be told in figures.

There is one episode of this period of which I may say a little more, that is the affair of the Secret Society. Putting two and two together, a good many years after the event, I am inclined to think that it was a mere item in the programme of strange and Arabian entertainment that was being produced for my benefit: the Secret Society was of the same order as the Incident of Mr. O'Malley and the Adventure of the Young Man who always left by the Spiked Wall, only of a more gorgeous and elaborate kind. And I must confess that it did me a great deal of good—for the time. To stand waiting at a closed door in a breathless expectation, to see it open suddenly and disclose two figures clothed in a habit that I never thought to see worn by the living, to catch for a moment the vision of a cloud of incense smoke and certain dim lights glimmering in it before the bandage was put over the eyes and the arm felt a firm grasp upon it that led the hesitating footsteps into the unknown darkness: all this was strange and admirable indeed; and strange it was to think that within a foot or two of those closely curtained windows the common life of London moved on the common pavement, as supremely unaware of what was being done within an arm's length as if our works had been the works of the other side of the moon. All this was very fine; an addition and a valuable one, as I say, to the phantasmagoria that was being presented to me. But as for anything vital in the secret order, for anything that mattered two straws to any reasonable being, there was nothing of it, and less than nothing. Among the members there were, indeed, persons of very high attainments, who, in my opinion, ought to have known better after a year's membership or less; but the society as a society was pure foolishness concerned with impotent and imbecile Abracadabras. It knew nothing whatever about anything and concealed the fact under an impressive ritual and a sonorous phraseology. It had no wisdom, even of the inferior or lower kind, in its leadership; it exercised no real scrutiny into the characters of those whom it admitted, and so it is not surprising that some of its phrases and passwords were to be read one fine morning in the papers, their setting being one of the most loathsome criminal cases of the twentieth century.

And yet it had and has an interest of a kind. It claimed, I may say, to be of very considerable antiquity, and to have been introduced into England from abroad in a singular manner. I am not quite certain as to the details, but the *mythos* imparted to members was something after this fashion. A gentleman interested in occult studies was looking round the shelves of a second-hand bookshop, where the works which attracted him were sometimes to be found. He was examining a particular volume—I forget whether its title was given—when he found between the leaves a few pages of dim manuscript, written in a character which was strange to him. The gentleman bought the book, and when he got home eagerly examined the manuscript. It was in cipher; he could make nothing of it. But on the manuscript—or, perhaps, on a separate slip laid next to it—was the address of a person in Germany. The curious investigator of secret things and hidden counsels wrote to this address, obtained full particulars, the true manner of reading the cipher, and, as I conjecture, a sort of commission and jurisdiction from the Unknown Heads in Germany to administer the mysteries in England. And hence arose, or re-arose, in this isle the Order of the Twilight Star. Its original foundation was assigned to the fifteenth century.

I like the story; but there was not one atom of truth in it. The Twilight Star was a stumer—or stumed—to use a very old English word. Its true date of origin was 1880–1885 at earliest. The "Cipher Manuscript" was written on paper that bore the watermark of 1809 in ink that had a faded appearance. But it contained information that could not possibly have been known to any living being in the year 1809, that was not known to any living being till twenty years later. It was, no doubt, a forgery of the early 'eighties. Its originators must have had some knowledge of Freemasonry; but, so ingeniously was this occult fraud "put upon the market" that, to the best of my belief, the flotation remains a mystery to this day. But what an entertaining mystery; and, after all, it did nobody any harm.

It must be said that the evidence of the fraudulent character of the Twilight Star does not rest merely upon the fact that the Cipher Manuscript contained a certain piece of knowledge that was not in existence in the year 1809. Any critical mind, with a tinge of occult reading, should easily have concluded that here was no ancient order from the whole nature and substance of its ritual and doctrine. For ancient rituals, whether orthodox or heterodox, are founded on one *mythos* and on one *mythos* only. They are grouped about some fact, actual or symbolic, as the ritual of Freemasonry is said to have as its centre certain events connected with the building of King Solomon's Temple, and they keep within their limits. But the Twilight Star embraced all mythologies and all mysteries of all races and all ages, and "referred" or "attributed" them to each other and proved that they all came to much the same thing; and that was enough! That was not the ancient frame of mind; it was not even the 1809 frame of mind. But it was very much the eighteen-eighty and later frame of mind.

I must say that I did not seek the Order merely in quest of odd entertainment. As I have stated in the chapter before this, I had experienced strange things—they still appear to me strange—of body, mind, and spirit, and I supposed that the Order, dimly heard of, might give me some light and guidance and leading on these matters. But, as I have noted, I was mistaken; the Twilight Star shed no ray of any kind on my path.

* * *

It was towards the end of 1900 that I perceived that as I had lost sight of the admirable Syon, so Bagdad was wearing badly enough. I have seen from the train the architecture of the "White City" in these recent years. It was never anything at its best, assuredly; never anything save foolishness. Still, lit up on a summer night, with its extravagant towers and walls, pavilions and domes and minarets, with all its fretted and fantastic work, with its still lakes and pouring waterfalls; in those old days before the war I have no doubt that it symbolised joy and enchantment to young and simple hearts. But afterwards, when long neglect had told upon it, when winter rains had wept upon its walls and soot showers had drifted on its pavilions, when the summer suns had scorched its whiteness, and black March winds had torn its feigned embroideries and false ornaments, when many autumn storms had beat upon its plaster battlements and the waterfalls were stilled and the lakes were become obscene pits of slime and rubbish—what an ugly mockery it stood there, an idiot's city fallen into ruin, a scenic fairyland in evil days. So my Bagdad became like the "White City", magic down at heel, its enchantments silly and clumsy tricks, its mystic architecture a shabby sham, its strange encounters, meetings with people who turned out to be bores or worse than bores. You know the story of the fairy gold: at night the man who had had happy commerce with the People of the Hills found himself enriched with boundless and wonderful treasure; but in the morning the marvel of gold had all turned into a heap of dead leaves; such was my case.

And here I am moved to wonder, as I often wonder, whether what we call "fairy tales" do not in fact contain a curious wisdom and the secrets of a very strange and mysterious psychology. Take this old tale of the fairy gold and its transmutation into ugly rubbish, as an example. To most of us it is a tale and nothing more than a tale; without any reason, without any meaning, without any sort of sense or significance in it. We accept it just as a piece of picturesque fancy and nothing more; the turning of the magic gold into leaves was just a happy notion of the unknown and remote individual who made up the story. But suppose that there is something more than this: rather, something quite different from this. I am well aware, of course, of the various explanations of the fairy mythology; the fairies are the gods of the heathen come down in the world: Diana become Titania. Or the fairies are a fantasy on the small, dark people who dwelt in the land and under the land before the coming of the Celts; or they are "elementals", spirits of the four elements: there are all these accounts, and, for all I know, all may be true, each in its measure. But is it possible that there is, now and then, a more hidden and interior sense in some of the tales of the fairyland and the fairies? I am inclined to think that this may be so; that the stories may be—occasionally, not always by any means—the veils of certain rare interior experiences of mankind; experiences, I may say, which are best avoided. The gold faded into dead leaves; it may be more than an idle tale. At any rate, it was a very dismal disenchantment to me when I woke up and found that I was not the Commander of the Faithful, that the fair Circassian was, in fact, a native not of Circassia but of Clapham, that Bagdad was not Bagdad at all, but a London "Exhibition" fallen into very bad repair and urgently in need of tacks and whitewash. The Palace was not habitable; rain was coming in through cracks and rents in the marble that was plaster on the head of him who for a time had been Haroun Alraschid, who now began to suspect that his real style and title was Silly Fool. And then I went on the stage, which is a world of illusion certainly, but of a much less harmful illusion than that of plaster-Bagdad and fairy gold and the hall under the hill.

I have wondered at times why there is no good novel of the stage. But a little consideration shews that there can be no such thing. George Moore wrote long ago a clever book called *A Mummer's Wife*. It is a capital book, and I should think a very faithful impression of a *Cloches de Corneville* touring company in the early 'eighties. I would say of an individual *Cloches de Corneville* company, for the characters strike one as portraits of particular people; there is nothing of the universal about the book, nothing of the essence of the stage life. And it is probably impossible to write the real novel of the stage, for the good reason that the stage is not one but many. In the old days, in the days of the Crummles Company, it would have been easier. The actor of those days was supposed, till he had proved his supreme eminence in one particular line of business, to be capable of all. He was to play *Hamlet*, he was also to go on in the Farce, he was to dance a hornpipe between the acts, he was always to be ready with a song; and, again, unless he were a very eminent actor indeed, he very rarely associated with people beyond the range of the call-boy's voice. The stage in those days was a world apart, and the men and women who trod it a race apart; the actor was a type, just as the sailor of Smollett's day was a type. But all that is long over; it would be very difficult to find a general formula to cover the life of the stage to-day. Commodore Trunnion viewed all existence as a voyage on board one of His Majesty's ships; and I knew a stage-manager who, playing skittles, avowed his determination to bring down "that O.P. skittle"; but the Commodore is dead, and the stage-manager is dying. In fact I should say that the average actor of to-day is far from being gratified when he is recognised as an actor; rather he is inclined to be ashamed of his profession. I remember that as I was talking to two stage friends on a London pavement an old man who was selling laces and studs and such matters in the gutter implored us to buy: "I was an actor once myself, gentlemen." I perceived that my friends were very far from being pleased. I think that the poor old man would have done better if he had said: "I was an officer in the Guards once myself, gentlemen." So, in brief, the actors are no longer the race apart of the old days; they mix with all sorts of people and have, naturally, become very much like all sorts of people. Some of them think that the change is for the better, others disagree. I venture no judgment save this: that they are certainly less picturesque, because less differenced than of old, and thus it is that nobody is likely to do much good with a story of the stage.

 I daresay that few people outside the profession are aware that the old players had a language of their own, or rather a language which they shared with another and a widely different craft. Not merely the technical language of the stage, though that had its curiosities too. For example, I once heard George Alexander at rehearsal say to one of the company: "Too much of the old, Smith, too much of the old!" And Smith, though he had been for many years on the stage, told me afterwards that he had never heard the phrase before, and didn't know what it meant. I knew what it meant, having associated, like Mr. Lillyvick, with members of the theatrical profession in the provincial, that is more or less, the less fortunate grade. "The old" means the melodramatic style of acting, the manner which used to be associated with the name of Barry Sullivan. When an actor said, "I gave them a bit of the old," he meant that he exaggerated somewhat both in his tones and in the business of the scene; in other words, that he made it "big" and "broad".

But this is not the language I mean. Once on a provincial tour I found that the stage-manager had somehow heard of my connection with literature, and was inclined, in consequence, to suspect me a little of being, as we should say now, a "high-brow" and to resent the supposed fact. So I put him through an examination. I asked if he knew what "omees" were, in particular as to the character signified by the phrase "omee of the carser". Then as to the idioms "nunty munjare" and "nunty dinnari" and so on. He broke down badly, but he put away his evil suspicions from that moment; he knew that if I had written books in my day I had turned over a new leaf and had become a reformed character: I knew the curious speech better than he did. It is barbarous Italian, and was the lingo of old-fashioned actors and thieves.

XI

It is a very odd experience to go on the stage at the age of thirty-nine. It is, of course, unpractical, since at that age a man is too old to learn the business properly; but it is a great entertainment. The change was so extreme. I had always lived a very quiet life. I had few friends, few acquaintances. My life was in reading books and in writing them. All my preoccupations were literary. Every morning after breakfast I went over what I had written the night before, correcting here and there and everywhere, generally convinced that the passage which had pleased me so much as I wrote it was, after all, not magnificent. I took the bulldog for a walk from 12 to 1, and another half-hour walk in the afternoon. Then two cups of tea without milk or sugar at 4, and the rigour of the literary game till 7, and again after dinner till 11. It was a life of routine, and all its adventures, difficulties, defeats, and rare triumphs were those of the written page. I did not know a single actor, and had no curiosity as to the actor's life, circumstances, customs, or manners. And then, one afternoon in February, 1901, I found myself stuck up with a number of ladies and gentlemen on a thing like a greenhouse flower-pot stand, and we were all required to express suitable and varied emotions as Shylock appealed for the fulfilment of the bond which Antonio had given him. This was the first thing I had tried to do on the stage, and I believe it was the most difficult. No doubt Mr.—afterwards Sir Frank—Benson was right in saying that it was the only way to learn how to act; but gesture, facial expression, pantomime, the knack of knowing how to be individual and yet to join in effectively with the crowd; all these things are extremely difficult, very much more difficult than the art of speaking an effective line effectively.

But—very likely because the change from my former way of living was so tremendous in every respect—I found the life an enchanting one. Of course I could not have begun under happier auspices; nay, I could not have begun under any auspices half so happy. It has been said, I think, more than once, and said by men far more qualified to speak than I, that if it had not been for the Benson Company, acting as an ordered art, with its technique and tradition, would pretty well have perished out of England. The old stock companies were gone, with their manifold opportunities for learning the actor's craft. The young man who went on the stage probably walked on for six months or a year in a London production, and unless he were an exceptionally bright young fellow he learned very little. Perhaps, if he were lucky, he was promoted from a thinking part to a speaking one and uttered the line: "You don't say so!" every night; but still he learned very little. If he became a good actor under this régime, it was a case of genius triumphing over circumstance. Of course good actors come from everywhere: from the academies, from melodramas travelling in the fit-ups, from the chorus of the musical play, from the ranks of the walkers-on in the long London run; but, as I say, these are cases of greatness overcoming difficulties. But under the training provided by the Benson Company it was a man's fault if he did not learn to act; it was pretty definite proof that there was no acting in his composition. I remember Henry Ainley saying in this very year, 1901: "Well, in the last fortnight I have played twelve different parts, and if that won't teach a man how to act, nothing will." This, I may say, was at the end of the Festival Season at Stratford-on-Avon, a strenuous and a delightful time.

But, as I say, I could have entered on the boards under no happier auspices. There was a constant succession of small parts, so graded with due tenderness both to the beginner and the audience that not much harm could be done by uneasy awkwardness, and much good was certain to be gained by the beginner. For example, I have a suspicion that the whole pack of us on that flower-pot stand in *The Merchant,* all of us beginners, were about as bad as bad can be; but it really signified little. The people in front were looking at Shylock and Portia, not at us; and I don't suppose that our incapacity diminished to any calculable extent the public entertainment. Then in the next piece, *As You,* I was a Forest Lord with a line. I had to say to the Banished Duke: "I'll bring you to him straight," and Oscar Asche took pains to shew me that I must speak it as I moved up stage with my back to the audience; but the fortunes of the play hardly depended on that line, while I was beginning to grow a slight seed of confidence.

And how all this was an utterly different world from anything that I had ever conjectured; I cannot express the gulf that yawned between the old and the new. In the former years I struggled with words and phrases and sentences and shades of meaning implied by them: now I strove to understand how something like an attenuated pigtail could become a highly probable fifteenth-century beard and moustaches in a couple of minutes, when skilled hands were laid upon it. And I was occupied with R.U.E. and L.U.E. and 5 and 8, and how to stand so that you command the stage as F.R.B. instructed me, and the endeavour to take in and profit by the kindly tips and hints and cautions given by the elder members of the company: here was a holiday, indeed, for a man who had tried to tear the secret of literature from the thorn castle where it is concealed, who had torn his hands and his heart sadly enough in the endeavour.

I have mentioned the tips and hints of the Elder Brethren amongst the Bensonians. This was a great part of the discipline and instruction of the course. It was not only what Benson said at rehearsal, it was also what Asche or Rodney or Brydone or Swete said after the rehearsal or after the show, and often what they said was, quite rightly, highly uncomplimentary. I remember when Henry Herbert—"starring" in America now, I believe—was playing in *King John*, it fell to him to pronounce the lines which speak of painting the lily and gilding refined gold. He spoke them, as I thought, with great spirit; but Brydone—dead not long ago—took him apart afterwards and talked to him for half an hour or more as to the grave mistake he had committed.

"You spoke the lines as if they were beautiful poetry," said Brydone, "and, indeed, they are. If you had been reciting them your reading would have been quite right; but not in the scene, on the stage. So-and-so—I have forgotten the name of the part—is raging against King John; he isn't thinking of the poetic beauty of the words he is using."

Now, I do not presume to judge whether Brydone were right or wrong in this criticism; such matters are too high for my small experience as an actor; but consider the enormous value to the beginner of living in such an atmosphere of thought and observation and consideration of the things of the theatre. Herbert may have come eventually to the conclusion that he had been right after all, and that Brydone was wrong; but, anyhow, he had worried the question out and weighed it in his mind, and looked at it and around it; and all that, it seems to me, is the very air in which good craftsmanship is born and nurtured and grows great and flourishes.

And so, apart from these after-confabulations and dressing-room counsels, a rehearsal in the Benson Company has always struck me as a liberal education in the player's art. Benson himself—the "Pa" of the affectionate and reverent remembrance of many hundreds of his grateful sons and scholars—has always been an imaginative poet of a high order; though somehow he has never written any poetry. Instead, he has produced Shakespeare, and perhaps he has chosen the better way. He has illuminated his text admirably, and his way was not to come down to the theatre with the whole scheme of things cut and dried in his head, with every intonation, every bit of business and every position settled immutably beforehand, but rather to approach the play, scene by scene, with a liberal and open spirit. The main conception he doubtless brought with him, but any light he could find in the process of rehearsal he would welcome heartily, no matter whether it came from one of the elder brethren or from the newest member of the company. For example, during the rehearsals of *King John* we had come to the scene wherein the Legate, Pandulph, reconciles the King to Holy Church. I was talking to the Legate at the wings during some brief interval, and ventured very tentatively to describe the symbolical embrace known as the Kiss of Peace as a possibly effective bit of business in the reconciliation scene. The Legate, interested, asked me to shew him how it was done, and we went through the business. But Benson, who seemed to be considering other matters down stage, had noticed what we were about, and he called out: "I like that: we'll do it." And done it was; and I had been a little over two months in the company and on the stage!

And another instance, taken from the same play, of a Bensonian rehearsal of those days. The scene was the discovery of the dead body of Prince Arthur. I had to say:

"What wilt thou do, renowned Faulconbridge,
 Second a villain and a murderer?"

Whereon Hubert furiously interposed:

"Lord Essex, I am none!"

And then I had to draw the cloak away from the corpse and exclaim:

"Who killed this Prince?"

And thereupon a debate arose. Should the words be spoken before the removal of the cloak? Should the cloak be removed before the uttering of the line? Should word and action be simultaneous? The point was discussed with the utmost earnestness, as a matter of vital importance, and I, feeling that I was in mighty deep waters, suggested in all humility that I should speak the words with an indicative gesture and that Hubert should step forward, appalled, and remove the cloak and discover the body of the Prince. But this started another subsidiary debate, and the rehearsal breaking off at this point, Brydone (Hubert) and Frank Rodney (Faulconbridge) were left on the Stratford stage, walking up and down, and wondering, in muttered undertones, whether it would be within the limits of possibility and stage propriety for Hubert to snatch that cloak away. Their faces were grave, earnest, and perplexed. Outside in the sunshine by the Avon I encountered "Pa". He looked at me with a certain waggishness in his eye, as if he suspected bewilderment on my part, and said:

"Well, Mr. Machen, what do you think about it yourself? "

"Indeed, sir," I replied, "I don't venture to have any opinion."

And I meant what I said, for I didn't think then, and I don't think now, that it befits the entered apprentice to express his opinion, or presume to have any opinion, in the presence of past masters.

Now it may be thought that I am "guying" the Company methods in this matter of Prince Arthur's funeral cloak. I am not doing anything of the sort. I only wish I had gone on in the craft, and were now myself entitled to walk up and down the stage, debating just such a point. The matter in itself was, no doubt, small enough: a stage-management in a hurry would have given a ruling and the scene would have proceeded; but under a stage-management in a hurry what would have become of the vivid interest taken in the smallest circumstance of the play by the whole company, from F. R. Benson downward?

And, by the way, I trust I am not giving the impression that the Bensonians of that day were a body of solemn pedants? I have not yet forgotten my admiration, my almost awestruck admiration, at seeing the manner in which the man who was to play King John drank homebrewed ale in a triangular parlour of the Windmill on the afternoon before the production. He drank in the manner of the ancient heroes, and he gave a very good performance at night.

But the Stratford Festival drew to its close. On the last Saturday we were rehearsing in the morning, playing in the afternoon and playing again in the evening. Some time in the course of the day I was told that I was to play Nym in the *Merry Wives* on Monday night at Worcester. I bought the play and looked at the part and got the cuts from the Prompt Book—and I wonder why I didn't drown myself in the Avon after the show as the easiest way out of the difficulty; and if anyone wants to know why, let him read the part of Nym in *The Merry Wives of Windsor,* and ask himself how he would like to learn that queer gibberish and learn how to play it in a couple of days, he having had three months' experience of the stage. But instead of drowning myself in the Avon, I . . . refreshed myself at a famous tavern of the town together with about half the company; and I think we heard the chimes at two o'clock in the morning, and it was reported that old George Weir, on being asked "to write something" in the hostess's book, had written the words: "When my cue comes call me and I will answeir."

And that reminds me: At the Bensonian dinner in the year in which this great actor, George Weir, died, F. R. Benson began his speech. His manner commanded the cessation of applause, and he raised one hand, and held it high, and said:

"This year, one amongst us has answered the summons of the callboy of the stars."

But to return to my small business. On the Sunday we travelled to Worcester, and I spent the rest of the day in a desperate struggle with Nym and "the humour of bread and cheese", and "that's the humour of it", in endeavouring to get into my memory phrases which are not merely old but old-fashioned, for Nym, like Touchstone, discourses for the most part Elizabethan catchwords which, three hundred years before, were "certain of a laugh", which the process of time and fashion has made meaningless, and phrases such as these are very difficult to learn.

But I learned them somehow or other on the Sunday, and the next morning came to the one and only rehearsal. It was not on the stage, more important things were happening there, but in the travellers' samples room of one of the Worcester inns. Of course there was no scenery, no costumes, no "props" of any kind. A few chairs indicated the set, quite sufficiently, I may say, to a man of experience, but dubiously enough to a man of next to no experience. Thus, when it came to my last exit, the Assistant Stage-Manager gave his instructions somewhat as follows:

"After you have said the last words to Page, turn round and go up the flight of steps L.C., here, between these chairs. When you have got to the top, turn again and say to Page, over his shoulder: 'My name is Nym, and Falstaff loves your wife.' Then exit Left along the terrace."

Simplicity itself, to an actor, but somewhat horrifying to a beginner. And then two or three of the principals were not there—they were rehearsing other scenes, very likely, on the stage, and the Prompter's: "Mr. Rodney will come on on that cue from the right upper entrance, where that table is, and you go up to him and meet him Centre and say so and so, and then he speaks the line so and so and you cross to the Right"—with much more to the same effect. And my breath was queer and catchy, even though it was only the rehearsal, and I wondered what my voice and I would be like at night!

Well, I was paralysed with stage-fright. But I got through, somehow; and I hope the Old Woman of the Company, Miss Denvil, as admirable an actress as George Weir was an actor, meant what she said after I had made my Exit Left along the terrace. She smacked me heartily on the back, and said:

"There! I always say the nervous ones are the best!"

So the tour went on, and in the course of it I received an odd bit of promotion. I descended from the flower-pot stand in the Trial Scene of the *Merchant* and became the Clerk of the Court. I think he speaks one line and reads a letter, and that is all. It is hardly to be called a part; if the man who had to do it failed at the last moment the Business Manager or, more likely, his assistant would be summoned and robed in the black habit and the square cap. He would be told the line and given the letter, and that would be all right. It was so small a thing that the man who "played" it was supposed not to care to do so under his own name, so I was either not in the bill at all or else I appeared as "Mr. Walter Plinge", the Mrs. Harris of the Benson Company, who often came in useful on occasions like this, or when there was a case of "doubling". "Plinge" was a name given to a person who kept a tavern frequented by the Company.

And so I was the Clerk of the Court, and solemnly proceeded to consider within myself what a Compleat Clerk of the Court should be like. I determined, firstly, that the boy at the back of the gallery should hear what I said; but this is a general rule—and by no means the least important—which applies to all acting. My second resolution was that a really convincing Clerk would not take the faintest interest in the very emotional procedure which seems to have characterised the strict court of Venice. He would listen to all the pleadings and all the agonies with a stolid countenance. When the Doge spoke of "brassy bosoms" and "hearts of flint" and "gentle answer, Jew" and so forth, the Clerk would become stonier and stonier in his indifference, possibly reflecting inwardly that he had always thought that the appointment was a purely political one, and that now he was sure of it. "Ad captandum arguments", "Old Bailey rhetoric", "Buzfuz on the Bench", "Trying to throw dust in the eyes of the Jew", such phrases, translated, of course, into choice Venetian dialect, might be supposed to flit through the purely legal and formalistic mind of the Clerk. As for the young advocate, whose credentials the Clerk had been obliged to proclaim, well, frankly, the Clerk could not understand how the Doge, politician as he was, could permit such unprofessional rubbish as the "Quality of mercy" speech to be uttered in court at all. "Mountain pines", "wag their high tops", "twice blest", "crowned monarch better than his throne": really, really! What was the Bar coming to? The Clerk's face and attitude have become perfectly stony in their supreme indifference; he might be a thousand miles away.

But! What is that? The Bond bad in law? The Plaintiff debarred from recovering, and not only that, but, *ipso facto,* liable to criminal proceedings of a highly penal character? Now, indeed, the Clerk of the Court is interested. Not that he cares twopence for Antonio or for Shylock either; but there does seem distinctly to be a flaw. The young Advocate must have a technical mind, that greatest of all blessings. The Clerk pricks up his ears, as if he were a terrier advised of the presence of a rat; he is intensely awake; he consults his authorities on the table before him; he is really inclined to think that a highly important point is at issue; he believes that the question, or something very much like it, was raised in the Dogeship of Bragadin, *c.* 1150. At length the Clerk of the Court is all alive.

I thought of all that, and I tried to render it as best I could. And I only mention this trivial nonsense because, to the best of my belief, it is the only instance in which I have found that doing my best and sparing no pains brought me the faintest sort of reward. As a rule, in my experience, the mere fact of taking pains has been rewarded with the malignity of scoundrels and the insults of fools.

But in this extraordinary and, as I must say, miraculous affair it was otherwise. The tour of the Benson Company drew to its close. It was now hot summer and we were playing a *matinée,* I think on the Whitsuntide Bank Holiday, in some theatre on the south side of the river; some theatre which in all probability is now devoted to "the pictures". It was glorious weather, there were few people in the house, and as one of the ladies of the company observed cheerfully in the wings, "People who come to see Shakespeare on an afternoon like this ought to have their noses rubbed in it." Ah, the good, gross gaiety: how few people have as this lady had, and has, the true art of it! Her remark did me a lot of good that languid, heated afternoon in the half-empty theatre; and I believe that the Clerk of the Court—we were playing the *Merchant*—was a shade wearier than usual in his utter boredom and contempt of the whole proceedings: till his moment came.

And a few days later Henry Ainley was saying to me in our dressing-room: "I am engaged by Alexander to play Paolo next year. And, do you know, Alexander said to me: 'You've got a remarkably good actor in your Company; and I couldn't even find his name in the cast. He was playing the Clerk of the Court that afternoon: he was very good indeed.'"

The Great George Alexander to speak thus of the little beginner in his little shadow of a part! Well, I suppose all such taps are vanities; but there was a very happy man that night in the dressing-room, and he plied the spirit-gum and fixed on his beard for the part of the Major-Domo in the *Shrew*—two lines—with trembling, unsteady, rapturous fingers.

A few weeks later I was engaged to play a small part in *Paolo and Francesca,* but that was for the early spring of 1902, and I had to fill in. So I joined a pastoral or open-air company (almost all of whom were Bensonians), and played with them for three weeks. Then I met a friend in the Strand and said "I want a shop," and found myself rehearsing next day the part of a comic Irish servant in a sketch called *The Just Punishment*—an entirely preposterous playlet. We did a fortnight of it—two houses a night—at the Hoxton Varieties and another East-End hall, the name of which I have forgotten. At the Varieties I dressed with a very pleasant black man; the rats ran about the dressing-rooms and passages like kittens. And the audience! There was no question of their being all right till you began to bore them. You made your entrance as the curtain went up, and found the whole house in an uproar. Most of it was light-hearted hilarity, some of it was argument, and they argue very forcibly in Hoxton, occasionally with broken bottles. The actor's business was to drown them, and get them to listen, and amuse them—if he could—and very capital training it was. But the sketch was not booked on—and no wonder—so I went to Mr. Denton's in Maiden Lane. He sent me to Mr. Charles Terry, who was taking out a melodrama called *The Silent Vengeance,* written by Mr. Harry Grattan round the personality of Mr. Silward, that wonderful animal impersonator. From first to last I played three parts in *The Silent Vengeance*—a solicitor, a doctor, and a barber—and it only ran six weeks. But for the last week of the run I had been rehearsing the part of an old actor in the farcical comedy of *The Varsity Belle.* Then at the end of a fortnight, for one reason or another, I had to change this rôle for that of a University Don; and there were over two hundred cues in the first act, and I had only a week for study! The manager was an entirely honest but boorish fellow, and I gave him my notice; "bunged in my notice" would be more idiomatic. The day I left *The Varsity Belle* company I got an engagement from an old Bensonian friend to play for a fortnight or so in Old Comedy down in the western country, and a delightful engagement it turned out. We all knew each other, or very soon got to know each other, and we drank beer and played skittles in tumbledown alleys behind old inns, and brewed bowls of punch, and in spite of these wild practices acted, I think, decently. Poor Ernest Cosham was the Comedian and Mr. Leon Quartermaine played the juvenile leads;

and I hope he has not forgotten a famous game of Blind Hookey in a little inn at Westbury-on-Avon, the only card game that I ever enjoyed. And the morning after our last performance I went up from Andover to town and listened to Stephen Phillips reading his play, *Paolo and Francesca*, to the assembled company. I had been a year on the stage, and I think I had had as varied an experience as falls to the lot of most beginners.

And here there is a great gap. There were other adventures on the stage; but enough, I think, has been said of these things. I have just told of that happy moment of June, 1901, when Henry Ainley repeated to me George Alexander's kindly praise of my acting. And, indeed, that was bliss, but I believe that I received the promise of a happiness that should be deeper and more lasting one morning towards the end of August, 1921. For that morning brought a letter ending my career as a journalist.

Poor George Sampson got into grievous trouble over his innocent speculations as to so innocent a thing as an underpetticoat. I propose, therefore, to say nothing about the craft of journalism, which I followed for many years.

Save only this: *Eduxit me de lacu miseriæ, et de luto fæcis. Et statuit super petram pedes meos: et direxit gressus meos.*

The London Adventure; or, The Art of Wandering

I

There is a certain tavern in the north-western parts of London which is so remote from the tracks of men and so securely hidden that few people have ever suspected its existence. For, in the first place, it is quite off the high roads of the leafy quarter once familiarly known as "the Wood", and then again, the byway in which it is situated does not suggest the presence of any house of public entertainment. Here are modest residences of stucco and grey brick, built for quiet people in the late 'thirties and early 'forties; their front gardens planted with trees of all sorts and varieties before the period when somebody settled that the only tree for London was the plane. Here and there in these gardens there survives an old gnarled thorn, a remnant, I suspect, of the time when "the Wood" was really a wood or a waste. There are no shops in the street, passengers are rare, and the whole region breathes quiet and repose. But far, as I say, from the high road, one of the modest residences displays a sign before its door, and is, in fact, a tavern. It lacks not custom. Jobbing gardeners drink gravely on one side of the establishment, and play games of Dominoes and Darts with the utmost decency; on the other there are some quiet bookmakers, sculptors, poets, and men of letters.

In this pleasant and retired spot I was sitting not long ago, enjoying gin and that great luxury and blessing of idleness, concerning which so much cant and false doctrine have been preached. It is, no doubt, perfectly true that a few men, a very few men, are born into the world to whom a great task has been assigned by the Almighty, and they are to perform this task or fail at their peril. Woe to the prophet who will not prophesy: doubtless. It would have been woe to Turner the painter if, instead of painting, he had devoted all his energies to that queer, disreputable life he led on the riverside by Chelsea, where he was thought to be an odd specimen of the retired mariner. There are the prophets in words and in paint and in other forms who have their work to do and must do it. But, for the rest of us, our "work" is but the curse of Adam, the slavery that we have to endure; about as blessed as oakum-picking and limestone quarrying and treadmill climbing and the other employments of the poor fellows that we call convicts, as if we were not as much convicts as they. We have been convicted of the offence of being born, and the sentence of the Court has been that we shall earn an honest living: an awful and a dreadful doom, if we had the courage to confess it. For, if we see clearly, we shall see that the men we call convicts and criminals have evidently chosen the better part. They have refused to abide the dreadful sentence that was pronounced against them at the moment of their birth. They have revolted, in one way or another, and the plan of things has got hold of them and pronounced a second sentence against them, and enslaved them, as it believes, in a much worse fashion. But the scheme of things is mistaken. It is not a much worse fashion. The convicted criminal is the victim of greater force. He cannot help himself: true: but he has no responsibility for himself or for his actions. He may think oakum-picking a loathsome occupation for a man; still, he is forced to do it, the choice is not his, but that of others. Violent bodily compulsion absolves him from all sense of degradation: if there be anything of the kind it is on the shoulders of those who order his occupations and compel him to follow them.

But this consolation is withheld from those whom cowardice or lack of enterprise or incapacity keeps in the narrow way of what is called honesty. It is, no doubt, sad enough, if you earn your ounces of bread and ounces of meat and ounces of potatoes by compliance with the strict demands of the warders and the Governor of the gaol, but it is surely much worse when the said ounces—that is livelihood—are purchased by shameful insincerities and smooth compliance. There are men—many of them—whose life it is to be shamed and insulted on Monday and then to be the good companions of the oppressor on Tuesday—lest they lose their living on Wednesday. There was once a very eminent journalist of Carmelite House. He was not only the distinguished servant but the friend of the late Lord Northcliffe, and he thought, no doubt, that he could make a personal and confidential appeal to the beloved "chief". And so John Robinson wrote to the effect that times were hard, that the income-tax on a bachelor was heavy—

and could his old friend increase his salary by a little?

He had his reply. It was posted up on the wall of some Common Room of the *Daily Mail,* for everybody, down to the office boy, to see. It ran somewhat to this effect.

"John Robinson asks me to increase his salary. He says that, as a bachelor, he is very heavily taxed. I would point out to John that he can easily remedy this part of his troubles by marrying one of my pretty typists on *The Times*."

I never heard that John Robinson beat the wretch who perpetrated this infamy. I think he remained in the service of Carmelite House. Probably, John shrugged his shoulders and said to himself, "A man has got to get a living." But he could have picked pockets, he could have become a burglar, a confidence trickster, a three-card man on a race train. There were many courses open to John; and if he had been caught and convicted he could have got a living in gaol by picking oakum—and held up his head. In gaol you have to obey the rules and the warders: hard rules and hard men. Still, that is the game that has to be played in gaol; there is no shame in it.

Hence, I say, my profound contempt for all those who praise "work" and the ways of honest living, which are, mostly, degradations somewhat below those experienced by the procurer of Soho. Hence, my profound gratitude for the bliss of idleness, for the happy state in which you survey the universe, somewhat in the manner of Socrates, who, so far as I remember, never did an honest day's work in his life, and made a very fine end. And, in this spirit, I was relishing the savours of things in general, thanking Heaven that I was at last, after long years, an idler once more, and sipping my gin and water, when a man entered the retired tavern which I have endeavoured to describe. He sat down opposite to me. His manner was threatening. He said in a very meaning tone:

"The leaves are beginning to come out"—and looked hard at me as he said it.

I shuddered. I was very much in the condition of the Young Man in Spectacles—some of my readers may know whom I mean—when he was suddenly accosted in the public-house by the emissary of Lipsius.

"At the first touch of the hand on his arm the unfortunate man had wheeled

round as if spun on a pivot and shrank back with a low, piteous cry, as if some beast were caught in the toils. The blood fled away from the wretch's face, etc. etc."

So I. I knew what that man meant. I had told him some months before that I was to write a book about London, that it was to be a really great book, this time. But, I explained, I was not going to begin writing it till the leaves were out on the trees, since the green leafage of the boughs made such a marvellous contrast with the grim greyness of the streets; of the streets of which I meant to write: unknown, unvisited squares in Islington, dreary byways in Holloway, places traversed by railway arches and viaducts in the regions of Camden Town.

And well I remember adding how once I had some mission to execute in waste portions of the world down beyond the Surrey Docks. I took an omnibus at the other end of London Bridge and went, I think, by way of Tooley Street, into something unshapen that I had never visited before; into places that might have been the behind the scenes of the universe; bearing, indeed, much the same relation to the ordinary London view as do the back of the backcloth and the backs of the wings to the gay set that the audience admires from the stalls. Everything was shapeless, unmeaning, dreary, dismal beyond words; it was as if one were journeying past the back wall of the everlasting backyard. Then a street of grey brick with stucco mouldings, not much gayer than the blank walls; and lo! from the area of one of the sad houses there arose a great glossy billow of the most vivid green surging up from the area pavement half-way the height of the ground floor windows; a veritable verdant mountain, as blessed as any wells and palm trees in the midst of an African desert. It was a fig tree that had somehow contrived to flourish in this arid waste; but to me a miracle and a delight as well as a fig tree.

Well; this was to be the kind of adventure out of which I had agreed to make a book; and thus it was that I had talked of waiting till the time of the opening of the leaves before I began it; and thus I shuddered when my friend came into the retired tavern and reminded me that the trees were indeed putting on their green and that so it was time for me to set about my task. Always, or almost always, I have had the horror of beginning a new book. I have burnt my fingers to the bone again and again in the last forty years and I dread the fire of literature. I know what will happen to me, just as the little boy knows what will happen to him when the dear old Head says: "Come to my room after morning school."

However, there was no help for it. The book was to be written; and I bowed my head before the message of the tavern; having, indeed, a very special reverence, almost an unreasoning awe, of signs and intimations given in odd ways in unexpected fashions, in places and surroundings which are generally accounted unreverend enough. In a former book I have described with some minuteness and—may I add—with absolute veracity what strange things I once experienced in chambers in Gray's Inn, in forsaken Rosebery Avenue, in all sorts of down-at-heel and shabby quarters of London; and I have never forgotten my almost incredulous amazement when I found out, seven years afterwards, that some of these experiences of mine had also been experiences of the monks of St. Columba's congregation at Iona in the sixth century—I think it was the sixth—of our era. But so corrupt and bewildered is our nature; on the one hand inclined to the crudest, most bestial materialism, to the simple, easy, natural explanation of all wonders, all miracles; on the other, so sickened with sham marvels, with pantomime-chorus fairies on photographic plates, with ghosts that gibber indeed in the vulgarest, silliest manner possible; so bewildered are we, I say, between these two sides that we hardly dare to testify to the things which we have actually known, seen, experienced with our own senses and our own souls, if these experiences go beyond the limits laid down in some twopenny "science" text-book. The ancients never found America because their "science" told them that when you once passed the Pillars of Hercules the air became full of feathers; and so we fail to discover a better world than America because we cannot find it in our manuals of chemistry, biology, or physiology.

De me fabula; but I do my best to conquer this "scientific" nonsense; and so, as I have noted, I try to reverence the signs, omens, messages that are delivered in queer ways and queer places, not in the least according to the plans laid down either by the theologians or the men of science. I shall never forget how one such message came to me of a dreadful afternoon some two and a half years ago; to the best of my belief in the January of 1921. I was sitting in a subterranean chamber of a tavern not far removed from that thoroughfare which Sir Philip Gibbs has styled so agreeably—and truthfully, I am sure—the Street of Adventure. It was just beginning to dawn on me after some weeks of doubt and wondering incredulity that I was in the power of certain people who had made up their minds for some unknown reason to subject me to the most shameful and humiliating mortifications that can be conceived.

At all events; here was I on this January afternoon of 1921, sitting at my table in the tavern room, quite overwhelmed with misery and despair. I am a married man, I may say; and so bound by certain just considerations of responsibility. I was not free to throw the money of these people into their collective faces, and then go forth to thieve or forge or rob blind men's dogs, or—in point of fact—to get a small living in a comparatively decent manner. I was to live on and keep those who depended on me by a prostitution of the soul, compared with which the prostitution of the body is a little thing. I was to lick spittle from the office floor. The office boys, the inferior hangers-on and servants of a great newspaper were to know all about it and to jeer at me as I went in and out and passed along the accursed corridors. I was to be pitied by the kindly lad who attended to the telephone, smiled at by the young man who ran the editor's errands. And the only hopeful end to this purgatory was in itself doom. After I had been tormented sufficiently I should be dismissed: and that meant ruin for my wife and children.

Ah; if one only had the courage to be truly wise! True wisdom is in the keeping of the saints—I am not confusing the saints with the bishops who are ready to die on the doorstep of the House of Lords if Marylebone people can get a glass of beer after 10 p.m., or with the ecclesiastics of all grades who have proclaimed their solidarity with the Labour Party. But the wisdom of the saints would have directed me that now the supreme chance of my life had come; that, here and now, to a wretched Fleet Street reporter, there was offered an opportunity for which many aureoled and glorious ones had sighed in vain. *Ama nesciri et pro nihilo reputari:* so spoke St. Thomas à Kempis, and he was writing to monks, and was probably thinking of the set mortifications of the monastery, of the schemes by which Baronius was wont to be discovered washing dishes when great princes came from afar to the Oratory to see him. But here was the real thing: the true mortifications that burned and scorched to the very marrow, to the inner heart; the most exquisite joy to the wise, to those that truly know the Gate and the Way. Here was the Shut Palace of the King laid open, here appeared the Bride in the Banqueting House, here from the Engendering of the Crow rose the Son Blest of the Fire. I could almost hear the song of those that feast within:

> *O pius, O bonus, O placidus sonus, hymnus eorum.*

But, alas, I was very far from wise. I sat at my table and ate and drank with a sick heart, with horror and despair very heavy at my heart, that January afternoon. And suddenly a man stood before me and said:

"Ah say, mister, could ya tell me how to spell *exaltavit*. Ma friend and I have been arguing about it, and we thowt ya might be able to tell us: ya seem to be as intelligent looking as anybody here. Ya know the words, ah daresay: *Deposuit potentes de sede, et exaltavit humiles*. Ma friend will have it that there's an 's' in 'exaltavit,' but I say 'no'."

I answered this not very difficult question to the best of my ability, and sat wondering. I think the gentleman stood me a drink in gratitude for the profound scholarship which had confirmed his position, and that we chatted, his friend, himself, and I, for ten minutes or so on indifferent subjects. Then we went on our several ways: I, if I remember rightly, to interview a gentleman of no particular consequence, living at the other end of nowhere, on a matter quite devoid of interest. But I had those words sounding in my ears all the while: *et exaltavit humiles*. I wondered; and again heard, *et exaltavit humiles*. And then I began to hope a little, to lift up a little corner of the black curtain of despair: *et exaltavit humiles*.

Now, to put an end at once to all false mysteries and mystifications: I may say that I got to know the man who had come up to me in the tavern fairly well. The only real mystery about him was his pronunciation of the Latin words: he said "exaltahvit" not "exaltehvit", and I have often wondered how he came by these true church tones. He was a man from the provinces, as I have indicated, and was following in London, not very successfully, some byway of commercial journalism, trying to get advertisements, we will say, for the *Basket Makers' Gazette*. He was, I should think, a very good and kindly fellow. We used to meet, for a year or more, at pretty frequent intervals, in the underground room of the tavern and talk about things over our tankards; chiefly, if I remember, about a patent penknife that Mr. Harrison wished to put on the market. When I last saw him, he told me that he had got a new job and "stood to be lucky"; and very glad I was to hear it. He was one of the two or three of the messengers that I have met in my life, and I never think of them without great wonder, awe, and reverence. Not in any personal way: when one hears Mass one does not want to know who or what the priest is, whether he is a good judge of poetry or, unfortunately, ill-tempered and over-fond of garlic. He is clothed in the vestments of his office, his gestures are not his own, he speaks words assigned to him from afar.

I asked Mr. Harrison the second or third time of our meeting as to his interest in a verse of the *Magnificat*. I found that his source was not the Breviary, but some poem of Longfellow's about Robert of Sicily; and—I am not quite sure—but I think that a possible cinema picture was in the background of these enquiries. But these words: *et exaltavit humiles*, sounded still in my heart—till they came true.

With due reserves and exceptions. For I was not *humilis*; or I would have taken the way of the true wisdom which I have indicated above; the way of those who rejoice in the sharpest mortifications, and are only glad when they are utterly despised. I was certainly not *humilis*, but I was certainly *humiliatus*; and the good God is content with a little when He cannot get all. He remembereth "that we are but dust"; and as Father Stanton said, commenting on this text: "You can't expect very much from dust." And as to the *exaltavit*: I think that I still recognise my old friends when I meet them in the street, my exaltation simply consisting in the fact that, so far, I have been permitted to live in a very modest way without swallowing an insult with every crust and excrement with every cup: and that is enough of exaltation for me, and bliss indeed, such as I never hoped to gain on that dreary January afternoon of 1921, when the plain man asked me how I would spell *exaltavit*.

It was just a coincidence? It may be so; and I am too keenly aware of the dangers and follies of credulity to deny that it may have been so. Yet, I am a practical man above all things, and coincidence or no coincidence, I know that I was comforted and sustained and enabled by that word through many months of horrible and shameful suffering. And, on the whole, I am really inclined to believe that this is the way in which things are done; that the betting man who backs "Black Boy" for the big race because he has seen a small negro the day before is not so wildly foolish after all. It is possible, just dimly possible, that the real pattern and scheme of life is not in the least apparent on the outward surface of things, which is the world of common sense, and rationalism, and reasoned deductions; but rather lurks, half hidden, only apparent in certain rare lights, and then only to the prepared eye; a secret pattern, an ornament which seems to have but little relation or none at all to the obvious scheme of the universe. Sometimes, in talking to my friends the Spiritualists, I urge on them that one reason for my disbelief in their message is my conviction that the two levels of life, the life here and the life of the world to come, are so utterly distinct. I have read, or rather dipped into, so many books which represent the spirits and souls of the dead as simply continuing their life in this world under conditions which are practically reproductions. The young man who on earth was interested in the affairs of the Mount Zion Chapel (Particular Baptist), Beulah Road, Tooting Bec, is still vividly interested in the pious activities of the old congregation. He communicates with his poor father to that effect: nay, he carries on the old controversies, and points out that Deacon Plinge is, no doubt, convinced by this time as to his error in holding that Moses had the Promise. Nay, if the people on my side went in for these odd orgies, I am sure that it would be just the same. We should have messages about the *Epiclesis* and the *Jube perferri* and the Ancient Liturgical Use of Incense in the Canon, and the superior spirituality of the Roman (or the Sarum) Rite, and so forth and so forth; not to say anything of the Unitarian doctrine obtained through the mediumship of the wonderful Mrs. Pipps, of Jamaica Plain, Mass., U.S.A. Frankly, I believe in not one single word of it all; and not on any pretence of any logical grounds, for what has logic to say of these matters? What would logic have had to say to the X-Ray hypothesis before it was proven? What would logic have to say to a passage which I wrote (in "The Great God Pan") in the year 1890? Here it is:

"Suppose that an electrician of to-day were suddenly to perceive that he and his friends have merely been playing with pebbles and mistaking them for the foundations of the world; suppose that such a man saw uttermost space lie open before the current, and words of men flash forth to the sun and beyond the sun into the systems beyond, and the voices of articulate-speaking men echo in the waste void that bounds our thought."

Well; so far as we know, it has not quite come to that yet. I remember that once, to my rage and shame and mortification, when I was a reporter, I had to take a taxi in a vast hurry and post off to Greenwich Observatory to ask the Astronomer Royal whether he thought that the Cavaliere Marconi was really receiving messages from Mars. It has not quite come to that yet; but it seems to me that the passage from "The Great God Pan" is a distinct prophecy of "Wireless"; and what would logic have said to it, in 1890, when that chapter was written? I use the word "logic", I may say, in the popular sense, well aware that it is an utterly erroneous one; but as friendly charwomen say when discussing these points, or deeper ones, "you know what I mean". Everything is a miracle before it happens: the reasoning faculties have nothing to say in the presence of the unknown. And it is an odd thing, by the way, that certain propositions which forty years ago would have moved the "scientific" people to mad mirth, which are now commonplaces of everyday demonstration, would have been heard with interest and respect, if not with instant acquiescence, in the early seventeenth century. If a learned German, bearing a name horribly Latinised, had published a treatise in 1615 or thereabouts, shewing how there was an art by which the words of a man speaking in Nuremberg might be heard, instantly, in Grand Cairo, nobody would have laughed. The matter would have been discussed: the old Aristotelians would have brought their abstract principles to bear upon it; the new Baconian school, I think, would have denied the possibility of such a thing; the Paracelsists and the Rosicrucians would have said that it was highly probable that such an art existed. But the proposition would have been discussed seriously. But; if the lady sitting next to Huxley at an 1870 dinner table had hinted at the possibility of such an achievement, that most amiable and excellent man would have sipped his claret and looked whimsical; wondering who had put such wild nonsense into a pretty woman's head. We know now that he would have been wrong; and, really, it is not a very profound axiom: we know nothing of matters concerning which we know nothing. And so this applies to the ghostly world—always allowing that there is any such world. What do we know? For all we can say, poor Raymond Lodge and his companions may still be sipping those synthetic whiskies-and-sodas and ætherised cigars by the gates of the New Jerusalem. Who is bold enough to say that it cannot be? Not I: but I am bold enough to say that it is not so.

For; I firmly believe that the two worlds have that gulf between them, that *magnum chaos,* which yawns, let us say, between painting and music. You may make analogies between the two arts; you can talk of the "colour" of this composition or that, just as you may talk of the "colour" of words: but, at last literature, music, painting remain worlds apart. So, I humbly venture to believe, it may be with respect to our life here and our life hereafter. There are relations between the two; just as there are relations between the life of an actor on the stage and off the stage. But the man who plays the Fool in *Lear* admirably, is not rewarded by instant promotion to the crown of Britain in place of Lear or King George (whom God preserve!). He has his reward: but it is after a different mode. It may run to a flat in one of the best parts of the West End, a charming old house on Romney Marsh, a French cook of admirable skill, the society of dukes, to the means of bestowing excellent and ample charity or—to anything, indeed, but not to anything connected with the antique Britain of King Lear. The two worlds are related and yet utterly apart; and so, perhaps, it is with us, and our two worlds; this world, and the world to come.

For, if we think of it, the antique Britain of Shakespeare's play is more than non-existent. It doesn't exist now; but it never has existed. It was first an old tradition, an ancient tale told about friendly winter fires on the mountains of wild Wales. It became a printed legend; a bit of pseudo-history: at last it grew into one of the many vast, enchanted dreams of the greatest master of letters. And so at last Smith plays the Fool in the magnificent West End production of *King Lear* and plays so well that he founds his fortune and can be sure of his two hundred a week or more and all that is implied therein—but not of the pettiest piece of promotion in the Britain of King Lear. And so, perhaps, it may turn out that this world of ours is but one of the dreams of the Supreme Artist. The moon in the sky may be just such an illusion as the moon which the master-electrician causes to rise so convincingly over the dusky garden. The storms of life—hailstorms and fire-showers as Carlyle called them—which beat upon us with such savage fury may, in reality, hurt us just as much as they hurt the actors who are playing Lear and Kent and the Fool in Act III, Scenes 1 and 2.

"Blow, winds, and crack your cheeks! rage! blow!"

and the rest of it: but you will not find these good fellows any the worse for the storm in the dressing-room a little later, or unable to relish their supper at the Garrick or the Green Room a little later still. For, you see, there was no storm; and so, likely enough, with us; there is no storm, and stage lightning cannot hurt anybody. Though, of course—to keep up the analogy—the quality of the meat and drink afterwards, when the stage-manager has rung down and the stage is dark may depend entirely on the skill with which we played our parts on the Heath, amidst all those sulphurous and thought-executing fires.

It is this sense, then, of the probable order of things at large that disinclines me to listen to the amiable Conandoylery that is now in such fashion in certain quarters. And, at the same time, it inclines me to believe that very high messengers—in the play, in the mystery which we are enacting—may be quite ordinary fellows in private life, or "off", as the actors would say. How very absurd it would be, if one of the Traitors in *Henry V* on being told by the King to get him gone, poor miserable wretch, unto his doom, were to reply: "I shall do nothing of the kind. You must have had onions with your tea to-night, and your collar was thick with grease-paint on Derby platform last Sunday; so on the whole I prefer to stay where I am." These very serious accusations may be perfectly well grounded; but they are impertinent in the proper sense of the word. It is not for us to laugh at the message, because the messengers don't wear their dalmatics in Fleet Street taverns or shew a glory about them. Indeed, if one thinks of it, such a course would attract an undesirable amount of attention.

This has been a little digression—I am afraid that there may be one or two more little digressions in the course of this work—designed to shew that one should hear and weigh all sorts of messages delivered in all sorts of places. And so I attended with respect and awe to the message that came to me in the tavern in "the Wood" this spring:

"The leaves are beginning to come out."

II

I think I have described myself as shuddering, in the Young Man in Spectacles manner, when I received the message about the coming forth of the leaves. But, really, I do not know why I should have shuddered. I had chosen the scheme for the book that was to be written myself; and I must still pronounce it to be a most excellent scheme. Moreover, I had thought of an excellent title. I was to call my book *The London Adventure*. It was only the other day that I thought I had found out that another man had used this title two or three years before me. *Pereant illi qui ante nos nostra dixerunt.* For I cannot part with my beloved Latin tags, as dark with antiquity and as well-worn as old farmhouse furniture. I love a friendly tag and shall continue to do so, in spite of a stern judge, "D.F.G.", who wrote about another book of mine in the *Boston Evening Transcript*:

"The whole book (*Things Near and Far*) shows the reflections of a conceited man of mediocre ability, who buries his talent in the ashes of the past, mumbles over it incessant Latin quotations, pats himself on the back because he knows so much Latin to quote and then—is continually irritated because the world hurries by without digging into the ashes, or listening respectfully to his incantations."

In spite of this grave man I shall continue to mumble: though I wish that the tags were not dropping one by one out of my memory; though I wish that I had still the profound Latin scholarship that I possessed as a small boy in the Lower Fourth at Hereford Cathedral School in 1875; when I could grapple with any question relating to *Mensa*, or even, if you liked to push matters to extremities, would run through *amo* with any man alive.

But as to this plan of mine, that was to turn into a book to be called *The London Adventure*. It originated in old rambles about London, rambles that began in 1890 when I lived in Soho Street and began to stroll about Soho and to see that here was something very curious and impressive; this transmutation of late seventeenth-century and early eighteenth-century social solidity and even, in some cases, magnificence, into a wholly different order. You turned down this street or that or the other, and you saw, at the foot of it, let us say, a house that had evidently stood in its day for something and somewhat. In the balance of its windows, flush with the walls, there was a certain symmetry and simplicity; and so about the doorway, its approach of steps, its pillars and its pediment. True; the matter was London brick, but here you could see the survival of the antique classic tradition, worthily embodied, though not in Parian marble. Here, you could say, once lived a man who played a great part in a great world, whose wig fell great about his shoulders, who sometimes wore a blue ribbon across his deep gold-laced waistcoat when he went abroad. Or perhaps an Ambassador: a Venier, representing the Most Serene Republic of Venice? But his Embassy was in Soho Square, opposite Mrs. Cornely's establishment. Here, at all events, was an ancient and a dignified house, dim with age; and you drew near and found that it had become? Perhaps a Pickle Factory, perhaps a Lithographic Printer's works, perhaps brass labels under half a dozen bells told of as many crafts plied within, or perhaps it was like the Soho house where Newman Noggs lived: a camping ground for poor people, a place where almost every room sheltered a family. Now all this interested me, and so I poked about and mooned about in Soho instead of doing honest work, and speculated as to its narrow alleys and its archways and houses, and its sudden alarums and excursions. For I remember going down Greek Street on a summer afternoon; instantly, without any reason that I could see, a crowd began to pour and buzz from all backways and hidden places and to gather in front of a house which looked as if it had been built for a Doctor of Divinity, *c.* 1720. Then people came down from the doorstep carrying queer objects with them which they bundled into a four-wheeler, and the crowd hummed with delight.

"Pore things," I heard a stout lady say to a stouter friend—both came straight out of Phiz's illustration of Kingsgate Street in *Martin Chuzzlewit*—"pore things: I daresay if the truth was known they only did it for the sake of their wives and families."

And then three or four men were brought out and bundled into another cab, and both cabs drove off. The crowd lounged away, with an expression that seemed to say that there would be a rarer smack about the gin than was common. I went into the post office—I think, but I am not sure, that the golden arm and hammer of the goldbeaters hung over it—and bought some stamps. The postmistress wore ringlets and black silk. She looked as if she had lived all her days in Uttoxeter, Tutbury, Tewkesbury, or Shaftesbury. And yet as she discussed the raid on the German waiters' gambling club—that was what I had seen—there was a certain complacency in her voice, a certain twinkle of a smile on her face, as she said severely:

"Really! This neighbourhood is getting too dreadful!"

I believe, in her very heart, she was proud of Greek Street, Soho. At all events things happened there.

Such were the beginnings and first elements of my London science, unless I were to take account of earlier wanderings in the 'eighties, when I roamed out north and west and saw the red brick villas and streets of shops gaining on the quiet fields and old lanes overhung with trees that then made a veritable countryside within ten minutes of Acton. But in writing this book of mine I was to dip rather into the later years; into the 1895–99 period when I first found out the wonders that lie to the eastward of the Gray's Inn Road, when Islington and Barnsbury and Canonbury were discovered, when Pentonville ceased to be a mere geographical expression. And there was a later time still that was to yield fresh fruit; the days when I ran errands that were often in themselves of inconceivable folly, but led me all the same into queer outland territories that otherwise I should never have seen. I remember once that in the war days I was told to go to Enfield and taste the newly brewed Government ale—some horrible teetotal concoction of those bad times. I had got the names of the taverns where this choice beverage was to be enjoyed, and I took train to Enfield from York Road, King's Cross. Outside Enfield Station I enquired for the public-houses on my list, and was met by the flat information that they were all of them about four miles away; they were not at Enfield at all, but at Enfield Lock. By some complicated process of tram and 'bus and walking I reached the Lock, and found that no one of my pubs knew anything whatever about the new drink, and so my journey was somewhat of a failure. But it was not a failure for me. I had passed through such unsuspected countries in my voyage and travel from Enfield through Enfield Wash to Enfield Lock, through fragments of market garden and fragments of wild thicket, by sudden apparitions of grey houses built in the early 'sixties when it had dawned upon the mind of some madman that the day of the Wash was at hand and that the time for "development" had come. These houses appeared with an awful unexpectedness; these settlements, of, say, half a dozen houses calling themselves Highsounding Terrace, 1860, manifestly supposing themselves in the first place to be but the nucleus of a whole town of thronging streets, and now standing up a grey island in the desolations of the Wash; waste lands and raspberry bushes and cabbages all about them. And now and again there would be a corner shop: a fortune was no doubt to be realised by the bold adventurer who would wait a few months, and then be ready to supply the thronging thousands with pickles, tea, cooked meat, and candles: here was the shop ready at the corner, prepared, at the point of vantage. Alas! there was a corner, but nothing but a corner; nothing but sodden fields all around. And then, again, a little onward a remnant of much older days: a Georgian mansion, of the seventeen-seventies or thereabouts, built of grey brick with plaster decorations in the manner of the brothers Adam; with its wall about it and its pillars adorned with grave urns at the entrance gate. There a substantial man, maybe an Alderman, had once lived; now, everything was falling down, broken, discoloured, desolate, uninhabited. And the next turn, very likely, would shew a very recent error. In 1900, perhaps even in 1910, a modern optimist had arisen and had convinced himself that a vast industrial population must soon be established in the land. He had built a bright red shop and there was a Butcher found to come and open it; but I cannot conjecture as to where his customers lived. Their houses were not in sight. And so forth and so on. And while I journeyed back to the office, I felt that I had been enjoying a rich and various experience.

And here let me point out that the point of view is totally removed from the ordinary tourist, guide-book point of view. I hope I am not without a due sense of the historic and literary interests of London, with which the guide and the guide-book are very properly occupied. I have my relish for the Temple and the Tower, St. Bartholomew's Church, Staple Inn, for the remnants of the Marshalsea; and it is a keen relish, too. But that is quite a different matter. That is partly a matter of literary and historical association, of the love of antiquity for its own sake; a curiously compounded pleasure. And I have remarked that the more noble, terrible, notorious the associations called up, the less I am moved, in my heart of hearts. Honestly, I have grave difficulties over Westminster Abbey, for example. Perhaps, because the Abbey has been the text for so many discourses, because it is one of the great commonplaces of England, and because *difficile est proprie communia dicere*. Perhaps, also, because, as I believe, the surfaces of its stones are not really old English but early Victorian, so that one gazes rather at an image and spectre of a church than at the very church itself. In a sense, therefore, Westminster Abbey is a sham antique; whereas the old Bell Inn in Holborn was a true antique, as the George in Southwark still is.

But, I confess that this love of antiquity for its own sake, apart from any particular literary or historical associations, has always been a great puzzle to me and still remains so. That high, grim wall of the Marshalsea, for example. I do not suppose that it is by any means of great antiquity; it is certainly not beautiful; but perhaps one may justify one's interest in looking at it by the plea of "Little Dorrit"—who never existed. And, by the way, why should we be interested in places more or less connected with the fortunes of people who never existed, outside the brains and the pages of the romancers? I do not know why we are thus interested, but I know that we are so and that this interest constitutes one of the gentlest of the pleasures of life. I confess, frankly, that when I go to Tower Hill I think much more of the residence of Mr. and Mrs. Quilp in that quarter than of the tremendous and awful events that happened there in stern fact. The dreadful end of actual traitors moves me much less than the thought of that "mixed tea, new bread, fresh butter, shrimps, and water-cresses" which were consumed with such a relish by the creatures of Dickens's brain, in the shady, lazy room with a view of the old Tower. So it is; and here, it seems to me, is one of the minor enigmas of life. There never was a Mrs. Quilp, she didn't live on Tower Hill and she never gave a tea-party in the room which she never occupied: what a wonder it is that all this fiction should be so much more impressive—to some minds—than solid and majestic fact. For me, Anne Boleyn, Lady Jane Grey, and all the "traitors" who passed into the Tower and perished awfully there are as mere shadows compared with Mr. Quilp, Mrs. Quilp, and that most engaging old lady, Mrs. Jiniwin. Perhaps, the explanation may be that the historic people are actual people, creatures of fact not of fancy; and that fancy is infinitely more impressive than fact, partaking, as it does, not of actuality, but of reality. In a certain sense, it is probable that Mr. Micawber is more real than any of us, infinitely more real than Dickens's own father, of whom he is understood to be a glorified projection. I once asked a Sheffield man if he would be so good as to give me a definition of steel. "Certainly," said he. "Steel is simply iron freed from all the other substances which are found associated with it." We are all of us associated with "other substances"; it is only the beings of true literature who are pure and without alloy, since their essences are simple and immortal.

But to return to the—more or less—chief topic of this discussion: the book that I was to write, the book to be called *The London Adventure,* was not to deal in the main with the historical or literary associations of London, nor even with antiquity as such, though sometimes antiquity would form part of the queer pattern that I had in my mind. For instance: the grey Georgian house with its solemn urns and mouldering ornaments fell into its place in the story of the journey from Enfield to Enfield Lock: but not from the artistic or antiquarian standpoint. It was part of the general queerness; a piece, a *tessera,* that fitted in very pleasantly with that hopeless 1860 terrace and that desolate 1900 shop, and the cabbages, and the raspberry plantations and, above all and before all, with the sense that I had never been that way before, that the scene to me was absolutely new and unknown, as if the African Magician had suddenly set me down in the midst of Cathay, that I was as true an explorer as Columbus, as he who stood upon a peak in Darien. For if you think of it: the fact that the region which is to you so strange and unknown is familiar as daily bread and butter or—more likely—the lack of it to multitudes of your fellow-men is of no significance on earth. I think that the first land that Columbus saw when he had made his incredible adventure of the Atlantic was one of the West India Islands. Well: you can imagine how awfully and splendidly that dimness on the verge of the sea struck upon his soul: but it was common enough, I suppose, to the Carib Indians who lived on it; and to the Mexicans and Peruvians and the other tribes their course of life was as natural, accustomed, and uninteresting as an At Home in South Kensington or a Chapel Tea in Dorchester are to the inhabitants of those agreeable regions. Montezuma, if I remember, and I remember these things very vaguely, had a special robe or headdress of feathers of some extremely rare bird. Very likely; but in itself that is no more amazing than the feather stoles which ladies carry now, no more wonderful in itself than the miniature of my grandfather, the Vicar of Caerleon, which my grandmother wore as a brooch. In Mexico you wore a feather robe; in Caerleon you wore black silk and a painted likeness of your husband as a fastening to it; in Peru the Government accounts were kept on strings with knots on them; in England they were kept, till recent days, on bits of stick with notches on them. It seems clear to me that nothing exists vitally, that is, as an object of wonder, surmise, awe, exultation, or mirth in itself. I write with all submission to Holy Church; but it appears that in the world of profane things, at all events, there are no sacraments *ex opere operato*. Are we not all in the same boat? I have just been listening to the *Agnus Dei* from Bach's great Mass in B Minor. I am assured, on the best authority, that it is magnificent: to me it is a disagreeable noise. Voltaire thought the works of Shakespeare a form of mania; Smollett, a very acute man, had exactly the same opinion of York Minster—he said it was a pity they did not build a "neat Grecian room" in place of the Cathedral; and a French gentleman of my acquaintance told me how he had once eaten roast lamb with "sauce menthe". "Je n'aimais pas ça," he said, with eloquent simplicity, meaning, I am sure, that he found the combination barbarous and disgusting; as I should find the Christmas dish of Germany, carp boiled in beer, disgusting and barbarous. It seems, then, I say, that nothing in the natural order is of itself, or absolutely; that to A. a little stucco villa of 1830 with a green verandah and a green latticed porch will give more pleasure than St. Paul's or Canterbury Cathedral affords to B.—just as Mrs. Quilp and her friends do me much more good than Anne Boleyn and *her* friends. And I confess that this conclusion tends to persuade me very strongly in favour of a former argument: that the storms of life are no more real than the storms of the stage, which depend on "Props". King Lear is not in the least dead: he is enjoying a mixed grill at his club. The Duke who had his eyes put out can see perfectly well and is regulating the admixture of soda and "spot" with clear and admirable vision. The play is a play indeed; but it is a play within a play, which we call life, which is also unreal, though after a different mode of being. And so I say that there is no such entity as the thing in itself, there is no absolute existence in things seen; and, against my own feelings, that even the rawest, reddest modern suburb, with those shops that are the same everywhere, with those villas that are the same everywhere, with that terrible, victorious invasion of green woods and peaceful lawns—more awful in a way, perhaps, than the German invasion of France—that even these vile, red stones may be transmuted into living, philosophical stones; as Robertus de Fluctibus has it. Here, if you will, even in these places, you can conjecture the sighs of the victim, the rapture of the priest; here the mysteries are celebrated, even as in Eleusis; the ritual is duly performed, though those who officiate are ignorant of the secrets in which they, nevertheless, share. I have always thought it a singular and curious thing that Freemasonry—in its essentials a most ancient rite—should still exist among us and exist vigorously, and be a high, important, respectable institution, patronised by Royalty, the right thing to belong to, as fine a thing in its way as the Church of England, by law established. The Freemasonry of to-day has, of course, been "reformed" like the other institution which I have mentioned; nobody, perhaps, quite knows what happened to it in the early 'twenties of the eighteenth century. Many things were removed, many things obscured; still the heart of the mystery remained, and remains still. And no doubt there are Freemasons, nay, many Freemasons, who know, more or less, what they are doing; but the vast majority of the Craft are certainly very little aware that they are celebrating the rites of an ancient mystery religion, originating, so far as the west is concerned, about the first century of our era, a contemporary, in fact, of Christianity itself. I remember that once in my newspaper days I had to see a brassfounder in Clerkenwell. My business with him was connected with a Ghost of a very singular kind; but I filled up an interval in our proper conversation with an enquiry as to the process of his business.

"Is brass cast in the old way?" I asked. "Or have all sorts of new methods and processes been introduced?"

"Brass," he replied, "is cast now as it always has been cast; as it was cast when the columns of brass were made gloriously for the

Temple of King Solomon."

"I know the name of the man who did that casting," was my answer. "And I know what happened to him."

My brassfounder looked at me.

"Are you on the square?" said he.

I said I was sorry, but I wasn't on the square; and we resumed our enquiry into a particular instance of that other ancient and insoluble mystery, the Poltergeist, which had been manifesting in a northern suburb. Now here was an intelligent and fervent Mason, but how little he realised that his Father in the Craft was much more than a Brassfounder, much more than a Master Builder, that he belonged to a race removed from man, and that his true name was, very possibly, Sabazius: that he was, perhaps, of the house of Osiris? I think this good Son of the Widow knew little of all this; and so, as I say, with the vast majority of the brethren. Yet, the ancient rite is duly performed, and so other ancient rites are performed in the rawest, reddest suburbs, as I once tried to declare in a story called "A Fragment of Life." There are, unhappily, in these days, people who profane these holy mysteries, some of them calling themselves, I am told, psychoanalysts, others professing a high-souled enthusiasm for the physical good of the race. And I believe that Coventry Patmore, if he had lived into our unhappy days and had seen these things, would have cursed the new profanation even more than he cursed the old; which is generally known as the Protestant Reformation. Patmore might have said, I think, that if the well-springs of nature were poisoned, if the water were turned into sewage; could even Grace transmute such water as that into Wine? The Miracle of Cana is a great wonder, doubtless, and a great symbol; but true miracles never contradict and defy nature; they rather restore nature to its first and unfallen state. Eyes are meant to see with: consequently the blind were given their sight. But if the waterpots of Cana had been full, not of water, but of liquid manure?

Well; I was saying, I think, that the book on hand, this famous *London Adventure,* would have to deal with the raw, red places all around the walls of London; places detestable in themselves, no doubt, from the artist's point of view, from the point of view of the lover of green fields and woods and shady lanes; but most of all detestable, I think, from my point of view, which is that of a man who loves ancient, memoried things; things of all kinds that have a past behind them, things of all kinds that shew use and the touch of men upon them, and have become, in a sense, almost human or, at all events, partake of humanity. I can look with a kind of pleasure on a very doorstep, on a doorstep approaching a shabby grey house of 1810 or thereabouts—if the stone be worn into a deep hollow by the feet of even a hundred years and a little over. That poor London stone in the back-street of the Gray's Inn Road, is in its very minor way, a *Lapis ex cœlis*—for I cannot accept my friend A. E. Waite's interpretation of the Lapis Exillit of Wolfram von Eschenbach. The feet of the weary and hopeless, the glad and the exultant, the lustful and the pure have made that hollow; and most of those feet are now in the hollow of the grave: and that doorstep is to me sacramental, if not a sacrament, even though the neighbourhood round about Mount Pleasant is a very poor one. For, it seems to me that here you have the magic touch which redeems and exalts the dull mass of things, by tinging them with the soul of man. What was that doorstep in the rough, in the rock, but a chunk of limestone, matter for the geologist or the road-mender, possibly, but for no one else? It is an instance, at the very bottom of the ladder, of the high miracle of veritable architecture, of Canterbury, Lincoln, Durham. Here you have, in fact, in the fact of the geologist, simply great heaps of stone dug out of the earth, and piled up on top of it. But the hand of man has so worked upon these rough masses, has so grouped them and carved them and carried them towards the skies, that you see the miracle of the dead raised to life, of the dull and shapeless mass informed with the living spirit. And—it is a lesser art, I admit freely—I see those worn and hollowed doorsteps round about Clerkenwell and the Gray's Inn Road and all the dim and desolate regions adjacent; I see them signed with tears and desires, agony and lamentation; and perhaps on those stones have stood the feet of those who have witnessed the Operation of the Great Work, and have seen the Son Blessed of the Fire. For strange lodgers sometimes take up their abode in quite shabby houses, in undesirable neighbourhoods.

My book, then, was to take all these things into account: the old, the shabby, the out of the way; and also the new and the red and the raw. But it was utterly to shun the familiar. For if you think of it, there is a London *cognita* and a London *incognita*. We all know about Piccadilly and Oxford Street, London Bridge and the Strand. Olympia has made us familiar with a little island in otherwise unknown Hammersmith; the Boat Race illuminates Putney, and the most inexperienced have ventured into the High Street, Kensington. But where will you be, if I ask you about Clapton, about the inner parts of Barnsbury, about the delights of Edmonton, about that region which was once called Spa Fields? Nay: how many people know their Camden Town in any thorough and intelligent manner? They may know the main artery of it by which the omnibuses go up to Hampstead; but not the byways, not the curious passages of Camden Town into Holloway. I remember once, I think it must have been in this borderland between the two quarters, coming at haphazard upon an unpretending street that to me was a whole chapter in social history. The houses were modest little places enough, standing back from the road, houses for small incomes, one would say. But each one of them had its little coach-house and its little stable; and for me here were compact histories of the *Sketches by Boz* period. Here lived, I suppose, people of the £250–£350 a year standard, as money was in those days. I conceive them as living quite carefully. There would be one little maid who did the rougher work of the house, who got up very early indeed in the morning and swept the rooms and lit the fires. But the mistress, or perhaps a daughter, helped her to make the beds and very likely—see Miss Trotwood—washed up the real china cups and saucers, and was responsible for the cakes and the tarts and all the niceties of cookery. The boy or hobbledehoy who looked after the pony and the basketwork chaise for six pounds a year, blacked the boots and did all sorts of odd jobs about the house and garden. I should suppose there were two joints of meat a week, but no more. There were eggs for breakfast, but no bacon. If master were "retired", then the principal meal of the day was between one and three of the afternoon: otherwise the boy, the pony and the chaise took him into the City in the morning and brought him back to dinner in the evening. The gig and pony were sometimes put up in dim stable yards and back places, the very site and existence of which, in our modern London, must remain a profound mystery; and what the boy did in the interval between morning and evening I cannot imagine. Perhaps, even probably, he drove back to Camden Town and cleaned knives and worked in the garden till five o'clock, and then set out again to fetch the master. Sometimes he would drive his mistress to Hornsey where Cousin Jane lived. Then master would walk back from the City and think nothing of it. It was all a very small life. On the sideboard—Sheraton, very likely, for people of slight means could not afford to buy smart modern furniture—there were cake and wine; sherry wine and port wine—ready for anybody, who might pay a morning call; but in the absence of such visitors, I do not think that the mistress of the house or her daughters often partook of these dainties. The cake, I daresay, was apt to get somewhat dry and the wine to grow somewhat flat and weary before the sentence was uttered: "We may as well finish them." Three or four times a year the family started early in the morning and drove off to Twickenham to see Uncle James, who was well to do. There was roast veal or goose for dinner, veal and ham pie or beefsteak pudding, Scotch Ale and Madeira. There might be salmon, there might be pheasant—according to the season—and if there were any sort of family anniversary, champagne might well be produced. If it were warm weather, the men of the party spent an hour or two of the afternoon in the summer-house overlooking the river, drinking punch. The ladies did their "work" in the drawing-room and told family histories. At ten o'clock, after a bowl of bishop and a sandwich with the alternative of tea and thin bread and butter, the bell was rung, the boy was ordered to put in the pony, and the party returned to Camden Town. There was probably, almost certainly "something hot" before going to bed; and this also was the case after one of the rare visits to the play. These people took no regular summer holidays; now and again they stayed for a week or two with relations in Somerset, and that was all, and in return, a son or a daughter of the relations in Somerset would stay for a week in the house in Camden Town, and for that week the family budget would be swollen. There would be ham for breakfast, something extra in the pudding way for dinner, a couple of theatres in the week, and oysters for supper afterwards, instead of the usual bread and cheese. Very few books in that house: odd volumes of Pope, Akenside, Smollett, The Rambler, Don Quixote, Drelincourt on Death, Law's Serious Call; none of them much read.

So much I saw as I passed down that street, Camden Town—Holloway, and I believe that most of it is truly seen; deduced rather, from the little coach-houses and the little stables; and all a vision of a mode of life that has passed utterly away.

But; I have just remembered. I was speaking of the Clerkenwell Brassfounder and his connection with a certain singular enquiry which brought us together for a brief season. I must not be too explicit, but while I tarried in Clerkenwell and met the metal workers at their taverns, I heard some curious things about an old London family, established in an ancient craft in that part for a hundred and fifty years and perhaps more. It is a modern superstition that all Londoners are, *qua* Londoners, things of recent date; that either they or their fathers came up to town from Inverness or Falmouth, Cromer or Pembroke. This is true enough, perhaps, of ourselves and of the Londoners that we know; but down below, beneath our cognisance of things, there is still the old town, the settled place, and the hereditary crafts, as if it were Cirencester or Wootton Bassett. Well, seated in the Clerkenwell Tavern, between the Brassfounder and a man who, I think, was interested in aluminium—or "ally", as he called it—I heard some odd tales of the race I have mentioned.

"There was the great-uncle," said the aluminium specialist. "He was a strange man. He wanted to spite his relations—I forget what it was all about. So he took three hundred pounds in gold, and put them in a pot and buried them. And there they were, till the navvies came to make the cutting for the Midland Railway and found the money."

"He was a very odd man from what they say," said the Brassfounder. "So was his cousin. He confuted Darwin."

"Really!" I interjected. "Surely not."

"Oh, yes, he did," confirmed the dealer in aluminium. "He proved that Darwin was all wrong by the Hebrew Alphabet—and by the stars."

"Yes; that was what *he* did," and thus the Brassfounder ended the discussion. But, as an afterthought:

"And I wish you'd get your paper to let us have the metal prices day by day; we should find them very useful."

And this was only an interlude in the real business which had brought us together. This, as I have said, was an affair of the Poltergeist, which had been raising sad havoc in a house of one of the remoter northern suburbs. The quarter, which I shall not specifically name, lest worthy people, who were horribly annoyed and distressed at the time, should be annoyed yet more, was one of those which still happily linger about us, and more especially in the northern parts of London. Happily, I say, because in spite of the rows and rows of cheap red villas, which we must expect everywhere, there are still remnants of a former age. There was the old parish church, not really of noble architecture, but deeply draped in dark green ivy and wearing somehow a venerable air, standing in the old churchyard on the side of the hill, with grave elms about it. Perhaps Edgar Allan Poe was at school not far from here, in the days when these northern suburbs could be justly described as "dreamy villages". Then, there was the principal inn of the place, an eighteenth-century building, "done up", of course, but not done up too much; and in the main street, here and there, midst the flaunting, flaring shops, a quiet house of the time of Queen Anne stood back amidst trees and lawns and flowers in a green and peaceful retirement from the jingle of the road. Then, of course, a stretch of brisk, bright shopkeeping, as up to date as you please; and perhaps in the middle of the red bricks and the plate glass a humble little gabled cottage, a remnant of the sixteenth century, somehow surviving into an age of progress. When I see such places, I always hope that the occupant and owner is a cantankerous and consistent old woman, who tells speculative builders and "developers" and estate agents exactly what she thinks of them. And here and there, in the side streets, the back gardens of the rubbishy little red houses still give on the fields and are bordered by trees of old growth.

It was in such a neighbourhood, then, that I was to investigate the doings of the Poltergeist; the rackety spirit. The afflicted family consisted of two elderly married people, their two sons, an aunt, and three grandchildren, a little girl of five and two boys of, say, nine and eleven. The story was the usual story. The grandmother, or the aunt, would be quietly cooking in the kitchen of an evening. Suddenly there was a crash; the window was broken and a lump of coal and some fragments of glass would be found in the garden outside. I saw the jagged holes in the kitchen window, and the glass and the coals outside. I saw glass and china which had been smashed, as I was told, in other rooms of the house. I talked to the various members of the family, who struck me as honest people in very considerable distress at these occurrences. I talked to the clergyman of the church which some of them attended.

I had been told that he had been an actual witness of some of the "phenomena"; he had seen, I think, some mantelpiece ornament shooting from its place and dropping on the floor on the other side of the room. I found that he was firmly convinced of the supernatural origin of these strange events. I asked him:

"Did you actually see that ash-tray—or whatever it was—shoot off the mantelpiece, fly across the room and drop on the floor?"

He asked me another:

"Do you see the ball at Lord's all through its course, from the moment that it touches the bat to the moment that it touches the ground?"

In short, I tried to make head and tail of the story. I made neither; I made nothing of it at all. I have said that the family struck me as an honest family. They had certainly nothing to gain by having their possessions—to the value of three or four pounds, I believe—smashed to pieces. And when the business became known through the agency of my colleagues and myself, they had still less to gain; for every night a noisy mob packed itself into their quiet, forsaken road and pressed at their gate, and howled at their windows. A number of journalists—I was not one of them—passed the night in the house and saw nothing and heard nothing. The little girl grandchild died; and I daresay the poor child's end was hastened, though not caused, as I gathered, by all the turmoil, within the house and without it. And the last I heard of the whole matter was, that one of the boys had suddenly become a victim to epileptic fits. And so the whole story passes into nothingness and oblivion, and presently, in a year or three years or five years, just such a tale comes from the neighbourhood of the Wash, or the High Wolds of Yorkshire; the scene a lonely farm instead of a small suburban house; and again the eager reporters rush to the spot; and again—there is nothing; no result, neither confirmation nor refutation. I wrote the whole story in a tale of mine called *The Great Return;* six years before I had any actual experience of the matter. Thus:

"Now and then such doings as these excite a whole neighbourhood; sometimes a London paper sends a man down to make an investigation. He writes half a column of description on the Monday, a couple of paragraphs on the Tuesday, and then returns to town. Nothing has been explained, the matter vanishes away; and nobody cares.

The tale trickles for a day or two through the Press, and then instantly disappears, like an Australian stream, into the bowels of darkness."

And that is exactly what happens. It happened in that affair of the Northern suburb which I was sent to investigate. Of course, I could investigate nothing. I listened to what I was told, I saw the smashed windows and the broken crockery and the lumps of coal; but that is nothing. The only person who can investigate the Poltergeist properly will be a member of the afflicted household with an open mind and keen and open eyes, without prepossessions on one side or the other. There are all sorts of difficulties to be encountered. I remember that in one of the articles which I wrote on the particular case which we have been discussing, I said that there was always a young person, a young boy or a young girl, in the Poltergeist histories. A correspondent wrote to me in correction. He said that he and his wife and a friend, a man, all of them of thirty years or so, had been annoyed in this manner and had never found any solution of their troubles. And then; take it that the whole thing is a fraud, the mischievous trick of the adolescent, the effect of the troubled mind in the troubled body. Very well; but how strange that the methods and ways seem always of the same order. We can hardly suppose that these young people have read up the subject, and simply imitate the mischief of other young people before them. It may be, of course, that it is all "natur'", which we know, on high authorities, to be both a holy thing and a rum 'un. It may be that it is an instinct in young males and females of a certain nervous diathesis to throw things and chunks about with devilish art and cunning, so that everybody is horribly puzzled. This may be so; but it is very odd, if it be so. It is almost as odd, but not quite so odd, as my own very tentative hypothesis, held with doubt and infinitely subject to correction and refutation: that a human being is a world and cosmos of forces that reach out to other worlds wholly, or almost wholly, unknown and unconjectured; that, in most cases and probably, as things are, for the best, these forces and powers are dormant and unsuspected; that occasionally and by accident they assert themselves and produce results which prove—nothing.

There is a scene which is very deeply impressed on my memory. It belongs to the old days of the Road when one wandered up and down England, from squalid manufacturing hamlets to beautiful, ancient, and utterly peaceful places. One day the morning stroll was by the green swelling ramparts of the Roman Wall, not far from Hexham; on the next it might lead us on the black and horrible track of Hetton-le-Hole, where the little brooklet in the valley throws up miniature beaches of coal-dust, where the players, in one instance, had to climb up a sort of step ladder to their bedroom, and then leap over a gulf between the top step of the ladder and the bedroom floor. For the white road of the old players led, and I suppose still leads, to endless variety: to the little Scotch towns of the border, where the language spoken is still almost unintelligible, where the aspect of things is very much that of a somewhat dingy town in the French provinces, an aspect which is further heightened by the fact that the humblest cooking is excellent, and that the fancy cakes in the small confectioners' shops surpass the cakes of Bond Street. And, thence, the road may wind away to Leamington or Cheltenham or Bath, to the ordered, beautiful towns of the eighteenth century. Or it may twist to Lincoln where you find yourself climbing up to the Cathedral by the way which is called Straight, or it may diverge to Tewkesbury with its noble minster and its admirable half-timbered, gabled houses, rich with fifteenth-century carving, or, just as likely, take you to Swansea, where they smelt twenty-two metals, and, on the whole, look like it.

Well, one of the twists and turnings of this famous road, where there is no money but plenty of happiness, took me eighteen years ago or so to the beautiful city of Bath. There was a "night off"—I forget how or why—and a few of us drifted that evening to the rooms of two of the band, there to drink whisky and smoke and talk and laugh in our vicious, abandoned way. The company consisted of two women and three men. Of the two men besides myself one was a middle-aged actor who had played leads for many years in "Number 2" provincial companies; the other was a youngish man, who had been a novice in a great Benedictine monastery, afterwards a student of sculpture in Belgium, and finally had turned to the stage. Well, there we were, spending our pleasant evening together, and I can hardly realise now, after those eighteen years, how with about twopence in our pockets and within a fortnight's notice of destitution—the fortnight's notice may appear on the call-board any night—we laughed at anything and everything and didn't even care that twopence which we somewhat dubiously possessed. And I have often wondered whether it ever struck the Benedictine Novice that there were certain resemblances between the life that he had abandoned—for lack of vocation—and the life which he had adopted. There are of course grave differences and I hope nobody will suspect me of doubting which is the higher calling; but there is this point of likeness: neither the good monk nor the good actor cares twopence! Each is rooted and fortified and secure: the one in God, the other in gaiety; the gaiety, I suppose, of publicans and sinners.

So, I say, we sat and laughed about the fire, when it occurred to one of the party, the old actor or the novice, I am not sure which, to say:

"Let's have a séance."

I stood out, being generally of Panurge's opinion when any particular course of action is proposed: "It is better to drink." But the other four sat down round a small rosewood table, in the middle of the room, under the flaring gaslights, and did some kind of hanky-panky with fingers and thumbs. I am afraid somebody was profane enough to recite the Pater Noster: the sitting had begun. I stood a few feet away, puffing at my pipe and looking with contemptuous and easy tolerance at the "four idiots", as I regarded them. But I must make it clear that, to the best of my belief, none of the four had any particular notions about spiritualism or knowledge of it: to them it was merely a parlour game, a substitute for poker.

But as I looked I perceived that the features of one of the party were becoming curiously intent, almost contorted, almost rapturously contorted, as with an acute and singular pleasure. I forget whether anything else of an audible or visible kind were going on. I am inclined to think that the former Benedictine in a burlesque voice with a burlesque earnestness addressed "the dear spirits" and implored them to shew a friendly temper and to rap or tilt the table; to do the decent thing in fact. There was no rapping, no tilting. The séance, with one exception, was getting bored, and some sort of a halt was called; and, I suppose, those fingers and thumbs were unlocked. But the interested member of the party called out in a voice of intense eagerness and excitement, much removed from her ordinary manner: "Oh, let's go on, let's go on": and the sitting was resumed. And oddly enough, I remember no more, so far as personal observation is concerned. I conjecture that I got tired of looking and had some more whisky and smoked my pipe in a corner arm-chair in a patient, resigned sort of way, wondering when they would all have done with their nonsense. But afterwards, when it was over, the lady who had seemed so highly interested during the former part of the proceedings, told me that the second stage had been dreadful, so far as she was concerned. A sense of great horror had come upon her, and with that a physical sense as of an icy breath in the little, stuffy, overheated room; and then, last of all, there had been the feeling of a presence, the presence of a dear friend, who had died suddenly some four years before. "Somehow, I felt that poor Blank was there," she said, and the sense of horror—overhaul Job for particulars of that sense—was so great that she very solemnly declared that she would never have anything to do with such matters again, even though it might be all a joke and a parlour game.

Now, I should like to note that being, as I hope, a fair man, I tell this true story, in a sense, against myself. I have no belief in the art of necromancy; I do not think that the spirits of the dead can be conjured into a parlour by people sitting round a table in the dark—or in the light either. Still; I repeat what I was told, and I am sure that the teller of the story told the truth; that is, repeated this particular sensation as it came to her.

And then: there are two important differences between this odd business in the actor's rooms at Bath in the October of 1905 and the real séance of the spiritualists. The four players were not in the least serious. They thought it would be fun, though I don't quite know what they expected would happen. At the séance proper everybody is entirely serious. They are investigators. They are intensely interested. They have a profound belief that the spirits of the departed can and do communicate with the living. They fervently expect to experience such communication before they rise from the table. With some of the sitters this is a matter of theory and science; with others, poor people, there is the aching desire to be quite sure that the beloved is not dead but living. In a word, these people are in earnest; they are not playing a game. There is no wild exaltation. And then secondly, when their desire is realised, as they suppose, there is no trace of horror. There is no sense of the awfulness of another order of being impinging on ours. It is all as cheerful as a tea-party. The spirits are gay, friendly, familiar; it is just as it was in the old days, when they were alive, in the common sense of the word. You are simply assured that John is still hearty and well, the very same John, with much the same interests as those of the John whom you knew and loved so well, with just the same little family jokes and turns of speech; and you go home after the séance cheerful and happy.

Well, these seem to me to be notable differences. Though I have told the story truly, as, I am quite certain, it was truly told to me; I still disbelieve in the presence of the spirit of poor, dead Blank in that actors' lodging-house in Bath. But I think that something happened; that the doors were opened; that the human spirit came into momentary contact with unconjectured worlds which it is not meant to visit.

I think of these things as I pass along the interminable wandering of the London streets; of the strange things which may have been done behind the weariest, dreariest walls.

III

Here, then, was the situation before me in this spring of the year. The leaves were out, as the dread messenger of the tavern had informed me, the stage of the London scene was fully set, and here was I well equipped with long-gathered material for a sermon on the great text that there is wonder in everything and everywhere, wonder above all in this great town that has grown so vast that no man can know it, nay, nor even begin to know it! I was thinking of a sentence I had written in a book of mine called *Far Off Things* to the effect that no man has ever seen London; and then, wandering a little—I am afraid that "wandering a little" is almost a hobby of mine—I began to consider whether, in this respect, London were the unique matter that I had considered it. For, referring back the axiom to its most august origin: we are ready enough to confess—if we be not occultists, who know everything—that no man hath seen God at any time. But are we prepared to admit that no man hath seen anything at any time? Yet, this is most indubitably the truth. We see appearances and outward shows of things, symbols of all sorts; but we behold no essences, nor could we bear to behold them, if it were possible to do so. We know what happened to the lady in the "haythen mythology", as the hedge-schoolmaster called it, who obtained her desire, that she should see her lover Zeus in his true essence, as Hera saw him. Her wish was fulfilled, and she was blasted and consumed in devouring flame. This is one of the old lies that are so much truer than the new truths; and it is like enough—Tennyson put the matter in a different manner—that if any man could see a grain of wheat as it is in its essence, he would instantly become a raging maniac. We see nothing real, we can no more see anything real than we can take our afternoon tea in the white, central heat of a blast furnace. We see shadows cast by reality. The more foolish of us gather up some of the shadows and put them in saucepans and boil them and then strain: and find out that water is really H₂O, which is true enough in its way, and will remain so: till it is found out that H₂ is shorthand for ten distinct forces, while O is a universe of countless stars, all revolving in their eternal order about an unknown, unconjecturable orb. And this, again, will be a good working hypothesis—till new discoveries call for an entire revision of all our notions on the subject. No; we see nothing at all; though poets catch strange glimpses of reality, now and then, out of the corners of their eyes.

And the recognition of these obvious truths cast me down a little. I had not, then, got the unique object for investigation that I had supposed. London, it was true, was unknowable, an unplumbed depth, but so was Caerleon-on-Usk, that you could see in its totality from the top of the hill; so was the pebble on the path. I felt I must have a little time to look around me and reconsider the matter; and while I did so, I thought it would be a good thing to glance through the notebook that I used in 1895, '96, '97, '98; in the period when I was writing *The Hill of Dreams, Ornaments in Jade*, "The White People", "A Fragment of Life", *Hieroglyphics*. We learn by experience, say the good men; but I believe the fact to be that experience causes us to forget most things that are worth knowing—as Wordsworth has observed in a somewhat higher manner in his *Ode*. And so, I said to myself, before I begin this magistral work about London, I will disinter the old notebook, which I kept when I was young, and understood one or two things far more clearly than I do now.

I opened it at random. I came upon what follows. I had utterly forgotten that I had ever written it. I did not know that I had once been clever enough to write gibberish.

> I wish to paint the ardent grace
> That shines upon my Mary's face,
> And speak of that within her eyes
> That sings to me of Paradise.
>
> She came to me from a distant shore,
> She came to me through a secret door;
> And when she walks, I know how they
> Must dance in a secret land alway.

> Her locks are scented with spices rare,
> Her Secret is one that no mortals share;
> For she goes ever in a light
> That shines upon no earthly wight.
>
> O Mary, bend to me your eyes,
> Instructing me in mysteries,
> Wherein all joys are found, that I
> Unto this dying life may die;
> And live for ever wrapt in Thee
> O present immortality.

This, evidently, was an extract from the notebooks of the young City clerk in "A Fragment of Life", the "inspired infant" who also wrote the lines beginning:

> One day when I was all alone
> I found a wondrous little stone.

To those who have not read this story it may be explained that Darnell, the clerk, was a man who "woke up" to real existence, to the sense of things that veritably are; and, without any education of the technical or formal kind, pottered with old books—he had evidently glanced into Vaughan and Crashaw—and wrote "poems", which, in spite of their rough, ungrammatical, conventional crust—"wight" is rather terrible—yet have a flame burning within them.

I read over the lines again, and thinking over them I was reminded of Henry James's story, "The Pattern on the Carpet"; the notion of a man of letters who had written many books and was quite surprised to find that one of his admirers had failed to recognise that all these tales of his were variations on one theme; that a common pattern, like the pattern of an Eastern carpet, ran through them all. If I remember; the novelist died suddenly, without revealing the nature of the pattern, and James ends very exquisitely, leaving us with the faithful admirer, who, we are to understand, is to pass the rest of his days in endeavouring to penetrate the mystery of this one design, latent in a whole shelf of books.

Well, I read my clerk's doggerel, and thought of the tale of the pattern, and began to wonder a little whether the "poem" did not furnish the key to the pattern of my carpet; nay, I would say to my "Orient carpet, nine by nine, brilliant colours, fifteen and six." "If you go to Dick's in the Seven Sisters Road, mention the name of Mr. Wilson of Fulham and ask for Mr. Johnston." But I was forgetting: all this happened years ago. Dick's now charge you thirty-five and six for the "Orient" carpet and Mr. Johnston is dead. He died violently; but they sent Mrs. Johnston his V.C. and she lives at Waltham Cross, and keeps a small school for very small children.

But I was thinking, as I have said, that here was something like the pattern of my cheap "Orient" square in brilliant colours. For this "Mary", to whom these lines that try to flame were addressed, was quite an ordinary young woman. Before her marriage to Edward Darnell, the City Clerk, she had been Miss Mary Reynolds, the daughter of an estate agent and auctioneer in Notting Hill, an auctioneer in a pretty small way. She was just a pleasant, amiable, conventional young woman, who had considerably more sense than her husband where money matters were concerned, did her best with his very small income, and was continually worried by the kitchen range and by the whims of her servant, Alice. Yet:

> When she walks, I know how they
> Must dance in a secret land alway.

Here, then, is the pattern in my carpet, the sense of the eternal mysteries, the eternal beauty hidden beneath the crust of common and commonplace things; hidden and yet burning and glowing continually if you care to look with purged eyes. Nay, I think that in this age, which has probably lost what I may call the epic sense, as it lives in villas and flats instead of castles, and goes in tweeds in place of chain mail, for us, I think, it is easier to discern the secret beauty and wonder and mystery in humble and common things than in the splendid and noble and storied things. I have been in Avignon, for example, and I hope I did not fail to realise its mystic beauty, as the sunset light glowed on its white machicolated walls. Here was a pure and intact relic from another world, from all the world of the beauty and romance and the music and the singing of old Provence; here was a city that was like the dying echoes of a magistral song. I could see all this and feel it deeply; and yet I was something like the old Japanese poet to whom an Englishman read *In Memoriam*. The Japanese understood not one word; but he wept—at the sheer beauty of the sound of the words. And so I, under the walls of Avignon, admired deeply but did not understand. A great music, a great voice, indeed, but not speaking in my native tongue. In one sense, it said a great deal; in another sense it said nothing. Nay, take the example of a man of supreme genius, such as Dickens. He made his tours in France and Italy, and the experience gave him little. The best thing that he got from France was the contrast between railway refreshment rooms in England and France ("Mugby Junction"). There is a very sunny and pleasant chapter on Sens in "Mrs. Lirriper's Legacy"; and, so far as I remember, that is all. Very agreeable, indeed, but not the vital, the tremendous Dickens; not, by any means, the essential Dickens who appears in Pickwick and his companions, in Micawber, and Mrs. Gamp, in Quilp, in the Flora of *Little Dorrit,* in the majestic figure of Mr. F.'s Aunt. Avignon and Rome and Genoa: great places, no doubt, and full of mighty eloquence, but the tongue was foreign, the idiom altogether strange. Charles Dickens was touched to the heart and the quickening spirit not by these, but by Camden Town by-ways, by the old inns of Southwark, by dirty streets in Soho, by the purlieus of the Gray's Inn Road. He understood their utterance, since it was in his native tongue. And so with Hawthorne: "Transformation" is a great essay in romance, but the achievement was in *The Scarlet Letter,* where the background was not splendid Rome but the arid, dusty Salem, Mass. And this, I suspect, is the reason why we are apt to be "put off" a little, if the first chapter of the new book has a Moated Grange or a Turreted Castle for its "scene", while we are drawn by an indication that the principal personages in the story live at Tooting Bec. And putting it higher still: he would be a bold author of these days who would write of man's first disobedience; we, it appears, are to learn of high things, if at all, through little things, and things of low estate. If we are to see the vision of the Grail, however dimly, it must no longer be in some vaulted chamber in a high tower of Carbonnek, over dreadful rocks and the foam of a faery sea. For us, the odour of the rarest spiceries must be blown through the Venetian blinds in some grey, forgotten square of Islington; the flame that is redder than any rose must come shining on "Bolton Abbey in the Olden Time"—is that the name of the famous picture?—hanging over the mantelpiece in the Canonbury lodging-house. And be it remembered, I regard these old tales as true tales, true, very likely, in the very letter, and as true now as ever. But, speaking as a man who has dealt with some very difficult and delicate literary problems in his day, I would say that the more commonplace the setting, the easier the task. You are to make wonder credible; it is clear that if your setting, your scene, at least is credible and familiar and accepted you are so far forwarded in the work that is before you. At least we believe in Acton and know how to get there; but what is the number of the lines of 'buses that runs to Astolat? Book from Waterloo to Camelot? It is doubtful, I think, whether the tickets to Winchester are really available for the other place. The fact is, I suppose, that I am a determined realist, that I demand a certain degree of assent in the reader to the propositions which are laid before him. I am sure that if I had been a man about town in Grand Cairo somewhere in the twelfth century, I should have found the *Arabian Nights* the most credible book imaginable; credible, that is, in the artistic sense, as Micawber is credible, though there never was, in actuality, any such person. But I cannot read *Phantastes* with any relish, simply because it tells you in the first few sentences that there is not a word of truth in it; that it is an allegory and nothing more. Bunyan now, succeeds and arrests because he is so vivid that we forget all about the allegory even in the face of the allegorical names of all the personages; the *Pilgrim's Progress* is a masterpiece of the picaresque, of the wandering hero, who passes through frightful dangers and difficulties and comes to a very good end.

But again to the old notebook; as I ponder and delay over the Great Work on London. Again, I open it; I wonder at the infinite labours of former years; at the efforts renewed again and again which have issued in so little. Here, thick on every page, are the notes of stories which were never even begun. Thus:

Maze Story

Girl who danced in the Maze was afterwards beset by the influence she had in that manner invoked.
—after the Hawthorne manner, somewhat.
The maze was constructed on a wild, bare hilltop, with innumerable blocks of limestone. It was called "The Way (or Path) to the City."

And then a great bulk of notes and suggestions for *The Hill of Dreams*.

> He wondered whether all the objects of nature are not purely symbolical: whether nature does not endeavour to talk to us and tell us amazing secrets by the signs and cyphers of trees and ferns and herbs and flowers and hills and streams.
>
> Suppose a Tuscan to come to a village of savages and talk in his beautiful speech, and suppose the inhabitants pronounced him a curious, gibbering creature and made him a slave to amuse the children by the strange sounds he uttered. Even so, perhaps, may be our state with regard to inanimate nature. The oak and the elm that we fell for our need may be wonderful signs: the brooks may indeed be books: the fern may be a great secret: the flower by the way the word of a great mystery: and whether we call the hills beautiful or dig coal from them, we may equally misunderstand their office.

And so on, pages on pages, long arguments, long lines of thought, heavy strivings to escape out of deep bogs and morasses, to get clear of false paths that led only to brakes of thorns; altogether the impression of a man who didn't know where he was going, losing his way in his endeavour to get there. Then: *The Hill of Dreams* at last finished, we begin again; we suggest plots for long stories or short stories on every page, thumping ourselves on the back all the time, and assuring ourselves that we can tackle successfully themes which would have appalled the very masters of romance. So here we go:

> A "young lady" of a country town comes running headlong through a wood, in a state of wild shame and confusion at something she has seen.
>
> She has been, contrary to her parents' wishes, to a certain spot disliked by the general opinion; there is a kind of superstitious dread against the place which has "hardened" into an instinct; people say it is not a "nice" place, without quite knowing why they disapprove of it.
>
> It must have, no doubt, some relation to Roman times—to the fauns.
>
> Some say it is "horrid"—"not a nice walk", Juniper bushes and Roman nettles.

Then:

> An "ethnological" story—would turn on the survival into our day of some primitive practice or desire.
>
> For example:
>
> An ordinary family living in the suburbs shut themselves up for cer-

tain days in the year to perform some horrible "cave" rites.

They have a language for these occasions, a "mystery" language: they have a code of morals, quite different from that of their everyday life.

They tear live animals for their food; they write in "cuneiform" on tablets of clay.

They worship a concealed image which is locked up in a cupboard for the rest of the year.

Incident in such a tale.

Someone finds a broken piece of a clay tablet inscribed with the secret characters, on the road. It is shewn to be modern, of clay found in the neighbourhood.

Who wrote the characters?

You have heard the tempest of the theatre: have you ever seen the wind-machine: the silk stretched over a sort of barrel, which being turned round by the property man, shrieks and wails? And here is another sketch for a terrible story:

Story of the man who made for himself a god; building was going on in the neighbourhood; foundations were being dug out; and he begged a wheelbarrowful of clay, thinking he would like to try his hand at modelling.

He is rather an ordinary young fellow, but he has read, with a dim sort of interest, one or two curious books (so his mind is in a measure prepared).

He lodges in the suburb, has no particular employments, no absorbing interests.

His rooms are on the ground floor, opening on the garden.

It is one of those houses which stand in a garden with a wall all round.

He has a good many acquaintances, one an artist in whose studio he sees modelling being done.

He makes an idol: to pass "the time".

The story is: that he is gradually corrupted and destroyed by the idol he has made.

First his life gains a new flavour; he becomes unconsciously an artist, and then, by degrees, an artist in sin.

He makes his idol foul, obscene; feeling ashamed of himself as he does so, yet letting the whim guide him.

Here now, the notebook takes the form of a somewhat cruel parody.

(Clement Scott) (Gray's Inn Road on Bank Holiday night).

"He saw the street lit for a great solemnity: the music was wild as of a bacchic orgie.

"The whisky seemed an occult draught, thaumaturgic, tremendous, the wine of a mystery, changed from common drink and changing the initiate.

"He saw the shy girl come in, timid, happy, unwilling. . . . He saw her come out, her dress gaping, and a light in her eyes.

"And the music: it was only three barrel organs, a cornet at one pub. and a French horn at another.

"But it made an awful and appropriate harmony.

"There were howls as of wild beasts and shrill screams, the roar of a returning party in a brake, and hissing whispers in the crowd—this was the choir.

"It seemed that a rite was being performed.

"He came home and found an article awaiting him: it began:

"'They were happy! Again and again they were happy! Who after this crowning mercy of a bright Whit-Monday will dare to repeat the calumny of the crusty chronicler? Who that has seen our merry millions at play will venture on the time-worn jibe that the English take their pleasure sadly? Possibly those superfine persons who bow down before the cult of the sunflower would have thought some of the fun a little rough, but who would give such persons a thought while there is fresh air on Hampstead Heath, brother, and sunshine at Greenwich?'"

And here is the outline of a nice Sunday-school story.

> Story of the painter, who paints a picture, which he keeps hidden and concealed.
> The lady to whom he is engaged comes one day to his studio by appointment: he is detained.
> He rushes in, in a mad hurry, with an awful interrogation in his eyes.
> She stretched out her arms and cried to him as he came in.

I think that is splendid; and yet I cannot help remembering a criticism of a real author that a friend of mine once delivered.

"Yes," he said, "Edgar Allan Poe is wonderful, amazing; there has never been anyone like him. *But,* somehow, one is, now and then, inclined to laugh."

Now, for a puzzle: what is the mystery hidden beneath this "outline"?

> There was an old stone in the wood, on which she often found cottage-

garden flowers scattered in summer-time.

She never saw anyone leaving the flowers.

There were cowslips and daffodils in spring; lilac blossoms, bachelor's buttons . . . in winter even, sprigs of box and laurel.

In summer great bunches of "old man" and cabbage roses and Sweet William.

Nobody in the village ever alluded to the stone or its offerings of flowers.

She was coming home late one night: heard a rustling, saw . . . a village girl (a singer in the choir) with a fresh posy in her hand.

She watched her lay down her flowers, and with staring, amazed eyes the ceremony that followed.

She found that nobody would acknowledge any acquaintance with the stone.

"The old people," she was told, "used to talk nonsense about it, a lot of silly superstition, I daresay."

She understood that there was a freemasonry among the frequenters of the stone.

And one day she went to the "houses" and cut curious orchids and many flowers of the steaming heat, and having made a wreath, went through the wood to the stone.

Here is the sketch of a little thing to be called "The Graven Image".

It was a burning hot day in Caermaen.

The river wound in and out, mystic between the reeds, in shimmering mist.

The blue-green woods were asleep and still.

The great mountain was in a dream. A deep silence, a hush of heat as if all the world were asleep.

Mr. X. and his friend Y. strolled out from the old house towards the walls, where the labourers were digging out a sunken tennis-court.

"We shall have a sloping bank all round to keep in the balls."

"Ah, what's that?"

It was a little bronze faun, preserved in almost perfect condition, in a layer of broken shards of pottery and dry sand.

Y. was enraptured. The find seemed fit for the day; it seemed to sing of the old summers when the vineyards glowed on the hill, and intoned the music of the flutes.

X. found it difficult to separate his friend from the statuette; he was willing to sit still, gazing at it, and finally he took it back with him, a present, to London.

It stood in a cabinet in his room. He vowed it had enchanted London, and that he could no longer see the dark fogs or the sooty air, but only the bright sunshine on the vines, and in place of the uncouth noises of the street, he heard Roman song.

There are many more of these shorthand sketches, and some of them were written, but most advanced no stage further. Then begin the notes for the book which afterwards became *Hieroglyphics*. The first sentence runs:

"Literature began with charms, incantations, spells, songs of mystery, chants of religious ecstasy, the Bacchic Chorus, the Rune, the Mass":

and, to the best of my belief, the thesis of the book is fairly well summed up in the sentence. There are pages of these notes, "worrying out" the main idea of the essay with infinite elaboration; and then things like this, which seem obscure enough:

He turned again to the monograph on *Labyrinths:* he looked at the plates: the various types of mazes (quote passage as to *dancing* with reference to mazes).

How does all this bear on the "psychology": what reference to ecstasy: the drama: the lyric of incantation?

It was a book that attracted him in spite of its dry, antiquarian air: he had felt that there was "something there".

Then the question of the *pattern.*

(Compare with the whorl, the spiral, Maori decoration.)

Why was this form common to all primitive art?

The problem perplexed him. He took it, as was his custom, for a long walk; and in the dreariest, most grey street of a grey, remote suburb, just as the men were coming home from the city, the thought, with a pang of joy, rushed into his mind, that the maze was not only the instrument, but the symbol of ecstasy: it was a pictured "inebriation", the sign of some age-old "process" that gave the secret bliss to men, that was symbolised also by dancing, by lyrics with their recurring burdens, and their repeated musical phrases: a maze, a dance, a song: three symbols pointing to one mystery.

Now, in the outline of this strange story—an ancestor, I fancy, of "The White People"—there seems some obscurity. As far as I can gather, the interest of the investigating sort of person, designated above under the somewhat vague style of "he", had first been attracted to this subject of labyrinths by seeing a girl, in the country—I am sure that the country in question was not far from Caerleon-on-Usk—drawing maze-patterns on the sand, or in a garden, or in her copy-book. Now see what happens:

> On D.'s—his name began with a D, then?—reaching home after his long walk and his discovery, he finds a letter from Gregg (the country correspondent, I presume) telling him that the girl who had drawn mazes had disappeared.
>
> "A hard-headed materialist, as you pretend to be, will no doubt be able to put me on the track. *Have you no suggestion to make?*"
>
> The letter left D. in a swoon of amazement, and a beginning of shrinking alarm. After the theories! He felt as a medium might feel who was suddenly aware that there was a real ghost in the room. He had called his theories credible, but was it possible that he would have to translate Latin into Saxon and confess that he *believed?*
>
> He had determined that the maze was the symbol of a "process", and here, the girl who strangely seemed to know the meaning of the occult and antique sign had disappeared.
>
> His mind went at once to the marvellous stories of magic transmutation, metamorphosis (Chants Scandinaves). He reflected how old the tales must be, of what secular antiquity, since human memory was so long. Persistently, the old stories told of those taken by *the fairies, rapt into the underworld,* recurred to him. He had rationalised all this into recollections of the Turanian "little people", but their forts had been uninhabited for centuries. And the girl had disappeared! What had happened to her? . . .
>
> The return: quite unconscious of what had happened.
>
> "But it seems," said Gregg, "that the country people have superstitions about the place where the girl disappeared. There is some hill or other there that they call ———, and they have a tale of a woman who went there and never returned. . . . It is strange no one in the neighbourhood has come forward from first to last. She may have had money; she may have come up to London; she may have gone to Ireland. We really don't know."

And so the story that was to be "The White People" vanishes into dense obscurity, with bits of "A Fragment of Life" here and there embodied in it, in a strange and alarming manner.

And so I run through the old notebook, through dozens of these "hints" and "sketches" and "outlines" and "arguments", most of which led to nothing in particular. I find it all a little pathetic, and a little puzzling. I find my destiny a hard one. Here am I, born apparently with this itch of writing without the faculty of carrying the desire into execution. I am faintly reminded of one of Socrates' tremendous "scores". He had, in his usual bland manner, demanded a definition of happiness. A rash man comes forward and says, pretty easily and confidently, that happiness consists in the gratification of desire—and really, on the face of it, most of us would say that the definition is not much amiss. To want something badly, and then to get it; to the natural man this seems happiness, or a very decent substitute for happiness. But not to Socrates. He pounced on the rash man, and said something to this effect:

"Then that beggar at the street corner must be happy above all other men. For he has the itch and vehemently desires to scratch himself, and he scratches himself all day long."

Whereupon the rash man—if memory serves—promptly collapses and gives it up.

But here am I much worse off than that Athenian beggar. I have the itch too, and vehemently desire to scratch myself, that is, to write, but I can't do it—save at long intervals, and after taking the most horrible pains, and racking my brains, and filling the fat notebook with hundreds of pages of plots and plans and elaborations and dark and crafty schemes. I dig deep, I burrow, far under the ground, I hew out my laborious subterranean passages, I blast whole strata of unsuspected rocks which suddenly interpose themselves between me and my end, I dwell down in that stifling blackness of toil, month after month, year after year, scarcely emerging to see the light of the sun and the glow of the green world. At last, after all these dark and dreadful labours, I succeed in laying my mine. I touch the button—and there is a feeble pop, which would hardly make a kitten jump. And, pray let it be very clearly understood, that I do not mean by this that the published book did not make an enormous sensation and become a "best seller". I was never fool enough to look for that result. The kitten that did not jump was not the great reading public, but myself; it was I who realised that the explosion—the result of all these efforts—was not, in fact, tremendous.

Long ago, at a tavern meeting—the good people will never credit what goes on sometimes in taverns—an old friend of mine said to me, over our beer:

"After all, we must agree that when God gives a faculty, He gives it with magnificent liberality. The measure is not stinted."

I think I agreed, to save the trouble of discussion, for it was past midnight—and "it is better to drink". But the dictum is not true, generally. Think of the immense number of the lives that have been poisoned and blighted by a stinted measure of faculty. I often ponder a saying of Oliver Wendell Holmes. He pointed out the misery brought about by a slight tinge of genius. "The man is spoilt," he said in effect, "just as fair water is spoilt and sickened by being poured into a glass in which there are dregs of wine." I would not limit the maxim to genius. The true tragedy is in the juxtaposition of desire and impotence. It must be horrible to long to write film scenarios—and to long in vain.

I repeat, it is all a little pathetic and a little puzzling. Most of us have always found the career of the *raté*, the artist who misses fire, distinctly comic. The poet who can hardly get into the corner column of his country paper, the novelist whose novels are simply "rot", the painter whose pictures are a joke; we laugh heartily at them all. But, on the other hand, we are not in the least inclined to laugh at the small grocer who goes bankrupt, or at the widow with children who fails lamentably in the stationery shop—tobacco, sweets, newspapers, and fancy goods included—in the new suburb. I do not know why this is so.

The jests of the good God are sometimes obscure.

IV

It will have been gathered, I think, from this book and from other books of my workshop that I am not altogether an enthusiast for the profession of journalism. Yet, looking back at those visions of strange places in London to which I have alluded, I am forced to confess that as a newspaper reporter I saw queer things and odd prospects which, otherwise, I should not have seen. In the general way, not in the direct course of the business, but rather as a side issue. Thus, I am sent to interview a distinguished fireman, who has just retired from the brigade with all honour—he had risked his life a dozen times or more, and had dreaded raging furnaces of flame as little as you and I dread the drawing-room fire. This is all very fine no doubt, and yet, by an astonishing paradox, the most tremendous heroism is a commonplace in man; there are many men, hundreds, perhaps thousands of men, who are willing to risk dying the death of the martyrs for two-ten a week—perhaps it is four pounds now—ready to face the roaring fires just in the way of business, as a bank clerk faces his daily accounts. This, astounding as it is, is commonplace, I take it; what was not commonplace to me was the infinite extent of Wandsworth. This fireman of whom I speak had retired from the Wandsworth Fire Brigade, and, fortified with his name, I approached headquarters in the old High Street of Wandsworth, in which I had lived thirty years before. The station gave me the address that I wanted, somewhere beyond the beyond of Wandsworth Common, and so I found myself traversing unknown and unconjectured regions, happy as always in the faculty of finding infinity round the corner of any street, within five minutes of anywhere.

I remember when I was quite a boy climbing up to a great mountain plateau in my country of Gwent. It was the beginning of the range that rises from the hollow of Pontypool and goes on swelling and falling and swelling to Abergavenny, and there dips down and surges up again and rises into sharp peaks of the order of the fairies and then marches onward in a solemn array past Llanthony, and so becomes the Black Mountains and goes into the very heart of Wales. But on this bright autumn day, just forty years ago, I climbed up into this high land—it was, in fact, a quest for a holy well still very famous in that country—I climbed up and up, and presently received that singular sense which always affects me in such places, the sense that all is moving not merely in space but in time. I mean, there comes a verge where the mountain visibly begins, where enclosures, hedges, fields, tilled and cultivated lands cease to be, where you come on the wild and know that you have come also into an older world before the time of sowing and reaping and gathering into barns. Up this big hill, then, I went—it is only a big hill, really, though we call it down there, Mynydd Fawr, the great mountain—and came out from the fields of some hill farm, where they harvest, if they harvest at all, in October, into a queer lane. High banks, jagged limestone rocks, and red earth on either side, oak trees, hideously dwarfed and contorted by winter winds; the bottom, huge slabs of limestone, with ravines between them where terrible December rains had torn the softer sandstone. This lane ended soon; and then the mountain began. Of short, sweet turf, it surged up in a slow, steady slope, studded with dark green islands of gorse, glowing with their autumn bloom; and then it still mounted towards another horizon; and the dark green and rich gold of the gorse gave place to strange circles and patterns of grey limestone rocks, something dread, threatening, Druidical about them, though they also had their decoration of yellow lichens. And so onward, slope rising to a still higher slope and no end or limit that the eye could see, there in that high, desolate place, lifted far above men and their habitations and their tracks and fields and homely fires. And I remember—I was only twenty then—feeling that there was an expression for all this in words: "For ever and ever. Amen." It was not till very many years afterwards that I learnt that the Welsh for "and ever shall be" is "ac yn y wastad"—and into the waste, the waste of time being understood. And, it sounds farcical, but I could read something of all this text into a newspaper expedition to find a fireman in his little villa beyond Wimbledon Common. I do not think that I have ever consciously borrowed from Blake, of whom I know very little, I am sorry to say, but I do remember that he makes the Farthing Pie House—it is now the Green Man, close to the Great Portland Street Station of the Underground—one of the limits of that Syon of his which is, somehow, London. But the unknown world is, in truth, about us everywhere, everywhere near to our feet; the thinnest veil separates us from it, the door in the wall of the next street communicates with it. There are certain parts of Clapton from which it is possible, on sunny days, to see the pleasant hills of Beulah, though topographical experts might possibly assure you that it was only Epping Forest. But men of science are always wrong.

And the mention of Clapton reminds me of a very strange and impressive scene I once witnessed there; this also in the course of my newspaper service. This, I should say, was not on those heights of which I have been speaking, whence one looks across a river valley to far wooded hills. This was in Lower Clapton, where it joins Hackney. My business took me to a great ugly hall, hideously grey without, painted within, if I remember, in dingy, bilious green, its gallery supported by cast-iron pillars. A raised platform or rostrum at one end, tiers of seats such as are in the gallery of a theatre behind it. In front of the rostrum something covered up with a blue and red flag; uniformed people grouped about this hidden object; above them massed bands with their bright brass instruments; the whole hall, floor and gallery, crowded; all the seats filled.

A Voice speaking from the platform:

"When I last saw her she was lying on her bed of agony in the hospital. Where is she now?"

Another Voice from the hall:

"In Paradise."

Many Voices:

"Alleluya, Alleluya!"

The first Voice again:

"The night before she died, they gave her clean, white sheets. She said, 'Oh, how kind of the doctor to send me these nice sheets!' I know who sent her those sheets. Who was it?"

Another Voice:

"The Lord Jesus."

The first Voice:

"Because she was clothed in innocence; in the white linen which is the righteousness of the saints."

Many Voices:

"Alleluya, Alleluya!"

The fact was that I was present at a great occasion. Major and Adjutant Jane Smith—I have forgotten her real name—had been "promoted to Glory". This was the funeral service at the Salvation Army Hall in Lower Clapton. It struck me as very remarkable, indeed; remarkable and impressive. Not so much because Jane Smith was, doubtless, a good and devoted woman, not because those who celebrated her faithful deeds and her pious end were, doubtless, good and devoted officers of the Salvation Army; but rather because of the form which the service assumed, that form being, as has been seen, a fervent dialogue. My mind was at once borne to another fervent dialogue:

> *Per omnia sæcula sæculorum.*
> *Amen.*
> *Dominus vobiscum.*
> *Et cum spiritu tuo.*
> *Sursum corda.*
> *Habemus ad Dominum.*
> *Gratias agamus Domino Deo nostro.*
> *Dignum et justum est.*

And here was the remarkable thing. You have at the one end the Jews and Greeks and Romans and the sweepings of all the Mediterranean shores that went to make up early Christendom; and at the other end you have the sweepings of modern London, people, for the most part, of very indifferent education, people in poor circumstances, drawn from very grey streets and humble, circumscribed surroundings, by no means addicted to the study of the science of Liturgiology, people utterly unaffected by motives of the æsthetic kind, the last people in the world to like things "prettily done"—to quote the Tractarian lady in *Bleak House*. And, above all, you have in the Salvation Army a set of people who have deliberately separated themselves from all ecclesiastical ways and customs and conventions, whose forms and phrases, so far as they exist, are borrowed from military terminology, who would regard a Methodist meeting as a rigid and cut-and-dried sort of business; here are these people, quite unconsciously, reverting to Catholic ritual, to that fervent dialogue between priest and people which the logical and learned Protestants have always detested. I once heard a very different funeral service. It was Joseph Chamberlain's funeral, and the rite consisted of the Church of England service, with the Christianity omitted, delivered as a solo by Principal Jacks. It was all unspeakably dismal, depressing, deplorable, unmoving—because opposed to all natural human instincts. The Salvation Army has got away, unconsciously, from this strange Protestant perversion; it has become in this one respect at all events Catholic, that is natural, in the proper sense of the word. There is nothing more natural to man than "back chat"; and this remains true, even when the back chat is ecclesiastically termed "Versicles and Responses". The Puritan ministers of 1660 wanted to have the English Litany turned into one long prayer; they may have been very good people. So the folk who like to listen in silence to long-winded after-dinner speeches may be very good people; but the natural man wants to get a word in, to answer back, with an "Habemus ad Dominum", or some little thing of that kind. Of course, it may be said that, in the case of the speeches, the interjection of "Hear, hear!" fulfils this need of humanity in an imperfect sort of way; and this reminds me of another service that I once attended. This was in a synagogue in the Commercial Road, down in the East End, and it was the Day of Atonement for the Sins of the People, and a very noble service it was. As I was rising to go, I had a whispered conversation with one of the wardens, concerning one or two points which were obscure to me, and I said finally:

"When the letters of the Name are made known there shall be Mercy and Compassion on every side."

To which he replied, cordially:

"Hear, hear!"

I think he must have been corrupted by our Western customs. I think he should have "responded":

"For at His right hand there are pleasures for evermore"—or in words to that effect.

But I was saying, I think that the newspaper business, though, like the toad, ugly and venomous, has yet its precious jewels scattered here and there on its squalid vestments. And I remember one enquiry of mine causing me to feel quite dazed, bewildered, uncertain; curious as to whether I had not somehow strayed into a world of illusion which was not wholly of our earth. For we, it is true, live in an illusory world, but there are other spheres of deception, beyond ours, and of a different order, into which we are scarcely meant to penetrate. So it is with the high geometry. I am sure that three-dimensional space is sheer fantasy and that a cube is as mad a dream as a griffin, or rather a much madder dream. But the geometers tell us that there is a fourth dimension beyond our three, and so on, as I understand, to the *nth* and to infinity; and I am sure that they are quite right—so long as we sleep, until we wake from nightmares to reality. But, in the meantime, I think that most of us prefer to take one set or order of illusions at a time, and are somewhat amazed and confounded at the intrusion of other systems of mania. I rather incline to think that the gentleman at the Mental Hospital who is, unfortunately, made of T.N.T. is a little disturbed by a visit from the other gentleman who is the Planet Neptune or, perhaps, the unrecognised Emperor of the United States of America. But: to our story.

In my newspaper days, I was on the reporters' staff of an evening paper, and the system or part of the system of such a concern is this. The gentleman who is called the News Editor—formerly the Chief Reporter—reads or causes to be read for him all the morning papers. Such items of news or comment that strike him as suggestive are cut out and pasted on slips. These are handed to the various reporters, and briefly, their business is to get something interesting out of the several matters that are handed to them. Thus, a brief paragraph may state that Trinity House has ordered that a Submarine Bell Buoy shall be placed off the Iron Reef, Morlach Head, where wrecks have been frequent. That much information strikes the morning paper as sufficient, but when I first became acquainted with evening journalism a dozen years ago or more, such an item of intelligence was one of the news editor's opportunities. A man would be sent to find out all about bell-buoying, to acquire accurate technical information, and then to make such information intelligible and interesting to the general public, as Mark Twain in his best book, *Life on the Mississippi,* succeeded in making the science of piloting a matter of high entertainment. This, then, was the older theory of evening journalism; and so, one fine day I was handed a slip from a morning paper relating to some threatened litigation over a recent will. There appeared to be one or two odd circumstances in the dispute, and I was sent to "find out all about it", and "see the man", and "see these things which have been left him".

So, off I went, and, I think, took a ticket to Reigate, and in the train read my slip and pondered the case. Briefly: a Belgian gentleman named Campo Tosto—he was of Italian extraction presumably—had lived for some years at a house of moderate size some three or four miles from Reigate—if the town were Reigate. This house was in a hamlet called Burnt Green. Mr. Campo Tosto had been "looked after" by a man and his wife. Their name was Turk. Finally, Mr. Campo Tosto had made a will leaving all he had to Mr. Turk, and some relations had raised objections. I should mention that the Campo Tosto bequest chiefly consisted of objects of late mediæval art.

Very well; I hired a dogcart from a very pleasant old inn at Reigate and was driven to Burnt Green. Naturally—it was my business—I asked the driver if he knew anything about Campo Tosto deceased. Well, a little. "Rather a queer old gentleman; didn't like people coming about his grounds; would shoot at them sometimes."

"Shoot at them!" I exclaimed. "Shoot at them with a gun?"

"Well; now and then, with a gun; but mostly with a bow and arrows."

I made no more enquiries. Presently we came upon the fortunate legatee, Mr. Turk. He was evidently delighted with his good fortune. About him buzzed four press photographers. He was protesting vehemently. He wished for no more publicity. The press photographers declared that nothing was farther from their thoughts than press photography; and as they spoke, they took four shots of Mr. Turk. All this was on the King's Highway, just by the house where Mr. Campo Tosto had lived. I opened my mission to Mr. Turk. I found him still averse from more publicity, even of the written kind. He told me that he would tell me nothing, shew me nothing.

"Except this," he added. "Give me that paper of yours." He took my copy of the *Daily News* out of my hand, deliberately turned it upside down—and read the article or the bit of news or whatever it was with the greatest ease and fluency. He explained his capacity of performing this feat—which, I may say, is a commonplace of the "Case Room" and the "Stone" in a newspaper office.

"You see," said Mr. Turk, "I was a farm-labourer for years, but lately I've had a lot to do with fuller's-earth."

But he would not yield farther. He allowed me to walk with him up the drive of the house which had been the residence of Campo Tosto, cunning with the bow. I wheedled. The press photographers, cleverer than I, took more shots. Mrs. Turk came out and denounced everybody. I was allowed to look in through the half-glass hall-door; that was all. Inside, I could see a huddle of fifteenth-century Flemish Madonnas, brass altar candlesticks of the "spike" pattern, carved oak chests. I drove back to Reigate in a "dwam", as the Scots say; really not knowing whether I stood on my head or my heels, feeling rather like an actor who has been "rushed on" for a small part in a mad drama which he has had no time to study. For consider; here was a man called Campo Tosto living in a place called Burnt Green, which is, practically, a translation of Campo Tosto. Here was a man whose property consisted chiefly in Madonnas and mediæval candlesticks, who shot at intruders with the bow, either long or short. Here was his heir, with the good old English country name of Turk. And here was Turk, who could read print upside down, because he had been a farm-labourer and a worker in fuller's-earth. I went home in that "dwam" and wondered what on earth I was to do, and at last wrote the whole, true story, just as it happened, and ended by wondering whether it were, somehow, a parable, written for our example, though, as I said, I could not conceive what the moral of the story might be. But my news editor would not print it. As he said, gravely:

"You must learn to recognise that sometimes there *is* no story. And, you know, you mustn't say that a man tried to read the paper upside down. That's virtually saying that he was drunk. That's a libel."

"But look here," I ventured. "This man didn't *try* to read the paper upside down. He read it upside down; perfectly. You can't call that a sign of drunkenness: surely?"

But the news editor shook his head. He understood, better than I, that one order of illusion must not be allowed to impinge on another. Anyhow, the singular tale of Campo Tosto and Burnt Green never adorned the columns of the Evening Paper.

*

Then, there was another odd adventure; and this struck me as a difficult problem then, and remains difficult to me now, though I have no doubt there is a perfectly simple solution—if one happened to know it. This was the case of an inquest on the part of our lord the King. Not on a corpse; but on a certain Treasure-trove, found on the coast or seaboard of the county of Suffolk. I say, Treasure-trove, and to the best of my belief that was the matter of the Crowner's Quest, though I have often wondered whether it should not have been of Jetsam. But here was the case: there had been a great storm of wind and waters, and certain mariners hovering on the border of the sea had noticed bright objects shining on the sand, thrown up, apparently, by the great wash of the deep. They had leapt down from their place of observation and had gathered what they could between the waves, and it was found that they had secured a very interesting catch of coins. Here again was the cutting from the morning paper, and off I went to Liverpool Street, bound for the east coast.

There was no railway station anywhere near the desolate spot where this odd incident had happened. The station where I disembarked from the train was full six miles away from the shore, and, so far as I remember, the population it served was lodged in an inn and half a dozen cottages. I hired a man and a trap and drove off over a level country in bitter February weather; the east wind blowing with the bite of the frost in it. It was fiercely cold, but I was a good deal warmed when the lad who drove me, talking of the crops of the country, spoke of "the peasen". Thank God! I said to myself, there is still some smack of old England left in the land. His father of a thousand years ago spoke of "peasen".

We came at last to a curious, desolate, unfinished-looking shore. Desolate? Hardly so dignified as that; there was no solemnity about its cold, barren raggedness. Sand-dunes, I think, but sorry sand-dunes, not big enough to be impressive; more a messy, sandy state of things than sand-dunes. There can be an awful solemnity about a region of sand-hills by a grey sea; but nothing of that here; it looked somewhat as if a speculative builder had heard that some people, with money, had got tired of wild, grey heights of cliff, and all that rather melodramatic, Wilson Barrett style of thing, and were going in for sand and coarse grass, and as if the said speculative builder had carried the sand to this stretch of coast at some expense and had sown the best kinds of coarse grasses, suitable to an eastern exposure. And, further, let us suppose that the speculative builder aforesaid had gone bankrupt in the middle of this enterprise, before he had got enough sand and grass together, and before he had run up more than three somewhat shabby bungalows. This was the aspect of that bleak and biting shore on the winter day on which I visited it, and lest I should be suspected of vilifying that Suffolk coast, I may say that Aldborough lay about five miles down southward, and that the shabby, starved poverty of that shore has been immortally set down in Crabbe.

The limit of land and sea is marked there by a cliff—if you may call it a cliff—rather, by a bank of sand ten, twelve, fifteen feet high. On this height, such as it was, the local fishermen had been standing a few days before, watching the raging storm and the great waves that blew in from the east. Suddenly, one billow, mightier than those before, had brought down a whole stretch of this sandy cliff. And as the wave washed back, the men on the inner heights noticed something bright and gleaming in the wash of waters. They retrieved what they could, and the learned being called in, pronounced that here were very ancient coins. I arrived, it seemed, in the very nick of time. I was shewn to a chamber in a martello tower, and here were the men in blue jerseys and some sort of official personage, and they were counting out their find and sealing them into little packets—to be ready, I suppose, for the Crowner and his quest. And it was an astounding treasure. Far am I from being a numismatologist, but, to the best of my belief, the earliest coins in the find were dated of the eleventh and twelfth century. I remember noting a beautiful mediæval French coin, a disc of gold, with the lilies on it. But the dates went on in a sparse scattering way through the centuries; here a coin, let us say of Richard I, then one of Henry III, then one of Edward II; a gap perhaps to Henry VIII; then a shilling of Elizabeth; and so forth, and so forth. And then; and here was the shock, here the true interest: two or three pennies of Edward VII, and a bronze medal commemorating the late Mr. Spurgeon, that esteemed Baptist pastor.

And, the questions are: What was this queer hoard? How did it come to be gathered together? Who gathered it? How did the great wave discover it? Was it washed up from the sea? Or was it washed down from the cliff?

I confess I find the problem almost as intolerable as the puzzles of Achilles and the Tortoise and the Lying Cretans. For, note, you cannot say that here was the collection of a numismatologist, even if you could get over the difficulty of such a collection being hidden in the sandy cliff or cast into the sea; both of them most unlikely places to keep coins in. For a man curious in old coins would never think of including the Edward VII pennies and the Spurgeon medal in his collection. To me there is only one tolerable solution, and even that is a very tentative one. The solution is this. A little way inland on that dreary coast there must be a well under a thorn or an elder tree. That well was once a Holy well, St. Somebody's Well. Those who made small pilgrimages to it and uttered their vows there were accustomed to drop offerings into the water. As time went on, the sanctity became hazy, the name of the patron saint was forgotten; but there was a lingering, decaying belief that there was something different here from the wells of common use. I remember a man of my age telling me that when he was a child, his nurse used to take him on an occasional walk to a well not far from Clifton. The small party would drink the water from their hollowed palms, and nurse would remark: "This water is so good that we ought to pay for it," and drop a penny or two into the well. And here, doubtless, was the odd end of a very old story. And so, I conjecture—I do not know—that there was such a well not far from the Suffolk coast, that a wave drove in by a subterranean channel and, as it were, sucked the bottom out of it, and bore away, as it washed back to sea, the votive offerings that had been dropped there, even from the days of Cœur de Lion to the days of Edward VII and Mr. Spurgeon.

But the queerest story of all was connected only incidentally and accidentally with the affair of journalism. It happened that I was on some newspaper business when it fell out, but this was merely by the way. It was like this. My errand, whatever it was, caused me to walk from somewhere about Earl's Court Station up the Earl's Court Road—I think it is—to Kensington. To the best of my belief I had never walked that particular track before, during all the days of my life in London. It was in spring and keen weather, and I was wearing my heavy cloak. But the clouds parted and the sun shone out with a sudden heat, and I crossed over from the sunny side of the road to the shady. This action brought into my head Captain Morris's verses, which I quote from memory:

> Some may delight in the country to dwell,
> But give me the sweet, shady side of Pall Mall.

And that, in its turn, reminded me of a passage in Boswell.

"We walked in the evening in Greenwich Park. He asked me, I suppose, by way of trying my disposition, 'Is not this very fine?' Having no exquisite relish of the beauties of Nature, and being more delighted with the 'busy hum of men', I answered, 'Yes, Sir; but not equal to Fleet Street.' Johnson: 'You are right, Sir.'

"I am aware that many of my readers may censure my want of taste. Let me, however, shelter myself under the authority of a very fashionable baronet in the brilliant world, who, on his attention being called to the fragrance of a May evening in the country, observed, 'This may be very well; but, for my part, I prefer the smell of a flambeau at the playhouse.'"

I was strolling along, thinking of this, and remembering that the fashionable baronet's title, given in a footnote, was Sir Michael Le Fleming, when I suddenly saw on a brass plate on the garden-gate of one of the houses the very name that had just entered my mind. Now it is very difficult to avoid lying in telling stories such as these. My impression is that the brass plate bore the inscription: "Mr. Edward—or John or Henry: not Michael—Le Fleming, Physician and Surgeon." But of this I am not sure: the name may have been "Mr. Edward Fleming", without the article. But, in any case, note the mad inconsequence of this odd incident. Here was I led by way of a heavy cloak and sudden warmth to the contrast between the sunny side and the shady side of the street, and so to Captain Morris's preferment of town over country, and so to a footnote in Boswell—and so to an uncommon name on a brass plate in the Earl's Court Road.

And, therefore? Why, therefore: nothing at all. That is the interesting point, the highly significant point of the incident. I am reminded again of the incident of the Poltergeist in the Northern Suburb, since I have been reading only this morning an interview with the Bishop of Zanzibar, now, in this summer of 1923, in England. The Bishop, who talks all like a man, says there are queer things in his diocese. He speaks of strange wedding ceremonies in which the bridal procession walks over the mothers-in-law of the principals; a curious matter, since I should have supposed that the ritual would have been reversed. But the Bishop had tales of things still queerer. He thought it might be easy enough to disbelieve in spiritual essences and powers exterior to man if one lived in England; in Zanzibar, he said, it was not so. He told a story, and I am sure that to the best of his knowledge, belief, and observation it was a true story, of a native mud-hut to which he was summoned. Briefly, the said mud-hut was disintegrating; not by the process of gradual decay, but in a manner of volcanic violence. It was flying into pieces, within and without, and nobody could see by what agency this was accomplished. Before the Bishop's eyes, as he went in, a portion of wall burst from its place and flung itself into the room. A piece of roof dashed itself on his head. Dr. Weston cleared the hut of all human inhabitants, and set a cordon of men about it outside, and still the place continued to "blow up" before his eyes. And then he fell to his exorcisms, and there was peace. And reading this; I remembered the broken kitchen window and the smashed crockery in the house in the northern London suburb; the frightened people, some wretched, some surly, who lived in that house. The Bishop did not say whether the mud-hut had a boy or girl amongst its inhabitants—it is likely that this was so—but it does strike me very forcibly that if you are to be a Rationalist as to this Poltergeist business, you must commit yourself to a highly improbable hypothesis. For you are to observe that if these bangings and crashings and smashings are the work of conscious fraud a highly technical method must be employed, and a method applicable to very different circumstances and surroundings. There cannot be two places, I suppose, much more apart in all their scene and apparatus than the modest villa residence somewhere on the York Road line from King's Cross and the mud-hut of Zanzibar; and yet, the story in each case is, practically, the same story. It is possible, I do not deny for a moment that it is possible, that the London Poltergeist was naughty little Johnny, that the Zanzibar Poltergeist was naughty little Ngachuga; but how very strange it would be if it turned out that there was a secret art of smashing and crashing known to the budding youth of the whole world, and a very subtle art also, which enables the trick to be done under the very eyes of the annoyed and the deceived.

Now, Dr. Weston, of Zanzibar, was inclined by these circumstances to believe in the existence of spirits exterior to the human order, as distinguished from the ghosts of the departed. He said that some of the people in his diocese called them *Djinns,* and, oddly I think, thought it lucky to have one or two about the house, and were willing to pay good Zanzibar money to the medicine man to get such ghostly lodgers. As to this, I know nothing; but, if moved by the evidence of the northern villa and the African hut, we confess that there is something not quite explicable in this Poltergeist business; to what end do we come? Why, to nowhere. There is no *ergo* to the Poltergeist, there is no *ergo* to my strange, true tale of the Earl's Court Road. But I do think that in each there is a hint of certain things. We move, as I have said before, in a world of illusions, but of illusions on one plane. We are mistaken if we think that there is, in ultimate reality, any such thing as a cube, any such thing as a cow; but, at all events, these two are apparently on the same surface of being. But, now and then, there are intrusions upon us from other worlds, probably quite as illusory as our own. And we are accordingly left stupefied. There is no "therefore"; no *ratio.* Suppose a mathematician, in the high matters of his science, to come upon a conic section singing a comic song. Suppose a gamekeeper trapping weasels—and catching Abstract Triangles, or a classical scholar finding the optative mood turning into white mice, with small, gilt bells. Thus it was when the coals shot out of the coal-scuttle at Farringay on the King's Cross Line, when the mud walls broke upon the Bishop's holy head in Zanzibar; when I saw the name "Le Fleming"—or Fleming—on the brass plate in the Earl's Court Road.

But, after all, from all this there does result this one moral, which may be regarded as more especially addressed to us writing persons—and our readers. And that is; that the world, the sum of things of which we are cognisant, is infinitely queer, that even in the rind or surface of it the strangest essences are lurking, that tremendous beauties, amazing oddities are everywhere present, wearing very often, to use the Wardrobe Master's phrase, Disguise Cloaks of the most commonplace pattern.

To take an instance low down on the scale: if you take up a clever Detective Story and read how the hero or villain or the victim or somebody turns scarlet or green when the quiet little country curate comes up to him in the billiard-room, and says: "We're going to do the *Nunc Dimittis* in Stainer in A, after all": if you read this sort of thing, I say, you are highly excited if you are a good man—I am an immense admirer of the early "Sherlock Holmes" myself—and you are on fire to pluck out the secret of the fantasy. But you regard it all as a mere fantasy; you don't for a moment believe that such things happen in what you call "real life"; you are a little ashamed of being even lightly entertained by "such rubbish", you tell your friends how deeply interested you are in Gchkvof, and in psychoanalysis and in the new theory of poetical rhythms. But you are completely in the wrong. Such things are constantly happening in real life, or, at all events, in the only life of which we know anything. I have given a mild instance: after all, a curate may be expected to discuss the *Nunc Dimittis* and Stainer—unhappily, so far as the latter is concerned. But if I wanted to be severely "realist", I should make a shabby sloucher of the streets accost my man, ask for a fag, and then remark: "Why, then, guv'nor, if you haven't got a fag, would you mind telling me what Ateh Geburah veh Gedulah means?" *That* is stark "realism", if you like. And the people who say that it isn't, really mean that they are more interested in vermin, skin disease, and incipient dementia, which are the chief matters to be found in their favourite novelist Gchkvof. And, mind! I do not deny for a moment that these things are a part of the sum total of the world. I despise Gchkvof, not because he writes of lice and the itch; but because he does not understand the significance of either. These people, as Coventry Patmore said, dwell in surfaces, and they don't even understand their surfaces. If they were to make punch—they never would, preferring methylated—they would never comprehend what exquisite poetry of the palate may be obtained by manipulating a lump of sugar and the rind of the lemon and the orange.

And this instance is, as I have said, an instance low down on the scale. Ascend to the heights and think if that young, sick, under-educated apothecary and despised dabbler in verses, mooning one night in the suburban garden up at Hampstead. Think of the young lady close at hand, with her marked preference for the military as contrasted with the poetic character, sipping a little warm sherry and water with nutmeg before going to bed—and the chance bird singing in the shrubs of these raw villas. There you have the elements which issued as the "Ode to a Nightingale", by John Keats, to the great, though secret, terror and dismay of the people who maintain that Keats was silly—he was: that Miss Brawne was sensible—she was: and that nightingales can't help it—they can't. I beg pardon: these people cannot now say that Keats was silly, since he is a classic; but they would have said so if they had known him in the days of his mortality. But it is curious, this reverence for the classic authors; after they are dead. Two or three years ago there was a play produced that dealt with Shakespeare and other illustrious wits of the Elizabethan Age. There was a tavern quarrel, and some confusion in the business, as I suppose, made people think that Shakespeare was represented as stabbing another dramatist. They were horrified. And I have often wondered why they were horrified. Where is the incompatibility between writing wonderful, supreme poetry and getting into a rage? And getting into a rage in the sixteenth century often meant drawing the little dagger. And why should not John Keats have been silly in his love affairs? Even great and successful members of the Stock Exchange and the Bar and mighty leaders of industry have been known to choose amiss. It is possible to win the deserved title of "The Go-ahead Grocer", and yet have a secret taste for skittles or gin—and even for both.

Let us remember from this instance of the silly—or at least, mistaken—young apothecary poet, of the sensible young lady, of the whistling bird in the suburban villa, and, finally, of the well-known Ode, that the most amazing things are latent in the commonest, most everyday, ordinary circumstances; and, furthermore, that these amazing things are the only realities in the matter, and the only realities that do matter.

Strangeness which is the essence of beauty is the essence of truth, and the essence of the world. I have often felt that, when the ascent of a long hill brought me to the summit of an undiscovered height in London; and I looked down on a new land.

V

I had just finished the preceding chapter, when I received from my learned and ingenious friend, Dr. Hubert J. Norman, a paper on "Genius and Insanity", a reprint, I believe, from the *Proceedings of the Royal Society of Medicine*. It begins with the statement that: "For many centuries it has been recognised that there is a definite correlation between genius and insanity." I wrote to Dr. Norman, thanking him very much, and denying everything, like Mr. Gregsbury in *Nicholas Nickleby*.

For, if we come to think of it, it is we, we others, the rest of us who are not men of genius, that should be certified and shut up. I was speaking of Keats, who made the Nightingale Ode out of his own somewhat misplaced passion, and his tuberculosis—if Dr. Norman pleases—and that commonplace Fanny Brawne, and the whistling bird in the grounds of the raw Hampstead villas; well, that man, according to our doctor, is the madman, and we are sane. Not so: if life be anything more than feeding and sleeping like a healthy and well-kept pig; most utterly not so. And, frankly, if we adopt the extremest material view, we cannot say that human life, in its essence, is at all of the same order as the pigsty life. There are things common to both: pigs and men alike desire to be kept moderately warm in cold weather and moderately cool in hot weather; to have enough wash or enough *consommé;* and I am quite willing to allow that, ultimately, *consommé* and wash are the same thing. But there, if you think of it, the likeness stops sharp and finishes utterly. Let us be materialists if you please; but if we survey mankind from China to Peru, according to Dr. Johnson's advice, we must admit that human existence mounts into scales and descends into scales that are altogether beyond the pig register. The Chinese, for example, may be very foolish in making beautiful porcelain, but they have done it for ages; we must surely admit that making beautiful porcelain is human, proper to man, though not proper to piggery. And this vice—if it be a vice—of ornamentation is not the product of a late, corroded civilisation; for all the savages that we know will put twirks and twirls and quillets on their domestic pots and pans; and the man behind the ages scratched the likeness—and a spirited likeness—of some prehistoric reindeer on a surface of bone; after he had gnawed the meat away. Really; it seems quite clear that Art, which, I take it, is equivalent with the genius of Dr. Norman's thesis, is in the very bones of humanity, that it is the *differentia* of man, that which makes him to be what he is, that distinguishes him from sheep and goats, that nourish a blind life within the brain. And how infinitely strange it is that we, who are men because we are artists, should begin to suspect that if we are artists we are mad. Genius, art are, I take it, vision; the power of seeing further, seeing deeper, seeing more than we others see, with the secondary part of expression, the power of communicating in notes, or paint, or marble, or words the thing that has been thus seen. What a very odd thing it would be if, now and then in a generation, there were a man whose physical sight were telescopic, or microscopic, or both at once, who could read, let us say, the name on the ship's side while the vessel was three miles away, who could discern minute forms invisible to common eyes. And let it be farther granted that these reports of the keen-seeing man were amply confirmed by experience; the boat comes into port and everybody can swear that her name is, indeed, *Phyllis Ramsgate;* the microscope is applied to the object, and it is seen that the forms described are actually there. And then science steps bravely forward and assures us that the fellow is suffering from hallucinations. I think the analogy is fair: the creators of Falstaff and Don Quixote were mad—because they saw what we could not see in the heart of man, which we recognised as being infinitely and infallibly true, after the facts had been pointed out to us—by the madmen.

Ah! If I had but been one of this happy race of lunatics; how I would have shaken your hearts with the picture of Clarendon Road, Notting Hill Gate, somewhat bowery, somewhat stuccoey, vanishing into October mists and dimness forty years ago, on still, dull evenings; with the picture of the poor lad who lived in the little top room of No. 23, issuing forth and pacing the dull, still ways, dreaming, ever dreaming and burning for the great adventure of literature; seeing the stones glow into spagyric gold beneath his feet, seeing the plane trees in the back gardens droop down from fairyland, seeing a mystery behind every blind, and the infinite mystery in the grey-blue distance, where, as they tell me, for I have never sought to know, the street becomes dubious, if not desperate.

    If I were only one of those elect madmen I should have known how to make that vague district that mounts upward to the east and the north from Gray's Inn Road as wonderful as that village of La Mancha, "the name of which I have no desire to recollect". I should have been able to give the sense and feelings of the lives that are lived there, remote from all the thoughts of London, from all its central and mastering aims and visions and ambitions. Here live, I know, the people who are a little aside from all our tracks, and, perhaps, some of them have a wisdom of their own or a folly of their own which differ from all our common systems of sapience or stultification. I remember a man of genius who, somehow, utterly missed his way, living in furnished rooms on the side of the steep, 1850 streets that ascend the hill, and he took me round to dingy rooms in Acton Street—where Andrew Lang records an undoubted ghost—and there I shook hands with a negro gentleman from the West Indies, who laboured under a very strong suspicion of leprosy. Apart from this unfortunate black man, who, I hope, was wrongly suspected, I always look upon this strange, unknown region as the country of the people who have lost their way. For example: supposing you are meant by nature to be a tremendous Wesleyan, the Wesleyan who gets into the papers, and stands in the forefront, who is interviewed constantly and is heard at the Central Hall where the old, wicked Westminster Aquarium used to be, who meets Anglican bishops on terms of equality; and supposing that the moving finger writes that, after all, such is not to be your fortune: then you live in a dim square in the quarter I have indicated and attend the services of the chapel of the Countess of Huntingdon's Connexion, situate close at hand. And here I see Blaydes, who was doing quite well in the City in 1890, earning his £200 a year, with a promising love affair with a girl employed in the Daisy Insurance Company—she was one of the earliest of women to take to a clerkly life—I see Blaydes watching poor Gladys as she died of consumption in her chair, babbling, as she died, poor soul, of the hat she meant to buy for Easter; I see Blaydes, who had found a very nice villa at Sutton, with very creditable neighbours, certain to call, who dreamed of the children that were to be, and the social amenities and the sense of stability, the sense of having stayed the dreadful clock of eternity, so long as one clung to that good, red, square villa in Sutton, Surrey, of having stayed that awful clock for a little while, at all events, while one clung to Sutton, Surrey: I can imagine that hapless Blaydes drifting to two rooms in one of the steep streets—I think in the house that has a fine Chinese junk in ivory in the ground-floor window—and living on there for forty, fifty years; a broken, bemused man, who answers most politely when you speak to him, and then says nothing, and dies away into grey silence and the grey region receives him and holds him for all his days.

I am sure that they are all secret people who live there, to the east of the Gray's Inn Road; secret and severed people who have fallen out of the great noisy march of the high road for one reason or another, and so dwell apart in these misty streets and squares of 1850, wondering when it will be 1851.

And then there are places and regions farther afield, places on the verge of London, as unknown to the vast majority of Londoners as Harran in Abyssinia. To attain these, the general recipe is to take something that goes out of London by the Seven Sisters Road, something that touches on Finsbury Park, which, I take it, is the extremest mark of the *Londinia cognita Londiniensibus;* the caravanserai from which the caravans set out across the wilderness; the merchants telling tales of travellers who journeyed on just such a voyage and travail and were heard and seen no more of men; though some chroniclers, in the fashion of old Mandeville, and therefore not to be trusted overmuch, hardily affirm that these very rapt personages have been noted going to chapel on Sundays in Grinders Green, wearing silk hats and frock coats, or as doing their own marketing on Saturday nights, haggardly, awfully, as men dwelling under the command of a *djinneh,* on the heights of Tottenham Rye. Such tales they tell of them that scoffed at the predictions of the geomancers, and undertook the journey of the great caravan that sets out from Finsbury Park, a station on the Great Northern Railway—I have not duly noted its new name—from York Road. His Name is the Merciful, the Compassionate, the King of the Day of Judgment; and in the Halls of Eblis there is no backyard gloomier than the backyard in which York Road Station, King's Cross, is situate. O true believers: be not misguided by those who speak proudly of Euston and Somers Town: for they stray from the way of truth.

Alas! I am sane, as the doctors persist, and so I cannot shew these visions.

But, in sober truth, this equation of madness with genius seems to me in itself a very violent form of craziness. For, if one examines the facts and takes the great names: Shakespeare, Cervantes, Milton, Fielding, Molière, Dickens, Thackeray, Keats, Wordsworth, Tennyson: what an evident lie it all is. I am quite ready to allow that men of great power of mind have gone mad, that many second-rate poets have gone mad; but many first-rate farmers have gone mad, many agricultural labourers and plumbers have developed symptoms of dementia. The fact is, I suspect, that we others, who have no genius, have an instinctive horror and dislike and a kind of dim, unrecognised envy of those who have it. If I were an undistinguished major, not over smart with my men, I think I should be soothed by the scientific assurance that Julius Cæsar and Napoleon were, after all, only high-class lunatics. It is I, the major, who am the perfect soldier, the normal soldier. It is true, indeed, that there is this common bond between some—not all—men of genius and madmen. Each fails to see the objects of earth under his feet, the one because his eyes are dazzled with light, the other because he is stricken blind.

But here we are, still delaying over the great work, *The London Adventure;* and nothing done. I begin to reflect on the matter very seriously, as the summer wears on. It strikes me that I had better try an old recipe of mine, and start out, on a book of a totally different kind, in the hope, I suppose, that the one undertaking, going prosperously—as of course it will—may stimulate the other. I search my mind; I go back to an old notion on which I set my heart far away in the 'nineties of the last century. This was the symbolising of a story of the soul by the picture of exterior things. I would write of a man on his summer holiday, if you please, granting him of special grace a month instead of the usual fortnight. I would write of him as coming to my old territory, and as he ran down the shore of the Severn and the level lands to Newport noting something strange, in the shape of the wild Grey Hills to the north, something outland in those greeny dells of Wentwood, that hide in their lower slopes buried walls and temples. I would take my man to Caerleon-on-Usk and shew him the grey Roman walls mouldering there above the green turf, and shew him the red sunset over the mountain, and the tawny river swimming to the flood. He should go wandering away, this unfortunate fellow, into such a country as he had never dreamed of; he should lose himself in intricacies of deep lanes descending from wooded heights to hidden and solitary valleys, where the clear water of the winding brook sounds under the alder trees. He should be high on Mynydd Maen in the morning, in the fulness of the sun, and drink in the wind that blows there, and look out on the rolling billows of the land, and far down yellow Severn Sea; and finally he should come home again to London and perceive that wonderful things have been wrought in him; that these woods and hollows, these ancient walls and buried temples, this might and majesty of sun and wind upon the summit of the great mountain wall, these enclosed, still valleys of hidden peace and wonder; that all these things have discoursed to him a great mystery, whereby his soul has been renewed within him.

That is a tale that I have been thinking of telling since the eighteen-nineties, as I have said. It is only now that I have finally realised that I shall never tell it. Dear Cinara's dear reign is ended.

But then there was another notion, a very queer one. I have said in another place how much amazed I was when I realised in 1899–1900 that my books were coming home to me in an odd way enough. Casual acquaintance, hitherto of the most ordinary type, meeting me in the purlieus of Gray's Inn, would utter terrifying sentences which would remind me of "The Great God Pan" at its worst. Publishers earnestly requested me to found secret societies; Miss Lally and the Young Man in Spectacles became my constant companions, uttering astounding things and involving themselves in the strangest adventures; I found, with something of a shock, that I was living more in *The Three Impostors* than in Verulam Buildings, Gray's Inn.

Well, I was thinking the other day of these queer doings, when I remembered another circumstance, equally odd, as it appears to me. In 1896 I was deeply engaged in trying to write *The Hill of Dreams*. It was in the June of that year, and I had plunged into the difficulties of the

"Roman Chapter", where the hero—or idiot—of the story is rapt into the ancient Roman world of Caerleon, and listens to the music of those corrupted flutes, and walks on marble pavements that have been for so long broken underground, and drinks from such rich, curious cups as Caerleon churchyard now ostends—when they dig old Owen Morgan's grave. My man had seen the city walls, now grey and ghostly in their æonian decay, all firm and white and shining, and had heard the pealing of the trumpets when the watch was set, he had been a part of the ringing tumult of the tavern by the river, where the priests of Osiris muttered their secret jargon to one another. Very well, indeed; or as well as could be expected in the circumstances. But, remembering all this, there came into my mind a queer affair. I was deep in all these matters, as I said, in that June of 1896; and after one very heavy and terrific night at this dismal old game of invention, I went out for my customary midday stroll in the Gray's Inn–Bloomsbury quarter, still struggling in my mind with my Roman problems, and whimsically considering—without the smallest real belief, I may say—a vague shadow of an intimation I had received the night before that I was really present at the Latin play in the hollow theatre by the river; I was musing over all this, when I suddenly became aware that I had utterly lost the sense of direction. I was disoriented, though I was in a part of London most familiar to me; north and south, east and west had no more any meaning. I knew perfectly well that I lived at 4 Verulam Buildings, Gray's Inn; but as to where Gray's Inn was, considered from the view-point of—say—Lamb's Conduit Street, I had not the remotest notion. I got home somehow by complicated and dubious calculations, and in a somewhat confused and alarmed frame of mind. And odd as it may seem, this perplexity has never wholly left me. I emerge from the Tube Station at Oxford Circus, and take my bearings from All Souls', Langham Place, and thence, by a kind of dead reckoning, find my north or south, east or west.

So, here was the notion. What about a tale of a man who "lost his way"; who became so entangled in some maze of imagination and speculation that the common, material ways of the world became of no significance to him? A fine notion, I think: but dear Cinara's dear reign is over.

So here ends, without beginning, *The London Adventure;* and, indeed,

I have been in London all this summer of 1923. I had thought of calling the book "The Curate's Egg", but I have a distaste for boastful titles.

Supplementary Essays

Strange Roads

The strangest road I know is also the shortest.

Far in the West, a byway, thick and green with the ferns on its banks, and shadowed and cool with overhanging ash trees, diverges at a certain point, and offers the choice of right and left. The way to the right will take you to a castle, that most of us are content to class amongst old things. It was built, this castle of Manorbier, when the Normans first came into Wales, in the twelfth century. It stands now a ruin, and yet a noble place, with its walls sloping outward as they come to the ground—"battering", the builders call this device. It stands high on a sort of inland cliff or promontory, looking westward toward the bay, whose crimson bastions and bulwarks of old red sandstone are crowned with shimmering bracken and golden gorse and purple heather. A noble place, a noble aspect; Gerald Barry, called Giraldus Cambrensis, who was born in the castle, said that it was the fairest place that he had ever seen.

But this is, after all, the new castle, although it is seven centuries old. If you take the way to the left, you appear to go inland and away from the sea. A short lane brings you up to a high, windswept place, whence the blue sea is to be seen far away towards Tenby, but nowhere before you. And then you go down into a gentle valley, and here the road becomes a field track, which ascends another hill and passes through the yard of a whitewashed farmhouse, gleaming in the sun. Here is a height once more, and still no hint of the sea. The track has become a path which goes under tall hedges of thorn by pasture and ploughed lands; and then, at a turn of the hedge, far away below, suddenly appear the blue fields of the sea—foam-flecked, mingling in a haze in the distance with the blue sky and the shining air. But against the sky and above the sea there rises the fortifications of the old castle—a prehistoric stronghold.

The ground falls from your feet steeply down a great slope of gorse and heather and bramble, and then swells up green to the sky. And on this seaward height rise these smooth, rounded, turfy circumvallations, as if one huge green billow were piled high above another with a hollow place between them.

I suppose it was a fort of refuge, a place where a certain number of the tribe could hold out for a while with their backs to a precipitous cliff and the sea; and if you climb the green billows of the outer walls, you come upon the road I mentioned—the short road.

It seems to lead easily to the very heart of the fort, and I can imagine the hosts of the besiegers foaming up it, howling triumph, their rearguard pressing them on. An easy way, and then a sharp turn: and the short road rushes down swiftly to the sheer edge of the cliff, and to the hollow-sounding sea far below.

Another strange road I know is by Marlborough. It leads up from the town to the high downs—for all I know, it was the road on which Tom Smart was driving when he had the adventure of the chair, which turned into a little old gentleman in the roadside inn. It was in the dusk of a summer evening, and the road presently became hedgeless, a white track on a wild, silent hill. The down fell away steeply on one side, and I noticed, as I went along, that little paths went twisting and winding down the turf, pausing by very ancient, low, twisted thorns, and then trickling and turning away towards the dimness of the valley. Somehow, I know not why, these queer, winding paths by the old thorns made my companion and myself think of the People—that is, the fairies—and we turned back again towards Marlborough. And suddenly, quite instantly, without any preparation of a distant sound, soft at first, and growing louder by degrees, we both heard the sharp rattle of footfalls coming behind, and gaining on us. We looked back, fully expecting to see the figure of someone in a great hurry and making pace; but no one was visible. And, though the air was now growing dim and the general aspect of the country indistinct, yet the road, white and chalky, without the shadow of hedges, was quite clear before us. While we turned and stopped the sound ceased, but when we went on, wondering a little, the clatter of hurrying steps was at once renewed and increased, as if the pursuit or the flight had grown sharper.

It was not an echo; the road was soft with dust, and our own footfalls made no distinguishable sound. The noise that followed us was rather that of iron-shod feet beating on a track of granite. We were glad, I think, when we came to that part of the down which is just over Marlborough. Here some preparations for a fair were being made; tents were rising, and roundabouts were being jointed together, and red flares were burning. The rattle of pursuing footsteps ceased as we saw the glimmer of the lamps in the darkness of the little town below. I do not explain: I must simply suppose that we heard some noise which sounded like footsteps, but was not footsteps—that is all.

I spoke of the strange little, wandering downhill tracks by the thorns as suggesting to me, somehow or other, the thought of the Fairy Folk, so I think I should explain, before I go on, that I am not one of those happy people who have only to think of fairies to be hallucinated, whether visibly or audibly. I wish I were, for the actual roads of life are often, or always, gritty and punishing to tender feet, and it would be well and happy indeed if one could be rapt at the desire into the tender grass-grown ways of fairyland. And this reminds me, and again reminds me; but, first of all, of a gentleman of an ancient Irish family that I once knew. Irish, I call him, for his ancestors had been settled in Ireland from remote times, but they were of Norman-Welsh blood, and of the ruling caste, not of the peasantry. Well, this young fellow and I were talking literature together, and especially Mr. Yeats and the new Irish literature, and I was expressing some bewilderment at the fact that men of character, and of apparent good faith, talked of seeing fairies in their daily walks.

"Is it," I said, "some kind of symbolism? Or what do they mean?"

"What should they mean," said young Mr. Geraldine, "but the truth? Can't you see the fairies when you want to? I've only to wish, to see them; and I've often seen them sitting on the stone walls by the mountain roads in Galway."

And then again: Six years ago I was in Belfast. I was on a journalistic mission connected with the Ulster movement, which was perplexing and threatening in the September of 1913. I went with an open mind on the Irish question. On the one hand, I certainly had no sympathies with treason and disaffection, and I thought—and think still—that the Home Rule movement had been advanced by odious and cruel and criminal methods. On the other hand, as all my friends will testify, I am not an extreme Protestant—to put it mildly, or, as the rhetoricians would say, to use an agreeable meiosis—and I had a notion that I should find something extremely dour and harsh among the "Black Prodestans" of the north-east of Ireland.

Well, I went mainly, or almost entirely, among the people who were on the Orange side in politics, and I must say that I have never encountered a more cheery, kindly, or more hospitable folk. They could not do enough to shew me the sights and the ways of Belfast, and they laughed at the bigotries and the furies of the less intelligent of their party.

After I had looked round and about Belfast, I said I should like to see a little of the country, and one of these stern Orangemen immediately said he would take me out into the country in his car. We went some twelve miles out of the town, and when we were about half-way on our journey, there was something in the aspect of the country on either side of the road that impressed me strangely. I do not know how to put my impression into definite words, but, somehow, the wild hills that rose in the distance before us were of an outland form; the rocks that surged suddenly from the land to right and left suggested fortalices of a bygone people, and the very thorn trees that grew in the fields had about them an aspect of concealed mystery.

Some devil of mischief moved me to ask my host, a leading Presbyterian and an eminent solicitor of Belfast, whether there were many fairy castles about that part of the country. I expected to be withered. I thought that McPhee Gillespie would advise me to talk to my friends the Catholics, if I wanted to hear about drivelling superstitions. To my amazement, he replied in a matter-of-fact tone, in the tone that an Englishman would use if he were asked whether there were any county families of note in his neighbourhood:

"No, there are not many fairy raths about here; they're more Antrim way. But I can shew you plenty of fairy thorns. There," he said, pointing to an old, crooked thorn tree growing in the middle of a meadow, "that's a fairy thorn; and I can tell you that the farmer who rents that land—I know him well; he's a strong Presbyterian—would rather cut off his right hand than lay a finger on that tree."

We passed through a dreary village; the ugly houses full on the street, without a sign of a garden or a flower anywhere.

"It's uneasy here sometimes," said Mr. Gillespie. "You see, about half the people are Protestants and the other half Catholics. That's because we're getting higher. You see, the Ulster settlers took all the good land in the valleys and drove the Catholics away, and the higher you go, and the poorer the soil, the more Catholics you'll find." (He was a fair man.)

But I had noticed that, though there were no gardens, nearly every house had a mountain ash planted by its door. I said:

"You seem very fond of the mountain ash here."

"Well," he replied, "the people think that they keep away the fairies. And, as a matter of fact," he added, with a queer smile, "you'll see a good many mountain ash trees planted round my little place out here that I am taking you to."

Then Mr. Gillespie began talking about flax, and the new and improved treatment of it which had speeded up the linen manufacture tremendously; he was a thoroughly practical man. But when we got to his country house, I found, as he had said, that it was fended and hedged about by mountain ash trees.

The saddest of all roads is the road that has been murdered. I know such a road in Wales. It wound to right and left in a goodly and leisurely fashion up a long, steep hill. The road was narrow and deep down in the ground. Every fern grew in splendour on those high banks; the wild strawberry was there, richly scarlet; the fretted leaves of the wild geranium were as if they had come from the margin of a golden, illuminated thirteenth-century missal; the arums shewed purple rods in the spring and red berries in the autumn; meadowsweet flourished where wells of cold water trickled out of the limestone rock. And high overhead, strange, twisted, wizened oaks mingled their leaves across the road; and so here, on the hottest day in summer, there was coolness and a pleasant green shade.

The lane was narrow and steep, but it was well enough for the slow farm traffic, for the parson's trap and the doctor's gig. But a wealthy city man has a house and many motor-cars in that part. And so one year I found that beautiful lane destroyed. All the oak trees had been cut down; the road had been straightened, as if it were the permanent way of a railway; the banks had been sliced on either side in the fashion of a railway cutting. They were bare. Flowers and ferns, and all the intermingled wonderful growth of ivy and honeysuckle and briony had gone; the wells of cold water ran no more from the limestone rock.

With the Gods in Spring

We shall go on seeking it to the end, so long as there are men on the earth. We shall seek it in all manner of strange ways; some of them wise, and some of them unutterably foolish. But the search will never end.

"It?" "It" is the secret of things; the real truth that is everywhere hidden under outward appearances; the end of the story, as it were; the few final words that make every doubtful page in the long book plain, that clear up all bewilderments and all perplexities, and shew how there was profound meaning and purpose in passages apparently obscure and purposeless. These are the words which, once read, throw their light and radiance back over all the book; as the furnace fires blazing up suddenly at night in my own country in the west, shine far away among woods, and in dark valleys, and discover his path to the wanderer in a wild, dim world.

Doubtless there is a secret, an illuminating secret, hidden beneath all the surfaces of things; and perhaps the old alchemists were thinking of that secret when they spoke of the Powder of Projection, the Philosopher's Stone, that turned all it touched into gold.

There are many ways of the great quest of the secret. Some of them fill me with an immeasureable weariness. Not very long ago, there was a picture in a daily paper with an odd history attached to it. The picture was a head of the Christ. It was a photograph of a painting done by a lady who was said to have no artistic skill whatever. But she had worked under "spirit control", and produced this marvel. The great spiritualist authorities said it was the finest head of the Christ that had ever been painted.

Well, I looked at it, and said, "alas!" within my soul. I am not a painter-man myself, nor a critic of painter-men. But—if one has looked at certain of the masterworks with a humble heart, one has learnt a little, a very little, no doubt, but still something of the elements. The L.C.C. schoolboy learns at quite an early age that "dog" is not spelt "c-a-t"; and nothing will move him from this secure faith. So I, with this newspaper photograph of Mrs. or Miss Somebody's head of the Christ. I could see that it was feeble, sentimental, sloppy, with about as much relation to painting or religion as the poems of the late Miss Frances Ridley Havergal have to literature or the faith. Painting men told me that, technically, the work was far from good; and I have no doubt that they were right.

Well, a few days afterwards, another photograph appeared in the newspaper. This also was of a painting of the head of the Christ. This had been painted by another lady, a Swede, I think, some years ago; also, it was said, under spirit influence. It was obvious that picture number one had been suggested by picture number two, and indeed it was stated that the English spirit artist had had opportunities of seeing the work of the Swedish spirit artist. And then the English artist said that she had nothing to do with spirits.

There it is; and it is no matter, as old Mr. Kemble, the actor, used to observe. But the secret is not to be found by that foolish way.

It is long years ago; but I once saw a little glint of the secret, merely a flash of the great radiance, noted at the time, and adored, yet forgotten in a moment, and yet never at all forgotten, but remembered still through all the heavy years that have gone by, and growing clearer, it seems, as the days darken and the shadows lengthen on the hill.

A long while ago; forty years ago, or near it, my two friends, Bill and Jack and I set out for a walk early of an afternoon in March. We are all white-haired now; we have been grilled and roasted and boiled and fried in the fire of life; then, we were raw and merry, and I was the youngest and the rawest of the three. But we were all in the mood of adventure; we would go to Usk—a little town in our country, far in the west—and go to it by a new way. Now, one ascertains the surest 'bus route, or the quickest tubes, and sticks to the way when found; I should hate anyone who proposed to me the theory that it would be fun to get into the City from St. John's Wood by way of Clerkenwell or Pentonville; but we have come to the age of iron. So, then, Bill and Jack and I set out for Usk, and would find a new way of getting to that noble city of two thousand souls or thereabouts. It was governed by a

Portreeve in those days; I severed my connection with the Liberal Party when Lord Rosebery brought in a Bill about Unreformed Corporations, and, like an evil enchanter, turned the Portreeve and Bailiffs into a Local Government Board.

So we set out for Usk, and we took the high road that led to Pontypool under the mountains—not a bit like the road to Usk—and then left it by a lane which seemed likely to bear towards our desired end. Likely so to bear, but quite as likely not so to bear; for lanes twist and turn and bend in the land of Gwent; still, we were going to Usk, and therefore—mark that "therefore", rationalist—therefore, we knew that all lanes led to Usk: Bill and Jack and I.

It was a great day of March. The wind shrilled and rustled and shivered and shook all the dead woods. Though it was so keen and cold, it came, if I remember well, over the wall of the great and high mountain of the west, and drove the white and grey rolling clouds before it to eastward over the billows of the land, over those hidden valleys where the little brooks rush clear and swift under the alders, over the hills where the pine trees stand, over the solemn, hanging woods that were still and sombre in their winter wear. We went along our lane, laughing, because we knew—note that "because", atheist—that it was most unlikely that we should ever get to Usk, and because we knew that we should most certainly get there.

Presently the lane grew too probable. It seemed as if it were really leading us in the right direction. This was not to be endured, and so we chose the first stile that offered itself. I will say, frankly, that reason was not absolutely outraged; it was not infallibly certain that the path opening from the stile was more likely to lead to Constantinople than to Usk; still, it seemed an improbable track, and so we took it gaily.

I wish I could remember all that way. Ah! in these dim and late and dreary hours; if one could recollect the splendour of the dawn. But, to be true, I remember very little; only the wonder, which is always a wonder, of passing through a new land and seeing things which are strange, and thereby receiving a revelation of the unknown; and this revelation you may get as surely in a country lane as if you went to the uttermost parts of the earth. But somewhere on this walk, as we talked of Moll and Meg and strange experiences, unfit for ladies, that glint and twinkling of the high supernal light came to me.

We were skirting a wild little hill. It was a place of rough grass, winter withered; of bracken clumps turned brown; of brambles that had forgotten autumn berries, black and rich; of the twisted, ancient thorn tree, dark and dreaming of fairyland. And as we passed on our way, while the keen wind shook the bare, brown boughs as it went roaring down the valley to the brook, while the huge clouds rolled on to the sea; there I saw on the hillside, under a low black thorn bush rising from withered bracken, the green leaves and pale yellow blossoms of a daffodil, shaking in that high, cold wind.

Vere Deus. It was forgotten as Bill and Jack and I came infallibly by our impossible way over the bridge into the street of Usk, and to the Three Salmons, that inn of old and happy memory. Forgotten then, but remembered always: the shining apparition of the god.

Sixty Years Since

Ballantyne, the printer, objected to the sub-title of *Waverley*. Sir Walter Scott had named his book: "Waverley, or 'Tis Sixty Years Since." But Ballantyne thought the latter portion of the title tame and devoid of interest. He argued with Sir Walter that the manners and customs of 1745 were very much like those of 1805 or of 1815; nothing much had changed; the world was the same dull old place in the seventeen-forties as in the eighteen-tens. And I dare say that Ballantyne thought that it was so. He didn't know he had lived into a new age. Yet in the interval the cause of the Stuarts had gone down for ever; the French Revolution had happened; Napoleon had happened; and locomotion by steam was already beginning.

Sometimes I wonder whether we realise that we, we older ones, have seen some quite remarkable changes in the last sixty years. Not in the big way, the terrific and earth-shaking way of the War; not so much in the matter of Empires that are no more, and a map of Europe that looks quite a different puzzle from the old map: but rather in little things and trifling matters of not much account. Here, for example, is a very early recollection of mine.

I am not sure whether 'twere sixty years since or sixty-one years since; whether it were in 'sixty-eight or 'sixty-nine. It was, anyhow, a tremendously hot summer. The ponds had dried up, the brooks ran shallow, and the mountain was on fire. And on a day of burning heat my father and mother went in the queer little basket-work carriage to pay a call on Mr. and Mrs. Gibbon of the Wern.

They were people of most ancient race of the Border, and they were full of hospitality. Soon, the servant came in with a tray holding glasses, a jug of boiling water, and a bottle. And then and there, with the thermometer climbing up the eighties, the hot gin-and-water was handed round. I don't suppose the house of Gibbon had ever heard of "afternoon tea". I don't know whether there was such a thing. Tea was a meal, taken between five and six o'clock, and you sat round a table to eat it; the dining-room table.

Another small point. My father was a parson, a true parson; a rector, that is, not a mere vicar, curate, or canon, who are often loosely called parsons. And when he went abroad, either afoot or in the basket-work contraption, all the old women curtsied to him; not merely his own or parochial old women, but any old woman, anywhere. So did the little girls; the age in between had ceased to honour the cloth in this fashion.

Again: I am a schoolboy at Hereford in the mid-'seventies, and walking through the town on market day. I wish I had known then what a wonderful sight it was to see. The streets were full of country people, and the men were all dressed in fair white smocks, curiously embroidered. They had dressed in that fashion, I suppose, for a thousand years; and there is a show that is gone for ever. Years afterwards, in 1912, I think, I was down at Dorchester for one of the Hardy Play celebrations. There was an old man playing the fiddle in *The Three Strangers*. He was dressed for the part in a smock. He had been a village fiddler in his earlier days, and so he had come to act his old life as a part in a play, and to wear his old dress as a stage costume.

In my young days the horse was still a going concern. I remember a Monmouthshire man who was paying a visit to an uncle in Glamorgan. He might have driven to Pontypool Road Station, and thence taken train to Caerphilly. He did not do so; he got on his horse, slung a small portmanteau on the saddle, and rode to Caerphilly over the mountains. Perhaps it is fifteen years ago since I saw a man riding in the Strand one morning, not riding to the Row, but apparently to his business. He looked so strange amongst the motor-buses and the taxis that he might have ridden into the Strand from another age.

Indeed, it is time that we left the rude hills and woods of the west and got to more polished regions. I first saw the Strand in 1880. There were no splendid hotels, nor gorgeous buildings devoted to big business and the interests of the Dominions. It was a homely, snug, hospitable kind of street, where a man could eat well and drink well, and go to the play, and have "something hot" afterwards. It was the heart of the theatre world then, and about it were all manner of queer purlieus, green and stony: Clement's Inn and New Inn; sixteenth-century Holywell Street and Wych Street; and devious Clare Market, which, somehow, always made me think of highwaymen in hiding from the cursed crew.

In the London of that day everybody wore a high silk hat and a black morning coat; everybody, that is, who was not a mechanic on his job. Indeed, I have seen traces of an older fashion. It was in the middle-'nineties that, one Sunday morning, I saw an elderly Bencher—as I presume—shewing some ladies round Gray's Inn. He was clad in what we now call evening dress, with a white tie. And, farther back, I can recollect old gentlemen in Hereford going about with large expanses of shirt front, profusely and richly frilled.

And then, as to books, novels. That business was very differently managed then. Suppose you had your first novel accepted—happy man!—by Smith and Elder, or Bentley, or Tinsley. In the first place, before acceptance, it had to be of a considerable length; I think, about 120,000 words. You will remember that Messrs. Smith and Elder rejected Charlotte Brontë's book *The Professor* because it would only make two volumes. A novel was expected to fill three volumes, and it was put on sale at the price of thirty-one shillings and sixpence; a guinea and a half. I did hear of a man buying a new novel at that price; but the book was *Endymion,* Disraeli's last, and he was an enthusiastic local Conservative. But this was not usual.

The Libraries took the book in this, its first, state, and the Reviewers said what they thought of it. If it succeeded, it became a one-volume novel often in yellowish linen boards, and then a "yellow-back", at two shillings. I believe many authors found the system fairly satisfactory.

I hardly think that the dominion, pomp, and power of the Quarterlies lasted into my days. It was only rarely that we spoke of them; though in the mid-'eighties there were some fine and learned wigs on the green over an article by Professor Churton Collins in the *Quarterly Review*. To sum up the affairs briefly: the Professor had charged Sir Edmund Gosse with gross inaccuracy on many high literary points, particularly with the mistake of saying that the seventeenth-century prose treatise *Oceana* was poetry. Whereupon Swinburne replied in the *Athenæum* that the *Quarterly* had loved Tories and hated Keats, and so it didn't matter; a very pretty little controversy.

But, in the main, it was the Monthlies that engaged our attention, the grave Monthlies such as the *Contemporary* and the *Nineteenth Century*. The issue of the new number was an event; one wanted to know what Huxley would have to say to Gladstone, what Tennyson's new poem would be like. Somehow, I do not think that this state of mind, this curiosity, has survived into our day. And so with the Weeklies. From my earliest years I remember the *Guardian* on the rectory table; a bulky, prosperous, archidiaconal journal, printed on thick paper, with a supplement, literary and learned, in which you might well find an historical excursus by Professor Freeman, or a learned essay by Pater.

And, later, when it had pleased God to call me to another state of life; I remember, equally well, another bulky paper, reposing, not on the rectory table, but on the table of the tavern nearest to the stage door. This was the *Era*. I have not seen either *Guardian* or *Era* lately; but when I did see them, it struck me that they were not so stout as of old.

It was somewhere in the 'nineties that I was telling a friend of mine about a new and amazing discovery: certain mysterious rays, by means of which you could so photograph a man's hand that the print would shew all the bones. My friend looked and uttered incredulity and derision.

"But," said I, with indignation, "there's been an article about it in the *Saturday!*"

He changed his note.

"Oh, I *see*," he said, with submission, and profound belief.

Does any Weekly—save JOHN O'LONDON'S—receive such a compliment as this in 1929?

A Lament for London's Lost Inns

Amongst the pleasant recollections of old, vanished London that I possess, none is more agreeable than my memories of the old inns. I do not mean the inns which would now be called hostels—in an attempt to be older than the old—that is, the various Inns of Chancery, though of these I could tell a long tale. I remember well the joy of turning aside from the gaiety of the Strand when the Strand was the cheerfullest, most delightful street in all London, and, as I believe, in the world, and going up a little quiet way and so into Clement's Inn, with its fine Hall, its lawns, its peace and quiet, and its Garden House, a red brick, mid-Georgian house in the middle of a green garden. Once when I turned thus aside, the Garden House was empty, and I asked the rent. It was only £120 a year; but it was slightly beyond my means. And then there was New Inn, as peaceful as Clement's, which it adjoined, but not so green. There were some sad, broken fragments of it surviving off Aldwych up to two or three years ago, but I am afraid these are now gone. The main entrance to New Inn was in Wych Street.

"The gentleman next in esteem and authority among us is another Bachelor who is a member of the Inner Temple. He is an excellent Critic and the time of the Play is his hour of business; exactly at five he passes through New Inn, crosses through Russell Court, and takes a turn at Will's till the play begins."

Thus the Spectator, and thus, I think, we see one of the sources of the younger Dickens. Lyon's Inn, where the old Globe Theatre stood, was gone long before my day. Barnard's, which Pip in *Great Expectations* disliked so thoroughly, has been converted into the Mercer's School, its hall happily intact; Clifford's (one of the choicest specimens of the Inns of Chancery) survives in a fragmentary state, but, I am afraid, will not last much longer. Thavie's Inn, the residence of Mr. Jellaby, still exists by Holborn, but looks exactly like a street. I suppose it was rebuilt soon after the Society of Lincoln's Inn sold it in 1771. It was named after John Thavie, an armourer, who lived in the reign of Edward III. Thus do old, old names, even the names of lesser men, cling to our London byways.

But it is not of the inns of this sort that I am thinking, but rather of those inns of common, not of legal, entertainment. It is odd to note that the word is fast becoming—if it has not become—obsolete, together with tavern; the reason being, as I suppose, that the things themselves are gone, or almost gone. We have hotels and we have "pubs"; scarcely inns or taverns. One of the noblest of the old inns that I remember was the Bell, in Holborn, to which the Amersham coach used to run up to 1880, or thereabouts. Facing the street, it was seen to be a late seventeenth century building of dim and yet warm old brick, with a fine coat of arms in terra-cotta set into it. But within, under the archway, it was, in my recollection, almost a replica of the White Hart Yard, as shewn in the *Pickwick* plate, depicting the first appearance of Mr. Samuel Weller. There were two tiers of galleries leading to the bedrooms, running round three sides of the court. In a word, you turned from Holborn into the seventeenth century, as, by the way, you may still turn if you will take the trouble to walk under Gray's Inn archway through South Square into Gray's Inn Square. Then, near at hand, was Ridley's Family Hotel, with bow windows bulging over the Holborn pavement; a sound, comfortable, snug-looking place, where I can see archdeacons reading the *Times* after breakfast. Of the taverns of former years my chief recollections cluster round the Cock, standing where a branch of the Bank of England now stands, near the corner of Chancery Lane. I had several chops in that old coffee-room of the Cock, where Tennyson called for his pint of port, of which he wrote one of the finest things in the lighter vein that have been written in English or in any other language. Thus to the head-waiter:

> Live long, ere from thy topmost head
>   The thick-set hazel dies;
> Long, ere the hateful crow shall tread
>   The corners of thine eyes;
> Live long, nor feel in head or chest

> Our changeful equinoxes,
> Till mellow Death, like some late guest,
> Shall call thee from the boxes.

My occasional visits to the old vanished tavern were paid in its last days, in '82 or '83. I do not know what I could have been reading, what eighteenth century stuff was in my head—I was twenty at the time—but I had a vague idea that I should meet "the wits" at the Cock, otherwise, "the most respectable authours of the day". I should think I was about a hundred years too late. I met no wits at the Cock, and I found that the coffee-room began to empty soon after nine, when, according to my out-dated fancies, it should have begun to be brilliant. But the odd thing is that once upon a time the sort of thing that I expected to happen did really happen.

"I was about seventeen when I first came up to town, an odd-looking boy, with short rough hair, and that sort of awkwardness which one always brings up at first out of the country. However, in spite of my bashfulness and appearance, I used now and then to thrust myself into Will's to have the pleasure of seeing the most celebrated wits of that time, who then resorted thither. The second time that ever I was there, Mr. Dryden was speaking of his own things, as he frequently did, especially of such as had been lately published. 'If anything of mine is good,' said he, ''tis *MacFlecknoe;* and I value myself the more upon it, because it is the first piece of ridicule written in Heroics!' On hearing this, I plucked up my spirit so far as to say, in a voice just loud enough to be heard, 'that *MacFlecknoe* was a very fine poem, but that I had not imagined it to be the first that ever was writ that way'. On this, Dryden turned short upon me, as surprised at my interposing; asked me how long I had been a dealer in poetry; and added, with a smile, 'Pray, sir, what is it that you *did* imagine to have been writ so before?' I named Boileau's *Lutrin,* and Tassoni's *Secchia Rapita,* which I had read, and knew Dryden had borrowed some strokes from each. ''Tis true,' said Dryden, 'I had forgot them.' A little after Dryden went out, and in going spoke to me again, and desired me to come and see him next day. I was delighted with the invitation; went to see him accordingly and was well acquainted with him after, as long as he lived."

Thus it was at Will's, the Great Coffee House in Covent Garden, as Pepys called it. It was No. 1, Bow Street, on the west side at the corner of Russell Street, and was perhaps the most illustrious of London taverns, from the Restoration to early Hanoverian days. It was here that "old Swinney" described Dryden as holding court. He told Dr. Johnson that "at Will's Coffee House Dryden had a particular chair for himself, which was set by the fire in winter, and was then called his winter-chair; and that it was carried out for him to the balcony in summer, and was then called his summer-chair".

Decidedly, I was a little late in searching for the wits at the Cock.

One Night When I Was Frightened

Most mountaineers, I suppose, have had their moments of panic. Indeed, even to look at the photographs of their perils has often made me shudder. To see a man with his feet resting on a ledge a few inches broad, one hand grasping a craggy projection—and a thousand feet of space beneath him: there is horror in the very thought of such a pass. What the actuality must be I can scarcely conceive; and though the mountaineer clearly has nerves that are well-nigh superhuman, I suppose that once or twice in his awful sport he has known how terror seizes the heart. But the strangest fright that ever befell a mountaineer has been described lately be Professor J. Norman Collie, lecturer in organic chemistry at London University.

This was no case of physical peril. The Professor has climbed most of the peaks of the world, and perhaps he has outgrown all common bodily terrors. At all events, he told some fellow mountaineers how the most intense fear of his life came to him on Ben Macdhui (or Mhuichdhui), the principal peak of the Cairngorm Range; a big mountain, no doubt, according to the standard of the British Isles, and a small affair to an accomplished Alpinist.

It was thirty-five years ago, the Professor said, when the fright of his life befell him. He was coming down the mountain side in a mist, when he began to be aware of strange sounds. He heard a big crunch and then another crunch, as if someone were walking after him, but taking steps three or four times the length of his own. He said to himself, "This is all nonsense." But he walked on, and the eerie "crunch, crunch" sounded behind him, and he was seized with terror. He took to his heels and ran staggering blindly among the boulders for four or five miles nearly down to Rothiemurchas Forest.

And the Professor ends his tale by saying that this experience had made him quite resolved never more to climb to the Cairn of Ben Macdhui alone.

Now this tale of mountaineering strikes me as most impressive. It is much more impressive, to me at all events, than a kind of sequel added by Professor Collie. He had imparted his experience to a friend, a scientific colleague, I think, and this gentleman, Dr. Kellas, had also encountered adventure on Ben Macdhui. He had seen a figure, ten feet high in appearance, walking near his brother, who was sitting down near the cairn on the summit of the mountain. The brother, it turned out, had seen nothing, but an old man of Rothiemurchas Forest, hearing the story, accepted the appearance as quite in the natural order. "Oh, aye," the Highlander remarked, "that would have been Ferla Mhor—the big grey man." That is very fine, no doubt, but it is more in the Highland convention of the ghostly, and one cannot help reflecting that the imagination, helped by solitude and the grim height in the clouds, and the shapes of the mist and the shapes of the dim rocks, is quite capable of fashioning such giant shapes. Not that I would say a word against any well established Gaelic ghost; but each man has his own peculiar taste in the ghastly, and the footsteps of Professor Collie appeal to me more richly than the Ferla Mhor of Dr. Kellas. And there is another reason for my interest: I have heard those footsteps myself, or something very like them.

It happened a little more than twenty-one years ago. My wife and I were touring with Sir Frank Benson, in the summer of 1904, and, amongst other places, we visited Marlborough. It may be mentioned, by the way, that the tour was a semi-scholastic one, the chief attraction being the famous trilogy, Agamemnon, Libation Bearers, and Furies, of Æschylus. Hence Marlborough, hence other places of the same sort.

Well, it fell out that one night at Marlborough some other piece was put on, and neither my wife nor I was wanted at the show, and so towards dusk we strolled out of the little town, and climbed up a white road, and found ourselves on the Downs. And it came upon me as we strolled along that we were in a strange country. It was twilight and the distances were vague, but close at hand everything was clearly presented, and yet (as it seemed to me) not altogether in the light of the common world. As I remember the scene, the road we followed was terraced on the hillside; higher land was above us, and to the right the turf fell swiftly away to some valley that was but dimly visible. And here were little bent thorn-trees, very old and very crooked and very strange, and by them little narrow tracks wound in and out and crept away down the steep hillside to the unseen valley. And the night was still, and not a leaf stirred, and, of course, those tiny paths were sheep tracks.

We strolled along this queer way for a couple of miles, perhaps, and then turned to go back to Marlborough. The night was now upon us, and all that was clearly visible was the road, white with limestone dust. And then we both heard the footsteps. They came behind us, hurried, vehement, insistent, as if some one were walking for his life—such a phrase might be allowed. We both heard but took no notice; it was merely somebody in a great hurry. And I am not quite certain, but I think I half turned and gave a casual glance behind me as if wondering why so fast a walker did not overtake us, who were strolling along in all leisure. And there was the stretch of road, a broad white ribbon in the darkness, and not a soul to see. I made some remark, and we both stopped dead and turned round. Nobody to be seen, and not a sound in the silence. Perplexed, we went again on our way back to Marlborough; in a moment those rattling, violent footsteps rang upon the road behind us. An echo? Impossible; the road was thick with velvety limestone dust; our feet fell upon it in silence. We stopped again; again there was dead silence; we set out once more on our walk, and once more the loud steps beat faster and faster on our track. And so they continued till we came to the hill just above Marlborough, and then the night was silent.

To this day I have never been able to account for those footsteps on the Downs; but that is very far from saying that they were unaccountable.

The Ready Reporter

No process is more common than the passage from time to eternity, since it is common to all men. But the reverse, the going from eternity to time, is not generally supposed to exist, unless we accept Wordsworth's magistral ode in its literal sense. Yet it is fairly descriptive of the process which takes place when an author, a writer of books, turns journalist.

Take my case. For years I had been muddling about with books, or things that I believed to be books. I had written these books purely for fun; and if it be objected that I must have a queer notion of what constitutes fun, I would say that many people find it amusing to engage in boat racing, alpine climbing, and Rugby football, all of which strike me as horrible and penal pursuits. Anyhow, I wrote books because I liked it and, naturally, time did not enter at all into the rules of the game. With the successful novelist, of course, the case is different. With him, publishers are only too glad to make contracts in advance; and he, after due consideration of ways and means and previous engagements, binds himself to deliver a novel of so many thousand words on a certain date one or two or three years ahead, receiving a handsome sum on account of the anticipated royalties. Such an one, therefore, works under time conditions; but my position was not quite like this. I was in no way inconvenienced by clamorous publishers; I was under no contract of any kind. I believed I had a sort of notion for a story, and I began to think it over, with the rest of my days before me, if I would have it so. The time element was quite eliminated from all consideration of the matter, from every division of the work which might be held to be more or less in hand; more or less just as I chose. I could hug my notion all day to my breast, if I pleased; or I could banish it utterly for possible weighing or measuring in the future. I might ponder it on the mountains of the old land, or it might give an extra relish to a pleasant little dinner in Soho. And so with every stage of the business; time was not, so far as the book was concerned. And if the best came to the best, and there was no book, why, it didn't matter. There was nobody to reproach me for the non-deliverance of the copy.

It was after about eighteen years of this state that I passed, as I put it, from eternity into time. I accomplished this feat, to the best of my recollection, by holding forth with some vehemence at the house of a friend, on the Celtic spirit. The date was 1897, and there had been a good deal of talk about the Celtic spirit in literature. It was all quite harmless, for one must shout if one is to be heard; but there certainly was a feeling abroad that so far as literature was concerned, so far at least as the finer, rarer essences of literature were concerned, the mere Saxon was a mere ass. If anything well done was, on the face of it, the work of an Englishman or a lowland Scot, it became necessary to look up the pedigrees of these people; and in nine cases out of ten, Celtic ancestors, Irish, Welsh, or Highland, would be found for them, and thus the source of their genius was clear. Mr. George Moore went a step farther: for he said that the English language was hopelessly vulgarised; tarnished beyond all cleansing. He announced his intention of writing in Irish for the future, a resolve which, I am glad to say, he has reconsidered. I suppose I thought that there was a good deal of exaggeration in all this; at all events I lifted up my voice on the other side one night in Gray's Inn, and declared that no Celt had ever written a masterpiece. And the consequence was that my kind host got me a job on *Literature*, a newly-founded journal published by *The Times*. I worked in the office on "space rates", and since the lapse of years makes trifles interesting, I may mention that my monthly cheque varied from £35 to £40; by no means bad pay for those simple days. The work was easy, after the first struggle. It is so much simpler, having read a book, to say "pooh!" "rubbish", or "a masterpiece", than to find out the reasons on which these summary judgments are based; but this difficulty over, I would say that the reviewer's task is not as a rule severe. And though the time consideration entered, it was generally in a mild form. Now and then, in the case of a book of importance, a date was fixed for the completion of the review; but in most instances, next week was as good as this week. I believe that I was only once acquainted with the true rigour of the game, as I came to know it years later. The assistant editor came into my room and said it was the tenth anniversary of *The Star*—"and we ought to say something nice about them. Write a short note of congratulation, will you; and be as quick as you can—the printers are waiting." And I must say that I was a little astonished, and a little pleased, too, when I found that I could actually write a few lines, with the printers eager for the copy. I patted myself on the back, and murmured that one never knew what one could do till one tried. But this was an exceptional occasion: naturally there is very rarely any reason for rush or hurry on a weekly paper. Since those days I have met men on weeklies who have told me of the stress and pressure of their days, but I have declined to believe in them, for reasons which will presently appear.

I was a year on *Literature* and then, after a brief interval, migrated into a world in which time is of the first consequence; for on the stage, a few seconds may easily become an eternity. Then I worked for *The Academy*, and for a few weeks for *Vanity Fair*, and during two years I was a constant contributor to *T. P.'s Weekly*. All these were weekly papers; none knew what hurry meant. If a two thousand word article were called for, there would be a couple of days or more in which to write it; the margin of time is ample. It was not until I became a reporter on *The Evening News* that I knew what the word hurry meant.

I had already practised a little in the craft. I had written at intervals articles for *The Daily Mail* and *The Evening News* describing scenes amongst the debaters of Hyde Park, Trafalgar Square on election night, the London electric signs, the crowd waiting outside Buckingham Palace while King Edward lay dying: all this was some apprenticeship, but now for the rigour of the game, as I call it. In the old days of my book writing I had a notion that solitude, silence, and, preferably, the waste hours of the night were the true conditions of writing. Now I found myself in a room with half a dozen men and half a dozen telephones. Some of the men would be talking to one another; others would be talking over the telephones; and in the latter case here is a typical conversation which I heard repeated again and again. The reporter, it is to be understood, is making enquiries. He mentions the name of his paper in a clear, calm voice.

"*The Evening News.*"

A little louder:

"*The Evening News.*"

Louder still: "*THE EVENING NEWS.*"

From this moment, the reporter shews signs of irritation. He says:

"*The Evening News*—the newspaper—published in London."

That is no good, it seems. The poor man is roused to a pitch of bellowing, like Prebendary Taylor, and shouts in syllables:

"*Eve-ning News.*"

It ends by his spelling out the name of the paper, letter by letter, cursing his fate, the man at the other end, and the constitution of the universe. And the general chat goes on, and other telephone bells jangle loudly, and a man bursts into the room, looks at the clock, and begins writing for his very life. And there was I in my corner writing also, and getting accustomed to it all, and pretty quickly too. But an odd contrast with literary composition at Llanddewi Fach Rectory, four miles from anywhere; in the dark circle of the woods; time, midnight.

And what did I write about? I hardly know what subject escaped me. I remember one morning, soon after I joined the staff, I saw the editor of *The Tailor and Cutter* about a particular sort of hat said to have been worn by a supposed murderer. I had a long interview with Mr. Frank Benson, as he was in those days. I did a "nice half-column" about the new "Kelly's Directory". I forget what happened in the afternoon and evening, but I remember one evening on which I had three appointments—enquiries and interviews—after seven, and three-quarters of a column review of a book, which I had only received that day, to be written and posted before three o'clock in the morning. One day I got an order to write a descriptive account of a billiard match. I understand nothing of billiards, beyond the bare fact that it is concerned with hitting balls with cues. So I said, in effect:

> "Let's pretend for once that we know nothing about the game. But here are two men hitting balls with long sticks with the most marvellous, almost incredible accuracy; making these balls strike against the sides of the table at exquisitely calculated angles, and then after the most complicated manœuvres bringing these balls to rest again and again in exactly the same positions; let us consider the infinite potencies and potentialities of man in this and in all other directions."

The article passed, somehow, as a new way, if an odd way, of writing about championship billiards. One day I would be discussing the question of submarine bell-buoying with Trinity House; on another talking to a poor man in Stepney who had lost his donkey, the support of his old age. I find myself on a slippery sort of stairway going down to the river by Billingsgate calling out "Dutchman ahoy!" in a coarse, seafaring voice. The exclamation struck me as savouring more of Adelphi melodrama than of real life; but it brought a man from one of the Dutch eel boats in no time. I investigate a Poltergeist in North London in the evening. The next morning I look into the mysterious murder in South London, and then resume a series of articles I am writing on "War and the Christian Religion". I am a bit of a dramatic critic, I review most of the new books, I go out into the country to look for signs of spring, I find myself on a tender off Fishguard at half-past four on a December morning, watching the lighted *Mauretania* glowing over the dark waters: "as if," I thought, "Regent Street came sailing across the Atlantic". I board the *Mauretania,* catch Beerbohm Tree and have "a little chat" with him, I interview other people, and sit down in the gorgeous smoking-room, and tear away at "the story", as we called it in our barbarous tongue. Time to go back on the tender, and landing, I put the first thousand words on the wires, write the next thousand in Fishguard Station, telegraph that; and by nine o'clock am in the second portion of the express on the way to Paddington. Next day I attend a memorial service for somebody in St. Paul's Cathedral, interview an old mender of cane chairs, who remembers the days of basket-work carriages and mourns for them, and finish up with a column of book notes. The day after I am shot down in a bucket a great number of feet into the subterranean workings of the Tube extension to Liverpool Street. I did not like this experience very much, but I liked it better than an adventure that befell me off Plymouth. I had been describing a submarine funeral, which was conducted on the deck of a torpedo-boat, as near the fatal place as might be. I had listened to the shrilling whisper of the boatswain's whistle—which, for me, is one of the tremendous voices of the world. The torpedo-boat was back in harbour; the Admiral and the distinguished people had gone off in their gorgeous galley; and then they shewed me how Mr. Tomlinson and myself were to leave the ship. Over the side a rope-ladder hung loosely; beneath it was a small motor-boat, tossing lightly up and down. I think

Mr. Tomlinson made nothing of it; but it was with extreme distaste that I went down backwards, rung by rung, and then turned and jumped for the boat.

Now, I am in one of the courts of the Old Bailey. A dozen men, who have been out of the court for half an hour or so, come back. Mr. Justice Darling, his Chaplain, and the Sheriff in full costume take their places. A lean, dark young man takes *his* place in a sort of glazed pen. A few questions are put, answers are returned: there is a dead silence. And then a man in a black frock coat whom I had not noticed slides towards the judge; the judge's hand goes to a receptacle under his desk; and the Black Cap, a square of black, limp stuff, is adjusted over the judge's wig, and the four corners drip down about it, and Mr. Justice Darling begins to sentence Stinie Morrison to death. In the same place, on another occasion, two people are standing side by side in the dock: Seddon and his wife. The man has been found guilty of murder, the wife acquitted. In an instant, they bend towards each other, and kiss each other on the lips. Mrs. Seddon is taken below; Seddon is asked whether he can give any reason why sentence of death should not be passed upon him. With perfect calm, in the clearest, coolest manner, he proceeds to give his reasons, including a pretty elaborate statement of his financial position, with £ s. d. all neatly ranged in order and summed up. And then I hear him saying something about "the Grand Architect of the Universe", and see him making a certain gesture. The judge, it seems, is an eminent Freemason. Here is a paradox. This low, ill-graced Londoner, educated, I suppose, as education is understood in our day, cunning and cold and cruel enough to plan and carry out slow deliberate murder, is yet such a simpleton as to believe in fairy-tale Freemasonry, to think that he can turn aside the stroke of English justice by pleading to his judge their common brotherhood.

Indeed, the newspaper reporter sees many strange things. I have no space here to tell the singular story of Mr. Campo Tosto of Burnt Green, Reigate, who shot at strangers with bow and arrows; or the case of the Treasure Trove of the Suffolk coast, a collection of coins beginning with the twelfth century and ending with three pennies of King Edward the Seventh, and a bronze medal of Mr. Spurgeon. I must also leave in silence the mysterious affair of the J. H. V. S. Syndicate, which was concerned with the Ark of the Covenant and the Shekinah.

But there was one feature which almost all these "stories" had in common: they had to be dealt with at the highest possible rate of speed. If I remember rightly, *The Evening News* printed six editions in the day, and all day long the staff was engaged in "catching" these editions. With the earliest I had little to do; though once I met the football pilgrims from the north on Cup Day, between five and six in the morning, and described their joyous dispersal about the London streets. But with all the other editions I had much to do, and had many an agonising race with the hands of the clock, wondering whether I should be able to finish the article in time for "the six-thirty", the most important edition of the day. And then, one fine morning, I thought of a way in which a good deal of time might be saved. It was the day of the "Battle of Sidney Street". By ten o'clock in the morning I was on the roof of the Rising Sun: men of the Scots Guards in the street below, lying on Yiddish newspaper boards, firing; unseen detectives lying hid on all sides, firing; heavy reports of the soldiers' rifles answered by the crackling revolvers of the police officers; and now and again the rending explosion of an automatic pistol coming from a house in a red row of newish buildings—a house with a window open on the ground floor, where a yellow blind flapped to and fro. The "battle" had already lasted for three hours; nobody knew how long it might last; and it suddenly struck me that I should save a good deal of time by describing the scene as I saw it, there and then, instead of waiting till goodness knew when, getting back to the office, and beginning to set down my impressions on my return. I carried this plan into instant execution, described such incidents as struck me as they happened, and, when the red-brick house went up in smoke and flames, judged that my moment had come. I made a hurried exit from the Rising Sun, finished my description in a taxi, and handed it to the chief sub-editor just in time for the edition.

It was a method that I found applicable to many stories. A hero, for example, was being buried at Streatham. The funeral started at three; my instructions were to be back at Carmelite House by four sharp, bringing with me my sheaves: enough of them to fill three-quarters of a column. I waited near the dead hero's house, in a hansom cab, and as the drone of the pipes began—the hero had fought in the Crimea—I began to write. My hansom fell in, and we followed the procession to the gates of the cemetery. Then I drove to the nearest station, and got back to the office with the finished article and about two seconds to spare. The like method served with many memorial services at St. Paul's and Westminster Abbey, with the unveiling of the Queen Victoria memorial statue opposite Buckingham Palace, and above all with the Coronation of King George.

I think it was seven o'clock in the morning when I got to the triforium at Westminster Abbey; it was half-past two in the afternoon when I found myself, dazed and bemused, in the streets; and very soon afterwards the paper, with a full account of the Coronation, was being cried up and down London. Of course, there was ample leisure for the first four hours, and I could describe the scene at my ease. With the entrance of the Royal Procession, the hard and fast work began. I wrote on large quarto sheets. When I had half a dozen or so ready, I put them into a scarlet envelope and held it up above my head. A hand took the envelope, and I bent again to the work, trying to get the sense of splendour and glory, the sense of a mighty incantation, the sense of triumphant organ music and singing voices into the swift words, recording, let us say, a tremendous sentence ringing up to the vault:

Be thou anointed on the breast with the Holy Oil.

I am not quite clear what became of the scarlet envelopes when they were snatched from me. I heard a tale that a boy put them into a bucket, and lowered them from a window to the ground outside. There another boy ran with them and shot them in some pneumatic way to the General Post Office, whence their contents were telegraphed to *The Evening News*.

It was a tiring day.

The Treasure of the Humble

A Note on *The Secret Glory*

The humble have many treasures; and one of the greatest of these is the gift of vision. I do not mean by this the vision of the higher kind, or the sight of those things which it is not lawful to utter, nor even that lower gift which enables the palmist and the astrologer to do some very astounding things every now and again. The vision I speak of has nothing to do with this or that; and yet we poor folk certainly are enabled to see the secrets of many hearts, and this *ex opere operato;* from the very fact of our humble condition. I have been in my day both a strolling player and a newspaper reporter. Neither occupation, I fear, is held in very high esteem, and thus from both careers I have been enabled to gather certain very choice observations. For example, soon after I joined the reporting staff of the *London Evening News,* I was sent to interview an old actor acquaintance, on his commencing manager. I often used to meet him in places of theatrical resort when I was playing at the St. James's Theatre in 1902–1904. He was always very pleasant, and he invariably told me of his great quarrel with George Alexander. I forget what the quarrel was about, but I know it contained the brisk incident of Alexander suddenly popping out of his brougham in Bond Street, and shaking his fist in the face of the astonished player who was sauntering harmless on the pavement of that pleasant western thoroughfare, thinking no evil. Well, I had listened to this tale so often that I felt that it was almost a link between us, and years afterwards when the interview with the manager was "assigned" to me I was pleased at the opportunity of renewing an old acquaintance. He received me with cold dignity and observed: "You will of course understand that the last thing I want is vulgar puffery."

And it was as a reporter that I was once the guest of Keble College, Oxford.

And then the stage has its opportunities of a similar kind. Once on a time I was strolling in *Pastorals,* that kind of theatrical entertainment which is given in the open air—unless it comes on to rain, and then the company and some of the audience adjourn to the town hall or the village schoolroom, where two geraniums in pots and one aspidistra in the same, artistically arranged on the platform, represent, with a technique that is quite Chinese, "these woods" of the Forest of Arden, declared in the text to be more free from peril than the envious court. Well, in the course of one of these old pastoral tours, my management, Messrs. Garnet Holme and Harcourt Williams, had secured a "cert". That is, we were to give our show at a fixed fee from a gentleman who was entertaining all friends round Stow-on-the-Wold at a garden party. The gentleman lived in a noble fifteenth-century house in that noble old village. He was waiting for us at his arched doorway; waiting eagerly. Not exactly out of the spirit of antique hospitality: but, to warn the players to go up by the back stairs. As we went up he called another and a still more stringent warning after us: we were by no means to use any of the hot water from his bathroom tap. I am sorry to say that Henry Herbert—now a "star" in America, I believe—at once had a hot bath, not because he wanted such a thing, but because his was a spirit that revolted against all the forms and circumstances of oppression. Hungry and thirsty we came to that house after a long railway journey, hungry and thirsty we left it in the evening, though the tea spoons were clinking in the saucers, though the ice chimed musically in the big jugs of claret cup, though there must have been an abundance of broken victuals; bread and butter and cake, which would be thrown away or given to the pigs. I believe the gentleman was a retired potter of the Five Towns.

Then there was another occasion, like but yet unlike to the Adventure of Stow-on-the-Wold. Again, we were a company of Pastoral Players, again the management had got a "cert". But this time our host was the late Duke of Norfolk, not a retired potter. Well, need I say more? the Duke treated us poor vagabonds as if we had all been dukes and duchesses, with the kindest hospitality and the most genial friendliness.

So much in explanation of the gift of vision which is vouchsafed to the poor and humble; and now for that particular application of the doctrine which serves as comment to *The Secret Glory*. Those who have read that tale are aware that it shews a certain lack of enthusiasm for the ethos of our great public schools. Well, in 1904, my old master, the Admirable Sir Frank Benson, was touring some of the big public schools with a representation that had been at his heart for many years. This was the Aeschylean Trilogy: the Agamemnon, the Libation Bearers, and the Furies. The first school to be visited was Harrow. Of course, the whole affair had been arranged with the school authorities; the performance was given in the school Speech Room; and, I suppose, Harrow School was in a sense the host, and we, of the Benson Company, were the school guests.

In the Greek classics we read that guests and strangers are the children of God. But I believe that for many years the study of the classics has declined in our schools. It has been pointed out by many weighty authorities that Homer and Virgil do not lead to eminence in that form of swindling the public which is called "business" and more nobly still "big business". I am willing to suppose that young Harrow as long ago as 1904 had realised this, and was devoting its attention to more up to date studies: the manufacture of stinks and shocks and the careful and daily perusal of the *Daily Mail*. This curriculum, perhaps, fails to deal with the treatment due to guests, especially to guests of a humble kind. At any rate, the Benson Company was escorted up Harrow High Street—the street that goes up "the Hill" that makes your heart thrill when you think of the day when you came so strange and shy—by gangs of boys who were lavish of such courtesies as are usually bestowed on procurers and prostitutes. Some of the girls of the Company had their back hair pulled; the manly English schoolboys wanted to find out whether it were real: insults and offensiveness of every sort were rained on all.

At this time, there was a show on the Halls, a sort of Glee Party, called Somebody's Eton Boys. I was telling a friend the story of our reception at Harrow. He spoke of the "Eton Boys", and suggested that we ought to run an opposition show, to be called "Wood's Harrow Boys"—Dr. Wood was then headmaster of Harrow.

"If," he said, meditatively, "if there were any reason to suppose that we could find in the worst slums of London a gang of hooligans offensive enough to be able to play the Boys."

Thus, it will be noted, the poor strollers, by reason of their low estate, were given a vision of the heart of "the Hill" which would never be vouchsafed to the Prince of Wales.

So much for the ethos of the Great Public Schools, as it is dealt with in *The Secret Glory*. Another point in that work relates to the tributes which schoolmasters bestow on one another. I depict them as writing highly offensive folly concerning their colleagues. Not long ago, a few days, in fact, after the publication of *The Secret Glory*, I read a review of Edmond Warre, a life of a late Eton headmaster. Here is the sort of thing that Dr. Warre's colleagues wrote of him.

> "I distinctly feared," writes one of them, "Warre's accession. I feared the dominance of athletics, his own autocratic ways, his strict adherence to the routine of what I thought rather a narrow and dry 'scholasticism'. The change came, and never was a more delightful surprise—it was like a fresh wind from the sea blowing into the place."

Another:

> "I like to think," said a later colleague and successor, "that Warre regarded the school as a great army on the march, the pace of which must necessarily be kept uniform."

The Lower Master:

> Warre's visits to the schoolroom were tremendous, there is no other word for it. The door flew open and in he swept. The boys sprang up with palpitating hearts, and the master looked suddenly bewildered. Yet there was nothing to fear; the awe was that naturally felt in the presence of majesty.

Another one, on his *Boots!*

> They were not ungainly nor policemanlike boots, but only the Head could have wielded them—and "wield" is the only verb that fits the case. . . . he seemed hardly mortal in his bigness.

Yet another, on his Voice, which Vibrated:

> This vibration had an effect on one's spine like that of the fiddles in the overture to Tristan.

So here was a Head—very likely the poor man in real fact was as harmless and as decent a pedagogue as ever took the Sixth in Sophocles—who was like a fresh wind from the sea, who thought that every one of his thousand scholars must learn his lessons at the same rate, just as an army must march at the same pace, who gave the boys a well-known functional disease of the heart by opening a door, bewildered the masters—no great feat, it would seem—wielded boots that none else of men could wield. Bow of Odysseus—was of ordinary height but seemed hardly mortal in his bigness, and had a voice like fiddles!

I gave it up! I tried in *The Secret Glory* to parody the sort of rot that schoolmasters write about each other; but I find that my attempt was useless. These Eton masters on their late Head read like an extravagant parody of my parodies.

What can such fellows as these teach—save cant?

There was once (1830–1840) a Berkshire Tory Squire, an old Winchester boy named Hughes, who wrote a letter of grave rebuke to a son at Rugby. The son, a praepostor, was accused of having allowed an Italian image-man to be "ragged" by the boys. And the father, who seems to have belonged to that interesting though extinct species called "Christian Gentleman", wrote—I quote from memory—

> "Do you not know that it is the special privilege of a gentleman to protect the poor; and that he who despises the poor despises the ordinance of God in making them so?"

Ah, if old Mr. Hughes—he was the father of the author of *Tom Brown's Schooldays*—could have seen the Harrovians hounding their guests, the play-actors and play-actresses, through Harrow street!

My Murderer

Many, many years ago Oscar Wilde wrote a brilliant essay on "The Decay of Lying". It was, really, on the decay of romance writing. There were admirable things in it. For instance, this on the late Henry James—I quote from memory—"He writes novels as if novel writing were a painful duty."

There was a great deal of foundation for the whimsicalities of the essay then; there is more now, and if we had a De Quincey in these days there would be an essay "On the Decay of Murder, Considered as One of the Fine Arts". Really, this Landru person! Compared with the great murderers, the classic artists, as it were, he is a Fergus Hume or Guy Boothby. There is no subtlety about him; he loads his double-tie brush with scarlet paint; he is a scenic artist rather than an artist. As Coleridge so justly observes, the supreme artist obtains his terrific, soul-shattering effects by means which seem in themselves insignificant; it is the bunglers who have to paint the villa red before they can win attention. I may be partial, but I cannot help putting My Murderer—second or third rate assassin as he was—before this ostentatious Landru. We are much too ready in England to neglect home talent for foreign; there is not a single French detective story fit to compare with Sherlock Holmes at his best.

But My Murderer? I call him so with pride that is, I trust, pardonable, because he was the only murderer, to the best of my belief, that I have ever met. He is otherwise known as the Moat Farm murderer. His name was Dougal. Oddly enough, a common interest brought us together.

In those days I owned a cottage on the Chiltern Hills, 200 yards and more from an ill-frequented road. Behind it fields and a deep beechwood going down to Wormesley. I believe it was this name that captured Dougal. All true artists recognise the enormous importance of place names, and Dougal could not fail to perceive the exquisite fitness of this name, Wormesley, for his purpose.

For, the matter was: I wanted to let the cottage on Turville Common, and Mr. Dougal saw the advertisement and called on me in my London chambers. With him came the lady. I could write a volume about her. I can only say here that she—she is a type—is aged forty-five—fifty-five—is dressed in black and carries a small black bag. If you like to follow her into the obscurest bar of some obscure house of refreshment, you may note her sliding a small bottle out of this bag over the counter, and replacing it after the filling process.

Well, I must cut the story short. Mr. Dougal took my cottage for himself and the lady, whom he called falsely, but fondly, Mrs. Dougal. He had his reserves. He did not mention the purpose for which he required the little place—the murder of the lady—or I could have told him that the next house was much too near. Possibly, he thought I had suppressed material facts, for he did me down over three tons of hay, won a county-court action which I was fool enough to bring against him, and, with a final superb gesture, went away without paying any rent.

The lady—with the little property—had left before. She saw, I think, that something was amiss. It was some few years before Dougal found the more suitable Moat Farm in Essex and a lady of a more trusting disposition.

Precious Balms

Let the righteous smite me friendly and reprove me, but let not their precious balms break my head.—
                              Ps. cxli

[Preface]

MELINA PLACE
LONDON
May 1, 1924

My dear Spurr,

I am grieved, indeed, to hear your news about Precious Balms. You say that during your recent visit to America, you were made acquainted with some very serious misconceptions as to a phrase in the Precious Balms prospectus. This document stated that for a certain period I was "languishing in the cells of Carmelite House, serving a term of eleven years' 'hard' for a series of obscure crimes". And now you tell me that in the United States, this small piece of jocularity has been taken in the most serious way. People were anxious to be informed as to the exact nature of the crimes aforesaid, and confused Carmelite House with such establishments as The Tombs, Sing Sing, Pentonville, and Wandsworth.

I am extremely sorry. I had no intention of hurting anybody's feelings. I hope you will present my sincere regrets and apologies—in the proper quarters.

Yours sincerely,
ARTHUR MACHEN

Harry Spurr, Esq.
    Messrs Spurr & Swift
        Pall Mall, London

Introduction

Now and again I glance at the correspondence columns of a paper devoted to the affairs of those interested in writing—and find to my astonishment that authors have a great dislike of unfavourable criticism. I note, for example, the letter of a hurt and angry man, who protests that he has had hard measure from the critic of the *Cosmopolitan,* that the *Daily Mercury* has clearly not read more than three pages of his book, that "Judex" in the *Lyre* says he is ignorant of the elements of prosody: "a harsh judgment," the poor man exclaims, "when directed against one who has the privilege of signing himself 'M.A. Oxon.'" And sometimes the reviewer is entreated to remember that authors have their living to get; the suggested inference being, as I suppose, that the critic should do nothing but praise the books submitted to him. In fact, there are, it seems, authors who conceive that a word of blame is a word of injury, and that a harsh notice is a hardship.

In my opinion, nothing can be farther from the truth. Could anything be duller than a monotonous song of praise? Is it not obvious that there is no sport in easy paths? If this were not so, what would become of the Alpine Clubs? A mountaineer would not thank you for a free excursion ticket to Romney Marsh or the Bedford Level. Opposition, whether it be that of a mountain side or a body of critical opinion, is one of the chiefest zests and relishes of life; and so profoundly have I felt this that for the last thirty years I have hoarded up my "notices", with a very special eye of favour on those "notices" which are foolishly termed bad. Foolishly, for many reasons, some of which I have suggested; but chiefly because there is only one sort of notice that is really bad, and that is no notice at all. I do not know whether there are critical writers who desire to extinguish, make to cease, and bring to nought this, that, or the other author; but if there be such, I take it that they are far too skilled in their craft to think that a man can be blotted out by a column of words, be they fierce or jeering. Silence is the only fatal sentence; from that there is no appeal, for it there is no remedy.

But this must be done thoroughly; and here I would submit is the error of the critic of *The Referee,* the late David Christie Murray, who will be found quoted in the chapter devoted to *The House of Souls.* The writer desired to "slate" the book with all his heart, and devoted the entire front page of his paper to that excellent endeavour. He compared the book to an obscene waxwork anatomical museum at a country fair: "it poisoned everything". He was light: he said it was all "baby-Satanic-tommy-rot", that it was "buried nastiness". He declared that I was taking the ha'pence of the public and making a very decent "(and most indecent)" living by exhibiting the bestial side of my nature. All very well; but the critic tried to combine the method of the hearty attack with the method of silence: he neither mentioned the name of the book nor that of the author. This was faulty technique: for the next few months the Editor of *The Referee* was pestered by correspondents who wanted to know all about it; to ascertain for themselves the extent of the author's depravity.

A more delicate method was employed—in perfect good faith, very likely—by *The Bystander*. Here the critic gave the name of the book and of the author, and praised the stories. *But he pretended that I had no existence.* He said that he had a very strong suspicion that I was, in reality, Mr. Montagu Wood, the author of *A Tangled I*. He added that Mr. Montagu Wood's humour was recognised in "Pop" at Eton, and afterwards at the Canning Club at Oxford.

Now, let us be fair. Honour to whom honour is due; I confess that the dart of this reviewer penetrated my armour. I was genuinely annoyed—I was a lad of 44 at the time—at being practically wiped out of existence. But, on calm reflection, I wonder what Mr. Wood thought of it. Perhaps he, too, was not over-pleased. But I shall always think of *The Bystander* with the respect that one gives to a cunning craftsman.

There are some very tolerable examples to be found in the collection relating to *The Great God Pan* and *The Three Impostors*. Of course I reject the violent, especially the morally violent. These are not in the true tradition of the fine art of reviewing. When *The Manchester Guardian* said that *The Great God Pan* was "the most acutely and intentionally disagreeable" book it had seen in English, the *Guardian* blundered. Deplorable as it may be, we must confess that such a sentence constitutes a valuable free advertisement; and *The Manchester Guardian* did not desire to advertise the work. Indeed it said so; and thus blundered again. And so again *The Lady's Pictorial*: "Men and women who are morbid and unhealthy in mind may find something that appeals to them." This is all wrong. Again we must deplore the anfractuosities of human nature; but to say that a book is morbid and unhealthy is to perform the office of a spielman, not of a censor.

No; the way to go about it, if you must leave the safe way of silence, is to take things lightly. Thus, in *The National Observer:* "In all the glory of the binder's and printer's arts we have two tales of no great distinction." So *The Sketch:* "his bogles don't scare"; *The Daily Chronicle:* "his horror, we regret to say, leaves us quite cold"; *The Observer:* "one shakes with laughter rather than with dread". All these are very well; and another manner is, I think, successful. *The Belfast News Letter* suggested that "sensationalism is the order of the day, and must be pandered to to make the author's pot boil". There is something intimate in this knowledge of the author's very disastrous private affairs which has a strange, elusive charm. Another favourite of mine is Mr. Walkley's review of *Hieroglyphics* in *The Morning Leader:* here again you will find intimate knowledge of the writer's life which could not have been gathered from title pages. Thus, the opening sentence:

"I do not know whether Mr. Machen is to be described as an actor who amuses his leisure with writing books or as an author who fills up his evenings by appearing on the stage." But the article which follows, though decisive as to the demerits of the book under review, is much too long. Brevity in these affairs is of the utmost importance. If you want to say that an author is an unimportant ass, you should say it in a paragraph, not in a column.

Other reviews which I should like to recommend to the notice of the *virtuoso* are *The Manchester Guardian* on *The Hill of Dreams,* and on *Far Off Things;* also *The Boston Evening Transcript* review of *Things Near and Far.* The heading of this article is: "The Reflections of a Man of Self-Conceit". The article displays my mean, sponging, irritable nature in a very masterly manner. And the very choice collection of *Outlook* reviews should not be neglected. And I have said that in my opinion the review of vehement denunciation is not of the highest merit: but I except Mr. Murry's notice of *The Secret Glory* in *The Nation and Athenæum.* There is a completeness about it which satisfies.

Finally, it would not be honest to conceal that there is another side to this as to most other questions. I have had "good" reviews in my day, and I give a few specimens of these. The writers of these articles I leave to the judgment of their own conscience. I only hope that, in the words of Mr. Pecksniff, they have not voluntarily deserted the flowery paths of purity and peace.

The Great God Pan and *The Three Impostors*

The Observer:
  . . . He imagines for us the horrible results of attempting by means of a surgical experiment to make a young woman "see the god Pan." Interference with the nerve centres of the young woman's brain turns her into an idiot; but that is not the worst of it, for she becomes in due course the mother of a sort of she-devil who goes through life frightening people out of their wits, and eventually causes a "terrible epidemic of suicide" amongst fashionable men about town. What is it about this mysterious heroine which sends the friends of her girlhood crazy, which ruins her husband "body and soul," and which causes her later admirers to go out and hang themselves—this is never definitely explained. The intention evidently is to make us shudder by vague allusions to "awful unspeakable elements," which are "triumphant in human flesh," and produce "a horror one dare not name." It is not Mr. Machen's fault, but his misfortune, that one shakes with laughter rather than with dread over the contemplation of his psychological bogey. His art has been hampered by the limitations imposed upon it through his having to leave his ingenious horror "indescribable" and "unutterable" from first to last. Mr. Aubrey Beardsley has no doubt come gallantly to the rescue with the admirably-realised repulsiveness of the nymph designed by him as an appropriate frontispiece. But the general effect of *The Great God Pan,* as well as of the kindred tale which follows it in "The Inmost Light," is, we fear, hardly so creepy as it would have been if it had dared to be intelligible.

The Daily Chronicle:
  . . . His horror, we regret to say, leaves us quite cold. Gallant gen-

tlemen commit suicide at the mere sight of the accursed thing; here be murders, inquests, alarums and excursions—and our flesh obstinately refuses to creep. Why? Possibly because we have had a surfeit of this morbid thaumaturgy of late, and "ken the biggin' o't." Possibly, too, because, while Mr. Machen describes the (literally) panic terror of the various people who behold the monster, he never lets us have so much as a glimpse of the monster for ourselves. How can we be petrified unless we see Medusa's head? To be told that others have been turned to stone won't do. That is only what the soldier said: it is not evidence. . . .

Belfast News Letter:
. . . Sensationalism is the order of the day, and must, we suppose, be pandered to to make the author's pot boil; but, despite the ability in this direction—for the conception is cleverly carried out—we fail to see why such absurdities should be presented to intelligent readers. The Great God Pan, with his syrinx, cloven hoof, and pointed ears, may have been a serious bogey to the rustics Theocritus sings about; but to call in this mythical monstrosity's aid to work on our *fin-de-siècle* nerves is far-fetched, to say the least of it. Mr. Machen's ability is worthy of a better *motif* than mystifying innocent people about the devil, or poking fun at his intellectual admirers about the unseen.

The Westminster Gazette:
If Mr. Arthur Machen's object were to make our flesh creep, we can only speak for ourselves and say that we have read the book without an emotion. There are nameless horrors hinted at in every other page, which make other people turn green and sick, but it is beyond the power of the most susceptible reader to shudder at the shudders of these fictional people. The story is, in fact, most elaborately absurd—so absurd, indeed, as to save it from the less agreeable charge of being nasty, as it would inevitably be if Mr. Machen meant us to take it seriously. We can at least congratulate him on having failed in the courage to make plain the mysterious horrors which are supposed to be in the background of this story, but the result is to leave an inchoate and confused series of impressions, as of a man who is trying to tell a story and fails to express himself. What the intention of the writer could

possibly have been we cannot even conjecture. Mr. Machen was possibly under the impression that he was writing a new *Jekyll and Hyde,* but *The Great God Pan* is as meaningless as an allegory as it is absurd from any other point of view.

The Echo:

Mr. Arthur Machen's story, *The Great God Pan,* published by Mr. John Lane, is a failure and an absurdity. His meaning, if there is any, seems to be the presentation, or rather the suggestion, of Pan as a hideous being or force behind nature, of which being the men who fall victims to an abandoned woman that appears in various disguises and under various *aliases* in the story catch glimpses, from the mere fact that they have yielded to her power—the obscene nature deity revealing himself in the person of the said woman. . . . Mr. Machen tells us that the victims saw the horrors, but that is not enough. Doubtless the horrors would turn out to be mere grotesques, even if we did see them. Not the ghost of a "creepy" feeling will this story produce in the mind of anybody who reads it.

The Speaker:

. . . If we may believe Mr. Machen, those doings are of the most horrible character; but as he omits to tell us what they are, and leaves us merely with the impression that she is "a bold, bad woman" of a very ordinary description, we are compelled to take her special horrors upon trust. Fortunately for everybody, and for the readers of the story in particular, she comes to a speedy end, though whether she is hanged or dissolved into "a substance as jelly" the record fails to explain. All that we know is that Mr. Machen writes of this unfortunate female as if he were in deadly earnest and she were something too terrible to be plainly revealed. There is another story, called "The Inmost Light," bound up with *The Great God Pan.* It deals with a lady who is represented as having been in every way as horrible as the heroine of the first tale; but as the only explicit fact recorded of her is that she frightened the passers-by by the faces she made at the window of her husband's house, the reader is left as much in the dark about her as he is about her sister in misfortune. . . .

The Sketch:

Mr. Machen's *Great God Pan* (John Lane) is concerned more with the nerves than with the imagination. We respect such things as, aiming at the ghastly, do actually make us afraid in the dark and give us hideous dreams. Mr. Machen's inhuman conceptions are put into ingenious forms, and exhibit many different clevernesses; only, his bogles don't scare. In his next attempt, however, he may come out on the right side.

W. L. Courtney in *The Daily Telegraph:*

"Really," laughed the Hostess, "is the Yellow Book a disease?"

"Assuredly," said the Physician, "a very virulent form of jaundice, due to an imperfect digestion and a morbid condition of liver."

"Yes," continued the Philosopher, meditatively, "and *Theodora* is a form of typhoid, due to ethical blood poisoning. *Little Eyolf* and *The Rat-Wife* are varieties of cerebral mania, Mr. Aubrey Beardsley's figures are salient examples of locomotor ataxy, and as for *The House of Shame* and *The Great God Pan*—well, there are some kinds of maladies which are not mentioned outside medical treatises!"

The Manchester Guardian:

The meaning of *The Great God Pan,* by Arthur Machen, is very carefully veiled, and on the whole we are inclined to think it is quite as well that it is so, since such glimpses as we are vouchsafed of it are singularly repulsive. In fact, so far as we have been able to make out, to shock would seem to have been Mr. Machen's sole intention. To achieve this desirable end he has ransacked the dark and hidden corners of Greek mythology, and so piled up innuendo and suggestion, to say nothing of the mere vulgar horror of five mysterious suicides and other unspeakable crimes, that we are afraid he only succeeds in being ridiculous. The book is, on the whole, the most acutely and intentionally disagreeable we have yet seen in English. We could say more, but refrain from doing so for fear of giving such a work advertisement. The same remarks apply to "The Inmost Light," the second story in the book, in only slightly lesser degree.

The Queen:
The Great God Pan comes near being a book of genius with its originality and weirdness; but it distinctly misses it, because Mr. Machen has not the power of indicating, even by a hint, the nature of the horror which made strong men destroy themselves rather than live with such a memory. There are two stories in the book, both dealing with villainous doctors, who make surgical experiments with the brains of living women in the hope, apparently, of turning human beings into devils. In each case the result is terrifying beyond human endurance, according to Mr. Machen, but he does not succeed in imparting any of the terror to his readers. . . .

The Westminster Gazette:
The English School of Diabolists.—I pass now to the fourth class, that of the lurid and nonsensical. These, I take it, are written under the inspiration of the French School of Diabolists. That school, as the reader knows, is possessed with ideas of black magic, spirits of evil, devils become incarnate, and numerous other nightmares of corruption. You are introduced to modern alchemists who use Latin incantations, pour mysterious fluids out of green phials, and by the black arts transform men into monsters, or penetrate the corrupt mysteries of their being. Several English imitators of this school have come into my hands recently, but the wildest is, perhaps, Mr. Machen's *Great God Pan,* published in the Keynotes Series. Here we have a physician who practises the black art, and by an operation on the brain releases for the time being the spirit of a woman, that she may visit the spirit world and "see the Great God Pan." She awakes, a lunatic "convulsed with an unknowable terror." Shortly afterwards she has a child whom we gather from certain lurid hints to be a she-devil incarnate. "When the House of Life is thrown open there may enter in that for which we have no name, and human flesh may become the veil of a horror one dare not express." (That is Mr. Machen's favourite style. The unnameable, the unknowable, the inexpressible, and the unmentionable have a nameless fascination for him.) . . .

Sex-Mania Incoherent.—The wild absurdity of all this really makes comment superfluous. But note the sex-mania in it all. It is an incoherent nightmare of sex and the supposed horrible mysteries behind it, such as might conceivably possess a man who was given to a morbid brooding over these matters, but which would soon lead to insanity if unrestrained. I imagine, however, that Mr. Machen's desire has simply been to emulate certain French practitioners in this line; indeed, the fact that he is so often reduced to gasping negatives proves that he has not made it clear even to himself what he is after. His work is innocuous from its absurdity, but the type is most truly decadent. . . .

The National Observer:

In all the glory of the binder's and printer's arts, we have two tales of no great distinction. Indeed paper and form are worthy of much better things. We look for literature and find the old, old tale of man or woman who is possessed of a devil. Mr. J. Sheridan Le Fanu made our youthful scalp tingle years ago with something of the nature (but infinitely cleverer) of these tales. The doctor who performs weird operations we have met before but not one so fortunate as the hero of "The Inmost Light," the second story in this volume. For this gentleman digs for the soul and finds it in the convenient form of an opal—a dangerous theory surely. Men have committed murder for less. Dr. Black murders his own wife, quite unnecessarily it appears to us, and it is her soul in the form of a jewel which he keeps for inexplicable reasons in a leather case in the back parlour of a toy shop in London. Mr. Machen does his very best to thrill, and relates his horrors in a style which should carry conviction but fails. The incidents are too loosely strung together, and the form of narration, bringing in as it does characters who take no part in the central idea of the tale, inevitably cools the interest of the reader. Again, there is no motive assigned to any action except a vague love of science which certainly fails to convince. Men do not pursue an idea as does Villiers in the first story—doctors do not kill their wives as does Dr. Black in the second tale—without strong incentive, and it is painfully obvious that in the present case their actions are a mere necessity to the author. Mr. Machen writes somewhat conventionally and without affectation. It is in construction that he is as yet markedly deficient.

The Lady's Pictorial:

This book is gruesome, ghastly, and dull. Mr. Machen has done his best with an impossible subject, but although men and women who are morbid and unhealthy in mind may find something that appeals to them in the description of Dr. Raymond's experiment and its results, the majority of readers will turn from it in utter disgust. From first to last there is not one human touch in the story, and not a trace of psychology to awaken our interest in the actions of any one of the characters. Dr. Raymond's apparent conviction that to see the Great God Pan would make up for any loss or suffering entailed by the sight, is almost childish; and as I waded through the dull list of horrors, which the too vivid imagination of Mr. Machen inspired him to write, I bethought me of the curious old legend, so exquisitely told in verse by Mrs. Browning, of the death of "The Great God Pan." It was waste of time for Mr. Machen to bring him to life again. . . .

The Guardian:

Mr. Machen has apparently tried to produce a novelty in fiction by borrowing from Mr. Conan Doyle some of the tricks of style of his detective stories, and uniting them with the rather gruesome studies in dehumanisation which Mr. Stevenson justified by the fine turn he gave them in his *Dr. Jekyll and Mr. Hyde,* and Mr. Rudyard Kipling essayed less successfully in "The Mark of the Beast." According to Mr. Machen's postulate, "a slight lesion in the grey matter" of the brain is all that is needed to "level utterly the solid wall of sense," and enable "a spirit to gaze on a spirit-world." Fantastically enough, this is called "seeing the god Pan," with whom it appears to us to have about as much to do as the vulgar figure which Mr. Aubrey Beardsley has placed on the title-page. The result on a lady of seeing the god Pan is that people feel cold shivers when they look on her, and that she initiates her male acquaintances into mysteries which either kill them outright with horror or send them home to commit suicide—also that she herself has eventually to be put to death by her husband or the amateur detective, and turns into all sorts of remarkable shapes in the process. Mr. Machen frequently informs us that his story is very terrible, and tries to keep up the mystery by breaking off every now and then as if his tale were too dread for words—but these tricks have also their ludicrous side. Perhaps the most discreditable paragraph in a not very creditable book is the "note" at the end of the first story, asserting that the woman of whom it is told "was born on August 5th, 1865, at the Red House, Breconshire, and died on July 25th, 1888, in her house in a street off Piccadilly, called Ashley Street in the story." Mr. Machen should make his choice between the art of fiction and penny-a-lining.

The Cork Examiner:

. . . Arthur Machen wants to thrill us, and sets about his task by mixing surgical experiments, devil-possessed women of weird beauty, Latin phrases, and fantastic art, reminiscent of craftsmen of ages agone, into a pottage which, for our part, we find mawkish. The trick of the thing is at once apparent. Ever so many circumstances, feelings, sights, thoughts, etc., are unutterable, unnameable, unknowable, and unwhisperable, and there are nameless horrors by the hundred. . . . In our judgment this is what children call "a frightened story," and, as an artistic piece of fiction, it calls for no serious consideration.

The Chronicle:

With this new volume Mr. Machen boldly challenges comparison with Mr. Stevenson's *Dynamiters*. The plan of the book is the same; that is to say, a number of short stories are woven into the fabric of a long one. Mr. Machen's literary method, too, is not unlike Stevenson's; there is the same careful turning of the phrase, the nice choice of epithets, the use of certain words in their correct, but not in their common meaning. . . . Mr. Machen's intention in all these stories is to give us a grue, to curdle our blood, to make us think twice and thrice ere we mount the stairs and face the possible horror awaiting us in our dimly-lighted bedroom. Well, all we can say is that he has failed where few writers have succeeded. Edgar Allan Poe has done this thing over and over again. Le Fanu did it once; so did the author of a volume called *Phantasms* reviewed in these columns some months ago; but here the delightful thrill never quite comes off. Mr. Machen lacks the power to create the necessary atmosphere, the atmosphere in which we shiver with apprehension as we breathe it. We all know how in dreams events in themselves commonplace and trifling enough, suddenly become ghastly, horrible, soul-devastating. And all because of our own state of mind. Now an author must somehow or other produce that state of mind in us before he puts us face to face with his creepy situation. He must compel "poetic faith" in us as Coleridge has it; bring us into the mental condition in which we are ready to believe anything. This Mr. Machen never once succeeds in accomplishing. We are interested in his stories, and pleased extremely with the exceedingly careful and polished style in which they are told; we enjoy his humour and marvel at his ingenuity, but that worked-for and longed-for grue never happens. . . . The fact is that to triumph in the particular literary line which Mr. Machen seems to have marked out for himself a certain peculiar sort of genius is, above all things, necessary. With this peculiar sort of genius the fates have not endowed Mr. Machen, and the sooner he frankly recognises his want of it the better, for he has many other and most excellent literary accomplishments.

The Dundee Advertiser:

As tragedy and comedy go hand in hand, so the weird is seldom far removed from the ridiculous. Arthur Machen's volume, *The Three Impostors,* furnishes an excellent case in point. The stories it contains form a connected narrative such as Poe himself might have evolved. These nameless horrors, however, weirdly fascinating as they are, have something in common with the dreaded gnomes and goblins by whose aid intelligent nursemaids are wont to charm little folk to sleep. What place the book will occupy in the literature of entertainment we cannot take upon ourselves to say. We can only regret that the author's singular inventiveness and great story-telling gifts have been employed in so undesirable a cause. What can any healthy-minded reader think of this: "There, upon the floor, was a dark and putrid mass, seething with corruption and hideous rottenness, neither liquid nor solid, but melting and changing before our eyes, and bubbling with unctuous, oily bubbles like boiling pitch. And out of the midst of it shone two burning points like eyes, and I saw a writhing and stirring as of limbs, and something moved and lifted up what might have been an arm." Such visions have before been given to little boys who complained of headache and divers other pains. The family doctor generally diagnosed the case as "mince pies and pickles."

Punch:

The Three Impostors, a novel ("Keynote" Series) by Arthur Machen, opens well, which, by the way, is more than the book does, being a bit stiff; but, though it has the machens of a good story in it, there is very little worth reading after page 64.

Glasgow Herald:

There are some books that produce a positive physical repulsion in their reader. Mr. Machen's extremely disagreeable story is one of them. One may be fond of the gruesome, and even take pleasure in an occasional sup of horror, administered in the piquant and artistic style of which Poe and Baudelaire had the secret. Mr. Machen himself, in his previous volume, led some of us to imagine that a share of the same gift might be found in him. But *The Three Impostors* changes our view. The horror in it is palpably and very literally sickening. Nothing but a smart turn in brisk air can cleanse the feelings of the person who has been unfortunate enough to read this volume through.

Black and White:

The Three Impostors, by Arthur Machen, lacks the vivid sense of actuality genius alone can impart to the grotesque. In less able hands, as Mr. Machen's, the weird tends to merge into the ridiculous. His connecting chain, too, is clumsily wielded, and you close the book, which opens with cleverness and promise, with disappointment.

The Observer:

The Three Impostors: or, The Transmutations, by Arthur Machen, is a puzzling book. It is both good and bad; good in the clear presentation of some parts of it, in clever handling of some difficult characters, and bad because of the indefinite and unreal impression which, as a whole, it leaves on the reader's mind. It also reminds us a little too strongly to be agreeable of a work with which it cannot for a moment be compared—with Mr. Stevenson's *New Arabian Nights.* . . .

Birmingham Post:

This is a singular effort of the imagination, suggestive of a mixture of Conan Doyle, Douglas Jerrold, and the author of the "Murders in the Rue Morgue," seasoned with grim touches of German mysticism. It is not over-delightful reading, but to those, and they are legion, who are fond of being steeped in blood and mystery the book will commend itself highly. It is cleverly constructed, and that is about the best thing we can say of it. No doubt the author's true intent is all for our delight; but, all the same, it is a matter of wonderment to us how it is that men with evident literary talents, which might be pointed to fine issues, should exercise their brain power in the noble cause of bewildering the brains of other people, and this without an adequate purpose.

The Guardian:

We never expected to see the day when we should be tempted to regret that Stevenson had written *Dr. Jekyll and Mr. Hyde.* Nevertheless, when we had waded through the pages of Mr. Machen's last production, we were disposed to feel that even that book was dearly bought at the price of so repulsive an imitation as that contained in *The Three Impostors.* For the impressive and true use of the præternatural in *Dr. Jekyll and Mr. Hyde,* we have senseless and sickening—we can use no other word—pictures of mysterious scenes and of men returning to the bestial form which are meant to inspire terror and intense dread, but really leave us entirely unmoved, although he may imagine that his reader, like his hero, is left "white and shuddering with sweat pouring from my flesh." Language seems almost to fail the author at times; he heaps up epithets of horror, the words "bubbled and boiled out" of one man's mouth "in the fury of his emotion"; another person stands "shuddering and quaking as with the grip of ague, sick with unspeakable agonies of fear and loathing"; a doctor goes to see a patient, and reappears with "an unutterable horror shining in his eyes." If we are not mistaken members of the medical profession would welcome the chance of investigating such a case as that of the gentleman who took the witches' Sabbath drug. Wearied with this hysterical rubbish the reader hurries on to the end, to find in the last chapter that the unfortunate youth who has got tired of the fauns and the mysteries, and all the rest of the Greek burlesque, has been murdered amid most horrible tortures, which, together with his sufferings, are graphically described.

Pall Mall Gazette:

... Mr. Machen errs by never trusting sufficiently to his reader's imagination, and his most elaborate horrors leave us "more than usual calm," except when, by borrowing from Catlin, they make us feel slightly unwell. It is impossible to admire the construction of Mr. Machen's romance so much as if one did not know one's Stevenson. Its framework, with its amateurs of the odd in London; its set of characters who break at sight into ingenious tales of absolute and elaborate falsehood with no particular motive for using the decorative imagination; its choice of a tobacco divan for the amateurs' place of meeting, and sundry other details, is curiously reminiscent of *The Dynamiter*. So, again, the incident of the powder, strangely altered from its pure condition until it obtained the power of "riving asunder the house of life and dissolving the human trinity," and giving a human form to "that which lies sleeping within us all," argues an uncommon boldness in the man who ventures to use it after its being worked into *Dr. Jekyll*. However, if Mr. Machen thinks he can wear the armour of Achilles with grace, that is his affair. He has a sense of style, as witness his pictures of the deserted house and his conception of the possible history of a street. He is strong enough to walk alone, in fact; and we heartily wish him a little more invention and a little less anxiety to make his reader's flesh creep.

Saturday Review:

Mr. Machen is an unfortunate man. He has determined to be weird, horrible, and as outspoken as his courage permits in an age which is noisily resolved to be "'ealthy" to the pitch of blatancy. His particular obsession is a kind of infernal matrimonial agency, and the begetting of human-diabolical mules. He has already skirted the matter in his previous book, *The Great God Pan,* and here we find it well to the fore again. This time, however, it simply supplies one of a group of incoherent stories held together in a frame of wooden narrative about a young man with spectacles. This young man falls into a circle of Black Magicians, who are practising indecorums and crimes at which Mr.

Machen dare only hint in horror-struck whispers. . . . But it fails altogether to affect the reader as it is meant to do. It fails mainly because Mr. Machen has not mastered the necessary trick of commonplace detail which renders horrors convincing, and because he lacks even the most rudimentary conception of how to individualise characters. The framework of the book is evidently imitated from Mr. Stevenson's *New Arabian Nights,* a humorous form quite unsuited, of course, to realistic horrors. . . .

Lady's Pictorial:
If you like the Prologue read the stories. I did not like the Prologue, but I was obliged to read the stories. They are a shade less odious than *The Great God Pan,* but the comparison says but little in their favour, for, in the former, Mr. Machen gave to the world a most gruesome and *unmanly* book. I should like to know how the imagination of the author would work upon clean and wholesome lines.

The Athenæum:
. . . *The Three Impostors* produces on the normal waking mind much the same effect as a hearty supper of pork chops on the dream fancies of a person of delicate digestion: "velut ægri somnia, vanæ finguntur species." It is Mr. Machen's chief joy, in the words of one of his characters, to dabble "with the melting ruins of the earthly tabernacle"; to hint, rather than describe, the unholy joys and infamous orgies of those whose diet is framed in accordance with the recipes of the devil's cookery book, and whose esoteric acquaintance with the black art enables them to practise short cuts to the sundering of body and spirit. The result is never agreeable, occasionally disgusting, but seldom really blood-curdling, since in the last resort Mr. Machen generally takes refuge in a copious use of such words as "unutterable," "hideous," "loathsome," "appalling," and so on. . . .

The Graphic:
. . . It is a pity, I think, that he does not confine himself to the marvellous pure and simple, and eschew the gruesome—that he should not be content with following in the footsteps of Stevenson in-

stead of entering into competition with Poe. For Mr. Machen, though he has, it must be admitted, an occasional inspiration of "the creepy," is too anxious to produce "goose-flesh" in the readers, and in his desire to do so he is apt to seek his efforts in what I cannot but consider an "unsportsmanlike" fashion. For instance, he is too much addicted to the artifice of describing by telling you that things are indescribable. This is a device which, though perhaps not absolutely illegitimate, ought obviously to be very sparingly used; but in *The Three Impostors,* as even more conspicuously in Mr. Machen's earlier volume in the same series, *The Great God Pan,* it is employed to an extent which is almost provocative of parody. A writer must, of course, leave something to our imagination; but when we are continually meeting with creatures whose aspect is too hideous to be portrayed in human language, who utter words too awful to be repeated, and take part in orgies so abominable and revolting that they must for ever remain nameless, even the most indulgent reader may reasonably begin to feel that he is getting rather short measure for his money.

The Echo:

    . . . *The Three Impostors* is plainly based on Stevenson's *Dynamiters.* The story opens in the same way, by a meeting of the principal characters in a West London tobacco-shop, and we have brought before us the same kind of house of mystery, and extraordinary men who haunt Italian restaurants, talk in archaic language, and unceasingly tell each other stories. Mr. Machen would have stood a better chance of favourable judgment if he had not so needlessly invited comparison with one of Stevenson's masterpieces. He has a powerful imagination, and a careful, laborious style. The adventures he tells, centred around a golden coin of Tiberius, are exciting enough to satisfy the most jaded palate. There is no effort made to retain even a reasonable verisimilitude, and probability is cast to the winds. A gentleman looking in an Oxford Street bun-shop is accosted by a stranger, who takes him into an Italian restaurant to dine. There the stranger pours out, with little provocation, a long tale about how, when starving and shabby, he had answered an advertisement for a private secretary, been accepted, gone to America, and the adventures he met with there. Another sits down in the gardens of Leicester Square, when an unknown young lady turns on him and narrates all her family history. Some of the tales are as weird and horrible as anything written in recent years, and there are murders without number. Frankly, the subject matter of *The Three Impostors* is not to our taste. . . .

Literary World:
. . . There are scoundrels who stop at nothing to get possession of magic seals and coins; there are foul creatures that come out of man; there are attempts to make our blood run cold. These all signally fail. We remain unthrilled; we pass from Mr. Machen to our luncheon as easily as we change from one coat into another. He never stirs us. He tells his stories well, and that is all. Why are we so unmoved? Does the fault reside in us or in the author? We are willing to admit that as reviewers we run a risk of having our sensibilities blunted. We do not cry or tremble as easily as we wept and shook a few years ago, but we *can* shed an occasional tear over a book, and we *can* shudder when the real literary magician has us in his conduct. To this title, however, Mr. Machen has no claim, a fact which explains our passive acceptance of his tame horrors.

The New Age:
Mr. Arthur Machen's attempts are the more ambitious and elaborate and the least successful. He well illustrates the limitations and dangers of this class of composition. With all his fertile fancy and constructive ingenuity he cannot create that magic atmosphere of creepiness that we presume it is his chief object to attain. Both *The Great God Pan* and *The Three Impostors* are clever and ingenious stories; but as blood-curdlers they are almost failures. All the materials are there, none of the conjuring paraphernalia are wanting, but alas! we are not in the least deceived by the tricks, and vainly wish that the would-be magician would prevent us from seeing how the thing is done. The fact is that, while recognising the value of "suggestive" writing, and the imaginative effects to be obtained from obscure hints of "unknowable" and "unspeakable horrors," he works this style—that ought to be used with fine reticence—to death, and reduces the "suggestive" theory *ad absurdum*.

Louis Weitzenkorn in *The New York Herald:*

To climb Mount Everest is a great achievement, but there is always a secret hate in the heart of the man who did it first for the man who ascended after him. I do not mean to write this article on Arthur Machen and compare him to Mount Everest. Let us reserve the crests for an Ibsen, a France or a Plato. What I mean by my first sentence is that Machen, at present, seems to be the prized property of a very few persons. He has escaped what Ernest Boyd is pleased to call the æsthete, 1924 model, and sunk to the next lower circle of the intelligentsia, who have an exceedingly happy time springing him upon the ignorami. It has not been my achievement to have read all his work, and there is not enough genuine entertainment in him for me to do it unless *The World* pays me for the job. But I have managed to stow away *The Hill of Dreams, Things Near and Far* (a truly beautiful book, by the way), *Hieroglyphics,* a volume issued under the presentation of Vincent Starrett called *The Shining Pyramid,* and his latest publication here, *Dog and Duck.*

Without going through the rest of his writings I feel rather confident that I know something of him, and so far I have not yet read, in the encomiums of his enthusiasts, the one characteristic of Machen that, to me, lifts the man out of the ruck of those who just have a "beautiful style." It is idle to talk in praise of Machen's writing, as writing. He has polished up the language to a glittering surface. Each word he uses is carefully chosen, so carefully, indeed, that the writing often becomes of greater interest than the substance and the thought.

His latest volume, *Dog and Duck,* is Machen taking a day off. The book is uninteresting except to his worshippers, it being a kind of vaudeville, essays under such titles as "Why New Year?" "April Fool," "Roast Goose: With a Dissertation on Apple Sauce and Sage and Onions." (Notice the recurrent "ands" for a clue to the man's careful style.) In the volume there is nothing of the Machen which brings him, for me, out in the first rank of the modern minors. But in *The Hill of Dreams* and perhaps, strangely, that imitative of Stevenson, *The Three Impostors,* there is the trade-mark of the man, a psychological insight almost uncanny. Machen has plumbed to the foundations, not of obscenity, but of the obscene.

For something over a decade I have watched what is known to the surface observers of Greenwich Village as the Greenwich Villager, the type of the kidding newspaper story, of the Webster Hall dance and the table-d'hôte, where bootleg liquor hides behind the entrée. They are a much more interesting study under the lights of Arthur Machen than the Sunday magazines know. Nor is it true that they alone are a lost tribe in this world. What they represent, I should say, in a rough guess, is about 20 per cent. of the habitable Occident and more of the Orient, and their kindred are to be found in all corners. One, specifically, is a prominent restaurant proprietor. Another is a fairly well-known business man, a third is an editor—in fact I could run pretty near the plane of professions and pick out striking examples of men and women who fall in the category discovered, so far as I know, by Arthur Machen.

It is an exceedingly difficult task to express the thing, to present with clarity what I think Machen means in his major efforts. In *The Three Impostors* there is an episode that symbolically pictures what I mean.

A young man is infected by some loathsome disease. As the malady grows upon him he takes to his room, locks himself in, and his food is left at his door. Finally his sister discovers the food is untouched. Several days go by and the door of that room is unopened. Then the ceiling above the inhabitants below the room begins to leak. The door of the horrible chamber is burst, and upon the floor is a slimy mass from which two human eyes glitter.

I think Machen has intended a symbol here. It is quite possible, of course, that I am doing that famous trick of interpreting into an author something he never senses. Thanking myself for the compliment, I believe, however, that Machen has deliberately intensified a certain type of human being, too populous, alas, and that this slime with its eyes, and the eyes are the most significant part of the picture, is the emphatic point Machen makes. I know this, that after reading and swallowing and then chewing the cud of this particular fantasy I found myself casting up accounts with the world and making of myself a kind of census-taker. I began to remember that certain persons I knew were slimy. Perhaps if I put it this way I would be clearer. Certain persons I knew were possessed of a hidden sexual rottenness, and those persons fell under vastly different indexes. Let me make it specific.

A young man, connected with the theatre, to almost every one who met him was "clean cut, charming, boyish." I think I, alone, held a violent dislike for him, in spite of the fact that he was kindly, confidential, open, toward me—an almost irresistible combination. I was accused of jealousy. My oath of neutrality was sneered at. However, he was then the particular idol of a particular girl. That was two years ago. A few nights past I met that girl and asked about him.

"You never saw such a change," she said. "His face is grotesque. Over it is written the most bestial lines I have ever seen. Everything that was in his soul has come out—in his face. He is horrible."

I think Arthur Machen has penetrated to the bottom of a certain type of man. He chooses to add to this type a touch of the unnatural or supernatural, the latter a wrong term. He speaks of mysterious demons, hill people, horrors that feed upon and devour human beings. He plays upon mythology and Welsh legend, which is all very well; but beneath this penchant for legend there is revealed in this writer a knowledge of vile degeneracy, of inherited devilry that is as accurate as simple mathematics. These invented demons of Machen destroy and devour. In our own specific haunt of so-called Bohemia there exists the type of person who devours and destroys, and beyond this section of the city there are scattered innumerable individuals, the more dangerous because the better disguised, men and women whose foundation is slime, who cannot be caught and held because they slide from beneath the grasp and one says: "I cannot quite catch hold of this person, I cannot quite pin him down, he slips away from me, and yet I have him under my hand, I want to hold him and it makes me sick to feel the touch of his soul."

Those who have read *The Hill of Dreams* will recall the mystical woman of the slums who flits in and out of the night like a bird of darkness, who, not touching the story, gives it an odour—the odour of decay and flesh. To me, as the book has gotten farther away from my first reading, I get to thinking of this woman as a human skull possessed of two full, rich, red lips, the only living thing upon the bones. Perhaps I am heightening the symbolism of Arthur Machen, but then he has revealed in his method specific creatures to me, creatures, however, of the same general base, the same compound of greasy, poisonous elements.

Of course, that which Arthur Machen has been tortured with must necessarily be expressed in symbolism. Gorgeous, magnificent symbolism that is at once satire and tragedy. For these inhuman characteristics in human beings present unexplored windings and twistings. So far psychology does not light up the crooked pathways and metaphysics give little to the pragmatic mind. This unwholesome or unholy nucleus of certain persons is a basic quality which is not a quality, it is something which can be felt and never named, sensed and never touched. It is directly inhuman, remorseless, impenetrable. It is partial atavism, perhaps, but I can't see how much and to guess would be poetic.

All of this does not say one word to the person who has not come up against this quality, who has not felt it, not been made aware of "something wrong" in some one, who has not been pained and stricken with the fear of having looked at a weird and uncanny manifestation. The place to find it most often is in the eyes.

Hieroglyphics

A. B. Walkley in *The Morning Leader:*
   I do not know whether Mr. Arthur Machen is to be described as an actor who amuses his leisure with writing books or as an author who fills up his evenings by appearing on the stage. He was a member of the Benson Company and is now to be seen in a small part in *Paolo and Francesca.* He wrote some years ago a clever, disagreeable book, *The Great God Pan.* He now publishes *Hieroglyphics,* which has attracted me (it is just as well to confess frankly the queer reasons which prompt one to take up new books) by its quiet binding and clear type. Unfortunately the type is clearer than the matter. The book proves to be a discussion, in the form of a monologue, of the question, What is Literature? But the monologue is verbose and the reasoning circuitous— Mr. Machen prefers to call it, after Coleridge, a "cyclical mode of discoursing"—indeed the question is not so much argued as begged. It would be unfair to Mr. Machen to compare him with Tolstoy, who in putting a similar question, "What is Art?" has been as lucid and logical as Euclid himself. Apparently Mr. Machen does not want to be logical. He says that there are only two parties in the world, the Rationalists and the Mystics, and as he happens to "plump for" mysticism, he despises logic as one of the vain shibboleths of the other party.
   Now it is this partisan attitude, this desire to see only one side of the truth, which I think spoils Mr. Machen's book. There is room in this world for both rationalists and mystics (as well as for rationalist mystics and mystical rationalists), and neither side can claim all literature for its own. Being a mystic, Mr. Machen finds the touchstone of all real or, as he calls it, fine literature, as distinguished from mere reading-matter, in "ecstasy." What does he mean by that? "Substitute, if you like, rapture, beauty, adoration, wonder, awe, mystery, sense of the unknown, desire of the unknown. All and each will convey what I

mean; for some a particular one term may be more appropriate than another, but in every case there will be that withdrawal from the common life and the common consciousness which justifies my choice of 'ecstasy' as the best symbol of my meaning. I claim, then, that here we have the touchstone which will infallibly separate the higher from the lower in literature, which will arrange the innumerable multitude of books in two great divisions, which can be applied with equal justice to a Greek drama, an eighteenth-century novelist, and a modern poet, to an epic in twelve books, and to a lyric in twelve lines." Well, of course, "higher" and "lower" here are mere question-begging terms. If you choose to call what appeals to the sense of the mysterious "high" and what appeals to some other sense "low," there is nothing to prevent you. But all that you have established by your classification is the fact that you, being what you are, prefer one sort of thing to the other sort. This is not criticism, it is mere personal whim.

The essential whimsicality of Mr. Machen's classification comes out when he proceeds to illustrate it by specific examples. *Pickwick*, it seems, is literature, while *Vanity Fair* is not. Homer and Dickens are on the same shelf—the shelf labelled "literature"—while Jane Austen and George Eliot are on a lower shelf, labelled "reading matter." Why? Because the authors in the second class only give us pictures of life, adroit rearrangements of what we know; they do not appeal to our sense of the miraculous, our craving for the unknown, like the writers of the first class. *Pickwick* is not a representation of life; "the book is rather the suggestion of another life, beneath our own or beside our own, and the characters, those queer, grotesque people, are queer for the same reason that the Cyclops is queer, and the dragons and dwarfs of mediæval romance are queer. We are withdrawn from the common ways of life; and in that withdrawal is the beginning of ecstasy." What is here said about *Pickwick* is true, so far as it goes, though the comparison with the *Odyssey* is rather forced. All *picaresque* novels—*Gil Blas* or *Roderick Random* or *Pickwick* or *Lavengro*—have something in common with the *Odyssey*, but not much. The *Odyssey* still remains noble poetry, and these others still remain rather ignoble prose. And no parallelism between the *Odyssey* and *Pickwick* will persuade me that the true *differentia* of the latter is its sense of mystery. It is for the fun of the book that the world cherishes it. But, like other mystics—notably M. Maeterlinck—Mr. Machen seems to be somewhat lacking in a sense of humour. For proof of that, you have only to read him complaining of the "limitations" of Miss Austen's characters or complacently calling the creator of Mrs. Poyser "poor draggle-tailed George Eliot."

One imagines for the moment that Mr. Machen is really a humorist of a very subtle kind when he compares the brandy-and-water drinking in *Pickwick* with the Dionysiac orgies from which Greek tragedy sprang. He drags in Rabelais with his *dive bouteille*. "After all, what does this Bacchic cultus mean? We have seen that under various disguises the one spirit appeared in Greece, in the France of the Renaissance, and in Victorian England, and that in each instance there is an apparent glorification of drunkenness. . . . We are to conclude that both the ancient people and the modern writers recognised Ecstasy as the supreme gift and state of man, and that they chose the Vine and the juice of the Vine as the most beautiful and significant symbol of that Power which withdraws a man from the common life and the common consciousness, and taking him from the dust of the earth, sets him in high places, in the eternal world of ideas." The "symbolism" of Mr. Pickwick's milk-punch! The "ideas" of a drunken man! Into such absurdities do writers fall when, like Mr. Machen, they set out with the preconceived notion that all great literature is a form of mysticism, instead of quietly examining the question without any preconceived notions at all.

The truth is Mr. Machen's new dichotomy of Literature and Not-Literature is simply the old dichotomy of Romanticism and Realism. Pater defined the Romantic as the element of strangeness in beauty, and what Mr. Machen is in fact pleading for is the recognition of nothing but Romantic Literature as great or fine literature. In other words he wants to narrow down recognised terms to fit the limitations of his particular tastes. Well, it won't do. He calls himself, somewhat obtrusively, a Catholic, and says that "literature is the expression, through the aesthetic medium of words, of the dogmas of the Catholic Church." Keeping the word "catholic" untainted by any sectarian meaning, I should be inclined to say that "catholicity of taste" is precisely what Mr. Machen lacks.

The Academy:

... Enter Mr. Machen in the part of Boswell to a talker both "literary" and "obscure," who offers a test whereby to separate literature from "fine" literature or, in effect, talent from genius. One listens respectfully to a reading hermit, because, on the face of it, a hermit's opinions should be matured by study and conceived in the calm of one who rolls no logs and grinds no axes. But, to get an unpleasant thing said once and for all, Mr. Machen's hermit is an indolent person, careless of accuracy, who has grudged the labour of justifying some extraordinary depreciations. He is, in fact, for all his anonymity, an egoist, whose object seems to be brilliance rather than elucidation. . . .

The Bristol Mercury:

Hieroglyphics is a somewhat figurative title for the latest book of Mr. Arthur Machen, author of *The Great God Pan*. It reproduces a series of monologues by and conversations with a kind of philosophical literary hermit whom the author discovered in a quaint old house at Barnsbury, an almost mythical region lying between Pentonville and the Caledonian Road. Now and again one discerns a faint and far-away flavour of Coleridge and Lamb in the dissertations, but the philosophy is not of the most profound. . . .

The Globe:

It is to be hoped that the title of this book, by no means a happy one, will not deter anybody from making its acquaintance. For it is a very readable book—at least, it will be found so by all who take any interest in things literary. It might very well have been called, "What, really, is Literature?"—a large question, which the author, Mr. Arthur Machen, does not succeed in answering convincingly. His main theory is summed up in one of his sentences, early in the volume: "If Ecstasy be present, then I say there is fine literature; if it be absent, then, in spite of all the cleverness, all the talents, all the workmanship and observation and dexterity you may show me, then, I think, we have a product (possibly a very interesting one), which is not fine literature." How this theory works out in practice is seen in another sentence: "Here is *Pickwick,* and here is *Vanity Fair;* and, applying my test, I set

Pickwick beside the *Odyssey,* and *Vanity Fair* on top of the political pamphlet." It is impossible to treat with seriousness such propositions; but that is no reason why *Hieroglyphics* should be neglected. There is a good deal in it, mostly incidental, with which we quite agree—such as, for example, the judgment passed on *Dr. Jekyll and Mr. Hyde.* The book is suggestive and therefore interesting. Mr. Machen ascribes it to an "obscure literary hermit," whose conversations he professes to reproduce; but there is no apparent necessity for such machinery. Mr. Machen should have the courage of his opinions—if they are his. Anyway, *Hieroglyphics* can be recommended to the well-read and the thoughtful.

The Daily Mail:

Mr. Arthur Machen, after diligently applying a microscope to sundry literary reputations, has detected a number of spots, which he enumerates in *Hieroglyphics.* This sheaf of essays is undeniably clever; but it leaves an impression of cynical iconoclasm, which sees false gods in books which have fallen under the curse of popular approval. Mr. Machen finds, for instance, that Jane Austen's works are not literature, and that Dickens reeks of Camden Town. Nevertheless, the book is piquant reading, and contains some shrewd pieces of analysis.

Pilot:

The device by which vendors of patent wares tempt curiosity by giving them some curious name is hardly worth the imitation of men of letters, and we admire neither Mr. Machen's title nor his other artifice of throwing what he has to say into the form of monologues delivered by a Coleridge-loving hermit in Barnsbury. His theme is the old one of "What constitutes Literature?" and his answer is given in the single word Ecstasy. The process by which the answer is reached has the merit of simplicity. Literature is explained to mean "fine literature" and (in an unguarded moment) "imaginative literature." "Ecstasy" is "the withdrawal, the standing apart from common life," and it is obvious that this is only our old friend "imagination" under a new and less happy name. Thus only imaginative literature deserves to be called literature, and what constitutes imaginative literature is the quality of imagination, a conclusion which we can reach without going to Barnsbury, but which yet, ere it is attained, gives Mr. Machen occasion for passing some excellent criticisms on the books he reviews. Thus he illustrates his axiom, "Only the Idea is pure art; with Plot and Construction and Style there is an alloy of artifice," by some admirable remarks on Stevenson's *Dr. Jekyll and Mr. Hyde,* and comes near the root of the matter in his criticisms of Mr. Hardy and Mr. Meredith. That he recognises his quality of "ecstasy" in *Pickwick,* despite its cockney atmosphere, is creditable to his generosity. That he adopts *Vanity Fair,* which he never tires of reading, as the supreme instance of "observation expressed with artifice" (and, therefore, outside his definition of "literature"), shows some blindness. Take away Thackeray's deep religious feeling, and the criticism would be true, but by the same process the *Agamemnon* may be reduced to the rank of a bad French novel, and the *Œdipus Rex* to a tale of horrors. To blunder thus seems the Nemesis of the straining after novelty which has made Mr. Machen attribute the worth of literature to its possession of "ecstasy," and the ambiguous definition he has given to this word. To stand apart, not from common life, but from the common view of life, is surely the criterion of true literature, and we are surprised that Mr. Machen should come so near as he does to making the subject rather than the vision (we are careful not to say the "treatment") of it the main test.

The Morning Post:

. . . He talks (like the Walrus) of many things, of office boys, of Coleridge, of words that end in "ings"; of Homer and of Dickens, of literature, of art; of books that bore and "lonely" books, which have "a soul apart." . . .

The Star:

"By what rule are we . . . to judge exactly in the case of any particular book whether it is literature or not?" When I read that question in Mr. Arthur Machen's new book *Hieroglyphics* I pricked up my ears. Here at last, I thought, is the divining rod for which I have yearned. No longer need I vex my soul over the judgments delivered here every Saturday. Fancy a rule which will make me infallible! What is it? "A single word." Out with it! "Ecstasy." Is that all? "Substitute, if you like, rapture, beauty, adoration, wonder, awe, mystery, sense of the unknown, desire for the unknown"—Stop! these words are not "substitutes" or synonyms. They are, I suspect, merely amplifications of another word, romance. Your solution, in fact, is merely a statement of your attitude. You are a romanticist, and I like you, for I am one myself. But your golden rule does not help me, for it leaves me still under the necessity of questioning my own soul. By "ecstasy" you mean YOUR ecstasy, not MY ecstasy. For every man has his own private ecstasy. When you get to work I find that your ecstasy is whimsical. You earmark words and use them in a Machenian sense. You prefer to speak of "feelings" when you mean "the things of life," and you reserve "emotion" for "the influence produced (*sic*) in man by fine art." I challenge the distinction. It is arbitrary. "Thus it will be with emotion that we witness the fall of Œdipus, the madness of Lear, while we feel for our friends and ourselves in misfortune." This will never do. "Emotion" is simply a poor Latin synonym for the fine Saxon word "feeling." How on earth can I confine my "emotions" to literature and my "feelings" to life? No, Mr. Machen, your sophistry won't help me to discover masterpieces for the readers of that "great pale bird," *The Star*.

And, really, your "ecstasy" leads you a mad dance. It makes you rate "George Egerton" above George Meredith. Mr. Meredith, you say, "not only fails in the body of art but even more conspicuously in the soul of it." Clearly, your ecstasy is not mine. While you shut Meredith out of literature you let *Dr. Jekyll and Mr. Hyde* scrape in! After that, nothing you say surprises me. Indeed, it is a relief when you damn Thackeray with Meredith, and canonise Dickens with—Miss Wilkins. For by this time I realise that you have gone MUST. Your "ecstasy" is merely the motor-car in which your preferences go out for a nocturnal ride without a light at seventy miles an hour. It is a very good vehicle if safely used. It is by no means new either. Mr. Watts-Dunton has been employing it for a quarter of a century. Why, his famous discovery of "the renascence of wonder" has become a critical commonplace. Indeed, so thoroughly has it permeated criticism that the phrase is used as literary shorthand for the great generalisation which it connotes. You have, indeed, turned the shorthand into charming *Hieroglyphics,* but you go astray in the application. Your "ecstasy" over that "thick white cloud" in the Tale of Gabriel Grub is quite funny. And if you identify the brandy-and-water scenes in *Pickwick* with the Bacchic cultus, what about Jos Sedley's rack punch? What about Mr. Meredith's glorifications of old port? But much shall be forgiven you because you are a good Pantagruelist, though I think it is a mistake to identify Pantagruelism either with Dionysus and the Greek drama on the one hand or with Dickens and *Pickwick* on the other. Falstaff is the only piece of real Pantagruelism in our literature. And now, let me advise everybody to read *Hieroglyphics*. It is brilliantly written, it bubbles over with pugnacities, and it is alive in every line.

Glasgow Herald:
 . . . The author's main desire seems to be to utter a series of elaborate paradoxes, and he does utter them in a somewhat conceited fashion. Mr. Machen has no doubt got hold of part of the truth, for it is indubitable that the sense of ecstasy, or whatever else one chooses to call it, is a main cause of æsthetic charm. As certainly, however, it is not the whole secret of literature, which admits much more of the pure intellect than Mr. Machen will acknowledge. If there were nothing more in fine literature than he will allow, then our masterpieces of prose and poetry would be nothing more than so many pieces of music; but fine literature and fine music are of course very different things. One judges theories by their results, and there must be something radically wrong about a doctrine which excludes Pope and Thackeray from the fine literary canon—which makes them "artifice" and not "art." There is something wrong also about the critic who permits himself such trivial impertinences as "the egregious M. Voltaire," "poor draggle-tailed George Eliot," "our great false prophet Bacon, a wretch infinitely more guilty than Hobbes." Even dramatically, as the utterances of an obscure literary hermit, such things are not witty—nor yet funny, except in an unconscious way. There are, indeed, better things in the book, and the author succeeds at times in saying a clever thing, as in truth, considering the earnestness of his efforts in that direction, it were hard if he did not. But, on the whole, the essay is the expression of a thoroughly false, unwholesome, and effeminate theory of literature.

The Graphic:

Mr. Arthur Machen's attractive-looking volume with the above quaint title is a little difficult to understand—namely, why was it written and why published? It purports to be records of conversations listened to by the author during many visits to the house of a friend in Barnsbury. In the society of this friend, and in an "old mouldering room," art in general, and the art of literature in particular, seem to have been very thoroughly discussed. This unnamed friend may have been an author, though Mr. Machen confesses himself ignorant, but "he was always ready to defend the thesis that, all the arts being glorious, the literary art was the most glorious and wonderful of all." Mr. Machen has now constituted himself the Boswell of this Barnsbury friend, whose existence we take leave to doubt, and the result is a discursive volume of opinions, given conversationally, on literature and art—on what constitutes literature and what constitutes art, with some smashing of idols (as, for instance, George Eliot, George Meredith, and the already chipped Stevenson), all set forth with a certain amount of affectation in style by the author. Mr. Machen, in point of fact, requires what he is pleased to call "ecstasy" in a book before it pleases him. He has found it in the Mr. Hardy of *Two in a Tower* days, but not in the Mr. Hardy who wrote *Jude,* any more than in the work of the other writers mentioned above. It is well to know, though, that he fancies he detected this quality in *Keynotes,* which circumstance may comfort Mr. Meredith for his lack of it, unless, perchance, he admires that curious work. Those who would know more, however, of the ecstatic in literature must turn to the book itself.

The Pall Mall Gazette:

Mr. George Gissing's "George Ryecroft," in the *Fortnightly,* deals with a subject so like that of Mr. Arthur Machen's *Hieroglyphics,* that for a time one thinks that both authors must be writing of the same person. Both take as spokesman a sort of literary hermit, whose only companions are his books, and who therefore gives forth his views on men and their works with a real or assumed air of detachment. The setting, however, is a little different; for, while Mr. Machen's protagonist is a gentleman with a past, not uncomfortably buried alive in lodgings at Highbury, Mr. Gissing's is an ex-literary hack, who has been left an annuity by a thoughtful friend, and has retired to Devonshire to spend what fag-end of life the newspapers and the publishers have left to him. Yet both gentlemen prose a good deal, and awake in a contentious mind the doubt whether the general public really care so much for the opinions of literary men about books as they seem to imagine. Outside a certain circle the reign of the old favourite seems to be pretty well established, and although a new one is now and then adopted into the dynasty, the admission is always due to his own merit, and not to that of his backers.

The House of Souls

Thomas Lloyd in *The Sunday Sun:*
  . . . He seeks only to entertain by what he considers legitimate forms of art. Nevertheless, there is a distinct likeness between his professor and himself—even to the suffering from overwork and brain exhaustion. The tales strike one as the work of one who has overtasked his imagination in London streets and been overcome by nightmares produced by excessive reading of the discussions of the British Association. An unusual but not uninteresting case! Time and a rest-cure may work wonders—may lead to Mr. Machen's next book being altogether as acceptable as the first story in this, and the successor to *The House of Souls* becoming a house of bodies and hearts and minds.

Academy:
  . . . The particular mark at which this criticism is directed is the mystical tale called "The White People." This story, which is inset into a not particularly well-executed discussion on the nature and spiritual significance of sin, contains the narrative of a young girl, who as a child had lit somehow upon some of the secrets of Fairyland and whose initiation gradually widened as she grew. The thing is not wanting either in imagination or in a certain painful beauty of its own. It is, perhaps, the best-written piece in the book, and the childish, simple language, admirably suggested and maintained, heightens its undeniable pathos. But in the end the young girl is found dead, self-poisoned in time—whatever that may mean—and prostrate before an image which we are given vaguely to understand is symbolic of the "monstrous mythology of the (witches') Sabbath." We cannot satisfactorily follow the process by which this gruesome consummation is attained. Mr. Machen has been inspired, no doubt, by wild, weird places. Their anciently reported spells, as Emerson has it, have crept upon him, but

nowhere here does the enchantment of nature make for sober healing. And why should these influences be set to work upon a pure young spirit for sorcery rather than for sanctification? If Mr. Machen should answer: Why not? we can only say how very greatly we should prefer the alternative. The other experiments with the "gurgoylesque" are at least legitimate. Weird and resourceful as they are, however, perhaps they rather fail of horror in their super-psychical parts. Nothing elsewhere in "The Great God Pan" approaches the effect produced upon the reader by the callousness of the experiment of the doctor (in the preliminary chapter) upon the brain of the girl who had once owed her life to him, and that incident is nearer to the possibilities of a lust for science than any part of the resulting coil, in which the devil became incarnate for a while and was made woman. In neither this nor the clever arabesque entitled *The Three Impostors* (which might well have been called "The Murderers' Fantasia") is the elaborate surrounding scroll-work quite as effective as it might be; and in the latter extravaganza we lose touch with the main event through the plethora of side tales with which it is garnished, though a word of praise is due to the various literary and artistic characters upon whose vagaries and idiosyncrasies the action indirectly hinges. . . .

The Standard:

It is a pity that Mr. Machen has done several things in connection with his new volume of short stories. First and foremost, he might have very well dispensed with his preface. Mr. Machen is clever, of course, but his bland references to the example of Mr. Kipling and Edgar Allan Poe as "fellow-authors" does not convince—it only irritates. Also his diatribe about the Puritan elements in the English character is quite out of date. Nearly every man who has written decadent fiction within the past fifteen years has lashed himself into a similar fury because he fancies that it has been "tacitly, if not openly, ordered that the English novel is only great when it is a sermon, a tract, or a pamphlet in disguise." The success or failure of a book is not, as Mr. Machen seems to think, governed by hard-headed men of business, who have never disguised their intolerance of imagination, *quâ* imagination, and who believe that "English fiction must justify itself either as containing useful doctrine and information, or as a manifest transcript of life as it is known to the average reader, due regard being had, of course, to the salutary conventions of the social order." It is almost invariably limited by its own qualities. Only let Mr. Machen produce a work of genius—and his fame shall be known afar. Another source of difference which we have with this writer is the inclusion of the first story, "A Fragment of Life," in *The House of Souls*. That story, in its particular way, is almost perfect—tender, true, intimate, and restrained—in its exhibition of how a small suburban clerk and his wife came to awake from their dream of a London suburb, of daily labour, and of weary, useless little things, and saw the things that really mattered in life, with the result that "the voices of men and women came to sound with strange notes, with the echo rather of a music that came over unknown hills." Its mystical qualities are both rare and beautiful, and, as a work of art alone, it deserves to live. But the other stories of Black Magic—of Pan, and of fauns and satyrs and other fearful wild-fowl of the occultist's stock-in-trade—frankly, they are failures. In one aspect, they would shame any respectable sensational novelist who practises a certain amount of natural illusion. In another—they are ineffective. They do not drive home the intolerable horror of the mystery of Evil. They suggest, on the contrary, the Fat Boy in *Pickwick*. Mr. Machen may have ransacked the whole British Museum for quaint and far-off ceremonies, simply to make our flesh creep, but, in sober truth, all he has accomplished is an engaging air of looking mysterious until the time comes for explanation—and then—well, then we yawn. Now, his "fellow-author," Poe, would not have done this. If he had essayed to melt this too, too solid flesh, if he had striven to throw into atoms and reconstitute the primal elements of our existence, if he had essayed to summon the eternal spirits of evil, the blind forces of ill that are hidden in the constitution of man—we should have felt a rush of genuine terror, and the breath of genius would have touched our cheeks. As it is—Mr. Machen only imparts a certain hot-house kind of atmosphere to several perfectly familiar experiments, such as an obscure operation on a girl's brain, the secret of a wife's disappearance, the reason why certain men of fashion are driven irresistibly to suicide, and the cause of an obscure, and, truth to tell, rather squalid murder in a deserted passage. He never makes us believe in those Black Masses, or in his theory of demoniacal possession, or in that wonderful jewel, the size of a pigeon's egg, that glowed and glittered, and was really a woman's soul. He should realise that poor Aubrey Beardsley, and the hot, impetuous souls that wrought as he did, are quite dead, and now should turn his attention to other and truer fragments of life.

The Bystander:

My reference, a week or two back, to the new form of humour exploited by Mr. Montagu Wood in *A Tangled I,* a humour which amusingly combined epigram and satire with literary power and imagination, has moved Mr. Grant Richards, the publisher of the book, to draw my attention to another work of the same *genre,* entitled *The House of Souls,* by Mr. Arthur Machen. Certainly this book, which contains about six complete novels, is a notable production. If it lacks the sparkle of Mr. Wood's book, it is, nevertheless, the fruit of a curious talent which seems to be of so very striking a resemblance to that work that I am moved to a suspicion that it is the handiwork of the same brain. *The House of Souls* stories are conceived largely with the desire to mix up the humdrum in life with the transcendental—to indicate the "appeal of Theosophy to atheists, men about town, journalists, and hard-headed men of affairs." The touch of humour is to be observed in the descriptions in the various stories—particularly "A Fragment of Life"—of prosaic suburban ways and manners, which reveal a very intimate knowledge of the lower middle classes; and as to the Theosophical aspect of the stories, undoubtedly it is interesting to find this theme exploited in fiction, especially by so brilliant a descriptive and imaginative writer as Mr. Machen. I may add here, that Mr. Montagu Wood's humour was recognised in "Pop" at Eton, and afterwards at the Canning Club at Oxford, and that his skit, published some years ago, "An Island Story," was highly successful in those sets wherein it gained a reading. I am more than confident that his is a literary talent which will, sooner or later, reach a wide and a startled public.

Liverpool Daily Courier:

... It is by no means a new trick, of course, but Mr. Machen has it to perfection, and he is shrewd enough to heighten its effectiveness by sticking his nightmares in the very midst of the modern and the circumstantial and the familiar—by transposing Edgar Allan Poe into the key of *The New Arabian Nights*. Too obviously Poe, here and there, perhaps; and too unmistakably the manner of *The Nights;* but in these derivative days echoes of that sort will trouble none but the most fastidious of readers, and certainly not those who have a healthy appetite for robustious and not too conventional melodrama.

Illustrated London News:

"My dear Sir," says Dyson in *The House of Souls,* "I will give you the task of a literary man in a phrase. He has got to do simply this: to invent a wonderful story and to tell it in a wonderful manner." Judged by this test Mr. Arthur Machen can scarcely be said to have made literature. As the reader is conducted, Sherlock Holmes fashion, through the House of Souls (there are six storeys to it) its wicked arabesques, its old cabinets and prehistoric flints and faded pocket-books, wear an unconvincing, property air. When wonderful gentlemen like Dyson having drawn from some antique bureau a tattered paper or a black seal, and presenting it for a chum's inspection the chum exclaims, "Take it away; never speak of this again. Are you made of stone, man? Why, the dread and horror of death itself, the thoughts of the man who stands in the keen morning air on the black platform, bound, the bell tolling in his ears, and waits for the harsh rattle of the bolt, are as nothing compared to this. I will not read it; I should never sleep again!"—then is the breath held, and the mind prepared for any delicious thrill. But the Manuscript at length, or the black seal fully deciphered, prove well-nigh soporific. And both lack the power of evoking that spiritual terror which, leaving Hawthorne and Poe and Coleridge out of the comparison, surrounds *The Island of Dr Moreau,* by Mr. Wells, and is imprinted in "The Mark of the Beast," by Mr. Kipling.

Birmingham Gazette and Express:

. . . Whilst admiring the literary workmanship and the weird fancifulness of it all, one wonders what it means and why the tales were ever written. Do they purport to be works of imagination only, then the author has sought a singularly repulsive form of expression for his undoubted talent; do they seek to promulgate a theory concerning the link between the human and the bestial, between the natural and the supernatural in its most depraved possibilities of manifestation, then we would prefer to remain in ignorance, debating for not one moment the reasonableness or otherwise of such a theory. Really and truly, these awful stories strongly suggest the half-mad imaginings of a degenerate mind steeped in morbidity. They are too completely nauseous ever to have been permitted the publicity of print, and we sincerely trust they will secure few readers.

Literary World:
   . . . But when our author attempts to handle such occult matters as are treated of in "The Great God Pan," he seems to lose his footing. He succeeds in giving his readers an impression of very disagreeable horrors, but he does not succeed in giving verisimilitude to his record. We feel ourselves in the presence merely of a somewhat morbid imagination. Mr. Machen does not reveal, as he leads us to hope, any real arcana.

East Anglian Daily Times:
   . . . We have conscientiously perused the 500 pages which the volume contains, and our conclusion is that we would not willingly repeat the experience. We have supped full with horrors, and the lurid abominations which are very plainly hinted at have sickened us. It is probable that there are some whose literary digestion is strong enough to swallow such pabulum with impunity; but we fancy that the great majority of readers will rise from the book with a shudder of loathing. Certainly persons of a sensitive temperament ought not to read the gruesome tales after dusk. . . .

Light:
   . . . The promise of the first story is not redeemed, and the book is given up to the blacker side of magical beliefs, wrapped up in a garb suggestive of "Sherlock Holmes." It is not Spiritualism, and we prefer to believe that there is no truth in such auto-suggested horrors. The book professes to indicate "the dangers of unauthorised research," but

no such dangers as are here presented beset the path of the earnest and conscientious Spiritualist investigator.

Speaker:

Mr. Arthur Machen writes a somewhat curious preface to his collection of decadent stories in which he attempts to turn the Puritan's flank in an ingenious manner. He claims that "it is entirely from the Puritan standpoint that I wish to rest my plea for these tales of mine ... almost every page contains a hint (under varied images and symbols) of a belief in a world that is not that of ordinary everyday experience.... I contend that as an English novelist I am within my right in doing so; since Science, the guide of Life, has done as much, has admitted many transcendental conceptions into her scheme of things." This is a neat apology for the subject matter, which may be summarised by the line, "the flesh is aghast at the half-heard murmurs of horrible things," but it may surprise the author to be told that in these clever artificial and decidedly sickly romances, penned apparently under the joint influence of Oscar Wilde's and Aubrey Beardsley's artistic example, he has proved his Puritan heritage better than he knows. There has always seemed to us something a little pathetic in the desperate attempt of the small school of young Oxford hedonists to break away from the moral code of the healthy Philistine and encounter and glorify the mysterious forbidden pleasures of Sin. For their world was an artificial make-believe affair, with an exhausted atmosphere, in which affectation stood in the place of real pleasure. We can respect in a measure the Puritan who cries out that pleasure is a sin, because he shows us thereby that it has a secret fascination for him, but the man who can only enjoy pleasure by making out to himself that it is a sin shows himself a Puritan *manqué*. We are not surprised, therefore, to find that Mr. Arthur Machen's stories fail to thrill us, because the artificial horrors and nameless sins in which they abound are all carefully concocted and have practically no correspondence with the sins or horrors of real life. That is where our young school of modern hedonists fails in art; it is divorced from nature, and its would-be spontaneity is palpably a carefully laboured, artificial affair. And this is a great pity, for the refined sense of beauty that the young hedonist starts with possessing can only create a stale preciosity when it is divorced from the freshness of nature. Practically all the stories in *The House of Souls* are so much labour thrown away, and the more carefully studied are their "nameless horrors," the more meaningless are they, and the worse as art. Take, for example, the story "The Inmost Light." Here is a most deliberate attempt to make our flesh creep, and the only result is to make the reader exclaim "stuff and nonsense." A certain Dr. Black secludes himself with his beautiful wife in his house at Harlesden, and makes experiments in "occult science":—

> " . . each night I had stolen a step nearer to that great abyss which I was to bridge over, the gulf between the world of consciousness and the world of matter. . . . In that work from which even I doubted to escape with life, life itself must enter; from some human being there must be drawn that essence which men call the soul, and in its place (for in the scheme of the world there is no vacant chamber)—in its place would enter in what the lips can hardly utter, what the mind cannot conceive without a horror more awful than the horror of death itself. And when I knew this, I knew also on whom that fate would fall; I looked into my wife's eyes. Even at that hour, if I had gone out and taken a rope and hanged myself, I might have escaped, and she also, but in no other way. At last I told her all. She shuddered, and wept, and called on her dead mother for help, and asked me if I had no mercy and I could only sigh. I concealed nothing from her; I told her what she would become, and what would enter in where her life had been; I told her of all the shame and all the horror. . . . That night she came down to my laboratory, and there, with shutters bolted and barred down, with curtains drawn thick and close, so that the very stars might be shut out from the sight of that room, while the crucible hissed and boiled over the lamp, I did what had to be done, and led out what was no longer a woman. But on the table the opal flamed and sparkled with such light as no eyes of man have ever gazed on, and the rays of the flame that was within it flashed, and glittered, and shone even to my heart. My wife had only asked one thing of me; that when there came at last what I had told her, I would kill her. I have kept my promise." Page 286.

This passage is a very fair sample of the school to which Mr. Machen belongs, and it illustrates its utter artificiality. No thrill can possibly come, because there is falsity in every line and human nature is violated at every turn. The leading idea of the opal gaining an unholy lustre from the commission of an evil deed is paltry in itself, and the whole psychological interest should lie in the study of the man's warped human instincts. But Dr. Black is a lay figure in whom we do not even begin to believe, and so the piled-up structure of horror appears childishly inept. And so with the description of the strange sins in the story of *The Three Impostors*. The strange sins are not real sins, that is why they fail to interest even a morbid imagination. If the author would go into the street and pick up with the first wastrel he meets and describe faithfully the workings of the man's mind, he would thrill us fifty times more than can this collection of concocted effects all alien to the truth of life, and so all remote from human feeling. In its horror of nature, indeed, our young hedonistic school shows but another phase of the old Puritan's distrust of art.

David Christie Murray in *The Referee:*

AN IMPURE IDEAL
A CHALLENGE TO PURITANISM

The Philistine as Art's Helper.—Every now and then some person rises up in England to protest against the restrictions by which a vulgar and uninstructed Philistinism cribs, cabins, and confines the imaginative artist. Sometimes the protest is made by a man of genius, and whenever that is the case it is triumphantly proved by events that there was not the slightest real need to make it. The more daring and robust the assault upon the proprieties the more assured is the attention of an immediate audience. Mr. Swinburne's career affords an excellent example of this truth. In some respects he is an artist of unique character, but it was not by virtue of his artistry that he made at his first coming so prodigious a noise in the world. Mr. Swinburne's admirers now appreciate him for his literary excellences, but his earliest fame was accorded to him because of his so delicious naughtiness. A man of genius with a narrow intellectual field in which to disport himself, but with extraordinary gifts of melody and energy, he has found his proper place in the poetic hierarchy in his own lifetime, and to pretend that his fame was retarded by his defiance of Puritanism is a task for a fool—and a task which only a fool would undertake. The plain truth is that it is the very shortest cut to notoriety in this country to make a mock of morals, and there are not a few men and women who enjoy a public vogue simply and merely because they flout the Puritan Ideal, whilst if they had been content to ally decency with their native dullness they would never have been heard of beyond their own doorsteps.

. . .

There has been sent to *The Referee* for review a book the pretensions of which I think it on several grounds desirable to examine. In an oddly pompous preface the writer expresses his surety that his fellow-authors will sympathise with him in the difficult task of finding for a collection of short stories a general title which is not obviously impertinent. He opines that the title he has chosen "will at all events hint at the nature of the contents." To me it afforded no remotest suggestion, and it would be easy enough to write a book which would justify the title with at least equal completeness whilst it would embody the actual antithesis of its idea. Before I proceed to the exposition of that idea it is just to set out such reasons as the author has to give for its expression in a work of fiction. In France, we are told, "it is agreed that imagination and fantasy are to work as they will and as they can, and are to be judged by their own laws. He who carves gurgoyles admirably is praised for his curious excellence in the invention and execution of these grinning monsters; and if he is blamed it is for bad carving, not because he has failed to produce pet lambs." In England we are said to judge very differently, and "Imagination itself is expected to improve the occasion, to reform whilst it entertains, and to instruct under the guise of story-telling."

. . .

Where to Draw the Line.—It has to be objected here that the case is too broadly stated. It is not agreed that imagination and fantasy are to work as they will in France. There is a certain restraining sense which now and then moves the authorities to suppress a theatrical production like the *Timbale d'Argent* or a serial publication like *La Nature*. Fantasy is nowhere in any civilised community allowed an unrestricted play. There is a point at which all modern peoples divide the endurably coarse from the intolerably indecent and abominable. You must arrange with your own sensibilities the precise point at which you will say to fantasy, "Thus far shalt thou go and no further," but every civilised man has a limit beyond which he will not permit himself to be carried. And, what is of at least equal importance, he has a limit beyond which he will not knowingly allow those innocences, ignorances, and inexperiences which are under his guardianship or control to travel.

. . .

There are many examples of literary, pictorial, and plastic art in the hands of lovers of the curious which are kept under lock and key. The owners are not necessarily persons of unclean mind, and they generally exercise some discretion as to the choice of the people by whom these objects shall be seen. The common sense of the world—not the art-hatred of the Philistine, but just the common-sense common decency of the world—has decided that they shall be jealously hidden from the immature in years and experience. The argument advanced by our author is that perfection in the presentation makes the nature of the thing presented of little consequence. I am not disposed to attach an exaggerated value to that contention, but even if it were wholly defensible in respect to a work of art in itself, it is impossible to argue that it is of little consequence to whom it shall be shown. There is nothing more sacred than that ingenuous shame which the growth of civilisation has fostered as a guarding instinct against the violation of the mind. I make no fight for prudery—pruriency aping modesty, and topping frank indecency by its lie. I have had my say in *The Referee* more than once already about those egregious persons who from time to time seek an *arbiter elegantiarum* in the police-courts. But I stand for cleanliness in art, and, above all, I stand for it in the modern novel, and not only because the novel goes into the hands of boys and girls whose premature introduction to certain dark places cannot fail to have disastrous results.

. . .

A Public Pleasaunce.—Now here, of course, is an excellent opportunity for those ladies and gentlemen who think it one of the privileges of Art to be indecent to ask if I expect the writer of the novel to address herself or himself exclusively to the Young Person—if I intend to tie his or her soaring genius to a boy's coat-tails or a girl's pinafore. I say in answer to that query that it is not I who choose the medium through which the writers concerned have elected to reveal their genius to the world. I say that having chosen that medium for themselves they cannot rightly ignore certain responsibilities which the choice imposes upon them. The field of the novelist is a very spacious pleasure-ground indeed, and you may legitimately lay out in it almost any sort of garden plot or plantation, and may erect in it almost any sort of palace or cottage or mansion. But it is an open space, and it is dedicated to the delectation of the public. Incidentally the wanderer in its precincts may be instructed or warned or spiritually lifted, but his purpose in going there is primarily to be entertained. The operating theatre and the dissecting-room are out of place there, though there are some people who can take their pleasure in such places and get no harm. Most out of place of all conceivable things in a pleasure-ground which is free to everybody is the mural picture gallery of the unburied cities.

. . .

An Intrusion on Privacy.—When I was a boy I was taken by a middle-aged fool who ought to have known better into a waxwork anatomical museum at a rural wake. The sight left an evil taste on my mental palate for years and years. A rural wake is no place for an anatomical museum. That was a day of days, and Wombwell's menagerie and that booth of Thespis which belonged to Messrs. Bennet and Patch, and the swinging-boats and the merry-go-rounds, and the gingerbread stalls and the spangled lady on the slack wire, and Mr. Merriman and the shooting-galleries, and the whole gay, harmless medley make clear pictures in my mind this minute, though the rain and sunshine of a half-century have made many another of memory's paintings dim. And the anatomical museum poisoned everything. The contention I desire to combat is that a literary craftsman has some right to intrude the most hateful side of his mind upon others because he is an artist. But who says he is an artist? A man may write fiction and be no more of an artist than a ledger clerk. "He who carves gurgoyles admirably is praised for his curious excellence in the invention and execution of those grinning monsters; and if he is blamed he is blamed for bad carving, not because he has failed to produce pet lambs." But has he who carves "gurgoyles" the double right to carve revolting shapes and to plump them down in the public pleasure-ground for any unsuspecting wayfarer to sicken at?

. . .

A Buried Symbolism.—I offer a most emphatic denial to the assumption that "imagination and fantasy" are anywhere justly to be "allowed to work as they can and will," so long as their product is exposed for unrestricted sale in market overt. If I am to give fantasy free play I can quite easily imagine things which would excite the loathing of a savage. In every society which has raised itself above the intellectual level of the hog there are certain things which are not currently spoken of. There were certain obscure obscenities with which the ancients surrounded Nature-Worship. They expressed imaginatively the primal forces, and the emblems employed to represent them were candid and unashamed. Their open exposure and popular exhibition were the characteristic originally of a time of purest savagery and animalism. As civilisation grew these emblems became conventionalised, and finally they ceased to be symbolic. Some are in frequent use to-day, but their meaning is so completely lost to the popular mind that every modern cemetery displays an entire perversion of the meaning of one of them. Now, the root-idea of the book under consideration is the survival of all those old obscure obscenities into modern life. "It is in the character of a sober portrayer of a certain side of life," writes the author in his own person, "that I hope to add to the pleasure of many pleasant Sunday afternoons." I am armed beforehand against the simpering suggestion that I am impenetrable to the subtleties of irony. Solomon to the contrary notwithstanding, it is sometimes good to answer a controversialist according to his argument.

. . .

The Naked Untruth.—In pursuit of this purpose of adding to the pleasure of pleasant Sunday afternoons our author introduces his reader to a girl-child in a modern rural neighbourhood in Wales whose mind is unutterably debauched by her nurse, and who at the age of five has for her playmate the very bodily devil of licentiousness. The girl thrives under tuition to such advantage that when she comes to her demoniac womanhood she has arrived at a knowledge of evil so complete that the revelation of it drives men of the world to whom it is displayed to suicide. Speaking for myself, I can aver quite honestly that this sort of baby-Satanic-tommy-rot will not add to the pleasure of many pleasant Sunday afternoons. It is offered, as I have said already, with a kind of pomp, as a protest against the degraded state into which imagination and fantasy have slipped under the withering influences of Puritanism. Puritanism is as a red rag to the author. We all know, so he tells us, "how Hampden died that England might be free, first under the martial law of the Great Protector, and afterwards under the Whig oligarchy." We are instructed that the Puritans hanged witches in Salem, and flogged the Quakers, baptised foals in cathedrals, hewed down the statues of the saints, shut up the theatres, and gave us the English Sunday. It is not quite a true bill. Hampden did not die for martial law and the *beaux yeux* of the Whigs. Nor did the Puritans—a really forbidding body of men, to my fancy, amongst whom I wouldn't have lived for any money—spend all their energies in hanging witches and baptising foals in cathedrals. Like many a tribe which went before them, and many another which has followed after, they obscured a noble cause by gross excesses. But it does not become a professed Iconoclast to get dancing-mad at the sight of a hammer in another man's hand.

. . .

The Little Pig.—It is an assured thing in our author's mind that English Puritanism is going to take exception to his work. On the ground that it is a needless and offensive resurrection of the buried nastiness of early heathendom, I think it very likely that he is right. I was never very much of a Puritan myself, but my taste and inclination take me to the Puritan side for once. There was a dear old philosopher of a village doctor whom I knew years ago when I lived in the Belgian Ardennes. We were talking of the pornographies of French art one night, and with a shake of his wise old head he said, "Il y a, dans l'ame de chacun de nous, un petit cochon qui se grandit vite." I know my own little pig, and though I am compelled to find him house-room I have no liking for him, and I certainly have no desire that his manners should be corrupted by association with the little pigs of other people.

. . .

I have myself been a modest market-gardener in the field of fiction now these thirty years, and I have been careful never to introduce my little pig to anybody who has come to look at my very humble patch. I try to keep him unseen and lonely in his sty. My attempt to starve him out of existence has unhappily met with but indifferent success; but I'll be hanged if I will take anybody's ha'pence to make a show of him. I decline to put him on exhibition either for praise or pudding. And yet I know that I could make a very decent (and most indecent) living out of him. For my little pig is not at all like your little pig, and it is the master-passion of the Artist to be different. We all know that a good half of the talk we hear about Art for Art's sake, with its accompanying malediction on the English Puritan, means nothing more than that the artist is setting the little pig on view for the gratification of a prurient vanity.—MERLIN.

The Athenæum:
    . . . Like Poe, Mr. Machen sets himself to make the reader's flesh creep; like Hawthorne, he abounds with subtle and suggestive symbolism, and, had neither of these writers existed, his work would thrill the reader even more ingeniously, although it lacks the originality of the one and the poetic austerity and wealth of imagination of the other. He deals in ancient mysteries; he is for ever hinting at the macabre, the sinister, the unspeakable. His puppets peep and mutter through an atmosphere of forbidden knowledge and obscure rites of remote antiquity, which, however, he would seem to suggest are not so remote as they ought to be, after all. He is an adept in the art of elusiveness—so much so, indeed, that some of his most horrific endings fail of their proper effect, and the piled-up agony topples to a fall, leaving the reader with just the ghost of a suspicion of the author's sincerity, and a haunting reminiscence of turnip-headed spectres and clanking chains. . . .

The Saturday Review:
    Mr. Machen adds three new stories to the contents of two earlier volumes, and introduces the collection by a preface which is perhaps the best thing in the book. We remember reading "The Great God Pan" when it first appeared, and discussing it with brother-undergraduates. Most of us thought that the story was interesting chiefly as illustrating the difficulties which beset an ambitious English writer who wishes to describe transcendental beastliness. Probably we were right. Mr. Machen's literary monomania takes the form of postulating that behind the veil of matter, in the centre of the material universe, resides an obscene and terrible power, the revelation of which brings to mortals infamy and madness. This pretty fancy is hardly relevant to his spirited attack on Puritanism, for the Puritans had a lively

sense of the demoniac. As regards the execution of the stories, Mr. Machen has style, and a talent for the fantastic (though *The Three Impostors* is in its scheme reminiscent of Stevenson), but he has not the power of creating horror. One feels that he is carving gargoyles (to borrow his phrase) just for fun, and his readers' blood will not run cold, though possibly their gorges may rise.

Tribune:

The Great God Pan is finding himself extremely popular among the novelists just now. It was Mr. Benson who began it, earlier in the year, and since that time the number of novels in which we are vouchsafed manifestations of the goat-god—complete even to the hoofs, and with an attendant murky odour thrown in—increases almost daily. Of course it is natural enough, for nobody, not even a novelist, knows much about Pan, whence unlimited possibilities of mystery and thrills. Mr. Arthur Machen is one of those who see in him all the possibilities of a "hair-raiser." Were it not disrespectful it might be said that *The House of Souls* is exactly the kind of book which would have been written by the Fat Boy in *Pickwick,* had he been possessed of literary ability. Had he also been, be it said, familiar with the works of Robert Louis Stevenson. For never was book more obviously written with the desire "to make your flesh creep." What with Pans and witches and mysterious keepers of treasures in hills, the half-dozen stories contain quite a population of queer folk, not one of which but has the potentiality of raising the hair upon the reader's head, until it resembles the quills upon a more than usually fretful porcupine. Potentialities only, however, for, truth to tell, the author never quite succeeds in raising our hair. He tells us either too much or too little. He so constantly hints at quite unmentionable horrors that we find ourselves mistrusting them, and when he does occasionally, greatly daring, venture to unveil a horror or two, they are a wee bit disappointing. This is, of course, as much the fault of the subject as of the author. None of us can take the great God Pan, nor witches, nor warlocks, very seriously nowadays—even if surgeons with alarming surgical instruments are introduced into the same story to keep them in countenance by their up-to-date associations. Because we know very well that did Pan put in a bodily appearance in a British wood to-day he would be given in charge by a stolid and unemotional gamekeeper for trespassing in pursuit of game. Pan was killed by the Game Laws, if not before, and not all the King's horses and all the King's men can put him together again—alas! Of the various stories in the volume "The Inmost Light" comes the nearest to being convincing, while lovers of Stevenson would feel interested in the story series, *The Three Impostors,* which at times is very successfully reminiscent of that writer.

The Manchester Guardian:

The stories in the volume entitled *The House of Souls,* by Arthur Machen, are all addressed to the ancient purpose of making the reader's flesh creep. It is a favourite pastime for easy people to play with fear; from time immemorial men have amused their leisure by sitting round the fire capping horrors. It is not, we may concede, a very high form of art, but any essay in this kind must stand or fall by its success in imputing horror. Mr. Machen has written a rather arrogant preface, in which the following passage occurs: "He who carves gargoyles admirably is praised for his curious excellence in the invention and execution of these grinning monsters; and if he is blamed it is for bad carving, not because he has failed to produce pet lambs." Conceded! We may even call it a necessary postulate of the reviewer; if he is writing of gargoyles he has no business to say, "I do not like gargoyles"; he must look for the curious excellence in invention and execution, and it is not to be found in Mr. Machen's work. He understands what has long been known, that the emotion of fear is best induced by vagueness; he insists—rather heavily, indeed—on the mysterious power of the spirit, but he has not felt it; too often the horror adumbrated in his vagueness is no more than physically disgusting. Conjuring tricks with the grey matter of the brain, burning and mutilating of live bodies are the clumsy devices of an unimaginative man. The restrained intensity of feeling and economy of suggestion in such scenes as those of Maeterlinck's early plays are infinitely more moving than these violent assaults.—H. M. S.

The Hill of Dreams

East Anglian Daily Times:

This is the first complete novel by the author of *The House of Souls*. When writing of that work we expressed regret at the prominence accorded to an unhealthy atmosphere. The suggestions of hideous survivals in the under-world were not pleasant reading, and it is our duty to insist that their repetition in the present work is deplorable. No good can be effected by a discussion of such esoteric matters, and we could have wished that Mr. Machen had refrained from introducing such horrors into his book. The story purports to be "a study of the temperament of a young literary man, whose dreams lead him into strange places, and bring him to a strange sequel." Expressed more plainly, the plot is that of a crazy youth who undergoes some particularly unpleasant experiences, and finally commits suicide. Frankly speaking, it was the best thing that could have happened, for the "dreams" of this young man were repulsive. If the reading public must have this kind of mental food, we can only deplore the taste; but we protest with all possible strength against the dissemination of such sickly, and in some sense horrible ideas, as form the basis of Mr. Machen's latest effort. It is not denied that the author writes cleverly. That, however, forms an additional reason why his talents should be employed in producing something more admirable than *The Hill of Dreams* can be said to be.

The Outlook:

It is safe to compliment Mr. Arthur Machen upon having produced a book that stands, and will perhaps continue to stand, quite alone in English fiction. Fellows might be found for it in the modern letters of Germany and France, but not even the most determined of our own symbolists has produced such an elaborate account of the adventures of an exclusively æsthetic nature in the rough world. But apart from such praise as that acknowledgment confers, it is not at all easy to put a value on Mr. Machen's *Hill of Dreams*. It is written in a simple yet studied English that conveys in the deeper passages of the book as much of magic as words can impart; yet the whole work is so unreal and so charged with spiritual disease that there is scarcely a place for it in the widest utilitarian view. Beyond an impression of intense agony of the soul, it leaves little behind it, and there is nothing to the purpose that a critic can say except that the book evidently answered to something in the writer, and may answer to something in others. The growth of Lucian Taylor's fervently mystic and quite inhuman nature, perfectly pure, perfectly egoistic, is traced with power. Most of his outward tragedy is that of the artist's struggle with the world, and of his association with gross and ordinary British barbarians, whose manners are described with a cleverness and a rancour in which we can find nothing but weakness; the inward story—if such a web of shadows can be called a story—is one of some strange insight into the obscurity of an essential evil in nature, of a strange development of the passion of love in the soul of the ascetic of art, of his sufferings, his dreams, and of his final destruction by the shadowy power of ill that laid its hands upon him as a child, on the hill where once the Romans camped. An undefined horror penetrates all the story, like an invisible vapour. It is an extraordinary performance and a work of art; but art fallen, we think, on unclean and fatal days.

Birmingham Gazette and Express:
    ... There is much fine writing, but probably few other than literary craftsmen will follow with patience the detailed story of his striving after perfection in the use of language. The most pleasing part of the book is that which treats of his love for and idealisation of the simple, womanly country girl, Annie Morgan. It is scarcely a "healthy" book, but it is evidently the work of a man who has thought deeply and suffered much.

Manchester Courier:

It would be hard to classify *The Hill of Dreams,* by Arthur Machen, for it is both unprecedented and unusual. Moreover, it is unpleasing and unconvincing, though its writer possesses a wealth of imagery and a power not often met with. The little story there is concerns the life of Lucian Taylor, but the plot of the book is but a peg on which the author hangs a detailed study of temperament. Lucian is a "dreamer," with literary aspirations. His early life is devoid of all humanising influences, and his character is only explicable, and then not very satisfactorily so, when this is remembered. Despite education and cultivation, Lucian never possesses any feelings which a barbarian might not be expected to have. He never imposes the least restraint on his natural susceptibility, and both as a boy and a man is a sensualist. After living a life of failure, in which, apart from his vivid dreams, a passion for a country girl is the only important event, he commits suicide. The reader is left in doubt whether Lucian was a genius neglected by an unappreciative world or a fool totally incapable of understanding the beauty of the world. The writing of the book is astonishingly versatile. At times there is the gruesomeness of Poe, at others the charm of Hawthorne. The descriptions of country scenery show a love of the picturesque, and the chapters on London life a knowledge of the seamy side of nature. Though there is splendid capability shown in the book, it will not make a wide appeal because of its want of humanity.

Birmingham Post:

Mr. Arthur Machen's is hardly the sort of story that is likely to win admiration from the average reader of current fiction. Perhaps it is as well, for *The Hill of Dreams* is not a healthy book, and the power of fascination that it exercises is tempered with a certain instinctive feeling of repugnance. Let it be said at once that it does fascinate. It is filled with passages of rare beauty. Mr. Machen understands the magic of words; his sentences are as silk shot with rich, variegated, and harmonious colour; they have a fine rhythmic flow also; and page after page is filled with "a procession of images" (we quote the author's own words), "now of rapture and ecstasy and now of terror and shame, floating in a light that is altogether phantasmal and unreal." So far as charm of language and beauty of imagery go—and they go far—the season is hardly likely to see the rival of Mr. Machen's novel. The weakness is that all this accumulated beauty is something fantastic, exotic, and bizarre. Mr. Machen leads us through a forest of flowers; but they are *fleurs de mal,* in Baudelaire's phrase, sprung from miasmatic ground, and spreading a perfume by which the atmosphere is vitiated. Through his power of conjuring up visions of the world of long ago and living in a dreamland of his own Lucian Taylor claims some kinship with Du Maurier's *Peter Ibbetson.* By the circumstances of his death he stands related to the English opium-eater. But Mr. Machen has neither Du Maurier's light touch and sense of humour nor De Quincey's stern insistence on the penalties of such visionary delights. His attitude is too accurately that which another exquisite artist, Ernest Dowson, assumed in the sonnet, now fairly well known, "To One in Bedlam":—

> Oh, lamentable brother! if these pity thee,
> Am I not fain of all thy lone eyes promise me—
> Half a fool's kingdom, far from men who sow and reap
> All their days vanity.

So Dowson sang; and in the same mood Mr. Machen seems inclined, throughout the greater part of his book at any rate, to hold up his invertebrate hero—or victim—as a subject for sympathy and admiration. "Invertebrate" is too weak a word. Most of Lucian's peculiarities are definable in the terminology of specialists in mental alienation. He is a sufferer from what an expert witness in the American "cause célèbre" of the day called lately "exaggerated ego." Echolalia (in his attempts at authorship), melancholia, visual and auditory hallucinations—all these familiar phenomena of an unbalanced mind does he exhibit; and doubtless the specialist in such diseases might trace more. It is because his attitude towards this "lamentable brother" is too nearly that of Ernest Dowson and too far from that of (say) De Quincey that Mr. Machen has failed to produce a piece of great literature which is above all things sane and level-headed. On the other side of the scales must be put a fertile imagination, a great deal of acute psychological analysis, and an extraordinary sensitiveness to impressions of natural beauty. These are sufficiently enviable endowments, which one hopes to see Mr. Machen exercising in the future on some more happily treated subject.

Newcastle Chronicle:

Mr. Machen's story is all about a young man who adds to a temperament naturally neurotic a passion for examining the inner workings of his own mind, and a dislike for nourishing food. This combination of qualities reduces him to a skeleton, and enables him to see visions and dream dreams of the most fantastic variety. Those who are familiar with Mr. Machen's work will recognise in such a subject one particularly suited to his *métier*. Step by step he traces, with fine imagination, the workings of the disordered brain until the inevitable end of complete madness and death is reached. Only Mr. Machen, perhaps, would not have us believe that his hero is mad; preferring if anything to think that he is of a sanity and clear-sightedness altogether denied to the devotees of plain living and plain thinking.

The Morning Post:

Mr. Machen has chosen for his book one of those subjects that depend entirely on their treatment for their success or failure. *The Hill of Dreams* provides an analysis of the character of an imaginative young man consumed with literary aspirations. Unfortunately, the treatment of this theme is marred by the two faults of exaggeration and monotonous insistence on the psychological note of alternate despair and exultation. The delineation of moods must be made variable if it is to be palatable to the reader; otherwise weariness of the mind ensues as a necessary consequence. Lucian Taylor's continuous habit of selfish introspection ultimately leads him to madness and "death by misadventure," but these misfortunes do not induce sympathy in the reader when he has become satiated with the morbidity which itself brought them about. At the same time, the book has style and is full of so many well-written descriptions of scenery that one is inclined to forget about the dreamer and only to dwell in fancy on the beautiful "Hill of Dreams" which prompted his visions.

P.T.O.:

Mr. Arthur Machen's first long novel, *The Hill of Dreams,* fails in humanity. The hero's literary struggles are desperate; the hero himself is an abstraction. The author labours too much over his work for it to be wholly satisfactory; we are obliged to him for the pains he takes in these days of careless writing, but could wish the effort less apparent. In his pictures of Welsh scenery he is at his best; in suburbia he lays it on with a trowel, and makes himself more unhappy than ever he will make the worthy folk he dislikes should they chance upon his book. In a word, Mr. Machen has yet to find a story, yet to create real living people.

The Scotsman:

Mr. Machen's novel displays a singular ability in giving a sustained and varied interest to a theme of which the material is to the last degree simple and monotonous. He has no more story to tell than how a young man, a country clergyman's son, feeling that he had a gift for literature, went up to London, and kept writing and writing and writing while he lived in a world of dreams, quite misunderstood and untouched by the outer world of everyday circumstance, until at last he came to kill himself, having accomplished nothing. Such is the subject, and it seems, thus stated, to afford little matter enough for a full-length story. But the work goes with such a skilful psychology into the workings of the unhappy young man's mind, and shows such fine imaginative artistry in varying the light and shade of his emotions and contrasting his outward with his inward life, that it proves interesting from first to last without even for a moment disturbing its air of soft tranquillity. It is a story that will readily impress a reader of quiet tastes who can reach to the more subtle refinements of fiction.

The Athenæum:

... In the emotional adventures of the hapless youth who is a victim of a species of nympholepsy and intellectual loneliness combined, we cannot, after the first hundred pages, feel any adequate interest. His agonies while engaged in the long-drawn-out struggle with his stubborn literary gifts are too protracted, too remote from any human sentiment, to hold the interest of the reader. Their recital is almost as monotonous as, and far more fatiguing than, the artistic *débâcle* of the painter in Zola's *L'Œuvre*, which had at least some elements of humanity. But the spirit of place which informs the book, whether it is the forlorn, illimitable dreariness of suburbia that the author chooses to show us, or the mysterious and melancholy beauty of that wild Wales he knows so well, could only have found expression at the hand of an adept. It is perhaps a pity that so clever a writer as Mr. Machen should bestow such infinite pains on astonishing the bourgeois, who in all likelihood will never have the privilege of reading his books; it is an obsession that brings to mind the unprofitableness of flogging dead horses. But, after all, the main matter for regret is the utter formlessness and the arid inhumanity of his work. His Muse is a kind of Lilith—not a drop of her blood is human—and thus, except from the decorative point of view, he leaves us cold. . . .

The Daily Graphic:
A curious and fanciful book, which shows much misdirected ability. It is the study of the temperament of a young man, who devotes himself to literature, but his imagination is abnormal, and his mental condition diseased. The book is not of much practical interest, as one feels that his death, with which the story ends, is the best possible solution of his difficulties.

The Daily Chronicle:
Mr. Arthur Machen has written *The Hill of Dreams,* we take it, not with a view to saying anything in particular, but rather with a view to saying something in a particular—almost a precious—way. We fancy that he would not greatly object to identify himself with his hero, of whom he says:—

> Language, he understood, was chiefly important for the beauty of its sounds, by its possession of words resonant, glorious to the ear, by its capacity, when exquisitely arranged, of suggesting wonderful and indefinable impressions, perhaps more ravishing and farther removed from the domain of strict thought than the impressions excited by music itself. Here lay hidden the sensuous art of literature, it was the secret of suggestion, the art of causing delicious sensation by the use of words. In a way, therefore, literature was independent of thought; the mere English listener, if he had an ear attuned, could recognise the beauty of a splendid Latin phrase.

One would like to have Mr. Machen's criticism of that majestic line of R. L. Stevenson's:—

>Opulent orotundo strike the sky!

The Hill of Dreams is a long, and in many respects, a clever psychological analysis and demonstration of the mind of a young degenerate. It is a deliberate and careful study of morbidity. It is well written, but written not quite well enough. The good writing is just a thought too obvious; one cannot help noticing it. It has what Mr. Machen calls "the secret of suggestion," but it suggests some things which we would much rather had not been suggested. It is a thoughtful piece of work though, and it is often lighted up by swift and penetrating flashes of satire. We wish the word "sonorous" did not occur quite so often in it. "Sonorous" is a very good and effective word in its way, but, like "sinister," "sombre," and one or two others, it should be used sparingly. It does not do to make a pet of it.

The Manchester Guardian:

Without a refined susceptibility to sensuous impressions there can be no high art. But there is always a danger that the artist who recognises this theoretically may give rein to susceptibility and sensitiveness as such and be drawn headlong along the road to mere sensationalism. For in art, as in everything else, the ultimate value of a sensation lies always in its content. The fact that your sensations seem to you "exquisite" or "delicious" no more gives them artistic than it would give them moral import; in the one case as in the other, there is the further question to be asked, the question what kind of person you are who feel them so. Which question leads in its turn to other questions, all pointing unmistakably one way. Sensation, you find, gives you no principle either in art or in anything else. It can open no locked doors. Take it for your guide and there can be no doubt but you will be landed, sooner or later, in the ditch. Mr. Arthur Machen in his new story *The Hill of Dreams* drives perilously near this dangerous territory. He recounts the life of a hypersensitive youth of whom the world is not worthy, upon whose delicate nature the violence of healthy humanity rasps and jars, who therefore, shut up within himself, runs riot in a fantastic maze of morbid mystic fancies, constructs an impossible romance out of a chance meeting with a farmer's daughter in the dark (for whose sake he afterwards inflicts upon himself nightly penance with a gorse bough), and finally drifts up to London and laudanum and an untimely end. This kind of story could only fail to be suffocating in its effect upon the reader if the oxygen absent in the hero were supplied by some sort of exhilaration derivable from the background against which he moves. But he moves, alas! in an atmosphere as exquisite and as exhausted as he is. "He knew that he himself had solved the riddle, that he held in his hand the powder of projection, the philosopher's stone transmuting all it touched to fine gold, the gold of exquisite impressions." It is of these impressions, this "powder of projection," that the bulk of the narrative is composed. If your air is full of dust, it is no matter what kind of particles the dust is made of; let it be powdered gold, the effect is just as choking. Many objections might be advanced against a story like *The Hill of Dreams* on the score of its subject matter: the artist would be ready to dismiss these as ethical and irrelevant. But the unrelieved preciosity of the style is equally open to criticism, and this is the rock upon which the book finally founders. "Only in the Court of Avallaunius is the true science of the exquisite to be found." It would be wise to leave it unmolested there; here in these lower courts, this "land of sin and woe," there is nothing that more quickly tends to tedium.—B. S.

Louis Weitzenkorn in *The New York World:*

Arthur Machen's *The Hill of Dreams,* according to the introduction included in a new American edition, was written in 1897. It was published first in 1907. Mr. Knopf would have been much fairer to Mr. Machen had he left this book to perish in the dust of things forgotten. It has a great beauty of writing. The Machen style is clearly a deliberate and successful attempt to get melody into prose. But it strikes us that music is not the first element of a prose style; in fact it is one part that, under compulsion, might be omitted without injury. After all, the poets are entitled to something.

Our first demand from a prose work styled a novel is living characters. Except in the last three paragraphs, not one breath of life shows up in *The Hill of Dreams.* Mr. Machen confesses his plan to have been the writing of a "Robinson Crusoe" of the mind. As to that there is a touch of similarity here to *Peter Ibbetson,* and more to Jack London's *Star Rover.* Naturally enough, Machen didn't see this latter work of fiction before he began his. But it is to the analogy of *Robinson Crusoe* that we mainly object. After all, that cast-off sailor had a man Friday who was every inch alive. Good, deadly arrows fly through Defoe's book. Ships and savages and hot sunlight beat down.

Whatever there is of Lucian Taylor beyond the author's frail beating against life, is something of a masculine and British Carol Kennicott. That's crowding a reputation, even a fictional one, pretty badly, but the futile protest and final escape of Lucian Taylor through suicide doesn't follow as four does two plus two and as true tragedy must. Not once does the book move us to feel for this hero, who lives like an essay in the *Atlantic Monthly.* He and the British countryside aristocracy—the British Main Streeters—are so many children's toys. They are dolls that get from one end of the room to the other only when lifted up and moved.

Machen has written this book as if he had been young and angry. He seems to have wanted to nail his old neighbours to some sort of cross. He forgets that the Babbitts are the very ones who read *Babbitt* and make the author rich.

The book will not enhance Machen's rather high reputation here. His incident of the hanging of a dog by a set of children, not one of whom protests, will never be swallowed, at least by American readers. The rest of the book is just as impossible. We are willing still to take our knowledge of Main Street Britons from Mr. Bennett's "Five Towns."

The Secret Glory

The Manchester Guardian:
 It is a little difficult to know what kind of readers *The Secret Glory* is intended to please, and there is a temptation to believe that its author wrote it simply and solely for his own amusement. The greatest works of art are no doubt those in which an artist insists on satisfying his own standard of taste, but Mr. Machen's game on this occasion seems to have been rather that of "letting himself go." He begins with a vivid indictment of the English public school, but does not produce either an original or a convincing picture of its faults and failings; and he then proceeds to cut the painter and to launch forth into a juvenile description of a juvenile escapade in London which his schoolboy hero, half mystic, half Bohemian, is supposed to share with a young lady of his choice, though not of his class—the whole embroidered with wonderful pæans to punch and poetry, surrounded with a sort of religious halo, and penetrated with a peculiar flavour of what one might call inebriate innocence. There are perhaps deep lessons to be drawn from the perusal of these singular heroics, but we have not succeeded in discovering or profiting by them. The narrative itself is allusive and obscure. Huge jokes are supposed to be concealed on one side, and on the other the profound, impenetrable import of things. But, judging by what is actually communicated to us, we remain in doubt whether what is withheld was either very funny or very significant.—B. S.

Punch:
 I have always understood that what St. Paul calls "visions and revelations of the Lord" were sent to forward their recipients' progress in virtue; and that if glimpses of the supernatural resulted in *Schwärmerei*, or sin, they were the work of the Devil. On this hypothesis there is no doubt whatever concerning the origin of *The Secret Glory,* a latter-

day variant of the Holy Grail revealed in a Welsh farmhouse to the boy *Ambrose Meyrick* and his father; although its exposition is accompanied (if I may credit Mr. Arthur Machen) by a vision of "The Mystery of Mysteries." *Ambrose,* still harping on his mystic experiences, is sent to an exquisitely odious public school, where he becomes first a cowed and isolated dreamer and last a furtive and malicious rebel. Both reverie and rebellion are natural enough, the school being what it is, but they are not particularly creditable to a devotee of "The Mystery of Mysteries." Nor is a *liaison* with a sympathetic parlour-maid, though this is set down as part and parcel of the "wonders." Nor is *Ambrose's* subsequent career, which continues a marvel of irresponsibility until his extremely unconvincing martyrdom at the hands of "miscreants" in Asia. And, talking of irresponsibility, I cannot help wishing that Mr. Machen himself, who shows considerable savage humour in his guerilla campaign against the public school system, would occasionally come to closer grips with one or other of the problems his extravaganza has evoked.

Forrest Reid in *The Daily Herald:*

In *The Secret Glory* the happenings are neither sober nor probable, yet the effect is prosaic and even tedious. Here, again, it is all a matter of treatment, or, rather, in Mr. Machen's case, of the absence of treatment, for he has left his subject a mere kernel rattling in the dry shell of didacticism. I have seldom been so disappointed in a book. What has happened to Mr. Machen? Have we gained a missionary and lost an artist? His gift was always narrow, apt to lead him woefully astray when he departed from the presentation of states of abnormal, or morbid, consciousness; but it was vivid, haunting, and intensely individual. *The Secret Glory* is little more than an elaborate tract in which Mr. Machen champions mediævalism and tilts at his usual windmills—the public school system, athletics, suburban life, etc.

The Outlook:

In *The Secret Glory* Mr. Machen attempts to describe the rebellion of a Celtic mystic against Anglicanism and the public school traditions. I say "attempts," because neither Anglicanism nor education interests him sufficiently to make him barb his satire. But the mysticism excites his dark and fantastic imagination, and there are bursts, in the latter half of the book, of successful paradox. Ambrose Meyrick, who had seen the "Holy Chalice of Teilo sant," and had an affection for Gothic architecture, was well whipped for absconding from football practice. Thenceforth he exerted himself to be in all things the most loyal Luptonian, but at night he walked in strange places and heard the voices that outsing the Fairy Birds of Rhiannon. After winning a Balliol Scholarship and performing some remarkable cricket at the Oval, he broke away and joined a troupe of actors, and was for ever lost to Lupton and its like. An effect of a kind Mr. Machen certainly produces. He incants Welsh names, and, as so often on lighter ground, he displays a great power of giving a queer twist to the least uncanny events. Naturally, he fails to inform us what there was so remarkable in the Welsh Church which was ruined by "the Yellow Hag of Pestilence, the Red Hag of Rome, and the Black Hag of Geneva"; consequently, he fails to show why Ambrose should not have had all the spiritual experience desired in his own school chapel. True, Lupton Chapel was built in 1840, and the neighbourhood was slummy. But, then, Ambrose was capable of ecstasy in Bloomsbury and Soho. No, Ambrose's unhappiness is too like that of Mr. Bultitude when, in *Vice Versa,* this gentleman took his son's place at Dr. Grimstone's academy, and proceeds from an intelligible dislike of small boys.

The Evening Standard:

A schoolboy is also the central figure in *The Secret Glory,* by Arthur Machen. But Ambrose Meyrick is an unusual boy, not at all the sort of boy to conform to the average type turned out at such a public school as Lupton. It is to be hoped, by the way, that not many schools are like Lupton, or at least that there are not any public schoolmasters like Mr. Horbury, who takes such a savage delight in using the cane.

Mr. Machen's satire on the public school system, and especially public school games, is a little too heavy-handed to be effective. Neither boys nor masters are very convincing, and now and then the story gets lost in the mystical atmosphere with which Mr. Machen surrounds his hero. Altogether *The Secret Glory* is rather an incoherent and tiresome production, and certainly does not represent Mr. Machen at his best. Schoolboys and mysticism do not mix.

Liverpool Daily Courier:

Mr. Arthur Machen has attempted an ambitious character study in *The Secret Glory*. He has also tried to give us a new version of the Grail, introducing a mystical cup preserved in a cottage in Wales. But neither the character nor the cup are very convincing, and it must be said that Mr. Machen has this time failed to get into his story any deep sense of the mystical. His principal character, Ambrose Meyrick, is a queer chap, as he is meant to be, but there is no reason why he should be as irresponsible as he is, and less reason why he should finish up by getting himself crucified somewhere in Asia. These improbabilities would matter less, however, if Mr. Machen had made Meyrick vital, and his adventures interesting. The story never runs with sufficient sequence to ensure this. It is all confused with propaganda, and very bitter propaganda at that, against the public schools, and criticism of Welsh Nonconformity when it combines religious revival fervour with sensuality. Mr. Machen knows how to tell a story, but he does not demonstrate that capacity in this work.

Sheffield Daily Telegraph:

Ambrose Meyrick said that "people who pushed . . . always reminded him of the hungry little pigs fighting for the largest share of the wash"—but though a reasonable aversion to Extravertism is comprehensible, it is really unnecessary to be so exaggerated an introvert as the hero of *The Secret Glory,* by Arthur Machen. Ambrose carried his mental "Secret Doctrine" to perverse, even morbid, excesses; he lived in a *paysage intérieur* peopled by mystics and martyrs, and visions of the jewelled Grail hidden by the descendant of Celtic Saints in some humble cottage on the Welsh mountains; and all this was naturally incompatible with the brutal facts of life at an English public school. An unpleasant school, certainly, but not more so than most.

It is to be assumed that Ambrose possessed a sense of humour, since he could enjoy, and even parody, Rabelais, but there is scant evidence of the quality otherwise than as stated. Extracts from his famous book, *In Praise of Taverns,* are equally unconvincing.

Some of Mr. Machen's arguments on religion are interesting. "In my heart," he says, "I have always doubted whether moderate Anglicanism be Christianity in any sense, whether it even deserves to be called a religion at all," and he objects to Protestantism because of the fundamental heresy on which it "builds its objection to what is called Ritual. I suppose this heresy is called Manichee; it is a charge of corruption and evil made against the visible universe, which is affirmed to be not 'very good' but 'very bad'—or, at all events, too bad to be used as the vehicle of spiritual truth. . . . Incense, vestments, candles, all ceremonies, processions, rites—all these things are miserably inadequate; but they do not abound in the horrible pitfalls, misapprehensions, errors, which are inseparable from speech of men used as an expression of the Church."

Mr. Machen is trying to present Celtic Paganism in the guise of Christianity, he confuses the Greek philosophy of restraint, "Nothing in excess," with a mere negation. There is very little glory in the book. It is concerned with the tortuous byways of a perverse soul through which the free wind from the mountains has never blown.

The Morning Post:

Though issued as fiction, this is not a novel. It is composite of story, autobiography, essay, satire, philosophy, criticism, poetry, and too formless to be brought within any literary mode. Presumably it was not written all of a piece, and that just yesterday. Spatchcocked passages point to times when there were as yet no Boches, only Boers, and "'E dunno where 'e are" was still a music-hall ditty. These were the days of Ambrose Meyrick's youth, true; but—though this need not (and will not) trouble the shade of Mr. Blackmore—the most consistent romancer, as to time and place, would not now suggest the Valley of the Doone as even a bogus field for the adventure of the Sangraal. Other times, other fashions, even in that high Quest. Pieced or wrought whole, the book nevertheless is unified by one idea. The "secret glory" of its title is the imaginative life, to which its every line and circumstance is meant as acclamation and appeal.

There are in it, among others of rare and rich beauty, a thousand absurd lines and circumstances we could willingly blot. For Mr. Machen's own purpose, Lupton School is a prejudice; like its Headmaster it is too much "commerce with mortality." "A deeper transport and a mightier thrill" are communicated in wise, rapturous praise of wine and humorous discourse on the marriage of Panurge. Here Nelly Foran is cunningly kept with Ambrose, aloof and aloft in a fragrant old Bloomsbury whose "stinks" in reality were neither better nor worse than the Midlands'. More understanding still of its own "secret glory" would Mr. Machen's fascinating book have been had he realised that its ecstatic vision, being of the spirit and the imagination, is as likely to occur in a "Bethel with the stucco front" as in the Celtic Church with its Cup of Sacrament. But Mr. Machen, in his own exclusive way, does catch it, and for that we are grateful.

Rose Macaulay in *The Daily News:*

The Secret Glory is, like most of Mr. Machen's books, very odd. It is the story of a mystic, of the inner and the outer life. The outer life of Ambrose Meyrick is passed at Lupton, a typically commonplace and materialistic public school, whose masters talk of "playing the game" and write horrible school songs of the "Forty Years on" type; while his inner life, which is alone of significance or importance to him, is spent in exploring mystic realms of Celtic Christian legend with or without his dead father, a Welsh architectural enthusiast. "I do not know," writes Ambrose in later life, "how it all happened; I had been leading two eager lives. On the outside I was playing games and going up in the school with a rush, and in the inside I was being gathered more and more into the sanctuaries of immortal things." Ambrose's mystical adventures are described with a good deal of beauty; it is his contacts with actuality which strike one as distorted and unreal.

Both he and Mr. Machen loathe public schools and all pertaining to them with such intensity that neither of them can see straight. They set up a monstrous figure of savagery and idiotcy and call him a typical schoolmaster, adding that schoolmasters are just like schoolboys, the implication being that nearly all schoolboys also are savage and imbecile. Even public schools are not really quite as bad as all that; and Mr. Machen would have been more effective if he had been more temperate. There is quite enough to be said about the savagery and stupidity of schools without resorting to distortion. Psychological accuracy is not, indeed, the strength of the book, which is full of unlikely actions. For instance, was Ambrose really the kind of boy who, in his quest for beauty, would have absconded with one of the school housemaids? Surely his dead father would have told him that this was conduct unworthy of an inquirer into spiritual mysteries. But the whole book is a fantasy, and not to be judged as a tale of real life. Its curious occurrences and characters are made odder by the difficult, obscure, and fragmentary method of narration. There is, in fact, a good deal of silliness in the book, as well as some bad taste, but there is also a good deal of beauty, and the beauty and the silliness and the bad taste are all the work of a writer.

Middleton Murry in *The Nation and the Athenæum:*
Even if we wished we could not tell the story of *The Secret Glory*. Mr. Machen manages to combine an onslaught on the public school system with some watery Paterian mysticism. Personally we have an equal dislike of those who belaud and those who denigrate the public school system. Besides, "there ain't no sich person," there are as many systems as there are public schools. But Ambrose Meyrick, if he could have been jerked for a moment by his creator into a semblance of real existence, would justify the worst outrages wrought upon him by his equally incredible *alma mater.*

He is a sentimental philanderer with æsthetic Catholicisms, a mystic Celtic dreamer, a Soho Bohemian (before Soho was ruined, of course); but these crimes are as nothing compared to his incorrigible penchant for "poetic prose." Mr. Machen has encouraged him in it. He will have a great deal more to answer for in the day of judgment than the schoolmaster who tried to beat it out of him.

Far Off Things and *Things Near and Far*

The Outlook:

It is difficult to know quite what to make of Mr. Machen's two most recent books. *Far Off Things* was a rather scrappy chapter of what might have been an excellent autobiography not written in the first place for publication in book form. Like the new volume it spoiled a great deal of good material and was not organised in any way that tends to make lasting literature. For all that, both volumes are excellent reading. There is a great deal to be said for Mr. Machen. And he himself has a great deal to say. He is not quite at home in the twentieth century. Spiritually he belongs to the years before the 'nineties, to Charing Cross Road as it was in the days when he translated Casanova at the rate of thirty shillings a week. The Strand is not what it was, and he paints the difference for us in no uncertain terms. Nor do the modern restaurants know their business half so well as the old chop-houses did.

> So through this monstrous incursion of women with the war and nursery hours of to-day, the old tavern life has gone; utterly and for ever, I am afraid.

This is one of the chief grudges he urges against the modern age; and he can give us chapter and verse for it.

> Going there (to Herbert's) in these latter days I used to wonder why all the meats seemed to taste alike. . . . I had business, oddly enough, in their kitchen. One of the cooks showed me the joints roasting on the jack; and I perceived that three different meats were cooking at the one fire, while beneath, in a common pan, their juices mingled, ready for the basting ladle. It is not much wonder, I think, that veal and lamb and beef taste all much alike in this unhappy place, once so high, now fallen so low.

On another occasion, when he asked for Stilton cheese, the waiter replied that only English cheeses were supplied! And just as the food has deteriorated, so has the journalism. "Always remember that we appeal not to the cabman, but to the cabman's wife," said one of Mr. Machen's friends, a distinguished journalist; and Mr. Machen, who, to say the worst of him, prefers the cabman, might have been a little more disgusted than he is, and that is not a little. He does his best to fix a considerable share of the blame for our present condition on this "monstrous incursion of women."

Such things as these are not, however, the main features of Mr. Machen's confessions—for that is what his pages really are. He is most interesting when he hints at his incidental experiences as novelist, journalist, and actor. And here, at the same time, because of his brevity, he is most disappointing. Mr. H. B. Irving once said to him of his book *The Great God Pan*—"You shouldn't have done it; you destroy the illusion. Never take people behind the scenes. I never do." Mr. Machen's great mistake in his two latest books is that he never takes us further than the stage-door. Although he is telling us about himself all the time, we learn very little about him because he does not tell us enough of other people. We enjoy his story, but always with a sense of irritation that he has not dotted more of the i's and crossed more of the t's. Time and again, following on some succulent anecdote, he seems almost to be about to paint for us the whole moving pageant of the 'nineties, and just as often he turns aside to trace something else into other and less interesting channels.

The truth is *Things Near and Far* is not really a book at all because it was neither conceived nor written as a book. It is a collection of amazingly good snippets, a sort of prearranged notebook that might have borne such a title as "Towards Biography." One feels about it as about something that might have been, that almost was, but is not. One is left wondering whether Mr. Machen is a good journalist or a good author, for it seems fairly evident that he cannot be both, at all events, not at the same time, as he has tried to be in his two latest books.

Liverpool Daily Post and Mercury:

. . . It is debonair, it is graceful, it is dignified and extraordinarily at its ease, it is essentially belles-lettres; it is not much more than that; it is not specially memorable, nor does it presage very brilliantly of the book to come (in the indefinite future), where "an interior tale of the soul and its emotions" is to be told through the shapes of "hills and valleys, woods and rivers, sunrise and sunset, buried temples and mouldering Roman walls." Mr. Machen has humour, poetic sensibility, a sense of style; he is reflective, open to the influences of nature, appreciative of the town's common and uncommon interests, readily responsive to the appeal of art and literature. What perhaps his work lacks to make it true literature is virility, and it wants substance to make it really worth while, though it is—this must be one's last word—exceedingly pleasant.

The Morning Post:

Mr. Arthur Machen has his full circle of readers, who will be delighted with this sumptuous edition which Mr. Secker has so ably prepared. It is limited to a thousand sets; five hundred of which have gone to America. Mr. Machen loves the unusual and the mysterious. They appeal to his imagination and set him thinking on a train of thought which seems without end. Someone has said that few men can more agreeably fill a column. The remark finds justification in these volumes. This gift is the strength and weakness of his writing. It might be said of Mr. Machen that he has at once too much and too little imagination. Too much, that his ideas flow on like the summer brook; too little, that his style lacks incisiveness and the power of expressing instantaneously some thought.

"The Great God Pan" is a fair example of this weakness. He tells us in *Far Off Things* that he was persuaded to write this tale of horror by a wish to "pass on the vague, indefinable sense of awe and mystery and terror" that he had received in childhood days spent in the valley of the Usk, above Newbridge. The feeling that all the best in human beings is built on a treacherous morass which may engulf it at any moment has often been expressed. Mr. Machen's effort does not compare with Stevenson's *Dr. Jekyll and Mr. Hyde*. Its terror is dissipated through failure to bring any definite incident of horror before the reader. The alternative would have been to envelop the story in such a wealth of strangeness that the impression would have been created through atmosphere; the method of Poe. Mr. Machen is neither sufficiently dramatic nor sufficiently keyed to the weirdness of his tale. It certainly lacks resemblance to the dark gravity of deep woods.

From a consideration of this point we notice another peculiarity in Mr. Machen's work. It is not plagiarism, but the ignoring of any reference to ideas which other men have worked upon. True, there is no monopoly of thought, but we are led sometimes right up to a thought which has been superbly expressed before. It would seem more natural if Mr. Machen directed us to the poet or writer instead of enlarging in his own words on that idea. It would certainly be more effective from the point of view of art.

It may be that we are somewhat critical. There is much to enjoy and admire in these books with ever a word for the weak and distressed, and the fascinating hint of "worlds unrealised." But library editions are becoming increasingly popular, and we wonder whether they may not be overdone. These fine books are delightful to handle, but the thought creeps in if their matter is quite up to the high standard of production; whether anything but the very best should find a home in these limited editions, which rise so readily in mere marketable value. Still, Mr. Machen has his admirers. No doubt they will think nothing too good as a home for his thoughts.

The Manchester Guardian:

In *Far Off Things* Mr. Arthur Machen describes his rambling boyhood on the borderland of South Wales and his adolescence (a rather sad affair of lonely lodging and penurious journalism in London) as far as the publication of his first book. His memories have been laid up in lavender, and they emerge rather heavily scented. The result is the praise of old and simple things in a style that has too glib an antiquarianism to be pleasing over a long stretch. The reader finds himself predicting Mr. Machen's reaction to each situation as it arises and trying to forestall the phrase which the author's sentimental conservatism will use. For instance, when he describes how his mother made "fermety" or "frumenty" in the autumn he must allude to it as "a very honourable dish and a most ancient and Christian pottage." One feared in advance some such pomposity. It is the more pity because Mr. Machen is sensitive as well as sentimental, and when he allows his memories to flow in unprinked English he achieves a beauty apt to the object he describes, notably in his landscapes of the Usk Valley and the surrounding hills.

The Outlook:

Literature and the journalist do not always rub shoulders nowadays; at all events few people look to find anything claiming to be prose in the misprinted, smudgy sheets of our raucous evening Press, unless, perhaps, in newspapers published North of the Trent. So that it does not promise well to read in Mr. Machen's preface that his new book appeared seven years ago in one of the best-known London evening papers under the title "Confessions of a Literary Man." It sounds like Mr. Bennett all over again, and misgiving increases when he adds that the confessions were written to editorial order when he was a reporter. It is an old truth that Fleet Street has ruined more good writers than Fleet Street ever made. Only at a first glance does Mr. Machen appear to be an exception, for in spite of the extraordinary quality and power of his present book, though it challenges comparison with Gissing's best work and surpasses it in parts, Mr. Machen is quite clearly not the writer he might have been. *Far Off Things* is one of the most entertaining and familiar books one remembers; a vivid autobiographical chapter, condensed and complete in much less than two hundred pages, but it is without that distinctive art that makes Mr. Gosse's *Father and Son* one of the great pieces of autobiography of this or any time, and it has not just that sense for the right word in the right place which knits language into abiding literature. He cannot wrestle with the conventional:—

> Now winter has its splendours; but with what joy do we welcome the yearly miracle of spring. We and the whole earth exult together as though we had been delivered from prison, the hedgerows and the fields are glad, and the woods are filled with singing; and men's hearts are filled with an ineffable rapture. Israel once more has come out of Egypt, from the house of bondage.

That is the prose of the best journalism, but not the prose of the man who is, first and foremost, expressing the pure content of his mind with all his mind's power through the power of words.

But the real charm of the book lies elsewhere, chiefly in the zest with which he describes the places he has loved and the people he remembers, the curious, quiet anecdotes, his sense of poetry in all things, and, especially, his literary enthusiasms. Cervantes and Scott come into his range, and even De Quincey, who "wrote in the great manner because he thought in the great manner." He is inspiriting about Carlyle, and there is a tone of voice meant for the detractors of that great man in the quiet statement: "I know not any man of these days that is worthy to dust Carlyle's hat or to clean his pipe for him." But the journalist comes out badly in that sentence. The best thing in the book is his description of the Strand as it was in the 'eighties, and there is a curious parallel with one of Mr. W. H. Davies' best poems when he writes of Gwent and Twyn Barlwm. He is equally happy proving that the Rosicrucians never existed as in describing the conventional garret of authorhood's infancy, and there is one magnificent anecdote of a lesson in Welsh pronunciation:—

> I said, "Yn oes oesodd"—from ages to ages. "That is right," said my Welsh friend, "speak it so that it makes a sound like the wind about the mountains."

And, as he says himself, the spirit of that sentence is very near to the heart of true literature. Mr. Machen knows what true literature is. There is a good critic in the man who can define realism as "the depicting of eternal, inner realities—the 'things that really are' of Plato—as opposed to the description of transitory, external surfaces; the delusory masks and dominoes with which the human heart hides and drapes itself." Though he is digressive he is never garrulous, even when he writes about food and drink, and he does that well enough to whet the reader's appetite.

Far Off Things, if it is not a great book, is a book too good to be read lightly. It contains a great deal of wisdom and more than a little humour. The author throws out hints of a book yet to be written, in which hills and valleys, woods and rivers, sunrise and sunset will be described so that a story is suggested to the reader; something of Wordsworth's method, and certainly a method of poetry, though Mr. Machen does not seem to realise it in that way. Such a book he has in his mind, and if, when it comes, it improves on *Far Off Things,* Mr. Machen will have done his work better than he knew.

Liverpool Daily Post and Mercury:

Mr. Arthur Machen is a modest man: he says so himself; but his modesty is of that most profitable kind—to the world, we mean, of course—which inspired Montaigne, Cowley, "Elia," and other famous "egoists." In *Things Near and Far* he continues the tale he began in *Far Off Things,* published a few months ago, the tale of his life, outer and inner, public and private. He is, it is increasingly evident, a man of letters, a complete man of letters, and nothing but a man of letters. The landmarks of his life are either one or other of his books, or one or other of the events out of which a book is to grow. He has a positive flair for making literary capital out of life. He is a very appreciative collector of experiences, and always has plenty to say on any point; he is fairly fertile in ideas, though no great thinker; and he is interested and can communicate his interest—even in his own books and the reviews they called forth. That notable modesty of his takes on, by the way, in presence of those reviews, an aspect too like self-complacency to leave us quite assured of his ingenuousness. There are, however, many books less worth 7s. 6d. than this.

Daily News:

Far Off Things, by Arthur Machen. "Heaven lies about us in our infancy." Nevertheless, few sensitive men recall a really happy boyhood. Mr. Machen is one of them. The only child of the rector of Caerleon-on-Usk, in the romantic solitudes of Gwent, he looks back on his earliest days as a secluded yet intense experience. The power of association is strong; and the vein of mysticism which characterises Mr. Machen's writings both derives from, and is heightened by, the gleam of such fond recollection. With Sir Thomas Browne, he finds those years "a miracle . . . which to relate were not a history, but a piece of poetry."

We all know that the author of such diversities in unity as *Hieroglyphics, The Great God Pan,* and "The Bowmen," is a thoroughly illogical and genial spirit. The incredibly genuine sense of wonder that runs through his excursions in practical journalism somehow prevents us from being irritated as we ought to be. His new book is good, if not a "piece of poetry." We are glad to have his apologia, it is oddly convincing. It must be a great and unbalancing thing to find miracles all the way.

When Mr. Machen writes of his studies, his early yearning for London, and the hard times he knew in the capital, it is in the same untroubled spirit. His temperament is unchanged through all these years.

"Omnia exeunt in mysterium"—the thought brings him the mystic's consolation. If one loves the unfathomable, why go about to probe it? Yet he demands realism from literature: De Quincey was his first idol by virtue of this possession. The old inference is made clear again. The mystic lives not in experience, but in the aura with which he encases it. To us others this way of acceptance is an illusion, an escape from the perplexed soul. But can we make anything better of life?

The Boston Evening Transcript:

THE REFLECTIONS OF A MAN OF SELF-CONCEIT

An extremely pleasant philosophy harboured by literary folk of a certain class in regard to the stress of bread-winning is that there is monotony about such a humdrum occupation. It is not agreeable to work at something you hate when you long to be literarily productive. Nevertheless, despite Carl Van Vechten's sympathetic explosions all over the yellow cover of this book, we wonder just how much self-respect and inclination may war with each other in a young man's soul when the young man lives as Mr. Machen did in his youth. A book called *The Anatomy of Tobacco* was an early effort. That achieved, he seems to have lived on his father, a clergyman who had no money. He speaks of the situation thus: "My mother had been a hopeless invalid for fifteen years; my father's health had failed, and he had become very deaf; the poor living of Llanddewi Fach had grown poorer still through the agricultural smash of 1880; he was in dire and perpetual straits for money; he underwent most of the mortifications which are allotted to the poor. It makes me grieve to this day to remember with what piteous sadness he would lean his head on his hand; he had lost hope."

Thus Mr. Machen summarises his family's situation financially. He does not appear to have been much comfort to his father. He speaks now of "grieving." Better indeed if he had done a little honest work. He goes to London. He reads manuscripts for a bookseller. Some intelligent people like that sort of occupation. He calls it a "weary business." In fact, this book is filled with complaints, constant, unstinted in their outgo, because he, Arthur Machen, could not do exactly what he wished to do, on all occasions. There is a good deal of what we might term the pseudo-classic touch to his style. He likes to pose as an intellectual deserving of immortality. He is not content to be one of our leading contemporaries. He prefers, as in one instance, to "abide by the verdict of M. Octave Uzanne, who is said, I believe, to be a good judge of letters. He said that it (a certain work called *The Chronicle of Clemendy*) was 'le renouveau de la Renaissance,' and that I was sure of my place beside Rabelais and Boccaccio, on the serene immortal seats."

We quote the above from Mr. Machen because it is wholly typical of the man. Another remark in reference to George Moore's *A Mummer's Wife* shows his attitude toward the age in which he lives equally well. He complains because no good novel of stage life has been written. And then he adds that in the old days, the days of the Crummles Company, it would have been easier. That is nonsense. This age and generation is adequate for all, provided some effort at adaptation is made by those of us who have been too overburdened by the weight of the glorious past. A good novel can be written as well in the twentieth century as in the seventeenth, provided some one has the brains to compass it. The whole book shows the reflections of a conceited man of mediocre ability, who buries his talent in the ashes of the past, mumbles over it incessant Latin quotations, pats himself on the back because he knows so much Latin to quote and then . . . is continually irritated because the world hurries by without digging into the ashes, or listening respectfully to his incantations.—D. F. G.

Maurice Hewlett in *The Evening Standard:*

. . . "To be in the Strand," he says, sighing, "was like drinking punch and reading Dickens." So it was—but one can read Dickens the better without the punch, either within or without the pages. It was a strange chapter of literary history where human happiness could not be imagined or pictured without too much to eat and too much to drink. I will be sentimental with almost anyone, for the mingling of tears is as wholesome a vent as the chiming of laughter—but I cannot cry over the bad smells of yesteryear to save my life. When I remember Holywell Street I turn with thanksgiving to Charing Cross Road. It is nothing to write home about—but you can feel the wind in it. So much for that. . . .

Dog and Duck

Laurence Housman in *Now and Then:*

The brief essay is a friendly form of literature; it enables the writer to say zestfully just what is in his mind to say, and no more. The moment his zest diminishes he can leave off, and another day start fresh on a new subject. So, in small measure, it gives us the man, the natural everyday furnishings of his brain, the room he lives in, the mental paraphernalia with which his taste for life has surrounded him.

The brief essay is, therefore, a personal test of character. Its writer need not make you, or even wish to make you agree with his opinions, he may have that type of minority mind which prefers to annoy people; he may be unlovable, provocative, sceptical, superstitious—I could string you any number of unvirtuous qualities from which a good brief essay may be compounded—but he must be himself, he must be interesting, and he must have a point of view.

I have not the pleasure, or the pain, of Mr. Machen's personal acquaintance. I do not know whether I should like him; but I do know that he would interest me—that he is himself, and that he has a point of view. I think that often we should differ and sometimes quarrel, that his point of view occasionally invites as much ridicule as it casts on others, that it is now and then inconsistent. But the inconsistency is all of a piece with the character: he has a mind with a certain focus, outside which the view becomes blurred, perhaps a little distorted. It is the kind of mind which Mr. Chesterton invented for himself, the better to attract attention to the good which God had given him: he has a mind credulous toward folk-lore and the past, incredulous toward modern history and science; but he does not explain why folk-lore should be believed and modern history rejected—beyond giving us a few instances where folk-lore has been proved true, and modern history proved false; as to which one need only say that the means for correcting modern history are more abundantly to hand than those for correcting folk-lore. He is a romantic, and has a romantic detestation for the impossibilities of Euclid, whom he therefore dismisses as unworthy of the wise man's consideration. But I could be just as romantic in favour of Euclid, on those very same grounds. It is only by giving it impossible things to believe that Euclid provides the human brain with foothold for clear logical thinking. It is only, as Mr. Chesterton might say, by accepting the impossible that man can attain to true belief. It is on those lines that theology has provided us with a spiritualised Euclid of its own: and only by believing in its impossibilities shall we ever get to eternal life—which in itself is to the human mind an impossible condition, unless miserable science, through the theories of Einstein, is now going to help us to accept it. It is quite possible to be as romantic in one's acceptance of science as Mr. Machen is in his acceptance of folk-lore.

But it is when Mr. Machen is sceptical of human nature's ability to recapture the good it has let go that I quarrel with him most. As surely as I could train an intelligent child to be superstitious about going under a ladder, so surely could I train it to enjoy the bracing and rhythmical exercise of the Morris dance, on which Mr. Machen throws a black and a wicked doubt for which I do not readily forgive him.

This only means that in his twenty-eight essays, his *Dogs* and his *Ducks*, Mr. Machen has not always scored a complete "Duck," and brought his point home with conviction. For the meaning of which I refer the reader to the first essay, which gives the book its unexplained title. But every one of them is interesting and attractive, even when provocative.

New York Herald:

Some twenty-odd little essays by Arthur Machen have been gathered into a book carrying the title of the first essay, *Dog and Duck* (Knopf), on its cover. This singular combination refers to an ancient game that is still played in a Georgian setting in London, but before Machen gets through describing the game he takes the reader through a famous criminal trial of the eighteenth century. Carl Van Vechten says for the publisher that these essays are "in the Dickens manner," but we found little of that savour in "Roast Goose" or "Martinmas" or

"Christmas Mumming," just the kind of subjects Dickens wrote about but in a so different manner and spirit. But, on their own merits, they make very agreeable reading.

Boston Transcript:

This collection of rambling essays represents a late phase of its author's work and presents an interesting contrast with some of the earlier books recently reissued as the result of the growth of a Machen cult in this country. The newer Machen is revealed as a less eccentric, healthier, but not less sensitive writer than the old. There is in *Dog and Duck* and its companion essays little trace of the author's former prepossession with things occult and ghastly, while his more pleasing qualities as a writer are fairly well represented. When Machen writes with a gentle regret for things past or passing, such as old sports and old enjoyments, or the disappearance of the vulgar Valentine and the "fogs of yesteryear," he is altogether charming.

A number of the essays have a satiric tinge, often sharply pointed and telling, as in "Simnel Cakes," wherein Machen pays his respects to the professional etymologist, or "A Midsummer Night's Dream," with its observations of the development of the popular idea of a fairy. Elsewhere there is a good deal of matter that is trite and obvious, as when the author demonstrates that Shakespeare was a practical man of the theatre rather than a university "don," or that the Victorians were not strait-laced on all occasions. Briefly, in a number of the essays one perceives the journalist writing to fill space. There is much in the book that will not enhance Machen's reputation as a man of letters.

The Manchester Guardian:

The suspicion which assails the reader who is familiar with the present state of the "first edition" market as he takes up Mr. Machen's new book of essays is very natural. In a note on the dust-cover is the announcement that the issue is limited to less than a thousand copies, and that the author has autographed a considerable number of them. This, taken in conjunction with the news from America that at the auction of Mr. John Quinn's library two first-edition copies of Mr. Machen's earlier works were sold at impressive figures, irresistibly suggests that one, at all events, of the immediate purposes of *Dog and Duck* has been to "catch the market." If this be so, then the modern craze for book-collecting has for once been useful. The essays are selected from the author's most recent journalism, and the reader will have rich enjoyment in them. A characteristic corn-cob atmosphere is created in the very first pages, describing with a quiet and mellow humour the ancient pastime of "Dog and Duck," which is so simple, we are assured, that only a soft india-rubber ball and a garden surrounded by an unbroken path are needed; yet it takes a lifetime for the player to become an expert. Dissertations on valentines, simnel cakes, old port, the only good way to make chocolate, fogs in November, and Shakespeare, Bacon, collops, and astrology follow handsomely; and through them all we have ample evidence that Mr. Machen has kept intact his creed that, in his own language, "it is the love of splendour—the splendid robe, the splendid word, the splendid picture—which constitutes the vital distinction between man and brute. Many beasts have reason, the faculty of using means for a certain end. But only man has art, which is the love of splendour and the desire to create it." The wistful note introduced a year since into his *Things Near and Far* develops occasionally into a page-long phase of sighing ostentatiously and regretting angrily, for he cannot help remembering the glories of his own youth in London that are no more.—T. M.

The Times Literary Supplement:

About most of the essays in Mr. Arthur Machen's *Dog and Duck: A London Calendar et cetera*, there is a graceful tenuousness which compares interestingly with the fiercer note of the other few. While he is gravely and reflectively tuning his discursive pen to the changing seasons of the year, he is grave, tenderly reminiscent, a trifle elderly. He discourses of the New Year and French influence in Scotland, of bygone valentines in February, of March and simnel cakes, of May and the decay of joy, of July and why young men row races at Henley, of roast goose in September, of first fogs in October, and so forth. These essays, with the charming account of the (we suspect) apocryphal game of Dog and Duck which constitutes the first, are nearly all in the wistful note which is characteristic of this author.

Mr. Machen excels at the picturesque-peevish, when he complains that the joys which he knew in his youth are no more, that joy has vanished like the fogs and horse-omnibuses, that the race of Englishmen has perished to give place to a generation of inmates for a convalescent home. Then all of a sudden he flares up, and the hidden reason seems to be that some misguided doctor once tried to put Mr. Machen on a diet: at all events the flare-up takes the form of violent diatribes against any interference in the name of science, health, or intelligence with the freedom of the stomach to indulge in wine, beer, stout, roast beef, kidneys, oysters, and other fleshly delights. At one moment he attacks poor old superseded Euclid under this inspiration, at another he satirically concludes that on scientific principles we had all better spend Christmas in gaol; and he will fire off a broadside at any moment against those who object to self-indulgence, who disbelieve in a primitive roystering Shakespeare, and who show any tendency to explain away anything at all. They hate life, says Mr. Machen; but apparently he himself confesses to finding the actualities of life repulsive. One must get away from them somehow, then; young men do it by rowing themselves blue in the face, pure scientists by turning to abstractions, applied scientists by interfering with old ideas, and Mr. Machen by imagining that he knew what Merrie England was like, somewhere about Caerleon in the day of Chaucer. Now he need never be dull, for he can revile the present in musical language.

H. P. Collins in *The Outlook:*

Mr. Machen has the one great requisite of a popular journalist: he holds the reader's attention from the beginning to the end of his article, and holds it no longer. He is never dull; and he is never profound. To adopt a simile from the ingenious old game of "Dog and Duck" into which he initiates us: he brings his ball to rest between the chases without going to earth in "grounds" or "green," scores five points or maybe ten—he never rounds the last corner and attains the Duck for a score of forty.

Mr. Machen has a spirited and genial manner; but it does not proceed from a really robust and consistent personality. He is akin to Mr. Chesterton in his gusto, his love of good fare, and his faith in medievalism and Merrie England; but he has none of Mr. Chesterton's wit and intellectual vigour. In *Far Off Things* the author's mystical attitude brought him through in a qualified triumph; it has thinned unawares to sentimentality in these laments for valentines in February, Victorian bonhomie, and the fogs of yesteryear. He is vexed with Hewlett for his dislike of "the universe in general and human nature in particular"! It is nothing to the cheery tribe of Machen that there are and always have been those to whom history is not a pretty game, those who cannot afford milk-punch and those who cannot stomach roast goose and sage-and-onion. What Mr. Machen, for all his gestures, cannot stomach is reality. He lives in a world not of experience but of legend, where it will please many to visit him.

It is with relief, though as must needs be a touch of sadness, that one turns from Mr. Machen to these posthumous essays of Maurice Hewlett. From rose-coloured and enervating mists we pass to the keen air of Wiltshire and the keener stimulus of the voice that is now still.

Richard Church in *The Nation and the Athenæum:*

Mr. Machen is a good journalist because he writes clearly and simply, and, for some reason or other, makes us finish reading his articles. We may think that his god, Commonsense, is often an uncommon fool, a creature of shallow thought and indolent prejudice, but we read on and enjoy the author's company—often with a yawn. It is boring to hear that the world of to-day is degenerate, that the spirit of joy left England somewhere about the time of Elizabeth; for such talk recalls the conversation of the clubs, and the bores who always buttonhole us when we are particularly depressed by the weather or the political situation. Mr. Machen is inclined to overdo this old "stunt" of the golden days of thirty, forty, fifty, five hundred years ago. In one article after another it appears, like the conventional "sea-runs" in the Norse and Keltic folk-tales. Our exasperation may be due to the fact that these articles are read one after another in the book, whereas they should be, and originally were, scattered in the periodical Press. Mr. Machen has a hearty way with him, and a humorous and observant eye which informs a mind never weary of the pageant of passing events. In his description of old scenes and games, of personal adventures, of the flotsam and jetsam incidental to the daily life of his neighbour—and all the world is his neighbour—he is delightful and Dickensian. When he dogmatises he tends to become "lowbrow," which is equally as unpleasant as being "highbrow." The publisher is to be congratulated on the perfect production of this book.

The Other Side

Marc Logé in *La Revue Hebdomadaire*:

La littérature anglaise contemporaine possède peu de figures plus curieuses ni plus sincères que celle de M. Arthur Machen, mystique et satiriste, lettré et rêveur, qui traverse le prosaïsme de la vie moderne comme un étranger revenant de très loin,—du moyen âge pour le moins—et qui se trouve sans cesse choqué, peiné et dépaysé par ce qu'il voit et entend. L'œuvre de M. Machen compte déjà une vingtaine de volumes, dont plusieurs sont fort recherchés par les bibliophiles pour leur rareté. Et il vient de publier deux nouveaux récits,—autobiographiques ceux-là,—*Things Near and Far* et Arthur Machen, une *Bibliographie,* agrémentée de notes et de souvenirs, qui éclairent singulièrement sa si originale personnalité.

M. Arthur Machen passa une grande partie de sa jeunesse dans un presbytère du pays de Galles, dont l'ambiance mystique a mis sur sa pensée une empreinte ineffaçable. Il a, toute sa vie, été hanté par le profond mystère de la beauté, et toutes ses œuvres sont comme frémissantes d'un émerveillement incessant, qu'il s'efforce de communiquer à ses lecteurs. Et ce n'est pas sa faute si ceux-ci ne connaissent point le charme de Caermaen la Blanche, ou la magic du doux pays de Gwent. Ses héros, dont la jeunesse ardente et tourmentée doit ressembler, on le devine, beaucoup à celle de M. Machen, laissèrent envahir leurs âmes rares et étranges par des rêves que les gens sensés et ordinaires qualifieraient de folies. Mais M. Machen excelle à dépeindre ce qui se trouve "sur les confines mêmes de l'inconnu." C'est pourquoi il aime pardessus toute la Nature.

Pourtant l'impérieuse nécessité de la vie l'obligea à quitter ses bois, ses collines et ses montagnes de Galles pour Londres, où l'on vit ce mystique exercer consciencieusement à Fleet Street le métier de journaliste qui lui répugnait. Il possédait heureusement le don de s'intéresser à tout, même à ce qui lui déplaisait le plus. Mais, comme il l'a dit lui-même dans le *Lignes écrites en contemplant d'une hauteur de Londres une école communale éclairée par le soleil,*—"celui qui n'éprouve ni émerveillement ni mystère, ni crainte, ni le sentiment d'un monde nouveau, ni d'un royaume inconnu dans les environs de Gray's Inn Road, ne découvrira jamais ces secrets,—ni au cœur de l'Afrique ni dans les cités cachées du Thibet. 'La matière de notre travail est partout presenté,' disaient les anciens alchimistes; toutes les merveilles se trouvent à un pas de la gare de King's Cross" . . . Peut-être, lorsqu'elles sont transmuées par le soleil! . . .

M. Machen connut bien des vicissitudes; il fut reporter, puis libraire, et il peut ainsi satisfaire son goût insatiable de livres rares et curieux, et en particulier d'ouvrages occultes du moyen âge;—il fut traducteur,—il compila des catalogues; mais il continua toujours, malgré toutes les difficultés d'une vie laborieuse, à écrire et à proclamer la permanence de la beauté.

Il est pourtant curieux de noter qu'à côté de ce mystère de la beauté, il fut également pénétré par le mystère de l'horrible: et l'influence de Poë est nettement apparente dans ses deux œuvres de jeunesse, *The Great God Pan* et *The Three Impostors*. Pourtant sa conception de l'horrible diffère de celle de Poë, en ce que le pessimisme morbide de ce dernier l'entraînait, ainsi que ses lecteurs, vers un désespoir sans fond. M. Machen, dans sa foi, persiste à voir le soleil et la beauté filtrer à travers les ténèbres les plus denses et la plus terrible hideur.

L'œuvre la plus curieuse de M. Machen est, nous semble-t-il, *The Hill of Dreams,* dont le héros, Lucian Taylor, est un des caractères les plus troublants du roman anglais moderne. Lucian vit une vie de rêves peuplée de présences invisibles pour les autres: il circule dans l'aujourd'hui sans y appartenir; sa sensualité, éveillée par les caresses d'une petite paysanne perverse, qui ensuite se marie bien sagement avec un bon fermier,—se transforma, sous l'effet de son imagination et de son désir, en un étrange mysticisme maladif. Lucian ne vivra désormais que par son imagination qui est féconde et morbide, et sur laquelle la "magie celte" exerce une influence puissante. Sa plus grande joie fut désormais de "rêver,"—laissant son esprit errer parmi des idées à demi imaginées et délicieuses, en permettant à son cerveau vierge de vagabonder à sa guise. D'une sensibilité qui allait s'exaspérant avec les années, Lucian se retrancha de plus en plus dans sa thébaïde spirituelle, inaccessible à tous les êtres qui l'entouraient. Dans Caermaen, dans sa propre maison, on le considéra comme un demifou. Mais que lui importait?

"Il se plongea de plus en plus dans ses livres; tout ce qui était ancien et désuet était devenu son domaine. Dans le dégoût qu'il éprouvait pour les stupides questions habituelles: 'Cela rapportera-t-il? A quoi bon?'—il ne voulait lire que ce qui était étrange et inutile. La pompe et le symbolisme de la Kabbalah,—pleine de suggestions de choses encore plus terribles, —les mystères de la Rose-Croix de Fludd, les énigmes de Vaughan,—les rêves des alchimistes, faisaient sa joie. Tels étaient ses compagnons avec les collines et les bois, les ruisseaux et les étangs solitaires. . . . Parfois, lorsqu'il était plongé dans ses livres, une flamme de plaisir montait en lui tout à coup, lui révélant toute une province, tout un continent inconnu de sa nature, brûlant et embrasé,—et devant ce triomphe et cette exaltation il reculait, un peu apeuré. Il était devenu ascète dans son isolement studieux et mélancolique, et la fusion de pareilles extases l'effrayait."

Lucian se met à écrire et ses tourments redoublent, car il "devinait les immenses difficultés de la carrière littéraire, sans les comprendre clairement." De ses longues promenades solitaires à travers les bois silencieux et crépusculaires, balayés par le grand vent, il "revenait rempli de pensées, d'émotions et d'imaginations mystiques qu'il souhaitait ardemment traduire grâce au mot écrit"; mais il ne peut le faire, et connaît toutes les amertumes.

"Et dans ces moments-là, la vision habituelle du paysage l'alarmait, et les sauvages collines, arrondies comme des dômes, et les bois sombres lui paraissaient les symboles de quelque secret terrible de la vie intérieure,—de cet étranger, lui-même."

C'est ainsi que Lucian se débat et souffre dans les rets de sa propre imagination, alimentée par toute son hérédité celtique, qui crée autour de lui des visions tour à tour mystiques ou païennes, sacrées ou charnelles, qui torturent et broient son âme et son corps.

Comme fond, contre lequel se détache si douloureusement le pâle visage tourmenté de Lucian, M. Machen a brossé, avec une ironie mordante, mais sobre, un tableau de la société bourgeoise de Caermaen;—et le contraste entre la placidité prosaïque et repue des "county families" et l'âme inquiète du fils du pasteur, est indiqué par quelques traits fins et satiriques qui prouvent que M. Machen n'a point perdu son humeur à feuilleter avec amour les bouquins poussiéreux d'autrefois.

Son dernier livre, *The Secret Glory,* est l'histoire d'un autre jeune Gallois, Ambrose Meyrick, qui s'efforce, *lui,* d'accorder sa nature pleine d'élans, de curiosités et d'aspirations vers un idéal tout gothique, avec la routine conventionnelle prescrite et acceptée. Inutile de dire qu'il échoue. Mais ce livre est aussi la critique âpre et passionnée de ces "public schools" qui sont l'orgueil de l'Angleterre, et dans lesquels M. Machen ne voit, assez justement, que des machines à broyer toute individualité, et il condamne sévèrement l'esprit de ces grands centres d'éducation, où toute "excentricité est impitoyablement réprimée, où toute conscience individuelle est détruite." Pourtant Ambrose Meyrick échappe à temps à l'annihilation de sa personnalité, car il découvre la *gloire secrète* qu'il porte en lui, et cela la sauvera. La terre entière devient pour lui "un sanctuaire," toute vie un rite et une cérémonie dont le but tend à la possession de la sainteté mystique,—la découverte du Graal. Pour cela seulement,—pour quelle autre raison? toutes choses ont été créées? C'est de cela que le petit oiseau chante dans le buisson, en émettant quelques notes faibles et plaintives dans les soirées crépusculaires, comme si son petit cœur regrettait ne pouvoir élever que de si piteuses louanges. C'était cela aussi que celebrait la splendeur de l'aube blanche sur les collines,—le souffle des bois à l'aurore. C'était cela qui était figuré dans le cérémonial rouge du couchant, lorsque des flammes brillaient au-dessus du dôme de la grande montagne et que des roses semblaient s'épanouir dans les plaines lointaines du ciel. C'était cela aussi le secret que connaissaient les endroits obscurs des bois; le mystère du soleil sur la hauteur, et chaque petite fleur, chaque petit fougère, chaque roseau était chargé de célébrer secrètement ce sacrement. Ayant compris ces vérités, "tout ce qui était beau et merveilleux fit dorénavant partie pour lui de la sainteté; toute la gloire de la vie était dans le service du sanctuaire."

L'œuvre de M. Machen est inégale et parfois confuse,—mais il s'en dégage toujours un charme étrange et pénétrant,—une espèce de fascination qui provient sans doute de l'extase dont elle est tout imprégnée. Car l'extase, nous dit-il dans son essai intitulé *Hieroglyphics,* est révélatrice de l'art véritable; celui qui ne cherche à exprimer que le quotidien, le visible, l'ordinaire, usurpe le titre d'artiste,—qui n'appartient qu'à ceux qui savent croire à l'invisible, en se fiant à leur imagination et à leur désir, et tendre de tout leur être vers l'inconnu. Car l'art, pour M. Machen, ne remplace pas la religion: il en est une forme!

The Daily Telegraph:

Wonderful indeed are the changes and chances of the literary life! Many years ago—let us say thirty—a judicious student of fiction who happened upon one of Mr. Arthur Machen's early books might well have thought to himself, "There can be no keeping down an imagination and a power of style like these. Whether one likes it or not, this man's work is literature, and some meed of fame will undoubtedly be his." A generation which had revelled in *The New Arabian Nights* and in *Dr. Jekyll and Mr. Hyde* must, it seemed certain, have rewards in store for the writer of *The Three Impostors* and *The Great God Pan*.

And then year after year went by, and Arthur Machen remained practically unknown. One or two more of his singular books appeared, written exclusively to satisfy himself, and in total disregard of the existence of any school of public taste. The mystical tragedy of modern life called *The Hill of Dreams* is not a book for everybody; but it is undeniably the outpouring of a strangely gifted spirit.

The war broke out in 1914, and Mr. Machen invented a fable about the "Angels of Mons" which flew all round the English-speaking world, and was passionately believed by vast multitudes of simple people to be a plain account of an actual miracle; so that its fabricator naturally got no credit for them, and met, indeed, with no little abuse for strenuously declaring that the story was a lie of his own imagining. Then there came out a curious essay in mystical Christianity, about the coming of the Holy Grail to a secluded place in Wales. Next appeared a gruesome little nightmare of a story about an attempted revolt, during the war, of the animals against mankind, the truth about which was supposed, in the tale, to have been rigorously suppressed by the censorship. Then the oddest, certainly, of all that class of recent fiction which has occupied itself with savage criticism of the English public school system and spirit.

Still nothing seemed likely to win a wide recognition for this peculiar talent. And then, quite suddenly, one began to hear it talked about on all sides among literary people, and especially those of whom Mr. Machen was by this time old enough to be the father. Now, after a remarkably brief period of celebrity, as these things go, his *Collected Works* appear in nine stately volumes, beautiful with wide margins and severely tasteful binding; an edition such as any writer living might be proud of, and any lover of the externals as well as the substance of books might delight to see on his shelves.

It is only too likely that recognition in this very substantial form has come too late to give Mr. Machen more than a fraction of the pleasure which it would once have yielded. Indeed, one may say it is certain; for the two volumes of reminiscences included in this edition are sometimes very painful, though always quite absorbing reading. There is nothing in them so petty as mere embitterment; but they are the writings of a man who has suffered deeply. Most deeply, perhaps, during those recent years of journalistic hack-work of which he definitely declines to give any straightforward account, but of which melancholy glimpses are to be had from time to time in one of the most discursive works of autobiography ever penned. These were the years of acknowledged, and apparently final and irredeemable, failure, and they can hardly be lived down at such an age as Mr. Machen has reached.

Success was denied to his earlier books, it may be surmised, because there was so much less feeling then than exists now for the spirit of poetic mysticism which went along with the gruesomeness of those extraordinary tales. They were dismissed by some as "morbid," and perhaps they were, although morbidity, by all accounts, is the last quality which one would attribute to Mr. Machen as a man. But the horrors of sorcery and the embodiment of evil were mingled here with a feeling for beauty and a severity of style which became more and more apparent in Mr. Machen's later books; and all through his work runs that thread of sombre preoccupation with the life of the spirit which, contrasted as it is with an unusually vivid perception of the colour and detail of the life about him, makes his personal reminiscences so strangely interesting, and even his tales of diabolism more plausible than a man merely attempting to exploit a popular liking for "the supernatural" could possibly have made them.

Mr. Machen's talent is certainly one of the most marked and individual that has appeared in his generation of English writers.

Robert Hillyer in *The New York Times Book Review:*

Up from the Ranks of Grub Street Authorship

Ten years ago weekly explorations of second-hand bookshops in Boston never failed to yield me a copy of the American reprints by Dana Estes & Co. of Arthur Machen's *House of Souls* and his *Hill of Dreams*. They were a regular feature of the rubbish counter. For these I usually had to pay about 50 cents a copy—though I bought one *Hill of Dreams,* which I still possess, for 10 cents. I must have purchased about twenty of these books. I gave them to friends, I lent them to friends—it does not matter which; the volumes disappeared one way or another. It seemed at the time a method within my means of bestowing great riches on the people I liked or admired. Few of my friends went away without their copy of a book they had never heard of, but which they would read for friendship's sake. When I had only two copies of *The Hill of Dreams* left, and could find no more, I decided to suppress my prodigal instincts, but a burst of generosity brought on by some green chartreuse disposed of one of the two. The other one, saved by the banishment decreed to monastic liquor, is still with me.

And beside it on the shelf is Mr. Knopf's new edition of the book. *The Hill of Dreams* will never again be found on the rubbish counter; the old red edition is a collector's rarity; the new yellow one is a substantial proof of the advance of good literature in America. During the last ten years Mr. Machen's art has been recognised; he is almost the only example of a fine writer rescued from oblivion in his own lifetime. Yet he has made no concession to the world in general. He has not changed a word of *The Hill of Dreams* since he wrote it twenty-six years ago. It is the same book—a failure in 1907, rubbish in 1913, a success in 1923. Obviously, the world has made concessions to the ideas which he represents.

The triumph of mechanism, which is shown in its full glory by the late war and the wars that follow it, has, like all bad tyrannies, engendered a reaction. For years isolated voices were raised against it, but they spoke in syllables that were incomprehensible to the minds of men spellbound by the wonder of Things. In differing accents, protests came from writers as diverse in talent as Samuel Butler, Walter

Pater and Arthur Machen. People took it for granted that such protests were the inevitable whine of the Old Order against Progress, an explanation at once so simple and inclusive that it could dispose of any objection calculated to disturb their satisfaction in the machinery of manufacture and the machinery of life. The world, indeed, was fast stampeding into a herd which would not tolerate the existence of unconverted individuals. Then suddenly the machine itself went wrong, and threatened, like the machine in the ballad, to transform its inventor into sausage meat. There was a wild flight of worshippers from the crumbling shrine of Moloch—whither? Into Spiritism, Bahaism, neo-Buddhism; into every cult, in fact, that offered even a temporary shelter from desperation. This headlong rout into faddism of all sorts was a superficial earnest that the mind of the race was turning, had in fact turned, back toward an acknowledgment of the final mystery of life.

Of this mystery, Arthur Machen has from the first been the consistent exponent. His mind is that of a medieval Christian; a liberal monk, perhaps, who has taken many an appreciative peek at the classics in the library of the foundation. To him all that is beautiful builds walls of the celestial city in the mind of man; all that makes war against that beauty is unutterably evil. There is no middle ground. And *The Hill of Dreams* is the epic of this spiritual battle.

In the new introduction, written for the new edition, the author tells us that he intended to write a Robinson Crusoe of the soul: the soul, and not the body of a man, solitary amid an alien sea. It would have been impossible for Mr. Machen to write any other sort of Robinson Crusoe, for he never leaves the material world untransmuted; everything becomes, either for good or for evil, the shadow of an overwhelming portent. Thus *The Hill of Dreams* shows us life, carnal and ethereal, as heightened by the oversensitive imagination of the hero, Lucian Taylor. The boy grows up in the outland country between Wales and England; all the glamour and terror of ancient forests become a part of him. Left largely to himself by his pathetically frustrate father, the vicar, and repelled by the lapses of taste and decency in the provincial society around him, he wanders over the domed hills under violently blue Summer skies, the hard glare of Winter and the sad wet twilight of Autumn, while the Roman past and the Celtic past, whose ruined fortresses and tumuli are only half-concealed by the moss and the thicket, gradually take possession of his imagination and ally themselves in his mind with an already established love of medieval lore, ecclesiastic and occult. All hidden beauties become his preoccupation, but, driven inward by the vicious sordidness of actuality, corruption also fascinates him. Year by year this struggle between the rapture of the inner life and the staleness of the outer aggravates an intolerable situation to be solved only by expressing it all in adequate style. But words fail, and the reasonable mind finally collapses under the weight of the imaginative.

It is obvious that Mr. Machen does not want Lucian to become the victim of this combat between modern existence and the life of the imagination. He staves off the conclusion again and again until, forced by the inevitable, he yields his hero to fate. His unwillingness to surrender the youth may be accounted for by the fact that, up to a certain point, Lucian's life was his life—his autobiography—a circumstance which has made the book suspiciously bitter in spots. He satirises the moneyed, the hypocritical, the snobbish, with a fine cruelty and vivid fidelity to life—but are these shoddy creatures, after all, worthy of so much attention? Yes, perhaps—if their mere existence is an obstacle to the higher sanity. And they are such an obstacle to Lucian, who magnifies their imbecile gestures of futility into really monstrous evils. They are a part of that wall of loneliness which isolates a naturally friendly and convivial spirit, driving it in upon itself, until all the beauties that it loves become, for lack of some one to share them, horrors and madness.

Fortunately for Mr. Machen, he is of stronger stuff than the hero of his masterpiece. In his two-volume autobiography, *Far Off Things,* which appeared last Fall, and *Things Near and Far,* which has just been published, he describes the loneliness which enhedged him and the means he took to cope with it. Now in his middle fifties, he can look back over that struggle with no bitterness, but certainly with no complacency. One cannot be complacent before the materialism of modern life, which not only fails to help a man whose interests are elsewhere, but will not even tolerate him if it knows him for what he is.

Like Lucian, Mr. Machen was born in the Welsh borderland, faced poverty in its fearfullest form—"genteel" poverty—went to London hoping to obtain the necessities of life by writing, and ended by nearly starving to death on the wages of tutoring, translating and cataloguing second-hand books.

In bookshops, he came in contact with alchemical and occult works which were to influence, though not dominate, all his later writing. Much of the interest of *Things Near and Far* lies in his treatment of various phases of mysticism, from its faddish to its serious manifestation. Very wisely, as I think, he has carefully guarded himself against seizure as an "adept" by any Spiritistic or pseudo-Oriental cult. In his burlesque description of a séance, he closes the doors of Spiritism against him:—

> The room is in total darkness. One of the sitters proclaims with exultation that his nose has been tweaked by Joey, who, on this side, was a clown. John King, understood to have been a master mariner, sings "Tom Bowling" in a falsetto voice through a speaking trumpet. On this Cardinal Newman, known to be a lover of music, is gratified, and utters the word "Benedictine." . . . "This spirit's name is Milton. Henry—no, John Milton, the author of the 'Faery Queen.' He says that they are very happy. . . . All repeat the Lord's Prayer, and Sir Arthur Conan Doyle expresses his intense gratification. . . . Well, it may be so. But I hope it isn't, and I never shall believe that it is so."

And the Oriental fanatics receive small comfort at Mr. Machen's hands:—

> There is one thing that I hope I may be spared, that is the comment of the Oriental Occult Ass. . . . I do hope nobody will say, "Why, this is only Ruja-Puja! You get it all in the first chapter of the Anangasataga Raja! It's all perfectly elementary. Little Hindu children learn their A.B.C. out of it in the Svanka Visatvara."

Despite his contempt for the physical phenomena of the Spiritists, Mr. Machen concedes their possibility. His one question remains: Is this of consequence? And he puts the same question concerning his own experience. During a fit of the most uncontrollable melancholy, he sat down in his apartment in London, and attempted, by some mental process which he does not describe, to rid himself of depression. Suddenly the pictures on the wall

> trembled, dilated, became misty in their outlines; seemed on the point of disappearing altogether, and then shuddered and contracted back again into their proper form and solidity; that is the closest description of what I witnessed: with a shaking heart, and with a sense that something, I knew not what, was also being shaken to its foundations.

He was filled with dread, yet, at the same time, with an almost unendurable ecstasy. For a moment the fear of death was upon him. Then gradually the fright passed, leaving him in an exalted and serene frame of mind that lasted for an entire year. Concerning the physical phenomenon of the pictures, he remarks:—

> This is all wonderful? I suppose that it is; but let me here say firmly that I consider an act of kindness to a wretched mangy kitten to be much more important.

But the year of peace that followed was, decidedly, of consequence, since he was lifted above the petty emotions that degrade and destroy humanity, and he saw life in its true colours. His implied conclusion is, therefore, that no occult experience is of any consequence in itself; its sole value is to enhance the dignity, decency and happiness of the human race.

All of Mr. Machen's fiercest satirical passages against humanity are dictated not by hatred but love of humanity. Nothing is so maddening as to behold a beloved being or race of beings degenerate into Yahoos. We observe the same quality in Swift, who was the most virulent of satirists because he was, fundamentally, the tenderest of humanitarians. When Mr. Machen is at his bitterest, we find no desire for vengeance; merely an infuriated, baffled perplexity that his fellows should sink so low. And even this emotion he reserves for types; for individuals he exhibits a friendliness, a conviviality, an understanding, which are worthy of the rich variety of his nature.

Indeed, though the mystical side of his character is the most interesting and the satirical the most entertaining, his Rabelaisian gusto for the good things of life sets them both off to advantage. He can recreate London or Touraine with a phrase or give us the play of sunlight on the brim of an old cup filled with clear wine. All phases of life interest him, since he has entered into more of them than most men. For example, in the opening years of the present century he was one of a company of strolling players. The single chapter he devotes to this pilgrimage might well be expanded into a sort of Thespian Lavengro. And in literature, all of whose halls, ante-rooms and little dark corridors are known to him, we always find him where we should wish to find him—on the side of rapture and care against emotionalism and slovenliness. For to him "Literature is the sensuous art of causing exquisite impressions by means of words":—

> To win the secret of words, to make a phrase that would murmur of Summer and the bee, to summon the wind into a sentence, to conjure the odour of the night into the surge and fall and harmony of a line; this was the tale of the long evenings, of the candle flame white upon the paper and the eager pen.

His style approaches the gift of music, and will repel such readers as consider words to be utilitarian vessels for measuring out their quart or bushel of meaning. But those who find reality in "Kubla Khan," "The Fall of the House of Usher," or the "Dream Fugue" will find it also in the books of Arthur Machen, who is of that small group of Coleridge, De Quincey, Sir Thomas Browne, Poe and Malory—a group where each is a master. In a vision we use the language of vision, and if on waking we would interpret what we have seen and heard into the language of waking, we can only suggest. If we state, the magic slips out between the syllables. By the marvellous orchestration of his prose, its undertones and overtones, Mr. Machen has suggested to us his vision of the battle between Light and Darkness—a vision that is far more real than this seeming reality which shifts with the passing years. It is not strange that he has been misconstrued as the artist of Terror and of Madness; he has seen so clearly the titanic war in the troubled spirit of the world, compared to which all the wars that have scarred the body of the world are but as the twitching of a sleeper in whose brain the nightmare rages. And, because of the same limitation which makes Dante's *Inferno* infinitely more convincing than his *Paradiso,* Arthur Machen's lurid darkness shines with a grander beauty than his open day. For this reason the superficial minded will persist in calling that great book *The Hill of Dreams* a "morbid" piece of work.

Objections of this sort, which entirely overlook the real robustness of the author's nature, grow fainter and fainter as the world swings around to his point of view. In brief, Mr. Machen's outlook on life is similar to his opinion of occult phenomena: external facts, valueless in themselves, are only important as they affect the imagination or spirit of man. They are merely the symbols of the great sacrament that lies behind them. For him, literature became the escape from circumstance, and he could not, if he would, relinquish it or write what was not in him.

> And my total receipts for these eighteen volumes, he says, for these forty-two years of toil, amount to the sum of six hundred and thirty-five pounds. That is, I have been paid at the rate of fifteen pounds and a few shillings per annum. It seems clear, then, that my literary activities cannot be adequately accounted for on the hypothesis of mere greed and money-grubbing.

It is this kind of devotion that gives us our masterpieces, this slow-burning, indomitable desire, independent of all consideration but the building up, phrase by phrase, of an enduring structure. That America, long the source of uninspired materialism, should recognise so fully the value of Mr. Machen's work, is a happy augury for the future of our literature.

Octave Uzanne in *Le Livre:*

THE CHRONICLE OF CLEMENDY

Je ne sais si la dédicace de ce livre rabelaisien, je veux dire de haulte graisse, adressée au *Right Honourable, Illustrious and Puissant Prince,* Humphrey, duc de Glocester, chevalier de l'ordre très noble de la Jarretière, etc., etc., est une satire barbelée ou l'hommage sérieux d'un humoriste. Le noble duc me semble le mieux situé pour en décider, et là dessus je m'en rapporte bien à lui. Mais ce que je constate dès les premières pages, sans l'ombre d'un doute, c'est l'esprit, le goût littéraire, la connaissance familière et intime de la langue jusque dans ses sources vives, le renouveau de Renaissance, si je puis dire, qui éclate à chaque ligne dans ce qu'écrit Mr. Arthur Machen.

Des contes en eux-mêmes, je ne dis rien, sinon que, les ayant lus, je les relirai souvent, à petites doses, sans me lasser, comme on visite ces flacons qui contiennent une fine et réconfortante liqueur. Gervase Perrot de Clemendy, gentleman, seigneur du manoir de Pwllcwrw,—ce qui, au pays de Galles, je crois, veut dire "flaque de bière,"—et maréchal des pots aux assises de l'Ale, ne m'est, je l'avoue humblement, pas autrement connu. Il me suffit de savoir que, depuis "The Discourse of Ale," traduit, paraît-il, du latin, jusqu'au dernier conte des neuf joyeuses journées, il se montre franc compère, aussi bon Gaulois qu'Anglais rabelaisien peut l'être, gai à miracle, spirituel à plaisir, fécond en histoires réjouissantes où les personnages n'échappent au ridicule que par l'amour, comme le peuvent désirer et faire des créatures en chair et en os, différentes de sexes et de natures semblables; en un mot, tel que nous connaissons les conteurs d'Italie et de France: Boccace, Marguerite, le seigneur des Accords, Camille Blessebois, l'Arétin, Beroalde de Verville, le Pogge, La Fontaine, et tant d'autres, au premier rang desquels le traducteur anglais de Marguerite de Navarre et de la *Chronique de Clemendy* est désormais sûr de sa place. . . .

The New York Times Book Review:

Mr. Machen, it will be recalled, is that author who, in the late 'eighties and the early 'nineties, was so overshadowed by his contemporary, Robert Louis Stevenson, that it is only of late years that his own varied genius has received the praise that was its due. Machen has recently been republished in England and in this country, but *Dog and Duck* does not belong to his earlier work. Some of the essays may date back several years, either in whole or in part, but it is clear that most of the papers are new, and that such as may embody earlier material have been elaborated and rewritten.

In *Dog and Duck* Arthur Machen has treated of nearly a score and a half of subjects; but he has neglected to write on the subject which would be of greatest use to his reviewer—namely, the art of being casual. For the essay—the true essay, that is, as defined above, not the thesis essay or the editorial—must, of all things, wear the air of absolute casuality. In actual composition, of course, there may have been nothing of the casual; and the very contrary is probable, painful delivery having, very likely, followed on long gestation. But when the essay is spread upon the pages, when the last revision of the proof has been made, it is a literary product or it is not according as a reader will be left with the impression that it sprang as spontaneously as Minerva from the head of Jove. And now that we have been carried into mythology, it might not be amiss to press the figure a little further. Minerva was the Goddess of Wisdom; and the burden of the essay—again distinct from the thesis, the burden of which is knowledge—is wisdom;

and moreover, as Minerva, issued full-panoplied and radiant of jewels and gold. And one thing more; the true essay will have wit—not loud and boisterous humour, but the wit that mellows while it stings; in short, the wit of wisdom.

To return to Arthur Machen: Does *Dog and Duck* satisfy the demands of our questionnaire? There can be but one answer, an unqualified affirmative. And that is why the complaint was raised that Mr. Machen had omitted an essay on the art of being casual. How does he achieve his illusion of apparent chance, of absolute spontaneity, when we well know that his essays must have been deliberate, as deliberate as any poem? But let it go; the question is not to be answered of Machen any more than it can be answered of Stevenson or of Lamb.

The title essay, it appears, has to do with an English outdoor game of venerable age, although Americans, apparently, are unfamiliar with it. As Chase Mallard the pastime of Dog and Duck takes on veritable antiquity. Yet the reader will not follow Machen through any desire to learn the technique of this simple outdoor sport; he will, however, be infected with the gusto of the author in trailing the game itself back through several generations, mention of it in literature, and especially— for here one will come upon the Machen of that fascinating psychoromantic tale, *The Three Impostors*—in the part Dog and Duck played in a celebrated murder trial of the eighteenth century.

Yet, if Machen is entertaining and enlivening when he discourses upon antique sports, he is none the less so when he directs a flashing eye on "Valentines and Other Things," when he turns to the matter of holidays—as he does more than once—when he talks of April Fool, of Twelfth Night, of fogs, of February stars, of the vice of making collections (to which we all are prone), to the matter of splendour, to the art of unbelief. In his best vein—though to single out any one essay from the teeming sheaf is invidious—is the one to which he gives the title "The Poor Victorians."

> We all know [he writes] what the poor Victorians were like. We have heard all about them over and over again. To begin with, they were prim. They were proper. They went to bed early. Their only form of revelry consisted in tea parties. The laws of their lives were dictated to them by maiden ladies and the vicar's wife. As for the arts in the Victorian era, they could not properly be said to exist. Nobody spoke out: nobody dared to

be "daring." No picture was painted that went beyond the vision of the Young Person. No poem that the curate could possibly dislike was ever written. As to love, the word was, beware! Above all, there must be no faintest hint of the vital things, of any sort of realities. And so on and so on, the general conclusion being that the Victorians couldn't write, couldn't paint, couldn't think, and couldn't properly be said to be alive at all.

And thus, having stated the case of the moderns against the Victorians, Mr. Machen suddenly whisks from his pocket several documents. The first is a love poem by the Victorian Tennyson that does not in the least remind the essayist of Miss Pinkerton's Academy for Young Ladies or the vicar's drawing-room. And then, lest this be a little solemn, he adduces one of Swinburne's stanzas on "lazy, laughing, languid Jenny," who was equally "fond of a kiss and fond of a guinea." And from this frankness he turns to Rossetti; then to Dickens. He finds that there were theatres in Victoria's day, and theatre parties; that there were also supper parties, and rich food, and Burgundy. And, finally, having presented the evidence, he comes to the summing up.

> The truth is, of course, that the Victorian Age, more especially the early and mid-Victorian Ages, were times of jollity and times of liberty, both in life and in letters. Those people who took a dozen oysters in the Haymarket at midnight and strolled off to Covent Garden would not have believed that their grandsons would submit to be smacked and sent to bed like naughty children. And as in life, so in letters. What the mid-Victorians wrote, whether it were well or ill, was written with a relish. We have lost all that. Cubism, Vorticism, Post-Impressionism; verse that doesn't scan and doesn't rhyme; novels that make one think of a stupid post-mortem or a dissection: that is what we have in place of Tennyson, Swinburne, Rossetti, Dickens, Thackeray, the pre-Raphaelites and the great illustrators of this despised age, the wood-cutters whose work has become to us miraculous. Those poor Victorians!

Arthur Machen is himself—outside of this volume—a late Victorian; so that this is a defence and an excoriation by one who not only knows what he is talking about, but whose emotions have been aroused by the slurs cast upon his people. And there is one phrase of his defence that we shall do well to linger over for a moment: "Whether they wrote well or ill it was written with a relish." It is the relish for life—the relish of letters—that Machen in the *Dog and Duck* essays would have us recapture, would help us to recapture. And this is important: as he himself says, too few of our present-day writers either care to relish life or evince any desire that their readers should relish letters. Indeed, this is a phase of English literature which seemed, in the main, to end with Stevenson, and Machen's little book is one of the few modern volumes able in any degree to win it back to us. Thus is *Dog and Duck* literature in the highest sense.

In more than one essay does Machen go back even further than to Stevenson; his little homilies on customs, and especially those on viands and potations, remind one of Dickens. When he discusses "Roast Goose: With a Dissertation on Apple Sauce and Sage and Onions," he even outdoes Lamb himself. And all these papers are shot with shafts of wit, stuffed with matured advice; and if Machen, as a philosopher, might fail in a rigid test, even the most quarrelsome of metaphysicians will be forced to bow before his sagacity.

There is a curious note appended to the final essay of the book, a paper on what the author calls "The Art of Unbelief." The editor of *The Lyons Mail*, who had accepted and printed all of the preceding essays, refused this one with the words:—

> I cannot deal with the enclosed.... I am afraid my readers would not understand it; ... a mass of dissertation, some of which I would not ask our linotype operators to translate.

The essay deals with the survival of the primitive capacity for myth-making, a recrudescence of which Machen discovers in the absurd legends surrounding the death of Lord Kitchener which appear to have gained credence in some circles in which intelligence in respect to other matters has generally been shown. But either the "linotype operators" of *The Lyons Mail* are a peculiarly susceptible force of workers, or—and, one will conclude, more probably—the editor was strangely deficient in a sense of humour. Mr. Machen, however, turns the matter off with the good nature one would expect of him; the good nature which is characteristic of the book. "Such are the amenities," he says, "of that highway which Sir Philip Gibbs has so delightfully called 'the Street of Adventure.'"

Appendix

Eleusinia

THE ASSEMBLING

The day is dawning. Whither shall we bend
Our steps, and whither send
The herald on before us; mighty clouds
That have been thick about the path of night,
Now parting all asunder, let the rays
Of mighty Paean glance upon the hills,
And shew us here and there a marble tower,
With minarets that climb aloft, and gleam
Like silver crowns upon the hills of time.
Let us then climb those hill-tops, if with pain
And patient limbs we may attain thereto.
   * * * *

We then at last have come unto the brow,
And gloried with the rays of the young sun,
May look upon the valley underneath.
It is a plain far stretching to the sea,
Which rocks and tumbles on the distant shore,
While close beneath the hill on which we stand
There is a city shining like a bride,
Whose birth-place was in old Pentelicus.
And all the roads which lead into the town
Are crowded with the hurrying steps of men,
Who have been coming from the north and south,
And east and west;
That they may see the city on this day,
And celebrate the praise of Demeter.

* * *

Are they not weary toiling through the night?
Is it not long before the dawn is breaking?
Shall not the pilgrims gladden in the light?
When God shall burst forth, the powers of darkness shaking.

No, we are not weary, if the night is long;
Nay, it is not long before the dawn is breaking.
For there rises oft the solemn swelling song
While our holy priest his offering is making.

Demeter all holy, see we toil to meet thee,
From the distant parts of thy beloved land;
Demeter all holy, shall we ever see thee
Standing in thy majesty, while countless as the sand
On yonder shore, the multitude adore thee
As thou blessest all men with thy loving hand?
Athens is thy dwelling place:
Holy mother, give us grace.
In the town thy temple stands
Bright, all marble from thine hands,
While the gathering people kneel, journeying from many lands.
Is that thy priest who stands within the town?
Is that thy choir whose thunders roll and swell?
Hail to thee most mighty, great be thy renown,
While minstrels sing, and priests thy glory tell.
And now the glory of the rising sun,
Poured forth upon the city marble-built;
And all the crowd of worshippers was come
Unto the temple of the Goddess Queen.
And there they hymn her with resounding songs,
Which rise and fall like thunders, or the noise
Of mighty waters rolling on the shore.
And so the day goes on in worshipping,
Until the sun has hid himself behind
The purple hills that compass Athens round.

And the moon glitters in the pale blue sky
Upon the pilgrims, who have laid their limbs
Weary, but glad at heart, upon the beds
Of herbs, which all the city strews for them.
Such was the ending of the opening day.

THE SEA-SHORE

Now to the sea the mystai bend their steps,
To purge all stain of guilt from off their souls;
And as they go, in pure white vestment clad,
Each one and all implore the goddess queen
To pardon all the sins of the past life,
And wash them pure, and free from every fault.
Down from the temple through the narrow streets,
And gardens smelling sweet, and cool with leaves,
Till they have passed out of the city gates,
And come unto the plain beyond the town,
All through its levels in a mighty band,
Singing in praise of Demeter the Queen.
And then the shore—for every one must wash
His limbs therein, and have it for a sign,
That, as the flesh is pure and free from stain,
The soul within is in like manner cleansed.
So, the cool water sweeps away the stain,
And all have been absolved—the priest has said.

THE FAST

The dawn again is breaking o'er the deep;
Shall we still journey onward, or yet keep
The fast in Athens? The sea heaves
And murmurs, as the yellow autumn leaves
At eastern winds, and nought relieves
The masses of grey clouds, but ever dark
They stand; and on this day no song
Save of the lark.

* * *

For is not now this day a day of tears,
Kept through the long-past years?
Kept and is keeping,
In fast and in weeping.
Now in the city where they stand,
Sorrowing in dark attire,
Wailing at the priest's command
A dirge, while with a lamp of fire
Slowly he lights the sacred pyre
With sad desire.

See, for thy sake is weariness;
Queen for thy sake is great distress.
Let us not perish, kind earth mother,
Sister by sister, brother by brother;
But heavy with thy heaviness,
Mourning and weeping on the temple floor,
Let there be pity for our great complaint.
And as by the sea shore,
We, washing, all were freed from taint;
Turn to us, mighty Queen, and weep no more.

So passed the day in mourning and in fast.

The Procession

The day is dawning. Whither shall we bend
Our steps, or whither send
The herald on before us; the great plain
Pours forth a shout of praise and many songs;
Thunders which roll and sweep the summer air,
Rising and falling like the swelling sea,
And striking all the soul with solemn awe.
Into the heart they rushed like sweet dark wine,
And all the rocks were ringing with the sound

All through the plain in which fair Athens stands,
Until the sailors seaward heard the noise
Of many thunders, and their hearts were stirred,
And worshipping they too took up the chant;
So it rolled along
Over the clean sweet waves till Thetis heard,
Deep in her palaces beneath the sea.
So sweet a song they made, the music yet
Is not all silenced, some clear notes remain,
Though many waves of centuries have passed
Upon those pleasant days: but hark awhile
Unto the chorus, though the years have sped,
And the dim twilight of the world is come.

Goddess most fair,
Loving the gracious land
Of Greece, and the golden sand
Of all its shores, ruling with thy hand
Thy dear Athenian town, but present everywhere.

Are not we pleasing to thee?
Goddess and queen of the corn:
Holiest mother divine,
Grant us thy glory to see,
Bright as the coming of morn:
See how we kneel, and are present, and worship thy shrine.

Hail! thou most sweet
And gracious one,
Is it not meet
To praise thee when the sun
Pours forth his strong far-reaching heat,
And then at evening when his race is run.

Ah! like a summer sea
At eventide
Thy beauty is to me,
I care for nought beside,

Save only thee;
Let thine anthems be upraised, let no chorus be denied.

Ah! soft and sweet
The maidens' voices raise
Thy hymn of praise,
As through the winding street
With eager feet
They pass, crowned with roses and with bays.

If in the holy place
      Men worship thee;
And pray to see thy face,
      So we.

If in the inmost fane
      Thy glory stands;
Grant us to touch, being without stain,
      Thine hands.

If the priest veils his head
      And boweth low;
Make us too, pure, as thou hast said,
      As snow.

Keep us, who worship thee,
      Within thy sight;
Let us, though in the darkness, see
      Thy light.

So the whole city burst into a song
That reached us where we stood upon the hill;
And all the altars smoked with frankincense,
Which sailors, toiling in the eastern seas,
With many weary furrows of the deep,
Had brought unto the praise of Demeter.
And all the day the seven-stringed harp rejoiced,
And the procession passed along the streets,

Even until the darkness covered all,
And wearied with great joy the city slept.

THE DAY OF TORCHES

The sun has slowly sought his resting place,
And the dim twilight of the day has come;
The worshippers assemble in the streets,
Coming from all the byways of the town.
The priest is present; every one a torch
Carries on high, and joins the line of light
Moving towards the temple: let us go.
For there is neither song nor choral chant,
Only the solemn sound of many feet
Moving with one accord; and at the head
Slow walks the priest, holding a torch on high.
At length the long procession reached the place,
Holy to Demeter: then passing on
Through gates and dimly lighted passages,
Until they came unto the central hall,
All set with marble columns, dimly seen,
And here and there a lamp with rosy light
Burning before a statue or a shrine,
Lighting the dimness of the painted walls:
Until the place is full.
All through the night never a voice is heard
In all the echoing passages and halls.
All through the watches of the silent night
The lurid light of many torches shines,
On altar, statue, dimly painted frieze,
Of which the figures flicker, hardly seen
In the dim light of torches borne on high.
Still not a word! the watches of the night
Are passing swiftly: and the day is near.

    *   *   *   *
    *   *   *   *
    *   *   *   *

Still must they stand,
Waiting and longing for the dawn to come;
For every light burns dimly; and the soul,
Weary of anguish, sickened with the watch.
Paler and paler grows the torch's light,
More and yet more uncertain shew the walls;
And still no sign.   *   *
Not from the priest, or from the weary crowd,
But very silence.   *   *
   *   *   *   *
    *   *   *   *

See! the rosy dawn
Is come at last: the priest has given the sign,
"Depart in peace, thy vigil has been watched."

IACCHUS

The day is dawning. Whither shall we bend
Our steps, or whither send
The herald on before us? many strings
Are swept, and many echoings of song
Sound and resound throughout the city streets.
Is there a minstrel left?
Or any music which is still unthrilled
Among their choirs? ah! the voices rush
Up like a trumpet through the summer air.
Was ever song like this? the birds rejoice
And sing for gladness; but let us be still,
We are not worshippers; the years are fled,
And hushed the music, if a lingering voice
And echo of their gladness be revealed,
It is enough. Ah! that in early years,
Before the greyness of the world had come,
I could have worshipped also, but enough.
Perchance across the waste, and strain to hear,
What music then was made for weary hearts.
Hark! the chant sweeps and thrills,

Falling and rising like a mighty voice
Of many waters.
   *   *   *   *
   *   *   *   *

Through the city gates,
Unto the plain they pass a mighty throng,
For it is near the end, and a great joy
Fills every heart with praise and loud acclaim.

Sweet, we are thine, thy vision is not far,
But close the temple stair
And marble altars; faint not by the way
And fall not, for the fair
Queen shineth like a star
At close of day.
Press on yet faster, lest there be delay.

The maidens are not silent: what a strain
Of love and sweet desire floats along
Their clean sweet voicèd chorus: is there any song
Like to their music, pleasure and sweet pain
Are met together, mingled in a chain,
There is no failing; e'en the weak are strong.
The sweet soft scent of roses fills the air
With silent music, even as a dream
The lilies languish and the censers stream.
Sweet sounds and scents are mingled everywhere;
Far in the clear blue distance climbs the mountain stair.

Thus with their offering of solemn song
The glad procession sweeps along the road,
With dances and with music, till afar
They see the temple: with renewed acclaim
The waves of song burst forth as each one sees
The goal of his desire.
Clear in the summer air it stands and shines
Like music carved in marble, and a song.

What can we say or sing
Of such a moment, for the swelling chords
Are broken of the old resounding harp;
Let there be silence and a solemn awe.
And as we strain across the blinding storm
Of many ages; only semitones
Half broken, half resounding, echo yet,
Heard by a few who love the former time,
And dim remembrance of the far-off years.
Now peace awhile, the night is drawing near;
Peace, and let silence fall
Upon the temple, peace and solemn fear.

THE INITIATION

The night has come, a cloud of darkness falls
Upon the temple, save a lonely torch
Lighting at intervals the silent throng,
Who still are waiting there until the time
When all its glories shall be seen by them;
And still a silence.

The heart is sick with waiting, half afraid
And half expectant, is not yet the time?
But ever silence.   *   *
            *   *   *   *
              *   *   *   *

Hark the trumpet sounds!
Upon the steps the holy herald stands,
And bids the worshippers prepare to see
The glory of the goddess.
How awful darkness broods, and one by one
They pass within; but what is seen by them
Within the temple; who of men shall tell,
Only dim legends handed down and told
From age to age; but no man knows the truth,
Only they tell that sudden light was seen,

And then the darkness covered all again.
Anon the thunder rolls and breaks along,
Crashing and thrilling all the halls among,
And then the silence covered all again.
    *   *   *   *
    *   *   *   *
Sweet and fearful sounds,
Following in alternation till the soul
Was melted all within, the heart was still
And almost life departed, then at last
The glory of the goddess was revealed.

      FINIS.

Beneath the Barley:
A Note on the Origins of *Eleusinia*

In considering the matter of laying eggs, general principles alone are to be taken into account. The theory of the process of ovification is not at all affected by the fact that the particular specimen or specimens we are examining turn out to be addled.

That being premised and granted, I can now turn to the matter in hand: the writing of *Eleusinia*.

I was seventeen at the time; the year, 1880. I had left Hereford Cathedral School at the end of the Easter Term. I had spent most of the summer at Wandsworth and had seen London, then a rare and wonderful town. I had failed by reason of defective elementary arithmetic to pass the preliminary examination of the Royal College of Surgeons, and here I was at Llanddewi Rectory with nothing particular to do, and less to expect. I loafed about, wandering all over the country round Llanddewi, taking peculiar delight in turning into bridle-paths—narrow ways, with high hedges on each side—and following them till they brought me out into unknown country. I would go walking on and walking on, and the dusk fell and it grew dark, and I, with the vaguest notions of the lie of the land, would somehow find my way back to the Rectory and tell the story of my traffics and discoveries. And I wandered also in and out of the books in that unselected library which I have described elsewhere; and on the whole, I suppose, got the education, apart from the Humanities, which was most to my purpose.

I believe it was in November of that Autumn of 1880 that I set out one morning to walk to Newport; for no particular reason that I can remember. Probably, there had been a slight frost in the night; the day was shining and splendid, and there was a briskness in the air that made the walk—it would kill me now—go very well. I had climbed up the long hill from Llantarnam, and was on my way towards Malpas when I saw the mountain, from Twyn Barlwm to the heights above

Pontypool, all a pure, radiant blue under a paler blue sky; and the sun shone on the farm houses and cottages of the mountain side, and made the whitewashed walls shine gloriously as if they were marble. I experienced an indescribable emotion; and I always attribute to that moment and to that emotion my impulse towards literature. For literature, as I see it, is the art of describing the indescribable; the art of exhibiting symbols which may hint at the ineffable mysteries behind them; the art of the veil, which reveals what it conceals. So, in the eighteenth century phrase, I commenced author; and began, with little delay, to write *Eleusinia*.

Of that work, I propose to say nothing whatever; rather, I have said what I think of it in the first paragraph of this note: I have described the indescribable. But its subject-matter, the mysteries of Eleusis, is not without significance, if anyone should desire to consider my career in letters. I chose the mysteries first and I chose them last: seeking always that secret which is hidden beneath the barley—to use the phrase of Eleusis—the one secret which is concealed beneath the various assemblage of sensible appearances.

I wrote *Eleusinia* in a few weeks. I copied it out on notepaper, writing on both sides of the paper, and sent it to Joseph Jones, the stationer, in Broad Street, Hereford, directing him to print one hundred copies. I think he had some misgivings, but he fulfilled my instructions; and the brief pamphlet was produced somewhere about March 1881 and offered for sale at the price of fourpence.

The edition was rapidly exhausted.

At present; January, 1931, two copies are known to be in existence. One is in the possession of Charles Parsons, of Regent's Park, London; the other in the collection of Senator Mayfield, of Washington, D.C., U.S.A.

There are two manuscript copies: one held by Paul Jordan-Smith, of Los Angeles, California, U.S.A.; the other by T. Fytton Armstrong, of Twickenham, Middlesex.

Introductory Letter to "Confessions of a Literary Man"

The Editor of *The Evening News* has received the following letter enclosing the MSS. of a fascinating record of thirty-five years' life in London from the pen of a well-known writer:—

"'I said I should like to tell you some things, such as people commonly never tell, about my early recollections. Should you like to hear them?'

"'Should we like to hear them?—No, but we should *love* to.'

"'. . . I was born and bred, as I have told you twenty times, among books and those who knew what was in books. I was very carefully instructed in things temporal and spiritual. But up to a considerable maturity of childhood I believed Raphael and Michael Angelo to have been superhuman beings.'

"I have written these two passages from *The Autocrat of the Breakfast Table* on the first page of the MSS. I am sending you for publication in *The Evening News*. I am not so sure that the writer whose Confessions have come into my hands did not go much further in the matter of these childhood beliefs, and what is of more consequence, he has held to them through all the journeyings of his eventful and hazardous career. I say hazardous because the life of a Man of Letters in London any time this last thirty years must of necessity have been hazardous.

"And as to the other point in common. The writer whose MSS. lies before me was bred in the security of a parsonage, and has more of the genuine savour of books than anyone I have ever known. He has, I think, the gift, amounting to genius, of writing about books so as to make the magical essence and quality of them seem like the stuff and substance of the real thing, real in the sense that it discovers some point of contact with actual life and reality. By that I mean he is a good poet who has not gone wrong, as so many poets do. So it is no mere bookworm who has chosen to write of his adventures among the masterpieces of the soul. He has other qualifications, too, for the task. He writes of Life. He has a passion for detail, seemingly trifling; and yet it is emphatically by the small and almost childish things of life that we know ourselves and learn to know others. This passion for the thousand and one things that merged into a whole constitute personality is a characteristic of all the great writers of Confessions. My friend translated the incomparable 'Casanova,' so he has an intimate acquaintance with the best models.

"By way of disarming the reader who may think that these Confessions come wholly from the library, let me say that the writer of them is a man of the world, a poet, and a journalist, once also an actor; and, what is of more consequence to Londoners, a lover of London before everything else in the world."

Bibliography

Far Off Things. London: Martin Secker, 1922. New York: Alfred A. Knopf, 1922. In *Works* (Caerleon Edition). London: Martin Secker; Edinburgh: Dunedin Press, 1923, Vol. 8. London: Martin Secker, 1926 (New Adelphi Library). [First published as "Confessions of a Literary Man." *Evening News* (London) (19 March 1915): 9; (24 March 1915): 3; (25 March 1915): 3; (26 March 1915): 8; (27 March 1915): 8; (29 March 1915): 3; (31 March 1915): 8; (5 April 1915): 8; (6 April 1915): 6; (7 April 1915): 3; (9 April 1915): 8; (14 April 1915): 8; (15 April 1915): 8; (16 April 1915): 8; (19 April 1915): 3; (20 April 1915): 8; (21 April 1915): 8; (22 April 1915): 3; (23 April 1915): 9; (27 April 1915): 8; (28 April 1915): 8; (29 April 1915): 8; (3 May 1915): 3; (4 May 1915): 8; (6 May 1915): 8; (10 May 1915): 8; (12 May 1915): 8; ((18 May 1915): 8; (21 May 1915): 6; (25 May 1915): 6; (27 May 1915): 8; (28 May 1915): 2; (2 June 1915): 8; (8 June 1915): 8; (17 June 1915): 6; (23 June 1915): 6; (29 June 1915): 3; (12 July 1915): 6.]

Things Near and Far. London: Martin Secker, 1923. New York: Alfred A. Knopf, 1923. In *Works* (Caerleon Edition). London: Martin Secker; Edinburgh: Dunedin Press, 1923, Vol. 9. London: Martin Secker, 1926 (New Adelphi Library).

The London Adventure; or, The Art of Wandering. London: Martin Secker, 1924. New York: Alfred A. Knopf, 1924. London: Martin Secker, 1928 (New Adelphi Library).

Precious Balms. London: Spurr & Swift, 1924.

Eleusinia. Hereford [UK]: Printed by Joseph Jones, 1881.

"A Lament for London's Lost Inns." *London Graphic* 111 (21 February 1925): 280. In *Dreads and Drolls*. London: Chatto & Windus, 1925. New York: Alfred A. Knopf, 1926.

"My Murderer." In Vincent Starrett, ed. *Et Cetera: A Collector's Scrap Book*. Chicago: Pascal Covici, 1924. 97–99.

"One Night When I Was Frightened." *London Graphic* 113 (2 January 1926): 12. In *Dreads and Drolls*. London: Chatto & Windus, 1925. New York: Alfred A. Knopf, 1926.

"The Ready Reporter." In T. Michael Pope, ed. *The Book of Fleet Street*. London: Cassell, 1930. 143–53.

"Sixty Years Since." *John O'London's Weekly* 21 (13 April 1929): 23.

"Strange Roads." *Out and Away* 1 (December 1919): 87–92. In *Strange Roads* [and *With the Gods in Spring*]. London: Classic Press, 1923.

"The Treasure of the Humble: A Note on *The Secret Glory*." *Reviewer* 3 (January 1923): 719–24.

"With the Gods in Spring." *Out and Away* 1 (Spring 1920): 193–96. In *Strange Roads* [and *With the Gods in Spring*]. London: Classic Press, 1923.

www.ingramcontent.com/pod-product-compliance
Lightning Source LLC
Chambersburg PA
CBHW050323230426
43663CB00010B/1716